JUNG AND THE MONOTHEISMS

Jung and the Monotheisms brings together a range of scholars to provide an exploration of some of the essential aspects of Judaism, Christianity and Islam. The contributors include leading Jungian analysts and scholars, among them Baroness Vera von der Heydt, Ann Belford Ulanov and Murray Stein. They bring to bear psychological, religious and historical perspectives in an attempt to uncover the nature and psychology of the three monotheisms.

The book provides a fresh and profound source of interpretation and comparison of Islam within the western psyche. The editor, Joel Ryce-Menuhin, is especially concerned to bring both the essential and comparative elements of the religious psychology of Islam to the attention of the contemporary reader and to provide a forum for an increased dialogue between the three monotheisms.

Joel Ryce-Menuhin is a Jungian analyst. A former international concert pianist who has travelled extensively, he is deeply committed to furthering the understanding between Judaism, Christianity and Islam from a psychological viewpoint. He is an Honorary Research Fellow of the Centre for Psychoanalytic Studies, University of Kent, former editor of *Harvest*, the journal of the C. G. Jung Analytical Psychology Club, London, and the Founding Director of the British and Irish Branch of the International Society for Sandplay Therapy. He is the author of *The Self in Early Childhood* (1988) and *Jungian Sandplay* (Routledge, 1992).

Also available from Routledge:

Jungian Sandplay
The Wonderful Therapy
Joel Ryce-Menuhin

Analysis Analysed
Fred Plaut

Jung and Searles
A Comparative Study
David Sedgwick

Jung and Phenomenology
Roger Brooke

In Search of Jung
J. J. Clarke

Chaos and Order in the World of the Psyche
Joanne Wieland-Burston

Changemakers
A Depth Psychological Study of the Individual, Family and Society
Louis H. Stewart

JUNG AND THE MONOTHEISMS

Judaism, Christianity and Islam

Edited by Joel Ryce-Menuhin

London and New York

First published in 1994
by Routledge
11 New Fetter Lane, London EC4P 4EE

Simultaneously published in the USA and Canada
by Routledge
29 West 35th Street, New York, NY 10001

Typeset in Garamond by J&L Composition Ltd, Filey, North Yorkshire
Printed and bound in Great Britain by
Biddles Ltd, Guildford and King's Lynn

British Library Cataloguing in Publication Data
A catalogue record for this book is available from the British Library

Library of Congress Cataloging in Publication Data
Jung and the monotheisms: Judaism, Christianity, and Islam/edited
by Joel Ryce-Menuhin.
p. cm.
Includes bibliographical references and index.
1. Monotheism-Psychology. 2. Psychoanalysis and religion.
3. Jung, C. G. (Carl Gustav), 1875–1961. I. Ryce-Menuhin, Joel.
BL221.J86 1993
291.1'4–dc20   93-8077

ISBN 0–415–07962–4 (hbk)   ISBN 0–415–10414–9 (pbk)

Dedicated to
The Right Honourable Lord Menuhin, OM, KBE,
my brother-in-law, who has worked for
peace between religions all of his life

and to the

School for Peace in Neve Shalom/Wahat al-Salam,
a village in Israel in which Jews and Palestinians
have chosen to build a community together.

CONTENTS

CONTENTS

Part III Christianity

Part IV Islam

Part V The Song of Songs

CONTRIBUTORS

Sarah Ansari obtained an MA in Area Studies (South Asia) at the School of Oriental and African Studies, University of London, and then a Ph.D. from Royal Holloway College, University of London, focusing on modern Indian Muslim history and in particular on the history of the province of Sind (now in Pakistan). Her book *Sufi Saints and State Power: the Pirs of Sind, 1843–1947* (Cambridge University Press, 1992) examines the evolving relationship between the British and the hereditary Muslim religious leaders of the region. Dr Ansari was assistant editor of *The Cambridge Encyclopedia of India, Pakistan, Bangladesh, Sri Lanka, Nepal, Bhutan and the Maldives* (Cambridge University Press, 1989), and has written a number of articles and reviews on issues relating to the history of Muslims in the Indian subcontinent. Between 1988 and 1991, she was British Academy Postdoctoral Research Fellow at Royal Holloway College, and worked on partition-related migration from India to Pakistan, with special reference to the impact which it had on the subsequent development of the Pakistani province of Sind. She is currently Honorary Lecturer at Royal Holloway College, where she lectures in twentieth-century world history.

Nicholas Battye is a Sufi, originally trained in Zen. He has a BA in Religious Studies and an MA in Psychoanalytic Studies. After a first career as a documentary photographer, he now works as a psychotherapist in private practice in London. He is co-author of *Survival Programmes* (Open University Press, 1982), a nation-wide study of urban poverty.

William C. Chittick has been assistant professor of religious studies at the State University of New York at Stony Brook and is a former assistant professor at Aryamehr University in Tehran. He is a specialist in Sufism, and his works include *The Sufi Path of Love: Spiritual Teachings of Rumi* (1983), a translation of Fakhr al-Din 'Iraqi's *Divine Flashes* (1982), and *Faith and Practice of Islam: Three Thirteenth Century Sufi Texts* (1992).

John P. Dourley is a Jungian analyst, a graduate of the Zurich/Küsnacht Institute, 1980, currently practising in Ottawa, Canada. He is professor of religion in the Department of Religion, Carleton University, in Ottawa. He is a Roman Catholic priest and member of the religious order of the Oblates of Mary Immaculate. He has written extensively on the religious implications of Jung's thought and has four titles published with Inner City Books, Toronto, Canada.

Gustav Dreifuss was born in Zurich. He is a graduate of the C. G. Jung Institute and has lived since 1959 in Haifa, Israel, where he was a teacher and supervisor in the psychotherapy section of the Medical School in Tel-Aviv and Haifa (post-graduate), a training analyst of the Israel Association for Analytical Psychology and its past president (1978–82). The papers he has written between 1965 and 1988 have been republished in a booklet entitled *Papers*, in which the main themes are: 'Psychotherapy', 'Treatment of Holocaust victims', 'Jewish psychology' and 'The archetype of sacrifice'. Besides his private practice and university lectures, he was group supervisor on psychotherapy at Afula Hospital and at the Kibbutz clinic in Naharija. He lectures at Haifa University, interpreting biblical texts from a Jungian perspective.

Freema Gottlieb was born in London into a family of Holocaust survivors from Poland, Romania and Vienna. She was brought up in a Scots rabbinical household. Her father, the late bayyan Wolf Gottlieb, was Head of the Scots Rabbinical Court. A scholar at Girton College, Cambridge, where she read English, she studied Jewish subjects both with her father and at the Gateshead Women's Seminary. Her doctorate on Leonard Woolf is from University College London. Based at present in New York, she has written two books, *Jewish Folk Art* (Summit, 1986), co-authored with Joy Ungerlieder, and *The Lamp of God: Jewish Book of Light* (Aronson, 1989). Her articles, interviews and reviews have appeared in the *New York Times Book Review*, the *Times Literary Supplement*, the *New Republic*, the *Jewish Quarterly*, the *Jewish Chronicle* and *European Judaism*.

Vera von der Heydt trained in Oxford with John Layard, in Zurich with Professor Jung and Dr Yolande Jacobi and in London with Dr Gerhard Adler. She is a Professional Member of the Society of Analytical Psychology, a Co-Founder of the Independent Group of Analytical Psychologists, Honorary President of the C. G. Jung Analytical Psychology Club, Honorary Fellow of the Guild of Pastoral Psychology and a member of the British Psychological Society. Baroness von der Heydt was formerly Senior Lay Analyst of the Davidson Clinic, Edinburgh. She is a lecturer, a broadcaster for British and American television, and the author of *Prospects for the Soul* and of articles in several British and American publications.

Siegmund Hurwitz was born in Switzerland in 1904. He became a pupil and corroborator of C. G. Jung, working with him, Antonia Wolff and

Marie-Louise von Franz. He became an analyst of problems of religious psychology. He has written several books in German, one of which is translated into English, *Lilith – the First Eve* (Daimon Verlag, 1992). He has contributed many articles to psychological journals and Festschriften (Jung, Kirsch).

Andrew Louth was born in Lincolnshire and brought up in the north of England. He studied mathematics and theology at the Universities of Cambridge and Edinburgh. From 1970 to 1985 he was Fellow and Chaplain of Worcester College, Oxford, and University Lecturer in Theology, teaching principally patristics. Since 1985 he has taught at Goldsmith's College in the University of London, and is currently Professor of Cultural History and Head of Department of Historical and Cultural Studies. He was received into the Orthodox Church in 1989. He is the author of several books, including *The Origins of the Christian Mystical Tradition* (1981), *Denys the Areopagite* (1989) and, most recently, *The Wilderness of God* (1991).

Levi Meier is the Jewish Chaplain at Cedars-Sinai Medical Center in Los Angeles and a psychologist in private practice. He is the creator of the Jewish Values series, which so far includes: *Jewish Values in Bioethics*, *Jewish Values in Psychotherapy*, *Jewish Values in Health and Medicine* and *Jewish Values in Jungian Psychology*. His writings integrate the teachings of Judaism and psychology in a positive manner, demonstrating how knowledge of one enhances understanding of the other. Rabbi Meier is also Special Issues Editor of the *Journal of Psychology and Judaism*.

Joel Ryce-Menuhin, B. Mus., B. Sc. (Hons), M. Phil. was an international concert pianist before studying psychology at Bedford College, London, and training as a Jungian analyst. He is in private practice in London, and has lectured on five continents. He is Founding Director of the British and Irish Branch of the International Society for Sandplay Therapy (founder: Dora Kalff). His books include *The Self in Early Childhood* (FAB, 1988) and *Jungian Sandplay – the Wonderful Therapy* (Routledge, 1992). Joel Ryce-Menuhin is a training analyst with the Independent Group of Analytical Psychologists, London and has contributed theoretical/clinical papers to various journals, including *Harvest* (which he edited for nine years), the *Journal of Analytical Psychology*, *Chiron*, the *British Journal of Projective Psychology*. He is Consultant Editor of the *Journal of Sandplay Therapy* and *Harvest* and an Honorary Research Fellow of the Centre for Psychoanalytic Studies, University of Kent. Ryce-Menuhin is a past chairman of the Guild of Pastoral Psychology and the C. G. Jung Analytical Psychology Club, London.

Leon Schlamm is a lecturer in Religious Studies at the University of Kent at Canterbury. His main research interests are in the comparative study of mysticism, and his Ph.D. (1988) was on the phenomenology of religious experiences in Rudolf Otto's *The Idea of the Holy*. Apart from work on Otto, he has been interested in Jung's relationship to mystical experience for more than a decade, and is engaged at present in several research projects, including one on the status of Jung's mysticism (relating Jung's mysticism to a variety of cross-cultural taxonomies of mysticism by phenomenologists of religion) and one on the relationship between analytical psychology and transpersonal psychology (particularly the work of Ken Wilber and John Welwood). Recent publications include: 'Numinous experience and religious language', *Religious Studies* 28 (1992); 'Rudolf Otto and mystical experience', *Religious Studies* 27 (1991); and 'The Bible and Jungian depth psychology', in *Using the Bible Today*, ed. D. Cohn-Sherbok (Bellow Publishing, 1991). Apart from contributions to the teaching of the MA programme in Psychoanalytic Studies, Dr Schlamm teaches courses in Psychology and Religion, Understanding Myth, and Patterns in Comparative Religion. He is engaged in setting up the first taught MA programme on the study of mysticism in Britain (1993/4).

Murray Stein holds a master's degree of divinity from Yale University, a doctorate in religion and psychological studies from the University of Chicago, and a diploma in analytical psychology from the C. G Jung Institute of Zurich. Training analyst and teacher at the C. G. Jung Institute of Chicago, Dr Stein is in private practice in the Chicago area. He is honorary secretary of the International Association of Analytical Psychology. He is author of *In Midlife* and of *Jung's Treatment of Christianity*, and editor of the Chiron Clinical Series, *Jungian Analysis, Jung's Challenge to Contemporary Religion* (with Robert Moore), *Psyche's Stories* (with Lionel Corbett) and *Psyche at Work* (with John Hollwitz).

Sara Sviri studied Arabic and Islamic Studies at the Hebrew University in Jerusalem. She wrote her Ph.D. dissertation on *The Mystical Psychology of al-Hakīm al-Tirmidhī, a Ninth Century Sufi Master*, and was awarded her doctorate by the Tel-Aviv University in 1980. She has been a lecturer in Arabic and Islam both at Tel-Aviv University and at the Hebrew University of Jerusalem. She is currently a full-time lecturer at the Department of Hebrew and Jewish Studies of University College London. She has been lecturing on Sufi psychology at Birkbeck College London, as well as at various Jungian institutes and conferences. Papers on Sufism and related topics written by her have been published in various periodicals and compilations.

Ann Belford Ulanov is the Christiane Brooks Johnson Professor of Psychiatry and Religion at the Union Theological Seminary, a psychoanalyst in private practice and a supervising analyst and faculty member of the

C. G. Jung Institute, New York City. With her husband, Barry Ulanov, she is the author of *Religion and the Unconscious, Primary Speech: A Psychology of Prayer, Cinderella and her Sisters, The Witch and the Clown*, and *The Healing Imagination*. Dr Belford by herself is the author of *The Feminine in Christian Theology and in Jungian Psychology, Receiving Woman: Studies in the Psychology and Theology of the Feminine, Picturing God*, and *The Wisdom of the Psyche*.

ACKNOWLEDGEMENTS

I wish to thank Baroness Vera von der Heydt for her long personal friendship in London, which has intensified my awareness of the importance of the relationship between religion and Jungian psychology. During the period I was chairman of the Guild of Pastoral Psychology (Honorary Patron: C. G. Jung), I met many leading religious figures of British life. This encouraged my own relationship to comparative religion, which had already captivated me in early boyhood. Before I was twelve I had spent many long nights devouring all the books available in my childhood home, both western and eastern religous works.

I am grateful to Professor Andrew Louth for permission to use his paper, originally published by the Guild of Pastoral Psychology, as was my own paper, which has been extended to include an Islamic section. All other works are newly written for this book except for Siegmund Hurwitz's paper which was originally published in German in the Swiss journal *Judaica*, and the paper by William Chittick, which the publisher of *The World and I*, (February 1991, USA), has released to us.

Thanks go to contributor Nicholas Battye for first calling my attention to Jung's father's thesis and to the Jung Archive, Zurich, for their agreement to our using portions of Paul Achilles Jung's dissertation from Göttingen University to reveal him as an Arabist.

To the spirit of C. G. Jung himself, who heard me as a concert pianist in Zurich in 1957, I owe a resurgence of belief in the deepest dogmas of the monotheisms, their psychology and eternal meaning.

Joel Ryce-Menuhin

INTRODUCTION

During the recent international Gulf War, the Christian West, the Judaic
Israeli state and the Muslim world were all deeply committed to and
involved in political unities and conflicts of great complexity. At a time
when religious faith has played its part in violent political difficulties in
many parts of the globe, it is valuable, as an act of peaceful intent, to
consider the *unity-in-variety* of the three monotheisms. In discovering that
the Islamic–Christian dialogue is treated less extensively in the literature
than is the Christian–Jewish dialogue from the viewpoint of analytical
psychology, I proposed this collection of papers to Routledge, wishing to
bring together issues of paramount importance to the subject of Semitic
psychology that are common to, or comparatively vital to, the three
monotheisms.

As editor I shall introduce the five parts of this collection. While retaining
the essences of the monotheisms in each author's own sense of expertise and
style, the selection of papers makes its own synthesis.

Wherever one searches into the monotheistic religions, one finds moments
of historical true unity forgotten by later generations. For example, Pico
della Mirandola (1463–94), following on Ficini's Latin translations of the
Greek text, the *Corpus hermeticeum* for Cosimo de Medici (which demonstrated the prestige given by 1463 to Hermes Trismegistus, its probable
author), revealed the Christian links to pre-Christian conceptions *without*
renouncing the Christian context. Pico went so far as to see that the magic
described from Egyptian sources and the Jewish Kabbala, taken as previews
of the Old Testament of the Holy Bible, actually confirmed the divinity of
Christ! Pico learnt Hebrew to study the Kabbala and is worthy of reassessed
contemporary study.

There were aspirations just before and during the sixteenth century to
unify the 'mysteries' of Egypt, the Judaeo-Christian world and the classical
world of the humanists. Pope Alexander VI actually had the Vatican
commission a fresco full of Egyptian images and symbols. These views of a
unity-in-diversity continued for two centuries. Giordano Bruno (1548–1600)
founded his sense of religious universalism on the role of Egyptian magic.

1

So many sixteenth-century authors followed suit that Hermetic magic was declared a heresy. Philippe de Mornay thought Hermeticism would help men escape from religious wars. In 1581, he quoted Hermes, 'God is one . . . so that to Him alone belongs the name of Father and of Good . . . Alone and Himself All; without Name and higher than any name' (see Yates 1964: 177). This exhortation is startlingly like contemporary Muslim teaching, 'Allah is the one and only God.'

Here diverse confessions find common ground. Microcosm is seen as a goal of macrocosm through the divinizing of man, and macrocosm is at the same time the home or dwelling place of microcosm. Eliade (1985) suggests that these ideas were already extant in China, India and Greece, but were infiltrating in the sixteenth century in a new closeness mono-theistically towards a *rapprochement* between nature in general and religion.

One of C. G. Jung's most original contributions was his analogical work on psychological process as developmental in the same sense as the alchemists were searching for ultimate selfhood through the language of the refining of metals into gold. The first Latin translations from Arabic date from the twelfth century. The *Tabula Smaragdina* is attributed to Hermes. His formula was 'All that is above is like all that is below; all that is below is like all that is above, in order that the miracle of Unity be accomplished.' Western alchemists, in particular Paracelsus, believed one must descend into alchemy's first stage – the *nigredo* or a regression to a fluid state of matter – which in psychological terms is the *prima materia, confusa* or *abyssas* or the 'mother'. Paracelsus believed that 'he who would enter the Kingdom of God must first enter with his body into his mother and there die'. 'Mother' here equals the *prima materia*.

One of Jung's favourite alchemists was Basil Valentine, who emphasized the necessity to 'visit the interior of the Earth, and by purification you will find the secret stone'. The synchronism between the *Opus alchymicum* and the intimate experiences of the adept led Jung to interpret synchronicities during a patient's analysis with the greatest interest. The idea of alchemy in attempting to transform oneself, 'a dead stone' into the 'philosopher's stone', suggests a spiritual development hidden within the language of 'stones' that is paralleled in the Arabic alchemists through their concept of the *elixir vitae*. This 'elixir' was a therapeutic result of reaching the philosopher's stone, or *lapis*, or the power to make base metals into pure and incorruptible metals.

By the sixteenth century Heinrich Khunrath, a celebrated Hermeticist, identified the philosopher's stone with Jesus Christ, the 'Son of the Macrocosm'. If Christ had redeemed humanity, Khunrath thought, so would the alchemical opus ensure that nature would be redeemed. Isaac Newton practised alchemy, as his discovery of gravity did not satisfy him. Newton hoped that through alchemical experiments he would discover the structure of the micro-universe. J. T. Dobbs in her book *The Foundation of Newton's Alchemy* (1975) points out that

> Newton's alchemical thoughts were so securely established that he never came to deny their general validity, and in a sense the whole of his career after 1675 may be seen as one long attempt to integrate alchemy and the mechanistic philosophy.
>
> (Dobbs 1975: 230)

Christian Europe was then overcome by mechanistic science and has left behind the further pursuit of the Hermetic and the alchemical in general. Jung, however, has resuscitated and renewed widespread interest in the alchemical inner process as psychological within Christian Europe's general aim of seeking 'total knowledge'. The Arab source material inspires one to wonder if the Muslim world should now reappraise its alchemical past, searching for parallels to modern Islam and its spiritual inner development.

It is with a sense of excitement that, in compiling this book, I sought the help of expert psychologists, religious and historical academics of distinction and persons often of a personal religious integrity within their own monotheistic religious life. It is to each contributing author and to the publishing house of Routledge that I owe the possibility – as a Jungian analyst – of creating this book, and to whom I shall always be grateful.

That which is one is one; and that which is not one is also one.

(An old esoteric saying)

REFERENCES

Dobbs, J. T. (1975) *The Foundation of Newton's Alchemy*, Cambridge: Cambridge University Press.

Eliade, M. (1985) *History of Religious Ideas*, vol. 3, Chicago: University of Chicago Press.

Yates, F. (1964) *Giordano Bruno and the Hermetic Tradition*, London: University of Chicago Press.

Part I

ORIENTATION TO JUNG AND RELIGION

1

JUNG AND RELIGION
Its place in analytical psychology
Vera von der Heydt

Much has been spoken and written about Jung and religion. The significance
of his discovery of the religious dimension within the psyche has not yet
fully sunk in, and the practical implications for therapy are still a matter of
controversy. His interest in religious matters and his outspoken allegiance
to Christianity in spite of his criticisms of it have puzzled many people, as
such an attitude is thought to be inappropriate for a scientist of the twentieth century. However, physicists and particularly quantum physicists are
gradually changing this materialistic outlook as they are grasping the truths
underlying Jung's ideas.

Jung raised fundamental questions for psychology as well as for religion,
which in his mind are intimately linked. These questions can be answered
only by looking at Jung's complex personality, at what he was and what he
did. He was activated by two conflicting tendencies within himself, equal
in intensity. One side of him was remarkably open to immediate numinous
experiences: from childhood on he had dreams and visions with religious
overtones, and he was aware of their significance. One dream, the earliest
he could remember, and one vision are of particular importance for the long-
lasting effect they had on Jung, as they foreshadowed his mental and
emotional development. He was convinced that such manifestations came
from God, and that it was up to him to make sense of them.

Jung defined the term 'numinous immediate experience' as a happening
which bestows on one sudden insight into another dimension and affects
one's whole being. From very early on in his life God had been one of Jung's
most immediate experiences; he wrote to a young clergyman that all his
thoughts circled around God like planets, and were irresistibly attracted by
Him. He added that he would consider it a grave sin if he were to resist or
oppose this force. This was his instinctive, intuitive religious side.

The other side was his scientific disposition: he was curious and always
wanted to know and to understand; he observed and explored with great
thoroughness and patience, carefully looking for proof and evidence before
publicizing any of his psychological discoveries; he was averse to speculation. He was acutely aware of and disturbed by the two mutually exclusive

tendencies within himself, and he believed that this was the reason for his feelings of isolation and loneliness, and the cause of many misunderstandings between himself and others.

Jung had a formidable religious background. All his family were members of the Swiss Reformed Church, and many of his immediate family were clergymen. His father was a vicar. In the sixteenth century the founder of the Swiss Reformed Church, Ulrich Zwingli, had taught that the basic requirement for salvation is faith in the word of God as revealed in the New Testament; without faith one faces damnation. The sermon is the centre of worship and is the only sacrament. The substances in the Eucharist, that is the bread and wine, symbolize the body and blood of Christ, and the main purpose of the service is spiritual communion. Jung was immersed in this religous background, and theological issues were continually being discussed in his hearing.

The atmosphere in his home was a sad one. His parents' marriage was unhappy; his mother suffered from bouts of depression and had to be hospitalized from time to time, and his father was racked by religious doubts. Nevertheless, in spite of their troubles, they did everything they could for the little boy without realizing how frightened, lonely and withdrawn he was.

His mother taught him to pray and also spoke to him about the Lord Jesus who sits on a golden throne in Heaven, is very kind, and loves little children. This beautiful and comforting image was shattered when he was about three or four years old as one of the prayers he had been taught seemed to say that Jesus came down from heaven to fetch little children, and grown-ups too, and then would eat them to save them from being devoured by the devil. This frightened him, particularly since his mother disappeared occasionally and he did not know where she had gone. He wondered whether she might have been put into one of the holes he had seen being dug by men he knew from his father's church, before being eaten; he knew that those people were never seen again. Pondering about this during one of her absences whilst playing in the front garden of his home, he saw a figure descending the path in front of the house. This man seemed to be in some sort of disguise. He was dressed all in black; he wore a big black hat and something like a woman's skirt. It was someone whose views irritated his father, who called him a 'Jesu-eet' (German pronunciation). The child was petrified: he was all alone and he thought that this man was Jesus, who had come to fetch him; trembling with fear he ran into the house, hid under a table and waited for a long time before he dared creep out from his hiding place. He did not tell anyone of his fears or of this incident.

Soon afterwards the child had a dream. He dreamt that he was walking in a meadow. Seeing a large hole, he ran into it full of curiosity and rather tremulously went down a stone stairway until he came to a heavy curtain which barred his way. He drew it aside and saw that he was in a largish

8

dim-lit subterranean room with a flagstone floor and a blood-red carpet running from the door to the centre; there on a low platform stood a golden throne, and on it there was a huge thing of naked flesh looking upwards with its one eye at the very top. As he looked at it with horror this thing seemed to be slithering towards him, and then he heard his mother's voice from above calling: 'Yes, look at him: he is the ogre.' At that he awoke.

This dream haunted him all his life. He spontaneously associated the subterranean monstrous being on the golden throne with Jesus sitting on his golden throne in heaven; the one was the counterpart of the other; then the image of the heavenly Jesus merged with the figure of the Jesuit and with the ogre of the underworld. All three were one and the same in the reality of the child's imagination. This Jesus transmitted the idea of death, not of loving care: his mother's death, his own death. Jesus, himself a corpse covered in blood, hanging on a cross, was the God of Death. Jung automatically thought of this dream and this image whenever Jesus was mentioned in front of him in later life, and after his father's death he had to leave the room when this happened, as he got overwhelmed by emotion. He did not and could not listen to his mother's remarks in the dream, either as a child or as an adult; he only said that for a long time he had been puzzled as to what she might have meant. He could not hear her telling him that Jesus was not the ogre; he was too traumatized by outer events, by his inner fears, and what he took to be his mother's unreliability, and his father's lack of power.

In the period between childhood and adulthood Jung continued to reflect on the dream. Finally he interpreted it in rational terms as an initiation into the dark secrets of the earth and into the mystery of the phallus. Most important, however, was his belief that it marked the beginning of his intellectual life, as in a dim way he felt that he had encountered the problem of darkness and evil. On the other hand the dream also revealed that he had lost his faith in Jesus and the capacity to experience him in his totality; the light side of Jesus had been extinguished. Jesus remained truncated and was never again quite real or quite acceptable to him. The power of darkness prevailed in the figure of the Jesuit who cast his shadow over the Christian doctrine as he heard it discussed in his home.

Jung was in his twelfth year when he had the vision which opened his eyes to the mystery of the will of God. On his way home from school on a lovely bright sunny day, he looked up into the blue sky; he saw God sitting on his throne in heaven dropping excrement on beautiful Basle Cathedral, thereby destroying it. He was panic-stricken; he felt responsible for what he had seen, fully awake and in broad daylight; he believed that he had committed the sin against the Holy Ghost. He thought that the only way to ward off the inevitable consequence of eternal damnation was not to think about what had happened, though he sensed that God would not allow this. God wanted him to look, and to see. For three days and nights he fought against this; then he had to give in; the strain was too great. He anticipated being overwhelmed by feelings of guilt and sin and dreaded it. He decided to look, and to his amazement such feelings of peace and bliss emerged from within him as he had never known.

When he was recovering from the shock of this experience, questions arose in his mind. Why had God allowed this to happen? What was the purpose of leading a helpless human being into seeing things and thinking thoughts which he knew to be sinful from the best authority, namely from Scripture? Did God want disobedience? How did one know the will of God? These queries and uncertainties forced the boy to recognize that God could be terrible. It dawned on him that God wanted courage: the courage to be, to reflect, to decide; the courage to make an ethical decision, as Jung was to call it later. He had stumbled on to a dangerous sinister secret which separated him for ever from his father and all his family. Once again he was utterly alone, different from everybody else; and that was shameful.

At about this time his father undertook to teach him the basic tenets of his religion; the boy looked forward to those lessons, since he had been avidly reading theological books in his father's library. He started to ask questions which the father would not or could not answer; frequently he was told 'one should not think so much about things: one only needs to have faith'. This was impossible for Jung. However, he realized soon with dismay that his father, like himself, had not been given the gift of faith, but that unlike himself, his father refused to face this fact as a bitter reality even though he was in despair about his doubts. Jung overheard his father pray, and then observed the way in which he ignored his thoughts and feelings and pretended that all was well. Jung was deeply distressed by and even faintly contemptuous of this attitude and believed that his father died prematurely because of his reluctance to face this inner conflict.

Jung mourned his father, but he was also angry with him and with God, so that he almost turned against religion. However, he could not forget his numinous experiences and persisted in paying attention to his dreams, fantasies and visions.

After some hesitation, Jung decided to study medicine as being the best option for him. When he had to choose in which branch of medicine he wanted to specialize, psychiatry was at the bottom of his list. Psychiatry was held in contempt by the medical profession because mental illness was thought to be untreatable except by physical constraint or the administration of drugs; no one knew anything about the psyche. Whilst revising for the final State Examination, Jung picked up a textbook on psychiatry he had not come across before. With great excitement he read that the author considered psychosis to be a disease of a personality who is in an incomplete state of development. In a flash of insight Jung saw that psychiatry was the one area of medicine in which the two drives motivating him could meet, unite, and be used for the purpose of healing. His teachers were baffled by his choice; Jung felt their disapproval deeply, and it reopened the old wound of being different and an outsider.

He became fascinated by the psyche and in all the ways it manifests and expresses itself. He was the first psychiatrist who took a real interest in the ramblings of severely disturbed patients and in their dreams and visions, attempting to make sense of them. He detected links between psychotic apparent non-sense and numinous material and constantly tried to discover from where it originated. He no longer believed that all psychic manifestations came from God; his studies had convinced him that their origin lay within the psyche, but the question was within which part. His research work consisted largely of studying religions, philosophical systems, myths and fairy-tales in order to satisfy his own desire for greater insight into the nature of the psyche and for the sake of his patients.

During the years of his friendship with Freud, Jung's conviction of the existence of a religious dimension within the psyche became a source of friction between him and Freud, but any attempts to discuss these matters with him failed. Freud considered religion to be an obsessional neurosis linked to the repression of infantile sexuality and incestuous wishes, while God was simply an extension of the personal parents. Freud believed that an adequate analysis would free an individual from such delusions. Therefore religious matters could be left intact in a different compartment; there was no need to analyse them. Jung thought that such compartmentalizing would hinder the development of the total personality, as unanalysed beliefs and religious attitudes in a neurotic person would then remain in an infantile and undifferentiated state.

Jung thought of neurosis not as a sharply defined isolated phenomenon, but as a reaction of the total human being to an intolerable life situation resulting in inhibiting normal development. Therefore he was certain that the spiritual and religious side of individuals as well as their biological and somatic aspects should be included in psychological treatments. Any repression makes for trouble: Freud emphasized the dire consequences of sexual repression; Jung pointed to the damage done to human beings by the neglect of the religious impulse.

The inevitable clash came when Jung published his book *The Psychology of the Unconscious*, in which he put forward his own theories and ideas about sexuality, transforming Freud's concept of the libido, and disclosing his own views on the hidden highly religious aspect of incest. Freud was outraged. Jung had foreseen Freud's inability to accept his ideas, but he had not been prepared for the violence with which he would be attacked by Freud and all other colleagues as well. Jung had called one chapter of his book 'The sacrifice', thinking of Freud when he wrote it. In order to maintain his spiritual and intellectual integrity Jung felt he had no choice but to sacrifice his allegiance and his friendship, and finally give up his need for a father figure. He was called a traitor, he was ostracized, and his ideas were declared to be rubbish. He was being punished for speaking out against the *Zeitgeist*, the spirit of the time.

As a result of this dreadful outer turmoil, Jung fell into a deep depression; he was assailed and invaded by terrifying dreams, images, fantasies and negative emotions. It was only his 'demonic psychic strength' which kept these forces at bay. Eventually, however, he was able to reflect on this material. He was certain that Freud's notion of the unconscious, containing only repressed personal material, was too limited. It did not explain the psychic phenomena of an altogether different kind with which he was being confronted. He decided therefore to conduct an experiment on himself, to descend into his own abyss, and to face the fearful powers which were haunting him. He was determined to discover their meaning and to uncover their unconscious content hidden in the form of images. He knew the danger he was exposing himself to, as the material he was grappling with was similar to that of his psychotic patients who had fallen victim to the same kind of images. However, he felt that he owed it to his patients, as well as to himself, to attempt this exploration. He considered that his scientific training and the fact that he was taking this step consciously and deliberately were his protection; furthermore he was convinced that he was obeying a higher will which transcended his ego's fears and resistances.

This is what Jung did. This sets him apart from anyone else in his field of work. He exposed himself to his own darkness and to what he considered to be evil within himself. He looked at his feelings of guilt and shame, and endured them without justifying himself. Eventually he became aware of being embroiled and contaminated by destructive emotions which did not belong to him personally but to a universal shadow.

His curiosity about psychic processes had enabled him to watch and observe what was happening to him and to discriminate between the personal and the impersonal contents of the unconscious which were attacking him. He had made his great psychological discovery. He checked and rechecked his experiences with those of his patients and compared them with mythological motifs. It was then that he became certain of having found a dimension of the unconscious which had never been investigated, the place he had been searching for and whose existence he had surmised. He called it the impersonal or collective unconscious, or the inner reality, as it underlies personal experience and is the vast hinterland of human evolution. It contains the archetypes, the typical reactions to universal human situations which when activated are experienced in a similar way to that of the instincts.

A human being is born as a totality, with all its physiological and psychological dispositions, and with all environmental influences and conditionings that are its lot. Jung called the centre of totality the Self; this central archetype is the dynamic nucleus from which consciousness and its centre the ego evolves, and it is the source of all creativity. It is the place where the image of God is born, the dimension from where religious symbolism, feelings, thoughts and longings arise and filter through into consciousness. Jung had discovered that this area is a psychological reality and not only a metaphysical assumption.

However, since the Self is the core of a totality, it also harbours the destructive evil inclinations which exist in the human heart and in the Creator who created the human heart. He chose the term 'Self' deliberately from the Hindu concept of Brahman and Atman because he wanted to stress the implications of the idea of totality. Brahman is Self as the unknowable, infinite, transcendent Creator of the Universe; Self is also Atman, the totality and centre of finite human existence which can be experienced. Brahman–Atman include explicitly all opposites, all ambiguities of life, good and evil, light and dark. Jung thought that the knowledge of dark and evil coexisting with light and good in humanity and in divinity would not be conveyed strongly enough by a Christian term. He was mistaken; in a very short time the Self acquired all the qualities of an omniscient entity, always right, always constructive, and always to be obeyed.

The experience of wholeness is a psychic event; it has the quality of absoluteness, of being and not being, the eternal now. Is this the experience of Self or of God? Jung was asked. He refused to give a direct answer. He said that he never made any statements about God because that was the province of theologians. He only knew about the God-image in the psyche, and that empirically an experience of Self cannot be distinguished from the experience of the God-image. Self includes the ego; as the ego changes, the Self changes; totality changes; the image of God changes. God, God behind God, does not.

Without the ego, this offspring of the Self, there is no consciousness, no experience. It depends on the ego whether awareness of outer and inner reality is increased. It is the function of the ego to improve the capacity to relate and respond to people and events instead of only reacting to them. This is hard work. It is even harder to become conscious of the ego's tendency to cling to its omnipotence and omniscience; in its inflation it may deny its dependence on the source of its origin. Turning back, reconnecting, reuniting with the Self is the task of the ego; it means listening to and watching all outer and inner events and scrupulously observing them.

The purpose of the work, its goal, which is never reached, is wholeness or, the term Jung used, individuation. Human beings are born as a totality, but the way to completion is a quest and can at times be a thorny one. It includes the religious dimension and religious experiences. These have also to be investigated, and this may go against the grain as one might prefer to leave them in the twilight of dim awareness, afraid that they might lose their numinosity in the light of consciousness. However, courage to take that risk may be needed. Otherwise these experiences have no value; schizophrenic fantasies and those artificially induced by drugs fall into that category if for different reasons; no attempt to assimilate their content is or can be made.

The ego's awareness of the reality of the Self and the inner world and its efforts to reconnect with it are the essence of religion. The function of religion is to reconcile Self and ego and bring about their co-operation. Although the Self is greater than the ego, it needs the ego to manifest itself; in the last resort it is through the ego that the degree of wholeness an individual has achieved can be seen. The willingness, readiness and longing with which the quest for wholeness is undertaken Jung called soul.

Jung spoke as an introvert. He pointed to the two Latin roots from which the word 'religion' derives. One is *relegere*, 'observing carefully' and the other is *religare*, meaning 'rejoining' something; both indicate inner activity. Jung was attracted by the introvert eastern way of thinking which emphasizes that Self-liberation and enlightenment have to be achieved by personal inner effort alone. In western extrovert tradition the desire for union with God Transcendent and the hope of redemption by Jesus are conjoined with grace experienced in the innermost place of one's Self, the birthplace of God Immanent, the archetypal God-image.

The word 'religion' in colloquial usage refers to the denomination or the creed an individual subscribes to. A creed is a systematized expression of belief enshrining fixed dogmatic teachings, and enriched by forms of worship, ritual and outer observances. A creed is a valuable and positive framework when it keeps faith alive, and serves to keep contact with the unconscious. It can be a protection for the ego in terms of grief and danger, or when it is too frail to withstand the onslaught of immediate experience.

When dogmatic teachings have become empty formulas, a creed may stand in the way of spiritual development, as well as causing great anguish; Jung knew this only too well. Thoughtless, mechanical clinging to inherited religious conditioning will also impede development, and a creed may then be a haven for individuals who shun personal responsibility and involvement, and resist consciousness and maturity. A negative creed is a substitute for religion.

The link between religion and creed is dogma. Dogmatic teachings are concerned with statements about the nature of God. They are markers by which we chart our relationship with God. Jung valued dogma as the outcome of inner experience, and for the care with which it had been formulated, giving it a super-personal character and the quality of absolute truth. He spoke of the beauty of dogma, and he went so far as to say that only unthinking fools would attack it and its symbolism, but not lovers of the soul. He thought that dogma expressed all the things of the spirit which human beings can intuit or experience.

It is on these issues that Jung criticized the clergy. He accused them of teaching and preaching inner truths in the form of external concrete reality. The burning questions of God's relationship to the creature he created and

14

of the horrible reality and mystery of evil in humanity and divinity were evaded or answered in a manner which touched neither the heart nor the imagination. This kind of teaching has resulted in individuals not taking Christian belief on board through total indifference.

The clergy reacted to Jung's ideas about religion with suspicion and many misgivings; they thought he was advocating a new religion. Jung's definition of religion as an attitude to the inner reality and an activity of the soul was startling; his assertion that such experiences are accessible to psychology and that the religious function lies in the unconscious was revolutionary. Christianity and its practice were considered to be a matter of the conscious mind, the ego, and the will though also of grace, as faith is a divine gift as well as a virtue. Jung's claim that religion affects the total personality and that essential processes of religious life take place in the unconscious seemed to the clergy to be threatening the essence of faith. They believed that Jung was reducing matters of faith, which transcend the human mind and the senses, to the human sphere of psychic processes and archetypal experiences. It was also very disquieting that he spoke of the image of God as being in the centre of the psyche.

Jung found this disregard for the human psyche which he detected in these criticisms unintelligible. He wrote that it was not he who had created the psyche, and that speaking of God as an archetype meant that He already has a place in that part of the psyche which is pre-existent to consciousness. Jung was equally indignant when he was accused of putting the self in the place of God: again he was unable to understand how anybody could believe that he would substitute an intellectual concept for God. Eventually the clergy realized that for the first time in many years a scientist was taking notice of religious matters without accusing ministers of religion of dispensing opium or of fostering infantile neurotic attitudes. On the contrary, he was 'offering psychological proofs for the rightness of theological statements on empirical grounds'. Moreover, this psychiatrist was willing to enter into a dialogue with them on the grounds that 'the object of their mutual concern was the psychically sick and suffering human being'.

In spite of this more favourable attitude to Jung, theologians still found it difficult to accept his concepts, mainly because they criticized from an intellectual and theological point of view without having exposed themselves to a personal analysis. It appeared to them that Jung was challenging ideological and dogmatic formulations when in fact he was exploring how modern people were affected by matters of the Christian faith, and relating his findings to his own personal experiences.

Jung appreciated the immense difficulties confronting the post-First World War generation: the loss of certainties, of values, of illusions, played a part in the rejection of suffering and sacrifice. There was so much of it in external reality that the impersonal language of orthodoxy touched only a minority of people. The clergy recognized the truth of these statements, and many accepted that they had failed through lack of psychological knowledge to get the Christian message across in its fullness. They began to listen to what Jung had to say. Jung felt that aspects of the human condition and of frailty had been left out of Christian teaching and therefore aligned himself with those who declared themselves to be outside the Church, *extra ecclesiam*. He emphasized that while faith cannot be demanded, understanding is needed; perfection cannot be expected from a being so unconscious of his own nature as man still is today, and as unknowing in the negative sense of his instinctive needs as well as of his spiritual ones.

One of the aspects of Christianity which troubled Jung was the split within it. Jung showed tremendous courage in bringing this issue out into the open. No one before him had ever dared to say that this outer schism affects the psyche of every single Christian; therefore it must also have affected Jung. It is a split which perpetuates ignorance of the different ways in which individuals experience their ultimate inner truth; Catholic and Protestant attitudes are opposites and also complementary.

In spite of Jung's attempts to make his position clear, many Protestant and Catholic theologians could not understand that he would not let himself be tied down to any particular denomination. To the end of his life he called himself a Christian and remained a member of the Swiss Reformed Church; but he never went to church. When he was asked whether he had ever thought of joining the Catholic Church he answered that though he knew but little of Catholic doctrine the little was enough to make it an unalienable possession for him. But, he continued, he knew so much about Protestantism that he could never give it up. Jung was a Protestant, a Protestant in the mould of Johann Sebastian Bach or of Rembrandt. He was fascinated by Catholic doctrine, but many aspects of Catholic faith eluded him; it was not in his bones. He did not understand, for instance, that the concept of the *privatio boni* is an intellectual one debated by theologians but which is not relevant to the ordinary practising Catholic.

Jung frequently said that the theological way of thinking was completely alien to him. However, he had acquired immense knowledge of the varieties of religious experience; he respected genuine Christian faith and tolerated the vagaries of creed, though he always attempted to assist patients to find their inner truth.

People nowadays want to experiment with life and determine for themselves the value or meaning of ideas, moral teachings or rules of behaviour. Liberation from some manacles of the mind does not necessarily lead to greater spiritual freedom. People are getting more and more frightened of their own daring and of the absence of signposts they can recognize and follow. They suffer from a deeply repressed bad conscience, and therefore react violently against any notion of guilt, let alone sin.

'To take pity on one's own soul is pleasing to the Lord' is an old Talmudic saying. It is the self-knowledge Jung advocates. Human nature is complex, one's own included. There are warring instincts. There is the cosmic reality of good and evil; there is the longing for oneness, unity, wholeness. Once upon a time the shadow was simple to recognize; it consisted of one's evil inclinations, one's shameful ugliness. Today it is the good, the light, the beautiful which are twisted until they too fall into the dark abyss. These problems underlie neurotic symptoms, and they are the reason why healing in the psychological sense is a religious issue. Analysis was for Jung the first step in which early traumata caused by existential ignorance and the frustrations of being in the power and at the mercy of others are worked through, by separating out – analysing – the resulting inner chaos and confusion. However, the next step, synthesis, was Jung's main interest; his great concern was to facilitate the approach to the numinous. He maintained that this was the real therapy; as one discovers the secret hidden treasure in oneself, one is released from the curse of one's illness, so that the disease itself becomes meaningful. Jung fostered this essentially religious attitude as a protection against the over-valuation of mechanical intellectual thinking on the one hand, and as a corrective on the other hand for the idea that material prosperity is the only proof of a successful life.

Jung was over fifty years old when he began to study medieval Greek and Latin alchemical texts in earnest, and it took him about ten years to decode their bizarre, complicated symbolic language. The alchemists were Christians, but had included in their religious system matters which had been excluded from traditional Christianity; secrecy was therefore important as a shield against the Inquisition.

The alchemists' basic beliefs were the unity of the universe, the perfectibility of matter, and transformation of undesirable psychic contents as an operation on a given individual reality, and not one made from idealistic demands. Furthermore they acknowledged God as a totality in His polarity. Christ for them was the highest value, the gold, the light, the stone from the rock of Daniel which conquers all; by Christ's incarnation matter had been sanctified. However, paradoxically, the stone is also the darkness of matter from which Christ has to be liberated. This attitude appealed to Jung and was instrumental in transforming his fear of Jesus.

Jung identified with all these ideas, and considered the method by which the alchemists attempted to achieve the union of opposites, the *mysterium coniunctionis*, to be parallel with his own ideas of healing after the first stage of analysis has been superseded by synthesis. Their spirituality was nearer to the introvert eastern mode, and therefore closer to his own.

At one time Faust, the Faust of Goethe's magnum opus, had been more meaningful to him than the Jesus of the fourth gospel; Jung knew that Goethe had been an alchemist. Faust is saved through the love and the prayer of a sinful young girl who turns to Mary, virgin, mother, queen of angels, for help. To Mary, the feminine principle.

Jung, in his passionate outburst against God in his book *Answer to*

Job, expressed his anger and the anguish he had suffered from God's unconsciousness and cruelty. But he experienced Job's unshakeable faith in God as his advocate and redeemer, and finally, as the incomprehensible infinitely greater. God was transformed by man's conscious trust in His other side. God remembered Wisdom, Wisdom – Sophia – Mary; woman, the feminine. He became conscious of having to atone for His crimes by incarnating and taking upon Himself the sufferings and the sins of humankind. This was God's answer to Job. The tempestuous vision mediated to Jung insight into the ultimate task necessary for healing and wholeness, namely reconciling and uniting the antinomy in the divinity and thereby achieving a reunion and reconciliation between the human and divine under a new dispensation.

Jung was giving a seminar to students in Zurich on The Spiritual Exercises of S. Ignatius. He had been thinking a great deal about the prayer *Anima Christi*, and one night he awoke and saw at the foot of his bed, bathed in bright light, the figure of Christ on the cross. The image was very distinct, not quite life-size, and the body was made of greenish gold. This hypnagogic vision was extremely beautiful, but Jung was 'profoundly shaken' by it. Reflecting on it he realized that he had overlooked the analogy of Christ with the *viriditas*, the *aurum non vulgum*. Green gold is the living quality which animates the whole cosmos, even inorganic matter. This vision with its emphasis on the metal showed him that he had faced an alchemical conception of Christ as a union of spiritually alive and physically dead matter. These thoughts comforted Jung, because they reassured him that there was nothing inadequate in his Christ-image.

Jung's account of this strange numinous experience goes no further. He does not say why he was so deeply disturbed by the vision; he does not comment on his having needed the framework of alchemy to restore his psychic equilibrium. Had he, in spite of his denial, overlooked the union of the glory of the risen Christ bathed in light with the darkness and suffering of Christ Crucified? Jung certainly felt closer to the Son of Man and His suffering than to the Son of God in His glory. In his inner study, Jung had a stained-glass window with scenes of the passion depicted on it, and hidden behind a veil he had a large photograph of the Shroud of Turin.

Jung knew a great deal; he was enlightened, but he was a very humble man. He knew 'that even the enlightened person remains what he is and is never more than his own limited ego before the One who dwells in him'. He did not accumulate knowledge for the sake of knowledge, but for the sake of healing troubled minds; he never forgot the oath he had sworn to attempt to relieve suffering; his way was to penetrate ever more deeply into the secrets of the human personality. This was his main business, his magnum opus.

Over the front door of Jung's home in Küsnacht stood the words: 'Vocatus atque non vocatus, Deus adherit': 'Called or not called, God is there.'

REFERENCES

Heydt, Vera von der (1976) *Prospects for the Soul*, London: Darton, Longman & Todd Ltd.

James, W. (1902) *The Varieties of Religious Experience*, London: Fontana Books, 1960.

Jung, C. G. (1932) *Psychotherapists or the Clergy* and *Psychology and Religion*, in *The Collected Works*, vol. 11, New York: Routledge & Kegan Paul.

—— (1938) *Psychology and Religion*, in *The Collected Works*, vol. 11.

—— (1952) *Answer to Job*, in *The Collected Works*, vol. 11.

—— (1963) *Memories, Dreams, Reflections*, London: Routledge and Collins.

—— (1973) *C. G. Jung Letters*, vol. 1, London: Routledge & Kegan Paul.

—— (1976) *C. G. Jung Letters*, vol. 2, London: Routledge & Kegan Paul.

Wolff, Toni (1946) *Christianity Within*, pamphlet, London: Guild of Pastoral Psychology.

2

THE HOLY: A MEETING-POINT BETWEEN ANALYTICAL PSYCHOLOGY AND RELIGION

Leon Schlamm

Underlying all of Jung's mature writings on religion is a definition of it which emphasizes individual submission to and dependence on numinous experience, which has its source in the unconscious. Jung was generally suspicious of the creedal statements and metaphysical claims of religious traditions;[1] and in a manner which resembled the pragmatism of William James, he focused his attention on the practical value of numinous experiences for psychological development, while bracketing out any speculation about the objective reference of such experiences. It is in this way that Jung wanted to be understood by his readers as a phenomenologist of numinous experience.[2]

The purpose of this essay is to present a detailed account of Jung's relationship to numinous experience, and to demonstrate that while Jung was clearly a passionate advocate of such experience, his enthusiasm for it was, nevertheless, tempered by his understanding on the one hand of psychosis and on the other of the function of consciousness in the individuation process. Numinous experience – or the experience of holiness[3] – does in Jung's mind provide a meeting-point between analytical psychology and religion, but also, he believes, because of its teleology, draws attention to specific differences between them which it is the purpose of this essay to clarify. In order to do this, I shall compare Jung's comments about numinous experience with Rudolf Otto's account of it, which so profoundly influenced him during the last twenty-five years of his life. I shall demonstrate that there are indeed some significant similarities between their religious world-views, and that a familiarity with Otto's work will contribute to a better understanding of Jung's writings about religious experience. On the other hand, I shall argue that the differences of theoretical perspective and practical intention between Jung the analytical psychologist and Otto the theologian are equally significant.

I begin with a review of Jung's comments about numinous experience, which he defined as Rudolf Otto's term for a unique experience which is 'inexpressible, mysterious, terrifying, directly experienced and pertaining only to the divinity'.[4] In his 1937 Yale Terry lectures about the relationship between psychology and religion Jung offered a definition of religion which drew attention to the value which he attributed to numinous experience and its significance for an adequate understanding of analytical psychology.

> Religion, as the Latin word denotes, is a careful and scrupulous observation of what Rudolf Otto aptly termed the *numinosum*, that is, a dynamic agency or effect not caused by an arbitrary act of will. On the contrary, it seizes and controls the human subject, who is always rather its victim than its creator. The *numinosum* – whatever its cause may be – is an experience of the subject independent of his will. . . . It causes a peculiar alteration of consciousness.
>
> (*Jung, CW 11, para. 6*)

In his subsequent writings, especially those concerned with the Christian tradition, there are many further references to numinous experience. For example, he speaks of the 'deeply stirring emotional effect' of numinous, divine images[5] and of their 'thrilling power'.[6] These numinous, god-images possess mana (psychic power), and are therefore unusually persuasive from the psychological point of view.[7] Moreover, the power or vitality of these numinous, divine images makes them 'difficult to handle intellectually, since our affectivity is involved . . . absolute objectivity is more rarely achieved here than anywhere else'.[8] Indeed, experience of these numinous images, Jung acknowledges, can be overwhelming – 'an admission that goes against not only our pride, but against our deep-rooted fear that consciousness may perhaps lose its ascendancy'.[9] In this statement Jung draws attention to another important feature of numinous experience: its identification with experience of the unconscious,[10] and consequently the danger that it may threaten the stability of consciousness. This is particularly well illustrated in the following passage:

> In the end such [feeling-toned] complexes – presumably in proportion to their distance from consciousness – assume, by self-amplification, an archaic and mythological character and hence a certain numinosity, as is perfectly clear in schizophrenic dissociations. Numinosity, however, is wholly outside conscious volition, for it transports the subject into the state of rapture, which is a state of will-less surrender.
>
> (*Jung, CW 8, para. 383*)

Again, he declares:

> An archetypal dream . . . can so fascinate the dreamer that he is very apt to see it in some kind of illumination, warning or supernatural help. Nowadays [, however], most people are afraid of surrendering to such experiences and their fear proves the existence of a 'holy

21

dread' of the numinous [the experience of which comes from the unconscious].

(Jung, CW 11, para. 222)

Jung regarded such fear as to some degree justified, and was clearly worried that unconscious, numinous, psychic contents could have a possessive or obsessive effect on consciousness.[11]

However, in spite of these misgivings about numinous experience, generally he thought that it was tremendously valuable for our psychological well-being and knowledge of ourselves and, of course, absolutely fundamental to an understanding of the individuation process.[12] Accordingly, he could conclude that it does 'not belong exclusively to the domain of psychopathology, but can be observed in normal people as well'. 'It is not in the least astonishing that numinous experiences should occur in the course of psychological treatment and that they may even be expected with some regularity.'[13]

But what more precisely were these numinous experiences, which Jung acknowledged during the course of his clinical work as having such an extraordinary effect on consciousness? Clearly, for an answer to this question we must examine Rudolf Otto's account of it, upon which Jung leaned so heavily.

Rudolf Otto (1869–1937) introduced his readers to the term 'numinous' (derived from the Latin *numen*) in his *The Idea of the Holy*.[14] His purpose was to draw their attention to the distinctive features of religious experience, which he regarded as in danger of being confused with other, non-religious, experiences and thus forgotten. This, he believed, was particularly well illustrated by the fashionable practice at the beginning of the century[15] of reducing the experience of holiness to a moral experience, thus ensuring that what was uniquely religious about the holy was overlooked. To combat this spiritual malaise and intellectual confusion, Otto proposed that the experience of the holy be understood as a complex one, which is the result of the uniting of a rational (or moral) experience with a non-rational, irreducibly religious, numinous experience. The burden of the argument which followed was to provide an account of the non-rational aspect of the experience of the holy, which was sufficiently detailed to justify Otto's use of the term 'numinous'.

Otto speaks of three moments or aspects of numinous experience, the *mysterium*, the *tremendum* and the *fascinosum*, and suggests that they may appear either in isolation or in conjunction with one another. I turn first to an explanation of the *tremendum* moment of numinous experience, to which Otto gives particular emphasis.

The experience of the *tremendum* is characterized first by feelings of fear and trembling in the face of the awful aspect of the deity;[16] second by feelings of overpoweringness in the face of the majesty of the deity, which in turn produce feelings of one's own nothingness (what Otto called 'creature consciousness' or 'creaturehood'), that is the feeling of being but 'dust and ashes' in the face of that which is above all creatures;[17] and third by an awareness of the energy or urgency of the numinous object, which is particularly perceptible in the wrath of the deity and typically 'clothes itself in [such] symbolical expressions [as divine] vitality, passion, emotional temper, will, force, movement, excitement, and activity'.[18] Otto observes that it is a fearful thing to fall into the hands of the living God, and a thing quite unlike anything else. Experiences of the *tremendum* are totally unlike any non-religious experiences, no matter how threatening these non-religious experiences may appear. The fear of God in particular is a peculiar dread quite unlike any non-religious form of fear. It produces a unique form of religious shuddering or horror in the face of the totally weird, the spectral or the uncanny. The presence of the numinous chills a man in a way that nothing else can. Indeed, even fear for one's life is not like the fear of God, which is more like the fear of ghosts; it gives one the creeps. In the fear of God we see supernatural terror, which acknowledges what can only be called a dark side of the deity. Otto insists that divine wrath is morally unintelligible; it is incalculable and arbitrary, rather 'like stored-up electricity, discharging itself upon any one who comes too near'.[19] Yet he observes that this terrible side of the deity, far from diminishing its absolute value and authority, appears rather as a natural expression of it, an indispensable element of the numinous. Clearly, Otto's emphasis on the daunting and singularly awe-inspiring character of the terrible, dark aspect of the deity requires further comment in the light of Jung's thesis about the shadow in God, and I shall return to this issue later.

I turn now to consider the *fascinosum* moment of numinous experience.[20] If the *tremendum* repels man, then the *fascinosum* is that irreducibly religious aspect of the numinous which attracts him to it, since it promises him supernatural love, grace and a bliss which defies understanding. The *fascinosum* represents the supernatural beauty of the numinous which is quite unlike any natural beauty, and which creates in those who are religious a yearning for experience of it. It is not merely to be wondered at, but something which entrances religious man. He feels something that captivates and transports him, something that leads him to experience a strange ravishment, rising often to a pitch of dizzy intoxication; it is the Dionysiac elements in the *numen*. At its most intense the fascinating becomes the over-abounding, the exuberant, the mystical moment, which provides the religious man with the most satisfying experience he can have in this life, and he is likely to sacrifice much to attain it. In short, the element of fascination in numinous experience provides for Otto the blessings of salvation, which the non-religious man cannot begin to understand.

Finally, I turn to consider the *mysterium* moment of numinous experience.[21] Confrontation with it arouses the religious response of stupor, astonishment which strikes us dumb, amazement and utter incomprehension. In fact, the mysterious aspect of the numinous object is 'beyond our apprehension and comprehension, not only because our knowledge has certain irremovable limits, but because in it we come upon something inherently wholly other, whose kind and character are incommensurable with our own'.[22] The 'wholly other', as Otto defines it, is that which is completely beyond the sphere of the usual, the intelligible, the natural and the familiar. It falls outside the limits of the canny, and is contrasted with it, filling the mind with blank wonder. Otto concludes his account of the *mysterium* by calling it the supramundane, 'that which is above the whole world order'[23] and in contrast to it.

I turn now to an assessment of the relationship between these accounts of numinous experience of Jung and Otto. To begin with, it is clear that, with few qualifications,[24] the details of Otto's account of numinous experience are not inconsistent with Jung's use of the term.[25] Indeed, it is obvious that a greater familiarity with Otto's account of numinous experience can only enrich – rather than undermine – our understanding of what Jung means by the experience of the unconscious.[26] Moreover, there are several striking similarities between the definitions of religious experience of Jung and Otto which require specific comment. The first of these is the actual acknowledgement of an element of fascination in religious experience, the significance of which is all too frequently overlooked. What Jung and Otto agree upon here is that the quest for religious experience is driven by a peculiar kind of religious desire for a peculiar kind of religious beauty. This observation leads us to the second similarity between the work of Jung and Otto on religious experience. This experience of religious beauty is frequently accompanied by an experience which is in sharp contrast to it: an experience of religious fear, dread, horror or even disgust. This is demonstrated in Jung's work by his constant references to the ambivalent attitude of consciousness towards the contents of the unconscious. These unconscious contents can repel and attract consciousness at the same time, thus casting a spell over it which is difficult to dissolve. Similarly, Otto observes that the daunting and fascinating moments of numinous experience 'combine in a strange harmony of contrasts, and the resultant dual character of the numinous consciousness, to which the entire religious development bears witness . . . is at once the strangest and most noteworthy phenomenon in the whole history of religion'.[27]

However, it is the unusual emphasis Jung and Otto place on the experience of a dark aspect of the deity which provides the most impressive similarity between their definitions of religious experience. Just as Otto attributes particular importance to a divine wrath of the *tremendum* moment of numinous experience which is morally unintelligible, so Jung in his writings about the shadow in God – particularly in his essay *Answer to Job*, which explores archaic, divine brutality – emphasizes the fierce and terrible side of Yahweh, using language to which Otto would be to some degree sympathetic. The purpose, for example, of the apocalyptic visions of St John in the biblical Book of Revelation, Jung informs us

> is not to tell St John, as an ordinary human being, how much shadow he hides beneath his human nature, but to open the seer's eyes to the immensity of God [in other words, to open the seer's eyes to an overwhelming divine shadow] . . . . For this reason he felt his gospel of love to be onesided, and he supplemented it with the gospel of fear: God can be loved but must be feared.
>
> (Jung, CW 11, para. 732)

Clearly, Jung, as well as Otto, is referring here to extremely disturbing religious experiences which must be unfamiliar to most modern Europeans. In fact, what both Jung and Otto appear to be doing is to be offering the twentieth-century Christian or post-Christian[28] a serious intellectual, as well as spiritual, challenge which requires of him sustained reflection and honest introspection. They point out that Old Testament literature is filled with anthropopathic images of God, many of which are extremely dark and therefore irreconcilable with the traditional and all too familiar account of God as the shadowless embodiment of perfect goodness. Moreover, they are critical of those biblical interpreters – ancient and modern – who appeal to the authority of the New Testament and post-biblical scholasticism to justify the repression or suppression of such dark images. The result of such repression/suppression – so often identified with the Aristotelian intellectual tradition – is that one fails to understand the complexity and ambiguity of God.

Of course, many twentieth-century theologians have dismissed these observations about God as referring to a deity with whom they are completely unfamiliar; and significantly, Otto's work has received as much criticism in this context as that of Jung. In fact, one of the most frequent criticisms of Otto's account of religious experience in *The Idea of the Holy* has been and continues to be that in emphasizing the non-rational quality or the 'wholly other' nature of numinous experience, Otto appears to be transforming religion into something sub-rational – and therefore pre-Christian – rather than supra-rational.[29] Similarly, one of the most persistent theological criticisms of *Answer to Job* is that Christianity in Jung's hands is in danger of losing the struggle for liberation from the tyranny of those dark gods who exercised authority over mankind in pre-Christian times, and who have continued to be influential in the lives of a significant number of men and women of the last two millennia.[30]

However, Jung, like Otto, questions the Christian evolutionary perspective which is presupposed by this criticism of pre-Christian numinous experiences,[31] and argues that if we succeed in separating ourselves completely from those dark, divine forces of pre-Christian times, this will only be at enormous – indeed unjustifiable – psychological cost.[32] It is for this reason that Jung seeks to direct the attention of his readers to what he calls 'an eternal, as distinct from a temporal [Christian] gospel', which acknowledges that, contrary to the teachings of the Church, we have good reason to fear God, as well as to love Him, because 'God has a terrible, double aspect: a sea of grace is met by a seething lake of fire.'[33]

Clearly, there are some important points of agreement between the accounts of numinous experience of Jung and Otto which require acknowledgement. However, it is equally clear that there is a need to acknowledge and set beside these points of agreement some significant differences between these accounts, and it is to an examination of them that I now turn.

In fact, there is one fundamental principle of analytical psychology which provides the key to understanding what separates Jung's interpretation of numinous experience from that of Otto: the need at all costs to preserve the fragile autonomy of consciousness. I drew attention earlier in this chapter to the danger that unconscious, numinous, psychic contents could have a possessive or obsessive effect on consciousness. Here lies the road to inflation or even psychosis; and Jung was concerned to defend consciousness against the fascinating, and yet dangerous, forces of the unconscious which are so powerful that they may cause the disintegration of the personality.[34] Moreover, Jung understood one of the most significant aims of the quest for individuation to be the strengthening, or even the extension, of consciousness in the face of these powerful, numinous, psychic forces. Even while he was emphasizing the value of the conjunction of consciousness with the unconscious for the individuation process, he was at the same time constantly warning his readers of the need for consciousness to maintain some distance between itself and the numinous contents of the unconscious, if there was to be an authentic *coniunctio oppositorum*. Consciousness must maintain its independence, although not be completely disconnected, from the numinous, psychic contents of the unconscious, if there is to be real individuation.[35]

However, in sharp contrast to this depth psychological approach to numinous experience, Otto argues that the only response such experience can elicit, if its distinctive phenomenology is understood, is unqualified submission. In fact, this emphasis on submission is actually strengthened by another feature of numinous experience which I have so far not drawn attention to: what Otto calls 'creature feeling' or 'creature consciousness', man's self-evaluation as absolutely worthless in the face of the only object of value, the *numinosum*.[36] Moreover, this emphasis on submission is, according to Otto, particularly well illustrated in the life of the mystic, whose experience of the *numinosum* is more intense than that of the non-mystic. The characteristic notes of mysticism, Otto declares, are the annihilation of the self and as its complement the recognition of the deity as the only reality. What he means here is that the self-consciousness of the mystic is characterized by feelings of self-depreciation, the estimation of the self as something not essentially real or even as nothing.[37] Ultimately, the mystic must surrender his whole being, even his consciousness, to God.[38]

Clearly, this rejection of the delusion of the self by the mystic is incompatible with the individuation process,[39] in which neither of the opposites, consciousness or the 'wholly other', numinous contents of the unconscious, is devalued by their *coniunctio*. Individuation requires the holding together of the numinous contents of the unconscious – even stupefying experiences of the *mysterium*[40] – with consciousness; in other words, it requires the acknowledgement that there cannot be any experience of the *numinosum* without the presence of consciousness. This is what Jung means by his celebration of the miracle of reflecting consciousness, which confirms the existence of the world and without which the world would be without meaning.[41] Moreover, this emphasis on the presence of consciousness during any numinous experience receives further support from Jung's controversial dream which anticipated his writing of *Answer to Job*. The climax of the dream presents Jung being 'lead into the highest presence' by his long-dead father. His father kneels and touches his head to the floor Muslim style, while when Jung follows his father's example, his head does not go all the way to the floor: there is a millimetre to spare. This 'millimetre to spare' is that which prevents complete submission; which represents Jung's defiance and determination not to be 'the dumb fish'; which represents man's reservation in the face of divine decrees.[42] This is man's freedom, and this is his consciousness which must constantly confront numinous experience during the individuation process.

At the end of his life Jung declared:

> We do not know how far the process of coming to consciousness can extend, or where it will lead. It is a new element in the story of creation, and there are no parallels we can look to. We therefore cannot know what potentialities are inherent in it.[43]
>
> (Jung, *Memories, Dreams, Reflections*, p. 372)

This remarkably agnostic statement clearly suggests that Jung was uncertain as to what the relationship between consciousness and numinous experience might be in the future. However, it is obvious that such agnosticism would hardly have elicited much sympathy from Otto. Moreover, Otto would have been even more hostile to Jung's chronicling of the evolution of human and divine consciousness in *Answer to Job*. Such a depth psychological account of God's inner life – with its acknowledgement of God's lack of consciousness and His dependence on man to integrate His opposites of good and evil[44] – Otto would have branded pure theosophy.[45] He could have had no sympathy for the antinomian thesis which lies at the heart of the argument of *Answer to Job*: 'Whoever knows God has an effect on Him.'[46]

To conclude this chapter, I can think of no better way to demonstrate the difference between Jung's measured appreciation of numinous experience[47] and Otto's unconditional surrender to it than to present Otto's interpretation of the experience of Job. Whereas Jung is enraged by Yahweh's failure to recognize Job's transparent righteousness, and concludes from His monstrous behaviour that He is an antinomy who is not quite conscious of what He is doing, Otto argues that chapter 38 of the Book of Job presents an experience of the *mysterium, tremendum et fascinans* which is so huge in scale, so astonishing and overwhelming, that it provides a vindication of God to Job and a reconciliation of Job to God. Job, according to Otto, is 'truly and rightly overpowered' by his experience of God out of the whirlwind, 'not merely silenced by superior strength'. When Job declares 'Therefore I abhor myself and repent in dust and ashes',[48] this is not an admission simply of 'impotent collapse and submission to . . . superior power', but of an inward conviction that God is justified and that Job's soul has found spiritual satisfaction and peace.[49]

NOTES AND REFERENCES

1 Where – especially in the West in the twentieth century – their libidinal connection with the unconscious has been destroyed. Accordingly, he argued, they are no longer capable of attracting the psychic projections of the majority of human beings in society. In any case, Jung proposed that a prerequisite for progress along the path towards individuation was the dissolution of such psychic projections. For further discussion concerning Jung's attitude towards the creedal statements and metaphysical claims of Christianity, see, for example, C. G. Jung, *The Collected Works* (henceforth *CW*), vol. 11, part I; J. W. Heisig, *Imago Dei* (Lewisburg: Bucknell University Press, 1979); M. Stein, *Jung's Treatment of Christianity* (Wilmette: Chiron Publications, 1985); A. Moreno, *Jung, Gods and Modern Man* (Notre Dame and London: University of Notre Dame Press, 1970); V. White, *Soul and Psyche* (London: Collins, 1960); H. L. Philp, *Jung and the Problem of Evil* (London: Salisbury Square, 1958).

2 See the recent study of Jung as a phenomenologist by Roger Brooke, *Jung and Phenomenology* (London: Routledge, 1991).

3 While Jung understood the two terms to be synonyms, Rudolf Otto argues that the constituents of the experience of holiness are numinous experience and rational or moral experience. Only as numinous and rational experience are united is there, in Otto's view, an experience which can be identified as an experience of the holy.

4 C. G. Jung, *Memories, Dreams, Reflections* (London: Collins, 1967), p. 415.

5 Jung, *CW* 11, para. 454.

6 Jung, *CW* 13, para. 396.

7 Jung, *CW* 11, para. 558.

8 ibid., para. 735.

9 ibid., para. 275.

10 See, for example, *CW* 10, para. 874, where Jung asserts 'Consciousness experiences this supraordinate totality [the unconscious] as something numinous, as a *tremendum* or *fascinosum*'.

11 He argued that archetypes could have such an effect, which is why they should be understood as daimonia. See *Memories, Dreams, Reflections*, p. 380.

12 To a consideration of which I shall return later.

13 Jung, *CW* 14, para. 780.

14 Originally published as *Das Heilige* (Breslau: Trewendt und Granier, 1917); in this essay I shall be referring to the English (Oxford: Oxford University Press, 1958) edition.

15 Which was largely the result of the influence of Kantian philosophy on European theology.

16 Otto, op. cit., pp. 13–19.

17 ibid., pp. 10–11, 19–23.

18 ibid., pp. 23–4.

19 ibid., p. 18.

20 ibid., pp. 31–9.

21 ibid., pp. 25–30.

22 ibid., p. 28.

23 ibid., p. 29.

24 To which I shall give some attention later.

25 Jung was clearly convinced that his use of Otto's term was justified by the phenomenology of the experience of the unconscious and that he was not, as his critics believed, guilty of interpreting numinous experience reductively as a non-religious experience.

26 This is well illustrated when we reflect upon Otto's references on the one hand to the awe-inspiring, overpowering and energetic character of the *tremendum* moment of numinous experience – and clearly Otto's references to a specifically religious horror in the face of the weird, the spectral or the uncanny require special attention here – and on the other to the captivating, indeed intoxicating, supernatural beauty of the *fascinosum* moment of numinous experience, which a religious man will yearn for since it provides him with the blessings of salvation.

27 Otto, op. cit., p. 31.

28 And the twentieth-century Jew as well, at least the Jew who is unfamiliar with the Kabbala, which locates what Otto calls the *tremendum* within the being – some would say the psyche – of God, that is within the *sephiroth* of *Gevurah* or *Din* (transcendent power of judgement) and *Hod* (majesty). For further discussion of the psyche of God within the Jewish mystical tradition, see, for example, D. R. Blumenthal, *Understanding Jewish Mysticism*, part II (New York: Ktav Publishing House, 1978).

29 See, for example, P. C. Almond, *Rudolf Otto, An Introduction to his Philosophical Theology* (Chapel Hill and London: University of North Carolina Press, 1984), pp. 81–2; R. F. Davidson, *Rudolf Otto's Interpretation of Religion* (Princeton: Princeton University Press, 1947), p. 183; J. M. Moore, *Theories of Religious Experience* (New York: Round Table Press, 1938), p. 84. However, it is important to understand that while this emphasis on the 'wholly other' nature of numinous experience in *The Idea of the Holy* clearly determines the direction of the general argument of the text, it is accompanied by other theological claims which are by no means easy to reconcile with it. In particular, Otto performs his own *coniunctio oppositorum*, uniting the non-rational numinous experience with reason (or morality) to create the experience of holiness through the mechanism of what he calls – borrowing a term from Kant – schematization. Otto argues that in the evolutionary history of religions numinous experience is gradually filled out with rational or moral experience and that the connection between them is in fact a necessary one which is confirmed by inner feeling – in other words,

religious experience. Through such religious feeling we discover in the higher religions, particularly Christianity, that the most intense (potentially amoral) numinous experience cries out to be united with the most advanced form of reason to create a conjunction of opposites in which neither of them is qualified by the other.

30 See, for example Victor White's review of *Answer to Job* in *Journal of Analytical Psychology* 4 (January 1959), 77ff. It is also significant that Jung has been accused of conflating the supra-rational with the sub-rational and thereby of confusing what is angelic in man (the realm of archetypes) with the bestial (the instinctual realm). This criticism has come not only from representatives of the 'traditionalist' school of philosophy of René Guénon and Frithjof Schuon (see, in particular, Titus Burckhardt's 'Cosmology and modern science', in *The Sword of Gnosis*, ed. J. Needleman (Baltimore: Penguin, 1974), pp. 167–77) but also from one of the most influential writers in the field of transpersonal psychology, Ken Wilber (see his *Eye to Eye* (New York: Anchor Press, 1983), pp. 211–15, 239–43).

31 In fact, Jung challenges the Church's account of salvation history and rejects its 'exclusivist' claim that true and complete, divine revelation has occurred only once in history. His rejection of the Roman Catholic axiom *Extra Ecclesiam nulla salus* ('Outside the Church no salvation') is based on his 'pagan' conviction that the deities of all religious traditions are equally valuable because they have a common psychic origin. For further discussion of this issue, see, in particular, P.F. Knitter, *No Other Name?* (London: SCM Press Ltd, 1985), ch. 4; and also A. Race, *Christians and Religious Pluralism* (London: SCM Press Ltd, 1983); J. Hick and B. Hebblethwaite (eds), *Christianity and Other Religions* (Glasgow: Collins, 1980).

32 For Jung there is a terrible price to pay for the repression of those dark, divine forces of pre-Christian times. Not only will we cease to be invigorated by our experience of our numinous, unconscious depths; but those archaic gods, whose nature is sensual and brutal, will also eventually seek revenge from the psyche which has attempted to deny them. When this occurs, and they rise to the surface of consciousness, they will 'press the God of our ideals to the wall'. See *CW* 6, para. 150.

33 Jung, *CW* 11, para. 733.

34 Jung, *CW* 12, para. 439.

35 While individuation clearly requires consciousness to abandon its habitual defensiveness in its relationship to the unconscious and to seek to reach out sympathetically to its numinous contents – Jung speaks here of the need to 'open ourselves to [the *numinosum*], let ourselves be overpowered by it, trusting in its meaning' (*CW* 10, para. 864) – this need not be incompatible with Jung's desire to safeguard the independence of consciousness from the unconscious. What is important to understand here is that it is possible for consciousness to be strong enough to experience powerful, numinous, psychic images of the unconscious without being overwhelmed by them. (Incidentally, I assume that Jung is not seriously recommending in the above quotation that we allow ourselves to be *totally* or *permanently* overpowered by the *numinosum*.)

36 Otto, op. cit., pp. 9–11. The *numinosum*, for Otto, is believed to possess value independently of any actual experiences of it. This is a judgement which is obviously based on Otto's epistemological assumption that the *numinosum* is not only felt to have objective reference outside the self, but also *known* with certainty to possess such status. Obviously, Jung – as a phenomenologist of the psyche rather than a metaphysician – cannot accept this epistemological assumption.

37 ibid., p. 21. For further discussion of this issue, see my article 'Rudolf Otto and mystical experience', *Religious Studies* 27: 389–98.

38 Incidentally, this understanding of the mystic's self-consciousness is not inconsistent with Otto's later discussion in *Mysticism, East and West*, trans. B. L. Bracey and R. C. Payne (New York: Macmillan Company, 1932), pp. 118–19, about the experience of the religious exaltedness of the self in the mysticism of Eckhart. Eckhart experiences his self as exalted only because of its identification with the 'Godhead'. There is, however, no consciousness here separate from the deity. Indeed, in spite of the vast differences of religious language, Eckhart's observations about the absorption of the self in the 'Godhead' resemble the Sufi concept of *fanā*, the total annihilation of the ego, where only the divine reality remains. Clearly, Jung's understanding of the relationship between consciousness, the unconscious and the *numinosum* would be rejected by orthodox Sufis as heretical *hulūl*, the theology of the 'incarnation or indwelling' of the divine in man. For further discussion of this issue, see, for example, A. Schimmel, *The Mystical Dimension of Islam* (Chapel Hill: University of North Carolina Press, 1975).

39 Obviously Otto's position here cannot be reconciled with Jung's claim that 'Individuation does not shut one out from the world, but gathers the world to oneself' (*CW* 8, para. 432). While the self which is rejected by Otto's mystic is the ego rather than Jung's Self, clearly Jung will inevitably equate the mystic's total rejection of the ego with psychosis.

40 Jung, *CW* 7, para. 344.

41 Jung, *Memories, Dreams, Reflections*, p. 371.

42 ibid., p. 247.

43 This is an extraordinary confession of agnosticism from a man who has spent his whole life attempting to understand the psyche, and who discovers at the end of his life an unexpected unfamiliarity with his own inner world (*Memories, Dreams, Reflections*, p. 392). Even at this late stage in his life, it is clear that Jung was prepared to acknowledge a lack of certainty over important issues, and indeed confesses with Lao-Tzu: 'All are clear, I alone am clouded' (ibid.). Such candour regrettably tends to be ignored by those within the Jungian community, who canonize Jung's writings and speak of a Jungian Aeon.

44 These details – together with Jung's general argument in *Answer to Job* that the redemption of man and God depend upon divine/human collaboration – obviously resemble the esoteric teachings of the Kabbala, particularly its emphasis on the ability of man to integrate such opposing intradeical *sephiroth* as *Hesed* (mercy) and *Gevurah* (judgement). For further discussion of such integration of *sephiroth*, see, for example, G. G. Scholem, *On the Kabbalah and the Symbolism*, trans. R. Manheim (New York: Schocken Books, 1965), ch. 4.

45 Otto, op. cit., pp. 107–8. Otto defines theosophy as a monstrous, speculative 'science of God', which is based upon a mistaken, literal interpretation of anthropomorphic language about the deity. Significantly, he cites Jacob Böhme here as an example of a theosophist, presumably because, like Jung, he argues that God possesses two wills, one loving and the other wrathful.

46 Jung, *CW* 11, para. 617. Edward Edinger argues in *Transformation of the God-Image* (Toronto: Inner City Books, 1992), that this antinomian thesis was discovered by Jung, and was unknown to anyone prior to the twentieth century. However, Edinger is mistaken. The capacity of man to contribute to the transformation of God has always been an assumption of Kabbalistic theosophy and practical mysticism. What is, however, important to acknowledge is that it may be that Jung's depth psychology provides us at the end of the twentieth

century with an opportunity to understand the esotericism of Kabbala more deeply than ever before.

47 Which expresses what Peter Homans has recently called – borrowing a phrase from Paul Ricœur's study of Freud – a 'hermeneutics of suspicion' which confronts numinous experience. See his 'C. G. Jung: Christian or post-Christian psychologist', in *Essays on Jung and the Study of Religion*, ed. L. H. Martin and J. Goss (New York: University Press of America, 1985), pp. 26–44.

48 Job 42:6.

49 Otto, op. cit., pp. 78, 80.

3

THE DREAM OF WHOLENESS

Murray Stein

Panning through the gravel-like array of texts, ideas, images, stories and doctrines from the world's religious and folk traditions and their offshoots in philosophy and literature, one can quickly and without much effort identify many golden nuggets that speak of the ancient and modern human 'dream of wholeness'. There if, for example, Plato's famous 'myth', which depicts human beings as originally round and whole. Later they became divided into 'halves' and consequently spend their lives searching for their other severed, lost part. This accounts for the mating urge in all its varieties, hetero- and homosexual. Our longing for the 'other', for the soulmate, is, according to Plato, identical to our longing for our own lost original wholeness. We want to put ourselves back together again. So the sexual drive aims for wholeness, for restoration of what was once one unified and complete human being.

There are many other symbols and images that likewise depict and reach for wholeness. Ezekiel's vision of four living creatures, each with four faces and represented by a wheel within a wheel (Ezekiel 1); the Chinese Taoist symbol of Yin–Yang bound in a circle; the Gnostic images of Adam as Anthropos and of God as Mother–Father; Leonardo's drawing of the naked human being outstretched within a circle; the Tibetan mandalas; Nietzsche's poetic rendition of Zarathustra's return and his new doctrine of the 'higher person' – these are but a tiny sample of the important nuggets of gold to be found in even a cursory survey of the materials available.

In our century the most powerful statement concerning the issue of human wholeness has been made, I believe, by C. G. Jung. Not only was his vision of human wholeness the most central experience of his inner work, as he reveals it in his autobiographical *Memories, Dreams, Reflections* (p. 149), but Jung's entire psychological theory is founded on the presupposition of the human potential for wholeness and is an elaboration and detailed explication of that primary datum. His theoretical model of the self, as presented in his late work *Aion*, is an immense historical and cultural, as well as psychological, detailing of the concept of wholeness. His notion of individuation, which guides human psychological and spiritual development, is orientated by the presupposition that its aim is wholeness. His theory of psychic parts – the archetypal figures, such as the shadow, the persona, the anima and animus, as well as the personal complexes – depends implicitly on the notion that they are parts of a whole, the self, which coordinates and contains them. Jung's central guiding myth is the myth of wholeness.

Looking now at our western religious traditions, the biblical traditions, which include the three religions Judaism, Christianity and Islam, we can immediately see a significant departure from the ground plan of wholeness in them. All of them emphasize one aspect or another of wholeness at the expense of the others. If wholeness is inclusive, they are exclusive; if wholeness requires a balance among the various typical polarities such as masculine–feminine and good–evil, the biblical traditions are one-sided. The biblical God-image is defined as purely masculine and paternal. He is a Father God. And He is a jealous God: 'Thou shalt have no other gods before me' (Exodus 20:3) is not only *one* of the Ten Commandments, but the first one. And it means, in reality, that there are to be no other gods, full stop. This commandment requires the absolute, exclusive claim of one particular God-image upon one particular group of people. Their covenant with Him is a quasi-legal contract of mutual obligation, and the chief requirement on the human side is faithfulness to this one, sole Deity and to His will. There will be little tolerance among this people and its descendants, among which all of us who have grown up in the biblical cultural and religious traditions are included, for any other possibilities that wholeness might allow or even demand.

Chief among those features of wholeness suppressed by and within this tradition was the Great Goddess in all her forms. This act of suppression is stated symbolically in the story of the Fall of Adam and Eve, where Eve's affinity for the serpent (an animal representative of the Goddess) leads her to pay attention to her feminine instinct and to lead Adam astray. This is decisively punished by God. He places enmity between Eve and the serpent, thereby erecting a psychological barrier between woman and her own unconscious depths and blocking her connection to the self, as represented by the images of the Goddess. This also protects Adam, of course, from the power of the Goddess, and is further cemented by driving Adam and Eve out of the Garden of Eden, which is an image of the Great Mother as container. The Fall from Paradise has often been given a positive interpretation, as a necessary early separation of the individuating ego from its state of fusion with the mother. This makes ego autonomy and independence possible. Only in recent times has the ultimate outcome of this development begun to be seriously questioned by many therapists and cultural commentators. Perhaps this kind of separation/individuation does not lead to the best results, if the end product turns out to be a heavily defended ego that has difficulty with the modes of interdependence and co-operation because of an excessive and one-sided emphasis on individualism and ego-centrism.

With its strong bias towards patriarchal culture and its exclusive worship of a male Father God, the biblical tradition produced a particular type of conscious human attitude. It is an attitude that tends towards rigid perfectionism at the cost of compassion and towards one-sided valuation of the abstract and 'spiritual' at the expense of the physical and material. It denigrates the material world as 'nothing but' material, and it seeks to dominate the natural world and other 'natural' peoples instead of co-operating and communicating with and understanding them. It assumes a superior and exclusionistic attitude towards other religions, whose Gods are generally taken to be mere figments of the untutored pagan imagination. It denies the value of feminine elements in both men and women and tends to place women in second-class positions of power and leadership. The doctrine of 'no other gods' has split the wholeness of the human psyche, and while it has stimulated the growth and development of masculine ego development, it has undermined the human urge towards wholeness.

This is itself, of course, a one-sided and highly selective interpretation of the biblical traditions and their psychological implications. It lifts up certain salient features, which I believe to be the most significant highlights in those traditions, but it neglects to mention many other features that would contradict it. These other features can modify the view just put forward in significant ways, but they do not erase it or cancel its primacy. On the contrary, they confirm it. For the point to be made is that the one-sided favouritism given to the Father God, Yahweh, at the expense of the 'others', was subtly undermined and subverted in the Bible itself. These other elements, while played down in favour of the patriarchal Yahweh and His strenuous adherents, left traces in the Bible itself as they began to return in various forms and figures and themes in the course of the centuries during which these traditions were consolidated in written form.

There is, for example, the figure of Sophia in the Hebrew Wisdom literature, who, according to Jung, represents Yahweh's forgotten and repressed feminine side, His wisdom and compassion. Later, in the Christian Scriptures the figure of Jesus presents a less one-sidedly patriarchal, masculine image of God: there are women in His circle; He has some distinctly feminine qualities ('suffer the little children to come unto me'); and the hallmark of His ministry is compassion ('forgive them for they know not what they do') rather than strenuous righteousness. In fact, the New Testament's emphasis on love, and on God as Love, leads strongly in the direction of recovering the wholeness that was lost earlier in the warrior phase of development, when the Promised Land was conquered under the leadership of a savage warrior God and the enemies were obliterated under the force of His mighty hand, without mercy. Still later in the Christian development of the biblical tradition, the formulation of the doctrine of the

Trinity took this movement of recovery of original wholeness yet a step further, when it recognized a third figure in the Godhead, the Holy Spirit, whose pictorial representation would occasionally be in the feminine gender and whose definition, according to St Augustine, was the bond of love that joins God the Father and God the Son and binds the divine to the human.

These elements, then – Sophia, Jesus, the Holy Spirit – modify the one-sidedness of a purely masculine Father God, Yahweh, and also serve to undermine and subvert the purely patriarchal values espoused by the older and classical biblical tradition. This subversion was carried further in the Catholic traditions in the devotion to female saints and to the Virgin, all of whom in effect become 'other gods' in a surreptitious manner. And yet all of these only represent adjustments and modifications of the fundamental masculine archetypal pattern that governs the biblical traditions; they do not carry the change all the way to transformation.

There was an attempt to transform the tradition radically and to recover original wholeness much more completely and fundamentally, but this came from another quarter, which was eventually rejected as heresy. It was Gnosticism. The Gnostics, so called because of their reliance on esoteric teaching and belief in private revelation that led to direct *knowledge* of God (*gnosis*), radically relativized the figure of Yahweh, the Creator God. Over against Him they placed the Pleroma, the ultimate source of all being, of which Yahweh was but one, and not the greatest, emanation. They named this deity Yaldabaoth. The Gnostic critique of Yahweh and of the biblical version of creation and history radically upended the biblical account and cast it into the position of at best a partial truth. The truth of the matter, the Gnostics would say, is that Yahweh is only one small piece of the Whole. There are many other equally important or more important figures. In fact, Sophia is Yahweh's mother. All of these transcendent beings have their source and are anchored in the primordial Pleroma; this is the origin of all the gods and goddesses. When the Gnostics prayed to this Primordial Ground of Being, they would speak to a Mother–Father, the Ultimate Deity, a figure who contains the opposites and represents total wholeness rather than only one piece of it.

What was emerging in the theology and experienced revelations of the Gnostics was an image of God that recovered original wholeness far more completely than had been expressed in the biblical tradition. But from a historical, rather than a psychological and spiritual developmental point of view, the Gnostic vision of God was premature. So it was suppressed and violently denigrated for some seventeen or eighteen centuries until its rediscovery and recovery in our own time. Gnosis was a powerful intuitive spiritual impulse that emerged among a small group of religious geniuses and visionaries, but it reached ahead too far for its times and so was lost to history until the twentieth century. Perhaps we are in a position to integrate its methods and vision today.

Even in his early work on psychology and religion, Jung recognized the importance of the Gnostics. In his first major ground-breaking study, *Symbols of Transformation* (published in 1912/13), Jung makes many references to Gnostic writings and indicates that he had been studying them deeply. Available at that time only in the writings of the Church Fathers, he read them for their important insights into the workings of the psyche. Throughout his later career, Jung continued to read the Gnostic writers and to feel the deepest affinity for them. He traced his own depth psychology back through the alchemists to the more ancient sources of intuitive knowledge in the Gnostic writings. In fact, so identified with the spirit of Gnosis was Jung that he composed a sort of Gnostic text – 'The seven sermons to the dead' – in the voice of a famous Gnostic from Alexandria, Basilides. Modern depth psychology, Jung would argue, has its roots in the Gnostic visions and speculations of the early centuries of the Christian era. When Jung was accused of being a modern Gnostic by Martin Buber, he attempted to deny the charge by claiming to be an empirical scientist, but in other contexts he would have been proud to accept this designation.

It is regrettable that Jung died before the magnificent treasure trove of Gnostic texts discovered in 1946 at Nag Hammadi in Egypt had been edited and translated into modern languages. One of the most famous and significant of these codices was actually named after Jung – the Jung Codex – and was given to the Jung Institute in Zurich, which returned it to its proper home in Egypt in the mid-1950s. But Jung had long since prepared the intellectual and spiritual ground for the recovery and positive appreciation of the message of these Gnostic texts. His numerous writings on alchemy, on the heresies of the Christian tradition, on the biblical tradition and its one-sided patriarchal attitude, and his studies of symbols and archetypal images from historical materials and modern dreams had all added up to a solid foundation upon which an edifice of understanding of these strange ancient texts could be constructed. It is this understanding that is so valuable and essential for our times if we are to advance the cause of recovering psychological wholeness in our day and for the future.

The accidental discovery of these texts at Nag Hammadi in 1946 by a group of Egyptian shepherds was synchronistic. Coming at a moment in western religious history when they could be received without prejudice and when those who study them can so greatly benefit from the recovery of this ancient intuitive wisdom, this find makes it possible for us to see exactly how the biblical traditions can be further developed and transformed.

We stand at a moment in western spiritual history when the Mother–Father God-image has a chance of becoming integrated into the heart of our spiritual traditions, into the doctrines of God. The Judaeo-Christian visions of God are now going through deep internal change. This is a transformation process that has its roots within the collective unconscious of the western spiritual attitude and that is surfacing now in many areas. It shows its effects in the dreams of individuals and in their spiritual malaise and gropings, in theological developments such as feminist theology, in doctrinal developments like the promulgation of the dogma of the Assumption of the Virgin, and in practical theology that has paved the way for the widespread ordination of women and of gay men and women into the clergy. It can be seen too in the general restlessnes of a pluralistic culture that will not be contained within the narrow limits of a one-sided image of God any more and in the uncompromising demand for individual spiritual freedom to explore and to experience the mystery of God for oneself. The strictly patriarchal vision of God is dead. What is emerging is a Man–Woman Deity, a unified Pair, which promises the recovery of the ancient, primordial, archetypal dream of wholeness.

Now it can be argued with great persuasive power that we live in a post-mythological age and that in this age 'God is dead', as Nietzsche proclaimed at the turn of the last century. The myth of a God 'out there' in space somewhere, of a personified parent–figure who cares for us and looks after us as His children and sometimes punishes us for our bad ways, is an image that may give comfort to some but is hard to reconcile with our other cognitive maps. Such images, we now know or believe we know, are the by-products of archetypal structures that govern the psyche. They are projections of these structures into the heavens. We now read these images for their psychological meanings – what do they tell us about the state of the psyche of the person who is doing the thinking or imagining or believing? – and not for their potential ontological truths. Visions no longer give us information about the 'beyond' but about the psyche.

While images and visions are 'only psychological', however, they do also create personal meaning, orientation, and interpretative frameworks. Images eventually lead to concepts and to abstract notions that we use to educate, to condition, and to create social policy and physical reality. As Jung so often pointed out, every human artefact began with an image, with a fantasy. So images have great power and effect, and we must not underrate them just because we know something about their origins. And besides that, we may not know as much as we sometimes think we do about the source of archetypal images, for as Jung also cautioned more than once, we do not know much about what lies beyond the psyche and conditions it. 'Out there', the structures of reality may reveal themselves to us by similarly structuring our psyches archetypally and transforming our fundamental attitudes. We may all be evolving, psychologically, spiritually, historically, according to a transpersonal pattern of development.

One question today is: what does it mean for us in the western religious biblical traditions that the image of God is changing from a patriarchal one of God the Father, and even from the modified patriarchal one of God the Father, Son and Holy Spirit, to one that could be named God the Mother–Father, or God the Quaternity? Both of these – God the Mother–Father, and God the Quaternity (Four in One) – advance the recovery of the primordial dream of wholeness, but they do so with different nuances and emphases. And these are important.

The movement towards the perception of God as Mother–Father leads the way to the recovery of the maternal, feminine elements within the Pleromatic Wholeness that is God, elements that were dramatically displayed and fully articulated in the Great Goddess religions and images of antiquity. This movement reaches back to the Garden of Eden, where it all began, mythologically speaking, and recovers Eve (and her sisters, for example, Lilith) and the serpent, who represents the chthonic energy of the Goddess and Her worship. Now the serpent will again have a place in the home, as it had in antiquity, and the painful enmity between spirit and matter, mind and body, Heaven and earth, man and woman will be healed and overcome. This is the movement of holistic health and of proper concern for the natural environment in our time. The watchwords here are Balance and Harmony. This complex of values, whose icon is God the Mother–Father, must be and will be integrated into the core of the religious life and thought of the biblical traditions. What it promises is the healing of the split between spirit and matter that has been so endemic and central in western spiritual traditions and religions. This is truly transformational. Perhaps it is revolutionary. Certainly the fires that burn in the energy sources of this drive towards transformation are hot and occasionally erupt like a volcano. This change in the perception of God's singularity of gender is perhaps the hottest spot in the entire spiritual landscape today, and its implications are multitudinous and still quite unmapped. Much work, practical and theoretical, needs to be done in this area. Studies, books, discussions, experiments of all kinds are necessary and are underway. More will come.

The other great theme in the transformation process now underway in western religions is more subtle, less well known, but certainly as far-reaching. It is the movement towards conceiving of God as Four rather than Three (in One). The development of the God-image from One to Three was an important differentiation within the archetype, but it did not reach beyond the patriarchal archetype very far or in very great depth. It produced a psychological trend within consciousness of great energy and dynamism. Three is a number of masculine dynamism unfolding and expanding, and it was this energy that converted a minor sect of a minor Near Eastern religion into a global force, Christianity. Christianity enlisted politics, economics and military force and harnessed them all to its ends of converting the entire world. It produced an energetic and restless religion, not a peaceful one, and the latter-day representatives of this tradition – the explorers, the inventors, the empire-builders – exemplify this kind of expansive energy. The movement from Three to Four transforms this restless expansiveness into quiet emptiness and repose, features that are more characteristic of eastern, oriental religions. While Three is a number of dynamic change, Four is a number of stability and repose. The movement of change in the God-image from Three to Four, from Trinity to Quaternity, is represented today by the widespread integration taking place in western religions of eastern spirituality and its methods of meditation and contemplation. These have not been absent in the biblical traditions, but they have been recessive and relatively underdeveloped. Now they are becoming more prominent and will continue to grow in power and centrality. The Quest of the West will give way to images of the Quiet Centre, the Place of Peace, the Self in Repose. Centredness and repose are the watchwords of this movement.

So, Balance and Harmony from the one side of this massive transformational process; Centredness and Repose from the other. God the Mother–Father and God the Four in One. Both of these trends are the hallmarks of the post-modern search for wholeness. The ancient dream of wholeness is alive and well and in our time is taking these forms. It is a powerful and indeed irresistible historical movement, and we would do well to understand it and to become aware of its implications. It should be taken up most particularly into the centre of our western religious theologies of spiritual practice and be allowed to transform them. This will give them new life and relevance for the coming centuries, and it will also provide our evolving culture with some measure of continuity with its own historical heritage. But it will also demand great change in orientation from the religious traditions. The Age of Conquest and Evangelization is over: the Age of Depth and Wholeness is just beginning. After the Age of Jahweh and Yahweh–Sophia, and after the Age of the Father-Son-and-Holy-Spirit, we will have the Age of the Centred, Whole Human Being.

Let me conclude with an image for this new era. It comes from the dream life of an ordinary man. He dreamt that he entered an empty room. The boundaries of the room were not visible, although this was a contained space. On the floor of the empty room sat an adult figure whose gender was indeterminate but a bit more feminine than masculine. This figure sat in the empty room in the lotus position. It was a western person, and her/his gaze was fixed on the distance just over the dreamer's shoulder. End of dream.

This is a dream for the future, a dream for the new age we are entering. It presents an image of Balance and Repose, of human Harmony and Centredness. This image is the successor of the biblical tradition and its images of a mighty Father in the heavens and His Son hanging in agony upon a cross. It is an icon for our present and foreseeable future. Behold the image.

Part II
JUDAISM

EDITOR'S PREFACE

Hear O Israel, the Lord our God, the Lord is One.

(Deuteronomy 6:4)

Judaism always asserted the One-ness of God as a statement of monotheism, the term derived from the Greek *monos*, or One, and *Theos*, or God. A later Islamic proclamation maintained 'There is no other God beside God'; similarly, the Jews have always believed in the One and only God and rejected dualistic theology such as the Zoroastrian, or polytheistic pantheons such as the Hindu.

The concept of the uniqueness of God is inevitably tied to monotheistic doctrine. *Hageburah* describes, in the Talmud, the omnipotence of God. Two levels of this omnipotent control are the forces of nature, which are believed to be subject to God's will and the work of His hands, and the absolute control of all human activity. God is also *shekhinah* or omnipresent, standing above and beyond everything. This transcendence gives a doctrine of divine incorporeality. God is free from limitations of time, space, matter or nature, and hence *omniscient*.

In Judaism God's three factors – omnipotence, omniscience and omnipresence – guarantee His ultimate purpose as one moral law for all. Amidst controversy, Moses Maimonides (1135–1204) elaborated in his *Commentary on the Mishnah* thirteen obligatory articles of faith. Today these are sung as a hymn at the end of synagogue prayers. Briefly this creed is as follows:

1 Belief in the existence of a Creator and Providence;
2 Belief in His unity;
3 Belief in His incorporeality;
4 Belief in His eternity;
5 Belief that to Him alone is worship due;
6 Belief in the words of the prophets;
7 Belief that Moses was the greatest of all prophets;
8 Belief in the revelation of the Law to Moses at Sinai;
9 Belief in the immutability of the Revealed Law;
10 Belief that God is omniscient;

11 Belief in retribution in the world and the hereafter;
12 Belief in the coming of the Messiah;
13 Belief in the resurrection of the dead.

God as holy (*qadosh* in Hebrew) means He is set apart from everything profane. He is wholly 'Other'. As God is the source of both the cosmic and the moral order, the awesomeness and the mercy of God operate simultaneoulsy. The Jews describe God as 'jealous', admitting to no offence against Himself and yet maintaining a profound concern for the well-being of this chosen people. Everything, good or evil, results from God in Jewish belief. However, the problem of the origin of evil is by definition unanswerable, as God is infinite, beyond human understanding and reasoning. This imponderable aspect of God is revealed in the Hebrew phrase *lu yadativ hayitiv* – 'If I knew Him, I would be Him.' Divine sovereignty is everywhere proclaimed in Judaism, the most ancient monotheism. Judaism believes God's universal love will lead all of mankind to know that the Lord is One.

4

THE DARK FACE OF GOD IN JUDAISM

Siegmund Hurwitz

A Jew can live with God, in God and even against God, but never without God.

(Rabbi Levi-Jizchak of Berditshev)

What an easy time of it they have, the followers of a dualistic-orientated world-vision: in *Manichaeism*, over against the realm of light stands a realm of darkness, and the Lord of Light is opposed by the Lord of Darkness; and in *Zarathustra*, we find a clear division between the domain of the Lord of Light, Ahura Mazda, and that of the devilish Angru Mainyu. Man is being told exactly what is good and what is evil and how he should behave. But basically he is really the plaything of cosmic powers.

In contrast, the three monotheistic religions which originated in the Near East have had difficulties with this problem from the very beginning. They have always viewed the clash between good and evil as an event in which man is deeply involved. Because man has been endowed – or perhaps it would be better to say burdened – with a certain amount of free will, he himself becomes the vehicle for this conflict. In the process he is less the victim of forces over which he has little or no influence than someone who takes a full part in the struggle, playing the role of both organizer and judge.

GOOD AND EVIL IN THE HEBREW BIBLE

Interestingly enough, it is never clearly stated at first, either in Judaism or in Christianity or in Islam, what evil actually is. Rather, it is taken for granted that man knows all about it. That is why it is up to him alone to decide which path he will choose.

But this world-view was never able to free Judaism completely. Already, the Paradise myth, which many authors attribute to the so-called Yahwist, describes a first invasion of evil into a world which until now has been ideal and harmonious.

God's interdiction on the eating of the fruit of the Tree of Knowledge gives rise to a similar situation to that encountered in numerous myths and

45

fairy-tales. A forbidden room is entered or a forbidden fruit is plucked, and some atrocity immediately befalls the hero. But, like Adam's sin, this is obviously a necessary prerequisite for a new knowledge. That is why it is not for nothing that the Catholic Church describes the sin of the first man and the first woman as a *felix culpa* in its Easter Night Liturgy, since it was the prerequisite for realization of the whole act of redemption.

But what position does God take in this Paradise myth?[1] First, it was He, of course, who created the serpent who tempted Eve. Also, He had imbued the first man with a certain susceptibility to being led astray. In any case, the interdiction on eating the fruit of the Tree of Knowledge is more questionable from a pedagogical standpoint, for it is well known that a child will always do exactly what he or she has been expressly forbidden to do.

Although a certain knowledge is clearly necessary, this is almost always the preserve of the gods or the divinity. That is why its acquisition by men will always be punished. Just as Prometheus was bound to a rock on Mount Caucasus as a punishment for stealing fire from the gods and bringing it to men, so the first man and the first woman were driven out of the Garden of Eden as their punishment.

However, the question for whom the Tree of Knowledge was really created, if not for men, remains open. In the end, is it the divinity itself which requires a certain knowledge or self-awareness? Only in the later sections of the Torah (the five Books of Moses) is the opinion advanced that good is synonymous with a life led in accordance with divine statutes and evil lies in the non-observance or violation of these directives. This is expressed most clearly in the fifth book of Moses (Deuteronomy). The unknown author of this source book, which was discovered around 600 BC on the occasion of King Joshua's religious reforms, explains (Deut. 30:15–18a):

> See, I have set before thee this day life and good,[2] and death and evil;
> In that I command thee this day to love the LORD thy God, to walk
> in his ways, and to keep his commandments and his statutes and his
> judgements, that thou mayest live and multiply; and the LORD thy
> God shall bless thee. . . . But if thine heart turn away, so that thou
> wilt not hear, but shall be drawn away, and worship other gods, and
> serve them; I denounce unto you this day, that ye shall surely perish.

Here, for the first time, is a clear statement that the choice of good is to be interpreted as a life lived in accordance with divine Law. And it is up to man himself whether he chooses this path or not.

But what kind of Law does Deuteronomy mean? On this subject, the author continues (Deut. 30:11–14):

> For this commandment which I command thee this day, it is not
> hidden from thee, neither is it far off. It is not in heaven, that thou
> shouldest say, Who shall go up for us to heaven, and bring it unto us,

that we may hear it, and do it? Neither is it beyond the sea, that thou shouldest say, Who shall go over the sea for us, and bring it unto us, that we may hear it, and do it? But the word is very nigh unto thee, in thy mouth, and in thy heart, that thou mayest do it.

Consequently, the knowledge of good and evil necessitates a decision of the heart, i.e. of the feelings, of an inner authority, which one might best equate with the collective conscience.

In later biblical literature, the view of how man knows about the way of good and evil is explored in greater depth. Gradually, the teaching is developed that evil has its place within creation. Indeed, evil is even attributed occasionally to the Creator. This is what the anonymous author of the book of the prophet usually described as Deuteroisaiah says (Isa. 45:6f.): 'I am the LORD, and there is none else, I form the light, and create darkness; I make peace, and create evil: I the LORD do all these things.'

Similarly, the Book of Proverbs says (Mic. 16:4): 'The LORD hath made all things for himself: yea, even *the wicked* for the day of evil.' And the author of the Book of Lamentations (Jer. 3:38) asks himself the rhetorical question: 'Out of the mouth of the most High proceedeth not *evil* and good?' This question confirms the author's assumption that his image of God has a thoroughly dark and cryptic side.

In the book which most stirs the feelings of Jew and Christian alike, the Book of Job, the question of evil is posed with the greatest clarity. As Rivkah Kluger has convincingly established,[3] here Satan – the personification of evil – portrays a direct aspect of YHWH.

GOD'S 'RIGHT HAND' AND GOD'S 'LEFT HAND' IN RABBINIC LITERATURE

In the later writings of rabbinic literature, these views are taken still further. The Talmud and the narrative literature of the Midrash develop the teaching of the so-called *middot* (singular *midda*), i.e. God's attributes or behaviour. Among these, two *middot* take up a special position: on the one side is divine love, mercy and compassion, the *midda* known as *chesed*. On the other stands harsh judgement, divine wrath, the demonic side of YHWH, the *midda* called *din*. Man approaches these two sides of YHWH with two different kinds of behaviour, in that he feels love towards God on the one hand and fear of God on the other.

In the Talmud it says:

Rabbi Ishmael ben Elijah recounts: 'On one occasion I entered the Holy of Holies, to offer up some incense. There I saw God seated on his most exalted throne. I said: "May it be thy will that thy mercy outweigh all other attributes, and may you permit your children to experience mercy and not justice."'

(Babylonian Talmud, Berakot 7a)

The justice referred to here is to be considered somewhat negatively beside the loving mercy of God, i.e. as a harsh or severe judgement.

The two *middot*, *chesed* and *din*, are often portrayed symbolically as God's right and left hands. As long as severity is tempered by love, both are equally balanced and in complete harmony.

An old Midrash says:

Thus spake the most High, may his name be praised: If I were to create the world with love and compassion, then the sins (of men) would become uncontrollable. If, however, I were to create it with harsh justice, how could the world endure? Therefore I shall create the world with harsh justice as well as with love and compassion. In this way it may yet endure.

(Bereshit rabba 12:2)

These two attributes of God, love and harsh justice, were to become almost hypostases of God and occasionally even to be personified. Thus this Midrash already comes close to that Gnostic speculation which bridges the gulf between God and man. This trend was to undergo further development and consolidation in the literature of the Kabbala.

EVIL AS *PRIVATIO BONI* AMONG JEWISH ARISTOTELIANS

If we examine the problem of evil in Jewish religious philosophy, it is surprising how few authors have tackled this question. It was two Jewish philosophers, above all, Abraham ibn Daud and Moses ben Maimon (Maimonides), who dealt seriously with the question of evil, around the middle of the twelfth century.[4] However, both authors have astonishingly little original thought concerning the problem of evil. Both tended mainly towards the philosophical ideas of Plato and Aristotle, with their dualism of form and matter, good and evil. Thereby, they superseded the previous, more Neoplatonically inclined speculative way of thinking within Jewish philosophy. Like the Arabic Aristotelians ibn Sina (Avicenna) and ibn Rushd (Averroes) before them, both authors take the position with regard to evil that basically it has only an apparent existence. According to them, evil is not truly real; it is simply something lacking in so far as it denotes the absence of good. This teaching of the so-called *privatio boni* coincides to a great extent with the opinions of the high scholasticism, which flourished later and which characterized God as the *summum bonum*.

In Christianity, however, this teaching had its heralds among the Fathers of the Church. Origen had already described evil as an 'accidental lack of perfection'. Similar phraseology can easily be found in the works of Dionysius the Areopagite and Augustine.

If God alone is highest perfection, however, where does evil come from? Obviously, it must inhabit man. And so this gives rise to the familiar saying: *omne bonum a deo, omne malum ab homine*. Thus, on the one hand, in Christian scholastics, the figure of Christ is greatly elevated; on the other, man is totally devalued.

Within Jewish philosophy, however, the teaching of *privatio boni* was not generally accepted. Above all, it was those philosophers influenced by the Islamic–Judaic Kalaam who combated this thinking.[5] Thus Maimonides' teaching on the unreality of evil, like his attempt to oppose Christian dogmatics with a Jewish one, foundered.

EVIL IN THE KABBALA

At the same time as the medieval philosophy of the Jewish Aristotelians, Jewish mysticism, the Kabbala, developed in Provence and Catalonia. But far from considering evil to be non-existent, the Kabbalists saw it as a question of burning relevance.

Almost all Kabbalists are of the opinion that evil has a dual root. On one side, it inhabits man; on the other, there is a place where evil which has been detached from man can be found within the divine sphere. Here the Kabbalists differ among themselves, above all on which side they emphasize.

On the one hand, it is the first man, Adam, who, together with Eve and the serpent, brought evil into creation. Before the Fall, Adam was a purely spiritual being. All his actions took place in a spiritual sphere, in which the distant, unknown God – whom the Kabbalists call en Sof – had developed in his ten aspects. For in the mean time, the teaching of the *middot* had further developed into the teaching of the ten emanations, auras, primordial numbers or Sephiroth.

The sum of these Sephiroth constitutes the apparent world of God as he reveals himself. It is called the 'place of plantings' by the Kabbalists. Caring for these plantings implies leaving the Sephiroth in their collective unity, so that a harmonious equilibrium reigns in the divine world. On the other hand, the 'destruction of the plantings' implies something like a casting out of individual Sephiroth from their band. However, should a Sephirah be removed, the danger arises of its becoming independent or out of control, which according to some Kabbalists is the real source of the rise of evil.

The Book of Bahir

The question of evil is put most clearly in the first great Kabbalistic work, the Book of Bahir, which was written in Provence around the middle of the twelfth century. With regard to evil, the Bahir takes up the ancient rabbinic tradition of the two *middot*, but the author (or authors) shows himself (or themselves) to be thoroughly acquainted with the teaching on the ten Sephiroth as well. In one place, the Bahir expresses itself very clearly on the subject of evil:[6]

> And what is this *midda*?[7] It is *Satan*. That means that there is a *midda* with God, that is called 'evil'. It is in the *north* of God, since it is written (Jer. 1:14): 'Out of the North an evil shall break forth.' That means: all the evil that befalls the inhabitants of the earth comes from the North. And what shape does this *midda* take? It takes the form of a hand, and it has many messengers, and they are all called 'evil', although there are greater and lesser among them. They are the ones who plunge the world into sin, for *tohu* comes out of the North and *tohu* signifies the evil that confuses men until they sin, and all the evil desires of men stem from there.

What does the author mean in this extract? First, it is clearly stated that evil is active as an evil desire innate in man. Beyond that, however, there is a power rooted in God Himself, which is completely independent of any of man's actions. And thus arises a further distinction from the biblical–Talmudic teaching of the *middot*.

The Kabbalists' picture of God clearly shows a dark, evil side, an image that is totally alien to Christendom, which even to this day holds firm to the teaching of the *summum bonum*.

Evil is located in the North, in accordance with the prophet Jeremiah's verse which states that all evil always comes from the North. Thus, in the Bahir, the North is always equated with the *midda din* and the South with the *midda chesed*. Here, the evil from the North is called Satan and is thus personified. That Satan is directly described as a *midda* or attribute of God belongs to the completely new and extremely bold formulation of this work. In one place, Satan is even described as *El acher*, i.e. the other God.[8] Some degree of influence from radical Cathars, who held similar views, certainly cannot be ruled out.

Then the author of the Bahir poses the question of what shape evil takes, and immediately answers it himself. Evil takes the form of a hand. G. Scholem has established that in biblical literature, the word 'hand' always signifies the right.[9] In contrast, the Midrash – on which the Bahir bases itself in this instance – takes the view that 'hand' means the left. Like the Latin word for 'left', *sinister*, the left hand of God also signifies his dark, baleful side.

Finally, the Bahir gives an exegesis of the word *tohu-va-bohu*, which it analyses speculatively, identifying *tohu* with the North, evil, while *bohu* corresponds to the South and the love and mercy of God.

The Book of Zohar

In the Zohar, the classic work of the Kabbala, differing opinions about evil are found side by side. According to one view, sin started with the first man, Adam. It came into existence because he divided the original single Tree of Paradise into the Tree of Knowledge and the Tree of Life. In this way, however, a split arose in the world of the Sephiroth which, until now, had been united. Another opinion holds that beside the ten bright, pure Sephiroth might lie an equally dark realm of impure Sephiroth. In addition, however, yet another teaching suggests that evil might have arisen when the Sephirah *din* or divine wrath got out of control or became independent. Finally, there is a theory that evil could be a kind of waste or excretory product, secreted by the living organism of the divinity, like lees by wine or dross by gold. All these dark, demonic sides together form the 'realm of husks', a concept which later plays a central role in the Lurjanic Kabbala. It has been established that in the Provençal–Catalan Kabbala, evil that emanates from man is most certainly not overlooked. According to this, the sins of the individual are nothing but a repetition of Adam's original sin. But the emphasis is laid more and more on the view that evil has its real roots in the divinity itself. In the process, a single Sephirah is held each time to be the starting-point of evil. According to the Kabbalist Isaac Hacohen, it is the Sephirah *bina*, but according to the Zohar, the Sephirah *din* is the starting-point of evil. In fact, there are isolated Kabbalists who would like to locate the seat of evil in the last Sephirah of all.

Isaac Lurja

In Isaac Lurja's Gnostic–cosmogonic mythology, the problem of evil is even more fundamentally complicated. Whereas until now all Kabbalists had interpreted the development of the unknown God – en Sof – as rectilinear, in the sense of the Neoplatonic teaching on emanation, this is changed in Lurja. True, he does not completely reject the teaching on emanations, but he modifies it in such a way that it opens up totally new perspectives.[10] The starting-poing of Lurja's mythology is the beginning of the creation process, which proves to be a cosmogony when seen from the outside, but a kind of theogony when viewed from the inside. In the process, Lurja starts out from the formulation of a question which is as simple as it is original:[11] if God, as tradition teaches, is omnipresent and fills everything with his being, how can creation actually take place? A similar question had already been raised by the unknown author of the Gnostic–Coptic Codex of Nag Hammadi. Thereafter it had also worried certain Christian theologians, such as John Scot Erigenus and Meister Eckhart, without their being able to find an answer to it.

Lurja's answer to the question he himself posed goes as follows: creation

51

could only possibly take place once the distant God, en Sof, had first withdrawn into the depths of His own being. Thus, the first act of the creation drama is not an emanation but just the opposite, a kind of retraction. Through this withdrawal into His own depths – which Lurja calls *Zimzum*, i.e. self-confinement – an empty space is produced in en Sof. The divine emanations now pour into this original space and form their different shapes. Retractions and emanations now follow in continuous bursts, so that life pulsates within the divine organism like the ebb and flow of the tide or the systole and diastole of the heart.

But now, according to Lurja, the act of *Zimzum* represents a kind of restriction or limitation. With the start of the retreat and of the consequent creation, a moment of disruption occurs if the Sephirah or *midda din* – which corresponds to the restriction – becomes predominant. As a result, both harmony and balance are disturbed. This means nothing more or less than that the origin of evil has intruded into the creation. Indeed, evil is to a certain extent even a necessary prerequisite of the creation.

With this concept, Lurja went far beyond the teaching of the older Kabbalists. From now on, evil no longer has its origin in one single aspect of the divinity alone. According to him, the source of evil lies in the creation itself, and since the divinity wishes to fulfil itself through the creation, it becomes itself indirectly the creator of evil.

Other Kabbalists such as Israel Sarug and Sabbatai Hurwitz combated Lurja's teaching or tried to reinterpret it. But, without exception, subsequent Kabbalists held fast to the original Lurjanic concept.

Sabbateanism

The problem of evil crystallizes most clearly in Sabbateanism, i.e. in that heretical–mystical movement which is attached to the name of Sabbatai Zevi, who lived around the middle of the seventeenth century. Like Lurja, Sabbatai Zevi left no written records whatsoever in which his ideas are expressed.

The bases of Sabbatean theology come from a pupil of Sabbatai Zevi's, Nathan of Gaza. Later theologians further elaborated and completed his teachings.[12] Nathan of Gaza based himself in the first place completely on the Lurjanic Kabbala, which, however, he enriched with his own profound ideas. Above all, it was the teaching on the *Zimzum* as the starting-poing of evil that he took up and remodelled in his own particular way. According to Nathan, before the *Zimzum*, i.e. before the beginning of the creation, within en Sof there existed two opposing lights, which he called 'thoughtful' and 'thoughtless'. The thoughtful light is completely geared to creation, development and structuring and is therefore an active, working force. But besides that, in en Sof there is also a force or light which rejects creation. Through its passive inertia, the thoughtless light resists creation. According to Nathan, the process of *Zimzum* took place exclusively in the realm of the thoughtful light. This had poured forth in the upper part of the original space, where it had produced its various forms. During the subsequent *Zimzum*, however, the thoughtless light – which had not taken part in the creation – remained behind in the lower part of the original space. Thus, the creation process takes place only in the upper half of the original space.[13] As a result of its resistance, the lower part with the thoughtless light becomes the resort of evil, the demonic. Following Lurja's terminology, this is described as the 'world of husks' or as the 'depths of the great abyss', in which live the dragons or impure snakes.

When, after the *Zimzum* the divine light poured into the upper half of the original space, a few of its sparks fell into the lower half. And with them, the soul of the Messiah also fell into the depths. Here it fought with the powers of darkness and evil, because it was trying to fill the lower part, too, with thoughtful light. Echoes of ancient Gnostic myths of the fall of primeval man into the depths of the physis as well as of the myth of the holy snake of the Ophites should not be overlooked. However, a direct influence should be ruled out. Rather, it is a question of a true new creation or, psychologically speaking, of a spontaneous appearance of archetypal motifs.

However, the struggle between the soul of the Messiah and the demons of evil doesn't take place exclusively within the divine realm. According to the teachings of the alchemists and Kabbalists, every above has a corresponding below and vice versa. Hence it follows that this clash between active and passive forces, between structuring and resistance and between change and inertia, takes place in every individual human being, too.

Hassidism contributed few original ideas to the problem of evil. It, too, is based on the Lurjanic Kabbala, which, however, it did not further develop. In its positive, ascesis-denying optimistic world-view, it stresses above all that even husks can contain a divine spark. It is the task of the Hassidic saint, the Zaddik, to loose these sparks from the husks and thus to free them.

DEALINGS WITH INDIVIDUAL AND COLLECTIVE EVIL

How does a person rooted in the Jewish tradition behave towards evil? The collective Jewish – and also Christian – morality commands him or her to do good and avoid evil. The difficulty consists, though, in how to tell exactly what is good and what is evil in each individual case – because it is well known that evil almost always contains a grain of good and vice versa.

The self-aware, mature person has learnt from lifelong experience that he cannot simply live a life of unrestrained evil, since this implies a devaluation of cultured man. But he is also aware that he may not simply drive out individual evil – his personal shadow – since otherwise it may attack him from behind. So he has no alternative but to decide from one case to the next how he will deal with evil and how to fit it into his overall personality.

But how to behave towards suprapersonal, collective evil, towards the demonic side of the divine image? In Genesis, God regrets having created men and He drowns most of them in the great flood. Likewise, very few people were saved from Sodom and Gomorrah. Where was God's omniscience, which ought really to have told Him that men are inclined to do evil?

Later on, there is Abraham, who, without thinking, is prepared to make the gruesome sacrifice of his own son which is demanded of him. Didn't God know in advance how Abraham would behave? What purpose does this dreadful test actually serve? Clearly, certain doubts about His omniscience must have arisen in God, or, psychologically speaking, He behaved just like an unconscious man who has been plunged into desperate conflict by his inner doubts.

In the case of Abraham, we have not as yet come to a head-on collision between human and divine will, between ego and self.[14] But this situation changes completely with the publication of the Book of Job. Here, the pious, silently suffering Job, who is unaware of having committed any sin against God or man, first opposes YHWH and His destructive side. But precisely because he recognizes this dark side of God's personality and consciously accepts it, he is granted a divine experience which fundamentally changes his previous image of God. However, on the other hand, God, who cares almost passionately for mankind, would like to be recognized in His dual nature and consciously accepted by men.

Creation myths portray a reflection of that process by which consciousness develops out of the depths of the unconscious.[15] In the cosmogonic myth of Nathan of Gaza, this process of the dawning of consciousness is portrayed as a conflict within the divinity. One part desires creation, illumination, consciousness. Another part opposes this illumination – psychologically speaking, this dawning of consciousness – and thus becomes the original source of evil. Whereas in the Paradise myth the dawning of consciousness is portrayed as evil, here it is exactly the opposite, in that unconsciousness appears as the original evil.

According to Jewish tradition, man needs God's help with the act of redemption. But, on the other hand, God also requires man's assistance with this act of salvation, which in the view of the heretical Kabbala is portrayed as a kind of process of the dawning of consciousness. In so far as each individual man takes part in this event, each is also called upon to contribute actively to this development and thus to learn to recognize both his own personal shadow and also the dark side of the divine, to accept them and consciously to tackle the problem of what and why (*sich damit auseinander zu setzen*).

NOTES

1 If God is talked of here, the word doesn't have a metaphysical meaning. It means the empirically demonstrable image of God in man's psyche.

2 The Zurich Bible translates the Hebrew word *tob* ('good') by 'fortune' and the word *rac* ('evil') incorrectly by 'misfortune'.

3 R. Scharf (-Kluger), *Die Gestalt des Satans im Alten Testament* (Zurich: Rascher Verlag, 1948).

4 J. Guttmann, *Die Philosophie des Judentums* (Munich: E. Reinhardt, 1933), pp. 163f., 174ff.

5 Kalaam describes a religious–philosophical trend which occurs in both Islam and Judaism, and which crystallized out of the debate about the problem of anthropomorphism as well as about Islamic teachings on predestination.

6 *Sefer ha-Bahir, ha-nikra Midrasho shel R. Nehunyah ben ha-Kanah*, ed. Reuben Margolioth (Jerusalem, 1951), para. 161. Compare G. Scholem, *Das Buch Bahir* (Leipzig: W. Drugulin, 1923), p. 116.

7 Scholem translates *midda* by 'principle'. I have left it untranslated both here and later on.

8 This passage supports the thesis already put forward by Kluger (see n. 3), according to which Satan is an aspect of YHWH, but was not then known to her.

9 Scholem, *Das Buch Bahir*, op. cit., p. 117, n. 3.

10 G. Scholem, 'The doctrine of Creation in Lurianic Kabbalah', in his *Kabbalah* (Jerusalem: Keter Publishing House, 1974), p. 128ff.

11 G. Scholem, *Die Judische Mystik in ihren Hauptströmungen* (Zurich: Rhein Verlag, 1957), pp. 285ff.

12 S. Hurwitz and S. Zwi, 'Zur Geschichte und Psychologie eines Erlösers und seiner Bewegung', in S. Hurwitz and S. Zwi, *Psyche und Erlösung* (Zurich: Daimon Verlag, 1983), pp. 87–116.

13 G. Scholem, 'Shabbetai Zevi and the Shabbatean Movement', in *Kabbalah*, op. cit., pp. 270ff.

14 According to C. G. Jung, on whose psychology this work is based, the ego is the centre and battlefield of consciousness; the self is the centre and battlefield that contains both the consciousness and the unconscious.

15 M.-L. von Franz, *Creation Myths* (Zurich: Spring Publications, 1978).

5

JERUSALEM AND ZURICH: AN INDIVIDUAL SYNTHESIS

Gustav Dreifuss

A Jew in a Jungian depth-analysis (individuation process) will be confronted with his Jewishness and will have to find a personal solution. I valued the idea of a Jewish homeland in the land of Israel as early as I can remember, and more so after the catastrophe of the Holocaust had become known. I left my home town, Zurich, in order to settle in Israel. Zurich is the place of my Jungian analysis and my studies at the Jung Institute.

I grew up in a traditional Jewish family, and as a boy I was very influenced by the Jewish religion, especially by my grandfather, who used to instruct me in the synagogue. As a young man I was very active in the Jewish community, organizing special services for young people in the little synagogue of Zurich, and later became an active member of the committee for cultural activities of the Jewish community. Still later I was confronted with the problem of my Jewish identity from within.

My contribution must therefore be personal and valid only for myself. Most Jews of the West prefer to remain in their place of birth, giving expression to their Jewishness in different ways, as believing or secular Jews. I felt that the Jewish people had to make an effort to get out of the victim-psychology of being helplessly dependent on hostile surroundings, as was so horribly demonstrated in the Holocaust in Europe and the state of degradation of the Jews in Arab countries.

The following dreams show how the unconscious supported and lead me to the decision to leave Switzerland for Israel. One can, of course, introject that all these dreams had to be understood on a subjective inner level only. Yet, the repetition of 'Israel-dreams' over the years meant that 'Israel' had to be interpreted on an inner symbolic and outer concrete level. Why had I actually to leave my birthplace and settle in Israel? In other words, why did I act out the content of the dreams? It was a feeling and an inner conviction which grew in me over the years and brought me to the realization of the content of the dreams. Today, after more than thirty years, I know that listening to the inner guidance together with changing my outer reality was the right response and helped me to come to terms with myself.

During my analysis I had many religious dreams, and some of them were connected with Israel, a few of which are given here:

1 I sit in front of a great large book written in Hebrew letters. I have to translate the book and edit it.
2 I am in Israel and negotiate the purchase of a large piece of land. The price seems to be somewhat high.
3 I see many lorries full of books, on their way to Israel.
4 I fight, wrestle intensely, with a great man.
5 At the end of the day of atonement, the synagogue is almost empty. Mrs X sits next to me, weeping. She says that she simply has no satisfaction in the synagogue and that this is terrible. I comfort her and say that there are different ways to serve God.
6 I ride on a camel through the desert.

The large book in the above dream is, according to my association, the Bible, Mishna, Talmud, Aggada, Midrash and Kabbalistic literature – the basis of Jewish religion and culture. The dream might point to a demand to deal with, understand and make others understand the texts symbolically. The 'editing' means going my own way in the Jewish tradition and not following it literally.

The second dream tells me that I have to buy the land. It was not given to me by inheritance: I had to put energy-money into owning it. At that time I was not ready to pay the price. The land of the Bible alludes to the problem of nationality of the Jewish people. For two thousand years the Jews lived in dispersion, away from their biblical homeland. They were uprooted. This disconnection from the earth promoted an overestimation of intellect and spirit. Mother earth and in a wider sense, the feminine motherly principle did not have their proper place. Yet indications for the feminine in the God-image can be found in the three monotheistic religions: Shekhina–Maria–Fatima. Here Jung's important contribution towards understanding the changes in the God-image has to be mentioned, especially the inclusion of the Goddess, the feminine archetype, in the image of the all-encompassing God. Some scientists think that the masculine God-image can be explained as a resistance against the dominance of the Great Mother, an unconscious living submitting to the natural course of life. The male God-image was necessary for the development of consciousness, as the masculine God is identified with light. However, Jung stressed the importance of the reintegration of the feminine principle into the Godhead for a full and complete masculine–feminine God-image.

In the minds and hearts of Israelis there is a strong link between the content of the Bible and the land. The state of Israel and the idea of Zionism are based on the actualization of the Jewish spirit in the land of Israel. Archaeological sites all over the country prove the existing natural link between the facts in the Bible and the idea of coming back to the Promised

Land as recorded in Genesis. During the long years of the Diaspora, there was a disconnection between the people and its actual, Promised Land. The element of earth was missing in the life of the Jews. Without the element of earth, intellectual knowledge is elevated, but can become unproductive and estranged. Jungian analysis of the personal and collective unconscious reconnects the intellect with the repressed earth element which exists in the unconscious. This furthers a more whole personality, containing both male–spirit and female–earth qualities. My second and third dreams, however, insist on Israel, meaning the factual reconnection of the intellect-books and the land of Israel.

The dream of the wrestling with the great man reminds one of the fight of Jacob with the 'angel' at the Jabbok river, psychologically a fight between the ego and the Self, or realizing the religious function of the psyche and of the inner conflict between ego and the demands of the Self.

On the Day of Atonement, a day of repentance for sins and crimes between man and man and man and God which a person has allegedly committed, man asks for pardon and redemption. This is the day of a collective and private soul-searching. Mrs X is a friend with a deep connection to Jungian psychology. She is an anima-figure, an image of the soul, no longer nourished by attending the service in the synagogue. She is estranged from the Jewish cult, from institutionalized religion. She is comforted by being told that one can be a religious person outside organized religion. Listening to dreams, reconnecting with the unconscious, with the Self, is a religious attitude, an experience of the beyond, of God, of the Self, but extremely personal. Many people are frustrated by a traditional cult as practised. Yet, a deep-seated need is inborn, a need to remain in contact with the Jewish spirit. The Jewish heritage is in the psyche, in the unconscious.

The desert is a desolate place, dry, fearful and unexpected, with little change in scenery, very monotonous, ideal for contemplation, a place where snakes and scorpions live, and therefore dangerous. The desert is a place where one is very lonely and is expected to be strong if one is to survive. Therefore it is the place of godly revelation, where one is closer to God, to the Self (see Moses, Hagar, Jesus, Muhammad, and some of the prophets). The camel is useful in the desert, mainly because of its ability to endure hardships. It symbolizes a helpful animal within the individuation process.

Zurich is my birthplace; there I spent my youth in a peaceful and comfortable home, in a sympathetic city, prosperous and successful, in a beautiful landscape. The atmosphere in the city was relaxed, with hardly any anti-Semitic feelings, until the rise of Nazism and the persecution of the Jews in Germany, which changed the ideal picture of the city and became a problem for Jews and some Gentiles too. Zurich is the centre of Zwingli's Protestantism. Although this was known to me through what I had learnt in school and saw around me, it never affected me deeply. The deeper meaning of my Christian surroundings became clear in the late 1940s, during my analysis and studies in the Jung Institute. The Christian myth was alien to me, the rites were foreign, and the holidays did not apply to the Jews. We lived in seclusion, although freedom was exercised all around. Looking for my Jewish roots became more and more important as a source of reason and understanding for my feeling of being different. Zurich, Switzerland, was my homeland, but not my land. Yet, Zurich was also the centre of Jungian psychology, significant for my personal development and a source for a new understanding of my Judaism! Therefore, to this day, I feel a certain attachment and relationship to Zurich and to Switzerland, especially to the two villages of Endingen and Lengnau, where my forefathers lived in the eighteenth and nineteenth centuries.

Jerusalem-Zion, and all its many names, represents the essence of Judaism, earthly and spiritually, actually and symbolically. Israel has manifold meanings – the holy land, a Jewish homeland, a refuge for the persecuted Jewish people. Jews of different *Weltanschauung* live in Israel. Although I feel very much a Jew and my spiritual roots are deep, my understanding of Judaism today stands on an individual basis and is very different from that of orthodox Jews. My image of God is different from theirs; they observe the rites, they keep to the Jewish laws – Halakha – they even dress differently, and keep to themselves, and yet we are all Jews. And in this difference of interpretation of Jewishness, one has to live!

Monotheism is the common denominator of the three religions Judaism, Christianity and Islam. The prefix 'Mono-' means 'one and alone': in the religious context, the belief in one God; in a philosophical context, in monism, the teaching that the world is built only on one groundwork. But there is definitely a great danger in everything which is 'mono', namely the possibility of falling into extremism. In an early work published in 1912 under the title *New Paths in Psychology*, Jung (1964: para. 482) discusses

> the monistic tendency, which everywhere and always looks for a unique principle . . . monism, or rather psychological monotheism, has the advantage of simplicity, but the defect of being an exclusive and incomplete point of view. It signifies on the one hand exclusion of diversity and the rich reality of life, and on the other the possibility of realizing the ideals of the present and of the immediate past, but it holds out no real possibility of development.

In the three monotheistic religions one finds this monistic tendency towards the other religions within the religions themselves also. The shadow of this tendency is a lack of tolerance and a hubris concerning possessing the one and only truth: 'and when monotheism developed, God could only transform himself' (Jung 1954: para. 409). This quotation alludes to the change of the God-image in consequence of the development of consciousness. The God-image of the early Bible is different from the God-image that developed later; the God-image changed in Christianity and Islam too. Judaism is the parent religion of Christianity and Islam. The Jewish Bible is incorporated in the Christian Bible as the Old Testament and is the basis of the Qur'ān in Islam. The offspring cannot accept their parent. They think that there can only be one monotheistic religion, namely theirs. The continuous existence of the parent-religion somehow threatens their identity. Thus the persecutions, the pogroms and the Holocaust. All three religions look upon themselves as elected and chosen. This is inflation. From each point of view, the other two religions are wrong and a threat to themselves, because there cannot be two or three religions chosen by God. From analysis we know that children, after a period of aggression towards their parents, can accept them only when they become sure of their own identity. This means that there is still some doubt, and therefore no tolerance, with regard to the Christian and Muslim identity. From an archetypal point of view it is the father–son relationship which Frey-Wehrlin (1992: 173) has aptly described. The tragedy in this relationship is on the one hand the desire of the son to annihilate his father, therefore the aggression he feels, and on the other hand the father fighting his son for this threatened domain. The Jews as well feel that they are chosen, yet they are not actively aggressive towards their children, maybe because of their weakness during the whole history of the last two thousand years. In all three religions there is a lot of infighting and rivalry, for example, by Mitnagdim and Hassidim, Catholics and Protestants, and Shiites and Sunnites.

It is interesting to note that the command of the Bible 'thou shalt love they neighbour as thyself' has not become the foremost mode of behaviour in the three monotheistic religions. Fundamentalism, which is the source of fanaticism, is found in all three religions, and threatens the success of the continuing endeavour of ecumenicalism. Next to the religious believers there is a large population which does not affiliate itself to any official religion: this is the age of reason. Yet the search for personal experience of the 'beyond' is widespread, as can be seen in the fact that so many people are drawn to mysticism, eastern cults and psychological personal development. The source of this trend is the archetype of the Self experienced as the centre of the personality. On the collective level, one appropriate symbol for the common origin of mankind is the Anthropos – the primordial man, in whom the whole mankind is united in a feeling-connection (*Gefühlszusammenhang*). The Self as the central archetype of the collective unconscious is the 'highest God', beyond the Jewish, Christian or Islamic God. Awareness of the common origin of all human beings may give a feeling of a common denominator to mankind. Tolerance and acceptance is the way to overcome gradually this tragic state of antagonism.

A very interesting phenomenon which I experienced on a personal level while working in Israel as an analyst is that neither I nor any of my analysands ever had a dream about Jesus, which I did have while living in Zurich. Amplifications by my Christian analyst in Zurich were naturally from the Christian myth or Greek mythology – and I complied. Although Jung integrated in his work ideas from the Far East, like the mandala and Yang and Yin, the accent was on European Christian culture. Typical Jewish concepts and culture were missing in Zurich. In Israel it is the practice for believer and non-believer alike to have a day off on Saturday instead of Sunday and to celebrate the Jewish holidays which are the official holidays of the state also. For analysands born in Israel, amplifications connected with the Jewish cultural background – the Bible – the Old Testament – come naturally. Here is an example of an Israeli dream association. The dreamer has to enter a closed house in which a secret teaching is hidden. His association was that the Kabbala was the secret, not Eckhart – not Christian mysticism. The Kabbala as Jewish mysticism is widely known in Israel today.

Although it is situated in the Middle East, Israel is westernized, and so are its psychologies. Psychology and analysis are based on western culture and conceptions. So is Jungian psychology. Even the psychology of Freud, who was a Jew, has to be considered under the influence of his western Christian background in Vienna. His opposition to the religion of his father should be regarded as a rebellion against paternalism. Jung as a Christian deals in his psychology with a critical approach to Christianity. Jungian western psychology with Jewish modifications is the basis for my work as a Jewish Jungian analyst in Israel. A Jungian approach to Judaism helped me to integrate Jerusalem and Zurich, my Jewish and Christian background. I am a Jew living in the holy land. Coming from the Diaspora, I have a new feeling of mother- and fatherland, of integration of nature and spirit. I am aware of this most subjective statement, but I believe that today problems of identity and belonging can only be solved individually for those who have no full collective identity.

I want to stress that Jung's teaching about the archetypes and his concept of the collective unconscious point to the unity of mankind, of all human beings not only in the physical but also in the psychic structure. Yet, at the same time, he stressed the cultural differences of people according to historical processes which brought about splitting and many variations in language, behaviour patterns, religious developments, economics and perceptions of justice. But at the base of every human development we find the primal energy – the collective unconscious, the archetypes.

Even though there is a great difference between the concepts of messianism between the Jewish and the Christian tradition and belief, for me, from a psychological point of view, and in accordance with Jungian psychology, the Messiah is a psychic content, an archetype. In the individuation process the actualization of the messianic idea is important. The projection of the redemption to the end of the days or the coming of the Messiah in person, bringing redemption to mankind, is psychologically taken back and experienced time and again when a conflict is resolved and one is at one with oneself – in order to be confronted with a new conflict and a potential new redemption, and so on.

The awareness of differences in mutual honour between human beings is important, and should never bring about a feeling of superiority of one people over the other, as feelings of inferiority with regard to other cultures will not have any positive effect, but lead on to aggression.

REFERENCES

Dreifuss, G. (1975) 'Zeitgenössische Jüdische Geschichte und ihr archetypischer Hintergrund' ('Current Jewish history and its archetypal background'), *Analytical Psychology*. 6: 428–36.

—— (1986) 'The search of a Swiss-Jewish-Israeli', in J. M. Spiegelman and Abraham Jacobson (eds) *A Modern Jew in Search of a Soul*, Phoenix, Arizona: Falcon Press.

Frey-Wehrlin, C. T. (1992) 'Oedipus in Gethsemane: archetypal aspects of homosexuality', *Journal of Analytical Psychology* 37: 173–85.

Gorali, Moshe, *The Old Testament in Music*, Jerusalem: Maron Publishers.

Jung, C. G. (1954) 'Transformation symbolism in the Mass', in *The Collected Works*, vol. 11.

—— (1964) *Two Essays on Analytical Psychology*, in *The Collected Works*, vol. 7.

Kluger-Scharf, R. (1974) 'The idea of the chosen people in the Old Testament', in *Psyche and Bible, Three Old Testament Themes*, Zurich: Spring Publications.

6

THE KABBALA, JUNG AND THE FEMININE IMAGE

Freema Gottlieb

Jung had access through secondary sources to many key concepts of Jewish mysticism, and, especially when it comes to descriptions of the psychic accoutrements of femininity, his entire opus bears the distinctive mark of Kabbalistic influence. For example, in discussing gradations of consciousness, he uses a terminology similar to that employed by the Jewish mystics when touching upon such religious ideas as holiness and spirituality. The particular language I am referring to is the vocabulary of light – and by light I mean also darkness and all nuances and shades in between.

Jung resorts to this type of language both when he is talking of fragmentation and reintegration of the human psyche as a whole, and when he is speaking of the male/female dichotomy in particular. In regard to the latter, he admits freely, as do the Kabbalists, that the feminine anima is as often as not conventionally associated with darkness, negativity, even what we call evil.

What Jung seems to have picked up from the Kabbala is that there is something out of the ordinary, something disturbing, about femininity. Something that, in a logical clear-cut upstanding universe, both seem to imply, one might have done better without. And yet, without the feminine, there would be no life at all. Therefore, a necessary evil . . .?

In possibly the very first manuscript of the Jewish mystical tradition, the *Bahir*, the Book of Illumination, written down not earlier than the third century and not later than the sixth, it says that a king (God) had in mind to plant nine masculine palm trees (*Sephiroth*, emanations) in His garden but realized that, if they all were of the one sex, they would not endure. So he took the female part of the palm tree and transformed it into an *ethrog* (citron), a moonlike feminine shape, referred to in the Bible as the Tree of Beauty (Lev. 23:40), and then the entire orchard flourished.

So, in the *Sephiroth* (the realm of the emanations), *Shekhinah* or the divine presence, typified as feminine, was the lowest feminine kingship formed. Jung says something similar, but a touch more derogatory to woman. He says that originally the members of the Trinity, including the Holy Ghost, were all spiritual, and therefore all male, and that it was considered heretical to define the Holy Ghost as Sophia (divine wisdom), female. Nevertheless, room had to be found for the feminine. In the divine drama, there were already shades of a fourth personality, the possibility of evil, but this could be considered masculine, the sin of Adam, or the devil. But of course it was far more convenient at once to shift the blame for sin upon the victim and to include what was palpably missing, the female, and so, with the entrance of the feminine, as necessary link between spiritual and physical, there is the implication that the way has also been opened for the possibility of evil.

Jung equates this feminine with the Shulamit of the Song of Songs, Jerusalem, the Community of Israel, who introduces herself as 'black but beautiful'. On this juxtaposition Jung remarks in his *Mysterium Coniunctionis* that the heroine 'comes from the same category as the black goddesses such as Isis, Artemis, Parvati, and the Black Virgin' (1963: 420).

Though Judaism is supposedly a paternalistic religion, in the Kabbala we find possibly the highest compliment to the feminine paid by a monotheistic faith, and yet in this regard it is just compliments that hint at their reverse. If the *Shekhinah*, the divine presence *per se*, is given a female typology, it is, the rabbis insist, only because the entire function of the *Shekhinah* is in the inferior realms, nature, the physical.

The point about the *Shekhinah* is that she is the spatialization of spirituality. If not for the need of substance and square feet, she would telescope back into her Father. Spatialization or the impregnation of the womb of creation immediately implied feminization, at least as far as the human imagination is concerned, of the divine light itself. As soon as God required a 'place' for His light, the light as it were descended and became feminized.

When dealing with a lexicography of light, one might have been forgiven for believing that in the Kabbala, the *Shekhinah* would have been all light. However, because the further the light travels from its source, the dimmer it becomes, paradoxically this is not so, and she is frequently depicted veiled in black garments. Frequently the matriarchs, especially Rachel, the daughter, have to stoop to deception (the substitution under the wedding canopy of her sister Leah for herself) so that she can have children through ersatz means.

Jung also is well aware that the connotations of the feminine are often far from positive, connected as they are with the shadow side of existence, with darkness, the left, the Other Side, and the lower region.

In the Kabbala, this feminine impulse is law, restriction, form – the threatening power of the womb. As opposed to masculine grace, generosity, and boundless desire to broadcast sperm, the female stands for the limited powers of receptivity of the natural world. In herself only slightly darker than the heavenly light, she is not always crystalline or spiritual by any means, but also associated with earth, clay and the grosser forms of materialism. The darkness which is her sphere is mother to all *klippot* (husks), shells and veils between the soul and the divine mother of all appetite for self-gratification that leads to mortality.

At this point, we can touch briefly on the notion put forward by the sixteenth-century Kabbalist R. Isaac Luria of *Zimzum* (a divine contraction and self-darkening). 'Before all worlds were created', says Rabbi Chaim Vital, a disciple of Luria, and the one who wrote down his ideas, 'the Supernal Light . . . filled all existence, and there was no empty space [that was not filled with light]' (Ashlag 1969). Everything was light, everything was God, in fact, and there was no room for the world. In order to create the world, God had, as it were, to draw back, as one who throws a ball bends back before throwing the ball forward. When God created the world, His light was concentrated into a single point to form a primal space or vacuum to allow matter to come into being. First He retracted; then He sent His light back again into the hollow thus formed, drawing out from Himself a mere thread of His infinite light which He spun and spun until 'He stretches out Heaven as a garment' (Ps. 104:2). In relation to God or absolute light (male), this stream of light or divine presence (*Shekhinah*) and the various receptacles so filled, for example, Israel, the human psyche, the entire created world take on a female typology.

According to R. Luria's concept of *Zimzum*, from all His beautiful creation God only created one new thing: 'He who fashions light and creates darkness' (Isa. 45:7). God only created darkness, the darkness that permits the light to be seen, darkness having a negative and 'feminine' connotation. And again, 'in the beginning', says the Bible, 'God said: "Let there be light"' (Gen. 1:3), which, according to the opening words of the *Zohar*, the Book of Radiance, the bible of the Kabbala, means: 'In the beginning God created a Lamp of Darkness' (1:15a).

Jung's description of the 'inferior function' of the feminine anima within the psyche is based on the Kabbalistic notion of the *Shekhinah*'s role in cosmology. She has frequently, says Jung, 'a shady character; in fact she sometimes stands for evil itself. . . . She is the dark and dreaded maternal womb which is of an essentially ambivalent nature' (*Psychology and Alchemy*, *Collected Works*, vol. 12). This female ambivalence stems essentially from the fact that the womb-type function of the female makes her a link between physical and spiritual.

If the male represents essence, the female stands for emanation, the divine urge to emanate, to create. And yet, once one has reached the essence, is not emanation itself a rather thin spreading out of essentials?

If the enigma of the feminine is not taken as outright evil, still it is mysterious, obscure, subconscious. Therefore, says Jung, while the conscious functions, shared between father and son, are male, the female, mother and daughter, are taken as unconscious. In this allotment of male/female roles, there is undying hostility, says Jung, between the principles, the father and the mother, consciousness and unconsciousness, but the auxiliaries are weaker, so that it is possible for the third function – the daughter – 'to be raised to consciousness and thus made masculine. It will, however, bring with it traces of its contamination . . . thus acting as a kind of link with the darkness of the unconscious' (p. 152).

The idea borrowed by Jung of the feminine being a mediating presence between conscious and unconscious (the Holy Ghost, Sophia, Mary) is not new in the Kabbala, where, however, the contrasting spheres are between spiritual and physical. In the case of the Jewish tradition at least the feminine is not viewed as exclusively physical and in need of any type of 'masculiniz-ation' in order to rise to spiritual heights. The feminine is as at home in transcendence as in this world! The idea is that God has, in fact, a feminine receptive part of Him, a kind of consort as the Higher *Shekhinah* or the Mother, who has an earthly representative in the lower spheres, Rachel, the Community of Israel, or the daughter and, just as the lower *Shekhinah* fares in the material realms, so fares the Higher Feminine in transcendence. The whole reason for creation is that, through the efforts of the daughter in the world of substance, God should be reunited with His *Shekhinah*. Thus in the Jewish myth, far from the feminine becoming 'masculine', she comes into her own by reunion with lost aspects of herself.

For example, there is a tale concerning four rabbis in quest of the ultimate who hear the voice of the *Shekhinah* ring out from a cave: 'Lamps shall give light from the lampstand.' The *Zohar* continues: 'Here the Community of Israel [a female image] receives the light while the Supernal Mother is crowned, and all the lamps are illumined from her.' Israel, by the single act of kindling the menorah (the seven- or eight-branched candelabrum), is identified and united with the creative aspect of God through the menorah symbol.

Already in the Midrash, creation and art are feminine activities. Creation is compared to a king who wants to build a palace. He does not build it with his own hands but calls in an architect. This architect, 'master-workman', *Oman* in Hebrew, is the feminine wisdom in God, Sophia or Torah that was the blueprint for creation.

The *Zohar* comes out with the startling notion, already hinted at in the Midrash, that it was the feminine principle within God that made creation possible. This whole deployment of male and female creative strategies the *Zohar* describes in terms of darkness and light.

Only the Supernal Mother had a name combining light and darkness – light which was the supernal vestment and which God created on the first day and then stored away for the righteous, and darkness.

Because the darkness was destined to sin against the light [because man was destined to sin], the Father was not willing to share in man's creation. [Thus is God absolved of human evil] and therefore the Mother said: 'Let us make man, in our image, after our likeness.'

'In our image' corresponds to light [masculine]. 'After our likeness'
to darkness [feminine], which is a vestment to light.
[. . . Also 'In our image' to the light of transcendence; 'After our
likeness' to immanence.]

(*Zohar* 1:22a–b)

What the *Zohar* is saying is that the male transcendent God knew that man
would sin and was reluctant to create him while the Mother took the
initiative. Therefore man is created after the image of the Mother, not the
Father, side of God, 'since the Father was not willing to share with his
creation'.

Like Jung, the companions of Rabbi Shimon, the Master-Teacher of the
Zohar, seize on the (sexist) notion that man in his lowest aspect should be
in the image of woman, mother, earth, whereas the ideal transcendental man
is totally male. But R. Shimon disagrees and maintains that man in his very
highest aspect is both male and female.

That is why it says: 'And God said, "Let there be light" ' [Genesis 1:3].
Let there be light From the side of the Father.
And there was light. From the side of the Mother.
And this is the man 'of two faces'. This 'man' has no 'image and
likeness'.
[This represents the ideal relationship between the sexes.]
He [R. Shimon] then paused, and all the friends rejoiced and said:
'Happy is our lot that we have been privileged to hear things which
never were disclosed till now.'

(*Zohar* 1:22a–b)

Another way of describing the act of making the unconscious conscious (the
desideratum of Jungian therapy) is reintegration, and here there are sometimes many fissures – the conflict would seem to be between the One and
the Many rather than between male and female.

Jung's description of the many sparks of a primal World Soul or collective
unconscious is based on Kabbalistic and Hassidic notions of the 'breaking
of the vessels'.

The sequel to the Lurianic conception of *Zimzum* is that into the vacuum
that appears after God's self-darkening, lines of divine light pour back in.
Crystal vessels are formed to receive them, but they cannot contain
the richness and therefore burst, leaving *klippot* – shards or hard husks
covering seeds or germs of light – remnants of the withdrawal of infinite
light.

This fragmentation of the divine light results also in the externalization
of evil, forcing the lower *Shekhinah*, Rachel, or the daughter, to fall into
the world of materiality, her spirit pacing the boundaries, reaching out to
her children in dispersion even though this entails separation from her

husband. The aim of creation is to release those imprisoned sparks of *Shekhinah*-light, that captive princess.

Thus, the human psyche itself is seen as feminine. She, like Jerusalem, like the *Shekhinah*, like the Community of Israel, is known in Midrash, in the Kabbala, in Hassidism, as the 'King's daughter'. The Book of Illumination talks of God's bride or daughter as a personification of His kingly splendour. This 'daughter' is pure object and jewel reflecting the divine radiance to man – in herself she has utterly no personality but is merely and consummately a 'Beautiful Vessel', a pure objectivization of divine royalty and splendour. She is the pearl without price, the precious stone, Sophia, Torah, and the collective soul of man as fragmented into the separate rays and sparklets of the individual psyche.

In addition to the sparks being fragments of the individual soul, they are also transpersonal. Belonging to the collective unconscious, they float from one ego to another with the insouciant impersonality of objects or motes of dust; yet it is they who are the broken-up rays of God's 'jewel'. Intrinsically the soul of Adam Kadmon, drawn from the reservoir of souls, is quintessential light and was the very 'idea' on which the whole of the subsequent drama of creation was based.

> It is written: *These were the makers* [potters] *and those that dwelt among the plantations and hedges; there they dwelt with the king in his work* [1 Chr. 4:23]. *These were the makers*: They are so termed on account of the verse, *Then the Lord formed* [made] *man* [Gen. 2:7].
>
> *There they dwelt with the king in his work*: with the Supreme King of kings, the Holy One, blessed be He, sat the souls of the righteous with whom He took counsel before creating the world [*Ber. Rab.* 8:7].

Similarly in the Kabbala, although the self-chosen exile of the feminine (the *Shekhinah*) and her elevation provide the centre of the whole drama of existence, another way of looking at the same process is that the onus is on man both individually and collectively to effect a *Tikkun* (reintegration of sparks).

Therefore, the feminine plastic power of God, the 'Potter', could be said to have been made up of 'the souls of the righteous' before man himself had come on the scene. It was the potential good that man had in him that required that he should be created, no matter what potential evil or suffering lay in store for him also in his own nature. It was the light of *Adam Kadmon* (original man) – for what is goodness but the primordial light of the reservoir of souls that made it necessary that God create man.

Shekhinah is taken as the collective representative for individual masculine endeavours, the individual 'points' or scintillations in her bouquet. Thus, though the *Shekhinah* descends in order to turn her passive (feminine) stance relative to God into the more dynamic action of raising up the lights of the whole created world, how close or how far *Shekhinah* light comes down depends on man and on the generations of the *Tsaddikim* (the saints, Jewish chivalric knights). In relation to the lower spheres, the *Shekhinah* takes on an active stance made up of the heroic deeds of the individual *Tsaddik*, or good person.

The individual *Tsaddik* is only capable of bringing redemption to Israel and to man because he contains an image of the fragmentary souls of all men. In a process closely akin to projection in psychological terms, 'every individual sees in the *Tsaddik* his own share, or his image', says the Great Storyteller (Likkutei Amarim 32a). Not only does the *Tsaddik* contain within him a little bit of all men, but all men see reflected in him the image of their own potential.

Drawing on various alchemy texts, as we have seen, Jung also says that people are surrounded by multiple luminosities, like so many sparks or points of light, and that these portray the psyche as a multiple consciousness – that is, a multitude of luminous particles that in their sum constitute the self. This impressionist panorama represents the total content of archetypes of the collective unconscious.

These fragmented 'sparks' of an original integral consciousness correspond to the Jewish mystical concept of the 'breaking of the vessels' and the challenge imposed on man of effecting a *Tikkun*, or reintegration of the individual rays. Already an aspect of the Kabbala, this concept was taken over by Hassidism and internalized. No longer are the sparks only part of a purely cosmological process; they represent the fragmentation and reintegration of the individual psyche. And this is so even when what is described may seem to belong to the external world of objects. In fact, they are fragments of the original soul of the *Tsaddik* waiting to be reintegrated again within him.

In Hassidism, the *Tsaddik* only reflects on a heroic cosmic scale what is going on in the soul of every individual. Everyone is composed of various fragments or sparks of lower vitality that he tries to elevate and reintegrate with his highest self through attachment to the divine. R. Jacob Joseph of Polonnoye says that in a sense all the objects, the food and drink we long for, all relationships, all experiences, including our business transactions, and even the person we are married to, are all part of the original 'spiritual fallout' of our own soul: 'If a man deserves it by his good deeds, then he meets the sparks which by his very nature belong to him.' And personal salvation, says the Rabbi of Polonnoye, is the only means at man's disposal of bringing about redemption on the cosmic plane and rescuing the fragmented sparks of *Shekhinah* light.

Jung in his *Collected Works* claims that spirituality and meaningfulness are characterized by a certain effulgence or quasiconsciousness – numinosity entails luminosity. This light is the legendary *lumen naturae* which illuminates consciousness.

He makes frequent allusion to the cosmological myth of the fiery sparks of the world soul, particles of the 'Spirit of God' (Sophia, or Original Man, depending on which way one looks at it) that hovered over the abyss when creating the world but that are now dispersed or sprinkled in and throughout the structure of the great world. In these luminous fragments he sees a clear psychological meaning. Not only are they dispersed in the cosmos; it is in the unconscious (that these 'sparks of light' or scintillae) are hidden, in which the archetypes of a higher meaning can be extracted.

It is precisely from the darkness of the unconsciousness that certain 'germinal luminosities' or 'broken-up sparkles of consciousness' spring. The collective unconscious, with its 'disseminated luminosities' or multiple eyes, makes up a Jungian landscape, as symbol of the self, 'the one Scintilla or Monad'.

The sparks are like seeds of consciousness dispersed and buried in earth, darkness, the unconscious (characterized as feminine), the whole purpose of human life being 'to free the soul of the world of matter from its fetters [of materialism, or unconsciousness]' so as to bring more and more of them to full awareness.

In Jung's description of the scintilla, he seems to find the visualization of various kinds of inner landscape granted by the collective unconscious an aid to heightening of consciousness. The kind of pictures he calls to mind are very similar to various images Jews are faced with, for example, during the Hanukkah (Festival of Lights).

From the aesthetic point of view, it is uplifting on a dark winter's evening during Hanukkah to pass through a neighbourhood where many Jews live and see the sparkling forest of menorot studding the windows.

The menorah-studded perspectives of Hanukkah are reminiscent in turn of the descriptions of the blazing illuminations shed by the numerous golden menorot during the 'Rejoicing at the Place of the Water-Drawing' that was celebrated in Temple times. So intense was the blaze, says the Talmud, that 'there was not a courtyard in Jerusalem that was not illuminated by (what was taking place within the Temple precincts)' (Rosh Hashanah 16a).

Another way in which the panorama of menorah lights is reminiscent of rituals practised during other seasons of the year is an exotic variant on the custom of Tashlikh as celebrated in some villages in Galicia, Poland. Usually, Tashlikh is the ceremony on the afternoon of the 'Day of Judgement' (one of the names for the Jewish New Year) when Jews make an expedition to a fresh-flowing body of water symbolically to throw away their sins. In the village of Bolehov, in Galicia, the Hassidim used to form a procession and go to the water with lighted tapers in their hands. At sunset they would kindle small tufts of straw and cast them on to the water. In the gathering darkness, these floating lights would drift on the water, creating a magnificent spectacle graphically illustrative of the exorcism of sin. But this ceremony with the detached floating lights spells out something else also. The person is a mere catalyst, a nest for these motes of spiritual energy to float in and out of, and the whole riverside scene is a mirror of spiritual life both inside a person and also in his interrelationships with others.

There are other vistas, not directly connected with lights, that move us in the same way. Also during the Festival of Tabernacles, the sight of a large community of people waving the Four Species (palm-branch, citron, willows and myrtles) resembles nothing less than a living field of grain swaying in the wind of a religious emotion. The secret of their magic is, in fact, the power of individuals to mirror and affect one another within the larger perspective.

Jung analyses similar images of dazzling vistas composed of individual luminous quanta, scintillations or points of light composing a pointilliste or impressionist panorama, vast perspectives such as 'the star-strewn heavens', 'stars reflected in dark water', 'nuggets of gold or golden sand scattered in black earth', and a 'regatta at night, with lanterns on the dark surface of the sea' (Jung 1960: para. 396).

Since 'consciousness', Jung goes on to say,

> has always been described in terms of the behavior of light, it is not too much to assume that these multiple luminosities correspond to tiny conscious phenomena. If it appears in monadic form as a single star, or sun, or eye, it . . . must be interpreted . . . as the self . . . the symbols of the self hav(ing) a uniting character.
>
> (Jung 1960: para. 396)

These atoms of light are a (fragmented) visual representation, he says, of the collective unconscious – no wonder they take our breath away! – while at the same time portraying the individual psyche as a multiple consciousness, a multitude of luminous particles which in their sum constitute the Self. But they also, by plumbing deeper than the ego, go far beyond. By revealing the interrelationships between individuals by way of the basic few archetypes of man, they herald a heightened form of (collective human) perception and the possibility for a transformation of consciousness. It is in this way that Jung goes on to describe them as 'the eyes of the Lord that run to and fro through the whole earth' (Zech. 3:9), a description applied by the prophet Zechariah himself to the menorah-lamp.

A 'lamp' is a reflector image, so the 'lamp of God' is also the 'image of God': 'The lamp of God is the human spirit' (Prov. 27:20). And, as we know, man is supposed to have been created in God's image. When the human soul is so purified as truly to be God's image, the 'lamp' is transformed into a transpersonal human entity for the collective mirroring of the divine.

However, it does seem to mark a point at which the most spiritual part of the human and the most human part of the divine come together. An interpretation of the second verse in Genesis, 'And God's Spirit was hovering over the abyss' (Gen. 1:2), has been rendered as essentially the spirit of man: this is the soul of Adam or of the Messiah, or the primordial light of the menorah, the reservoir of souls from which the individual soul was formed. 'Spirit of God', individual human soul, reservoir of souls, and especially the soul of Adam, soul of the Messiah, come together in the form of the menorah!

Yet for other Kabbalists, the 'lamp of God' is not a collective human entity so much as that part of God that relates to man, that is, the *Shekhinah*. In essence these archetypes are meeting-points at all levels of the human and the divine. This is a case of reflection and irradiation at all levels.

Although not articulated in words, this is the actual impact upon us of the Hanukkah lights, when far and wide we see the individual 'points' of light imitating the starry sky. For each one is the spark of a soul, and all together constitute a living entity that is the image of God Himself. All souls mirror and refract one another, so that Cordovero was led to say: 'In everyone there is something of his fellow man. Therefore, whoever sins, injures not only himself but also that part of himself which belongs to another.' And this is the real reason for the command to 'love your neighbor as yourself' (Lev. 19:18). For, says Cordovero, 'the other really is he himself' (Cordovero 1976: 5).

While a single light may represent the individual soul, the menorah-candelabra, as a complex system, is the collective reservoir of souls personified as a feminine entity, the mother or 'bundle of life', the place where all identities merge – Jung's collective unconscious already hinted at concretely, pictorially, in the Kabbala.

REFERENCES

Ashlag, Y. (1969) *Ten Luminous Emanations of R. Isaac Luria*, trans. Levi I. Krakovsky, vol. 1, Jerusalem: Research Center of Kabbalah.

Cordovero, M. (1976) *The Palm Tree of Deborah*, trans. L. Jacobs, New York: Sepher-Hermon Press.

Dan, J. (1980) 'Interpretation of the Tetragrammaton', in *Kabbalat Rabbi Asher ben David*, Jerusalem: Hebrew University Publications.

Epstein, Rabbi I. (ed.) (1938) *The Babylonian Talmud*, London: The Soncino Press.

Gottlieb, F. (1989) *The Lamp of God: A Jewish Book of Light*, New York: Aronson.

Idel, M. (1988) *New Perspectives in Kabbalah*, New Haven: Yale University Press.

Jung, C. G. (1960) *The Structure and Dynamics of the Psyche*, in *Collected Works*, vol. 8, New York: Pantheon.

—— (1963) *Mysterium Coniunctionis*, in *Collected Works*, vol. 14, New York: Pantheon.

—— (1966) *Psychology and Alchemy*, in *Collected Works*, vol. 12, New York: Pantheon.

Kaplan, A. (1979) *The Bahir: An Ancient Kabbalistic Text Attributed to Rabbi Nehunian ben HaKana, First Century, C.E.*, New York: S. Weiser.

—— (1982) *Meditation and Kabbalah*, New York: S. Weiser.

Midrash Rabbah (1939) trans. into English by R. Dr H. Freedman and Maurice Simon, London: Soncino Press.

Scholem, G. (1941) *Major Trends in Jewish Mysticism*, Jerusalem: Schocken.
—— (1971) *The Messianic Idea in Judaism*, New York: Schocken.
—— (1974) *Kabbalah*, New York: Quadrangle.
The Zohar (1949), trans. Harry Sperling and Maurice Simon, London: The Soncino Press.

7

JACOB AND 'HEAR, O ISRAEL'

Levi Meier

EDITOR'S NOTE

In this paper, Levi Meier explores the central declaration of Jewish faith, the 'Hear, O Israel.' In addition to an in-depth analysis of the concept of the Oneness of God, he analyses the six words of the *Shema* prayer in detail. Essentially, he has written a modern psychological Midrash, i.e. utilizing his active imagination to suggest the feelings and thought processes of Jacob and the Children of Israel.

INTRODUCTION: THE CENTRALITY OF THE 'HEAR, O ISRAEL'

On Jacob's deathbed, he thinks of his grandfather, Abraham, who spread the message of monotheism to all peoples of the world. He envisions the entire history of the Jewish people and humanity, from the ancient past until the future arrival of the Messiah. Jacob gathers together all of his sons, the founders of the Twelve Tribes of Israel, and through divine prophecy, foretells their destinies.

Jacob is well aware, however, that the past will be interpreted and the future will be experienced by what he says on his deathbed. He is worried that all the trials and tribulations of his grandfather, Abraham, and his father, Isaac, as well as his own turbulent life, may lead to disunity and divisiveness among his children, and may affect their belief in one God. Among Jacob's concerns about potential conflict among his children is the fact that he has four 'firstborns' from four different wives – Leah, Rachel, Bilhah and Zilpah. However, he is careful to recognize each child's individuality and different maturational processes as he prepares to bless them.

Jacob has already become whole (Genesis 33:18), healed from his limping, partly through his reconciliation with Esau, and partly through having attributed positive meanings to the adversities of his life, such as being deceived by Laban. But the resolution of one remaining issue would grant

Jacob the ultimate meaning in his life. He yearns for the certainty that his children, the Twelve Tribes of Israel, the future of the Jewish people, will believe and experience the oneness of God that has always been with him, with his father, Isaac, and with his grandfather, Abraham.

The Midrash and Talmud state (Genesis Rabbah 98:3; Talmud, *Pesahim* 56a):

> At the time that Jacob, our father, departed from this world, he gathered together his twelve sons and said to them: 'Perhaps there is a doubt in your heart about the existence and essence of the oneness of the Holy One Blessed Be He.' They said to him, in unison: '*Hear, Israel*, our Father, just as your heart is complete and one with the Holy One Blessed Be He, so in our hearts there is total accord that *the Eternal our God, the Eternal is One*.' Upon hearing these beautiful, true sentiments, Jacob's doubts were assuaged and he declared: 'Blessed be the Name of the Glorious Majesty of God forever and ever.'

Based on this epic event in the lives of our patriarchs and matriarchs, the Jewish declaration of faith is expressd in the 'Hear, O Israel.' This declaration is formulated in the Torah as 'Hear, O Israel, the Eternal our God, the Eternal is One' (Deuteronomy 6:4).

The centrality of the 'Hear, O Israel' declaration is demonstrated in a number of ways. For example, it is the first prayer that Jewish parents teach their children, and the last prayer that a Jew recites before dying. Throughout life, Jews, old and young, recite this prayer at least twice a day, in the morning and evening, and before retiring at night.

Jacob and Jewish belief

Jacob sees himself as the essential link between his grandfather, Abraham, who spread monotheism, and the era of the Messiah, when such knowledge and recognition will be universal. Through the continuing daily recitation of the 'Hear, O Israel', Jacob is the focus not only of a core belief, but also of an ethical framework by which to live, based on monotheism.

The most striking aspect of the Midrash quoted above is that the children of Jacob addressed him in *unison*, with one voice, indicating their common understanding and belief. Furthermore, the way that they addressed their father is meaningful to us and to all succeeding generations of Jews. After they began with 'Hear ...', they paused and considered whether they should address their father as Jacob or Israel. The same divine spirit came over all of the sons, as they instinctively knew what to say. They chose their father's alternative name, 'Israel', representing a person who had struggled and had undergone transformation in his life. Israel's children understood their father's struggles. Perhaps even more importantly, they understood

75

their own, ranging from sibling rivalries to searches for ultimate meaning in their individual encounters with the changing images of God.

Similarly, all Jewish people throughout the generations continue to go through their own episodes of struggle and transformation. Our struggles in our relationship with God and with our opposites and ourselves lead to the realization that we are all 'Israel'. What keeps us together is the belief that God is with us, as promised to our forefather, Jacob/Israel, during his dream about the Ladder of Ascension (Genesis 28:12–15).

THE LANGUAGE OF THE 'HEAR, O ISRAEL'

The Torah's formulation of the 'Hear, O Israel' (Deuteronomy 6:4) presents a number of possible interpretations.

I suggest that the 'Hear, O Israel' may be understood in three different ways. One understanding is that this declaration is addressed to Jacob by his 'children'. That is, we continue the legacy of Jacob and address him as our father, when we declare that 'the Eternal our God, the Eternal is One'. This interpretation is in keeping with Jacob's words in Genesis 48:5, where Jacob 'adopts' his grandchildren, Ephraim and Manasseh, by publicly accepting them on the same level as his own sons, Reuben and Simeon. We are all the descendants, or grandchildren, of Jacob, and it is, therefore, natural that we should feel like his own children in declaring the central Jewish belief that is expressed in the 'Hear, O Israel.' This approach may provide an added dimension to our understanding of the rabbinical statement (Talmud, *Taanit* 5b) that Jacob, our father, has not died. He is a real presence in our daily lives, as we confirm in our declaration of belief.

A second interpretation of Deuteronomy 6:4 is that the 'Hear, O Israel' is addressed by each of us to the 'Israel' within each of us. Every morning and evening, together with Jews all over the world, we recite the 'Hear, O Israel' to the Jewish collective whole – from Abraham, our forefather, to future Jews who will witness the messianic era – as well as to each individual Jew and to our own struggling selves.

A third interpretation is that we address the God within each of us. The internal struggle between the divine and human aspects of our being may be alluded to in the name 'Israel', which means 'wrestling with God'.

Finally, each of us may choose to synthesize all or some of the above interpretations at the moment that we recite the 'Hear, O Israel', and our personal interpretation does not have to remain static. On any given day or at any given time of day, our inclination may be to focus on an aspect of the prayer that speaks to our soul at that moment.

Before we recite the prayer, we are obligated to pause for a moment of silence, giving us an opportunity to collect our thoughts and reflect on what we are about to say, as well as what is in our minds and hearts. This self-reflection will lead to true *kavvanah* (intention), both in reciting the prayer and acting upon it. As discussed below, those who truly 'hear' the words that they recite will respond by acting accordingly, in an ethical, godly fashion.

Essentially, by reciting the declaration of faith, one addresses God directly. Furthermore, by reciting the 'Hear, O Israel', one accepts upon oneself the yoke of the Kingdom of Heaven (*Ol Malkhut Shamayim*), i.e. the supreme obligation of walking in God's ways.

All of the above pertains to hearing God on an individual, personal level. However, this hearing can ultimately be translated into building a collection of individuals with common perceptions and common goals – a nation, a people. Abram's response to hearing the voice of God was to heed His words of *Lekh Lekha* (Genesis 12:1), 'go forth', leaving the familiar and comfortable perceptions and surroundings of his youth. This was the necessary first step in his building a new nation. During this process, Abram became Abraham (Genesis 17:5), 'the father of a multitude of nations', as well as the father of the Jewish people. Abraham's message of monotheism spread to the far corners of the globe, teaching a new way of understanding the human–divine partnership.

The words of the 'Hear, O Israel'

The 'Hear, O Israel' prayer consists of only six Hebrew words. In the Torah text (Deuteronomy 6:4), two of the Hebrew letters are written larger than the rest – the *ayin* in the word *Shema* ('Hear') and the *dalet* in the word *Ehad* ('One'). Together these two letters spell *Ed*, meaning 'witness'. Our rabbis interpret this text as indicating that those who say the 'Hear, O Israel' serve as witnesses from generation to generation to the truths that the living God is within each of us, there is but one God, and the God of our forefathers is also our God.

The 'Hear, O Israel' is divided into two parts: 'Hear, O Israel', and 'the Eternal our God, the Eternal is One'. The rabbis of the Midrash analyse this division to understand better the nature of the divine revelation at Sinai and the privilege of reciting the 'Hear, O Israel.' The *Midrash Rabbah* (Deuteronomy 2:31 (on 6:4)) states:

> From where does Israel have the privilege to recite the 'Hear, O Israel'? Rabbi Pinhas bar Hama said, from the act of revelation at Sinai, where God Himself uttered the 'Hear, O Israel.' Before beginning [the Ten Commandments with] 'I am the Eternal, your God', He called: 'Hear, O Israel', and all affirmed: 'The Eternal our God, the Eternal is One.'

Interestingly, after the giving of the Ten Commandments, the Children of Israel expressed their fear of continuing to hear the voice of God speaking directly to them. In Deuteronomy 5:21–4, right after the Israelites heard the divinely revealed Ten Commandments, they said to Moses:

We have *heard* His voice out of the midst of the fire. . . . Now therefore why should we die? . . . if we hear the voice of the Lord our God any more, then we shall die.

God listened to their request. The placement of the 'Hear, O Israel' following their request seems to imply that from now on God's voice will take on a different form. God will continue to speak to the people through their inner hearing of God's voice. This phenomenon will continue to be paramount in their lives and in those of all future generations.

Each word of the 'Hear, O Israel' has special significance and importance. Therefore, every word of the declaration is analysed in the section that follows.

Hear ('Shema')

The central declaration of Jewish faith is directed to our sense of hearing. This formulation is not surprising in view of the fact that it was through *hearing* the voice of God at Sinai that the Israelites unconditionally accepted the One God and His Torah. Throughout Jewish history, that voice has continued to resonate within each Jew – the voice that is the basis for belief and for action. Our rabbis expound on the fact that hearing is more powerful than seeing as a basis for faith. It is easier to *imagine* something infinite through the sense of hearing than through other senses, such as vision or touch, that are bound by finite dimensions. Furthermore, hearing leads to belief. One can perceive and touch idols, but one cannot hear them speak.

Rabbi Adolf (Avraham) Altmann, former Chief Rabbi of Trier, Germany, masterfully examines the imperative of continuing to hear the voice of God on a daily basis. He explores the central role of hearing during the revelation at Sinai and throughout Jewish history in his analysis of the 'Hear, O Israel' (A. Altmann 1928, 1991):

> God's Sinai voice has never turned silent for us; its echo continues throughout time. Only through this continued, inner, intuitive receptivity to that divine voice has Israel's belief in God remained.
>
> (p. 61)

Furthermore, as Rabbi Altmann points out, the ability to hear the divine voice is directly related to action and to ethics:

> The universe is filled with voices, but only those attuned will hear them. . . . God's voice of revelation cannot have become audible only once for all time. . . . If the Jew applies his heart to things that concern faith and that concern life, if he inclines his inner ear with its specific sensitivity, he will hear the voices. How can one direct the inner ear above all foreign outside noise toward the ancient voice calling from Sinai? The answer is, with the heart.
>
> (p. 65)

In other words, the ear must hear the language of the lips when the 'Hear, O Israel' is recited. Then, the actions of the individual must follow this divine call to act justly. If one hears the call from Sinai and its quiet, daily echoes, one is obligated to act on that divine message, in a godly, ethical fashion.

There are voices and calls which sound out loud, yet one fails to hear them, and there are others that make no sound at all, yet they are heard. The human without ethics passes by what cries out most in life without hearing, whereas one of high moral character hears even the most subdued call and traces its source. . . . If no one else hears the silent cry of the humiliated, the powerless, hidden victims, the Jew must hear it; that is the noblest ethical significance of the 'Hear, O Israel.'

(p. 63)

Israel ('Yisrael')

The second word of the central declaration of Jewish faith is 'Israel'. This brings to mind Jacob's pivotal encounter that led to his receiving an alternative name – Israel.

Genesis 32:25–33 presents an account of Jacob's encounter with an *Ish* (an angel, a human being as a messenger of God, or an internal struggle) and his acquisition of the name 'Israel'. That episode of struggle and wrestling may be understood as Jacob's *lonely night journey*. The experience of going through such a 'dark night of the soul' is one which all must undertake if they wish to achieve the goal of realizing their creative potential. Everyone goes through such a journey in life; not once, but many times.

In the biblical story concerning Jacob (Genesis 32:29), the name 'Israel' is explained as follows: 'And the *Ish* said: "Jacob shall not be your exclusive name; you will also be known as Israel, because you have prevailed with God and with men."'

Each person who recites the 'Hear, O Israel' may be engaging in a type of soliloquy, or dialogue with the self. Life presents itself in a manner whereby individuals have frequent, continuing struggles – with God, with the image of God and with humans. Thus, this monologue-prayer may be, in one sense, addressed to the God within. The divine promise is that individuals will prevail in their struggles and give birth to 'new' selves, of greater dimensions, as a result of these difficulties. The key word in the biblical account is *va-tukhal*, 'and you have prevailed'. By working through periods of difficulty and finding meaning and growth through this process, one may attain a higher stage of existence and understanding.

Life presents individuals with the opportunity to pass through sequential

79

stages and achieve continued growth. However, life often presents numerous difficulties in terms of relationships – with individuals, families, business partners, communities, societies and nations, as well as with God. Even on his deathbed, Jacob faced a new struggle as he wondered whether his children would continue in the way that he had directed them.

Jacob's struggles are significant in serving as examples for each person's life journey. The meaning of the ebbs and flows that we encounter in life experiences is sometimes easy to grasp and sometimes totally hidden from us. As a result, we are alternately angry, frustrated, depressed or elated.

Sometimes a difficult encounter allows us to resolve issues from our distant past. For example, we may have had difficulties with our parents that were never resolved. Yet, at a later stage in life, we may meet other individuals who share some of our parents' characteristics and qualities. By relating to these new people in our life, we may ultimately be able to work out difficulties that date back to our childhood, thereby achieving self-realization and individuation. Furthermore, by repairing our relationships with our parents, we may find new paths and directions in our approaches to God, since the image we have of God is partially based on our relationships with our parents.

Healing and the Higher Self

This entire process of continuing encounter, struggle, new understanding and personal growth leads to living life on an increasingly elevated plane. One can move from one plateau to another throughout life. This experience is the true meaning of 'healing'. Whatever happens in life can be used to heal relationships with people and with God.

In this way, through this process, one experiences growth and learns how to get in touch with one's Higher Self. This concept means achieving the ability to transcend the ordinary and to imbue the ordinary with meaning and spirituality.

In thinking about Jacob's struggle and his subsequent rebirth as Israel, one is also reminded that this struggle took place at *night*, a time that gives rise to dreams and other manifestations of the unconscious. In his commentary on this biblical episode, Maimonides (1974: 2:43) alludes to the possibility that Jacob's encounter with the *Ish* may have been some sort of vision that occurred while Jacob was in an altered state of consciousness.

On the basis of Jacob's visions during that night of struggle, Jacob might have been pleased to realize that the Jewish people to follow him would also pay careful attention to the interpretation of dreams and visions. Dreams and other aspects of the unconscious form part of God's forgotten language that Jews continue to use to explore both internal and external conflicts.

The printed text of the Torah includes notations to indicate how each word is to be chanted. After the initial reflective soliloquy of 'Hear,

O Israel', the text indicates that one should pause. Perhaps this is a reminder that after each 'Israel', i.e. after each internal and external struggle, one should try to assimilate the knowledge gained from the experience and the new perspectives before proceeding to the next stage of life.

As discussed above, when one recites the 'Hear, O Israel', one also addresses each individual Jew and the collective Jewish people, from earliest times to the distant future. Furthermore, the 'Hear, O Israel' serves as the last statement of a Jewish person facing immediate death. Commenting on this role of the prayer, Erwin (Morenu Shlomo Bunim) Altman, one of the sons of Rabbi Adolf (Avraham) Altmann, presented his own living testimony and analysis a short time before his own death:

> As the Five Books of Moses, which contain the godly testimony of His holy life, end with the words: *Le'ene Kol Yisrael*, 'before the eyes of all Israel', so a Jewish *Tzaddik* and every righteous person dies before the eyes of all his people, communicating with them in his last star-hour message. Even in death he thinks more of the people he is leaving behind than of himself. And he passes from this world with an entirely selfless fulfillment of a *Mitzvah*: comforting, encouraging, uplifting and inspiring the godly people of 'Alone-ness', his fellow *Bney Israel – 'Shema Yisrael!'*
>
> (E. Altman 1988: 162)

'THE ETERNAL OUR GOD, THE ETERNAL IS ONE'

The second part of the 'Hear, O Israel' is 'the Eternal our God, the Eternal is One'. This affirmation is equivalent to the *na'aseh ve-nishma* ('we shall do and we shall hear') declaration of the Jewish people at Sinai (Exodus 24:7), when they received the Torah. Therefore, Jews recite daily not only a confirmation and reaffirmation of monotheism, but also an acceptance of 'we shall do and we shall hear'.

In this declaration of acceptance, equal emphasis is placed on doing and on hearing. 'Doing' is the acceptance of the rituals. But the 'hearing' is equally significant. It means not only understanding the meaning of the rituals, but also continuing to hear the voice of God throughout one's life.

The practice of the *mitzvot* (commandments) heightens our awareness and sensitivities, imbuing ordinary events with spirituality and holiness. This is the underlying philosophy of the *mitzvot*. The ordinary daily routines of men, women, children, the old and the young involve activities that are needed to maintain, preserve and enhance life. Yet, all of these activities can be raised to a level of *kedushah* (holiness). Thus, Jewish commandments, practices and customs are not distinct from the ordinary, daily life of the person, family or community. The *mitzvot* take those things that are necessary to sustain life and imbue them with holiness and transcendence.

The Eternal (pronounced 'Adonai', written YHWH)

'The Eternal' refers to the quintessential nature of the existence and essence of God. This name connotes that God's time frame is unique – God was, is and will be. For God, these three aspects of time coexist simultaneously, rather than following one another in linear fashion. For a human being, this concept is incomprehensible, underscoring the mysterious, unfathomable essence of God.

In contradistinction, humanity lives in the present, reflects upon the past, and anticipates the future. But God's essence combines all times. When we acknowledge the eternal, we imagine ourselves experiencing the divine revelation, standing at Mount Sinai, accepting the Torah and hearing the voice of God. We reaffirm that acceptance for present and future generations.

Although this name of God, the Eternal, is mentioned in the Book of Genesis, it is first explained in Exodus (3:14). There, God said to Moses: 'I AM THAT I AM', following Moses' experiencing the divine presence in the burning bush that was not consumed. The word 'eternal' signifies that God will always be with the Jewish people. This is very similar to what God told Jacob, i.e. 'I will not abandon you' (Genesis 28:15).

It is significant that the meaning of 'eternal' is given after the episode of the burning bush. That encounter signifies to all future generations that God's eternal presence needs to be experienced in everyone's own life – daily, weekly or yearly – in different ways. When God calls unto Moses, he responds with one Hebrew word, *Hineni* (Exodus 3:4), meaning 'here I am'. Those reading about this encounter get the feeling that someone who experiences the divine responds with a sense of acceptance and surrender in the awesome presence of the divine.

The human response seems to be: 'I am Your obedient servant. I am grateful to be able to experience this aspect of life. I will go in the way that You direct me. I will carry this experience with me forever. I will bring it into other parts of my daily life in order to experience new forms of "God's presence in the burning bush."' Although we recognize that our earthly existence is temporal, every person can connect with the eternal presence of God in a spiritual manner.

The name of the eternal being is now pronounced 'Adonai', meaning 'My Master', indicating that we are the obedient servants of the will of God. We do not know the original pronunciation of this name. However, we do know that this name has so much sanctity that it was uttered only once a year, by the High Priest, on the Day of Atonement in the Temple's Holy of Holies. These limitations add an additional element of mystery to this supreme Name of God. The unfathomable mystery of the existence and essence of God, 'I AM THAT I AM', is something that every individual grapples with throughout his or her life in personal, unique ways.

E. Altman brought new meaning to the first message that God gave to Abraham as he undertook his lifelong task of spreading monotheism (Genesis 12:2), *Veheyeh Berakhah*, 'And be a blessing.' Altman pointed out that the same four Hebrew letters of 'be' (WHYH) are identical with those that make up the name of the eternal (YHWH), though they are arranged in a slightly different order. Thus, the ethical imperative of monotheistic belief is related to embodying the highest goal of human action, i.e. being a blessing.

E. Altman expounded on this similarity between the letters of God's name (YHWH) and 'And be (WHYH) a blessing.' In his amplification of this idea, he writes:

Man's destiny to 'Be a Blessing' can be conceived on various levels. It proclaims the constructive principle against any destructive tendencies. It means love in thought, words and action. But it has deeper dimensions. . . . 'And Be a Blessing' . . . addresses man's higher self, saying: by your faith and fulfillment of God's call, 'Be a Blessing', you reach a stage of understanding of its highest spiritual meaning: *Veheyeh* – you are that you were, you are that you are, you are that you shall be – a continuous potential source of blessing, as you are an eternal 'partner' within God's love and His eternity.

(1988: 146–7)

E. Altman emphasizes that this message is addressed to Abraham and 'to each individual in each generation, as each is created in the Image of God, which is a basic Biblical concept'.

This understanding explains the relationship between monotheism and ethics in daily life. When one acts ethically, others notice and respond accordingly. Furthermore, they want to know the basis for the ethical behaviour. What is its origin? What is the source of these absolute standards of justice, honesty and goodness? By living up to these elevated standards of behaviour, individual Jews can fulfil their ultimate mission of being a 'kingdom of priests and a holy nation' (Exodus 19:6), as well as a 'light unto the nations' (Isaiah 60:3).

Our God ('Elohenu')

As we proceed through life, we experience multiple images of God, even though we are aware that God is an eternal presence. These multiple images explain why the Torah utilizes several different names for God. *Elohenu* is the combined form of *Elohim shelanu*, 'our God'. This name includes the concept of God as not only an eternal presence, but also a judge. That the word *elohim* means 'judges' is clearly indicated in Exodus 21:6. Thus, we acknowledge that God has given us a moral standard to live up to.

This image of God as judge indicates that He yearns for His people to live up to standards which are beneficial *for them*. Hence, we are told 'to keep *for thy good* the commandments of the Lord and His statutes' (Deuteronomy 10:13). Even when God is experienced as the God not only of love, but also of judgement, we recognize that the judgement is based on love, and its goal is to help the individual and the nation.

The term *Elohenu*, 'our God', has additional meaning for us. It implies that the God of Abraham, Isaac, Jacob and Moses – the One each experienced during his life – is also the God who leads each of us in our life's journey. While we accept the special relationships that our forefathers enjoyed with God, nevertheless we have to personalize our own image of God. Our life journeys are just as significant as those of our forebears. Ultimately, we must recognize that during our lives – at high points and low points – God is with us, just as He was with our forefathers.

The Eternal (pronounced 'Adonai', written YHWH)

It seems unusual that this name appears a second time in the very brief 'Hear, O Israel.' One explanation is that this repetition differentiates between a transcendent, external, incomprehensible God and an immanent, accessible, personal God.

The first time that the Eternal's name appears, it refers to the transcendent God of history, such as the image that appeared to Moses at the burning bush. However, after we recite the *Elohenu*, we personalize and accept *our own* images of God. We thus experience God on a personal level and find our own Eternal – who was, is and will be with each of us.

Ehad ('One')

The Oneness of the God of Israel is a recurring theme in the Torah. The best-known source of this essential Jewish belief is the first two commandments of the Decalogue (Exodus 20:2–3), which are echoed in the 'Hear, O Israel.' As discussed above, each of us encounters multiple images of God during our lives, just as our forebears did. However, all of these are manifestations of the One God, who appeared to Abraham, Isaac, Jacob, Moses, Sarah, Rebekah, Rachel, Leah, and so forth. For example, when God appears to Jacob during his dream about the Ladder of Ascension, God identifies Himself to Jacob (Genesis 28:13) as 'the God of Abraham, thy father, and the God of Isaac'.

The concept of One God is fundamental to the ethical framework of the Jewish people. Only One God who is immutable can give one set of everlasting values, principles and standards by which individuals and a nation are to live. These standards are not subject to variation or to change, as they may be in polytheistic societies.

Furthermore, E. Altman (1988) relates the concept of the One to aloneness, and thus to reciting the 'Hear, O Israel' at the end of life. He writes:

> [The 'Hear, O Israel'] has many equally valid interpretations and translations, but the recitation and proclamation of the *Shema* at the very moment of death is probably meant in the sense: *Adonay* is our God from without and within, *Adonay* alone! This testimony reflects the most intimate direct relationship with God; man feels and realizes: I am dying alone, as nobody can accompany me, where I am going. I am 'on my own', as never before in my life, but just in this 'alone-ness', which I am facing now, I am closer to God's identity and His Alone-ness than ever before. In this true alone-ness, I experience and recognize my very own Divinity from within in the Image of God.
>
> (p. 161)

In addition to this 'identification' with the divine, I find great personal comfort in the image of Divine Oneness. This concept reflects the oneness that pervades much of life. Every day, I am aware of the oneness of humanity – the similar drives, fears, hopes, dreams and aspirations that we all share. We share one space, the earth, on which we strive to make a difference for the short spans of our individual lives. We share the same spiritual quests, which, although they take us along different paths, lead us to answers that we seek to universal questions. This awareness of oneness – that of the human experience of the cosmos and the universal pursuit of religious experience – can enhance our daily encounters with other individuals, communities and nations, thereby enriching our lives.

On a personal level, the recitation of the 'Hear, O Israel' allows us to listen to our inner voice, thus guiding us in achieving our highest potential and becoming our best selves. 'This ability to listen and to hear allows the voice of God to be heard continually on a daily basis. This is a central aspect of individuation' (Meier 1991b).

Every prayer must be recited with intention and with some level of understanding of what is uttered. However, the recitation of the 'Hear, O Israel' requires a particularly deep understanding that emanates from one's heart and soul. The sages placed the recitation of the 'Hear, O Israel' in a class above the other commandments. They mandated that this prayer should be recited with particular 'intention of the heart' (Talmud, *Berakhot* 13a–b). Therefore, one should recite the 'Hear, O Israel' with particular concentration on each word and concept contained therein.

Another unique feature of this prayer's recitation is the custom of prolonging the sounding of the large letter *dalet* at the end of the word *Ehad* ('One'). The prolongation of this sound heightens one's awareness of the other large letter in the prayer, the *ayin* at the end of *Shema* ('Hear'). As discussed above, these two letters form the word *Ed*, 'witness'.

When we recite the 'Hear, O Israel' with this level of intention and attention, we indeed become witnesses, bearing personal testimony to the historical revelation at Sinai and to the continuing revelation that all of us can achieve in our daily lives. Furthermore, we become witnesses to the fact that each of us is a link in the long chain of tradition, enhancing the meaning of our own lives, and passing on our personal testimony and our own spirituality to this generation, as well as the next.

SHEMA, YISRAEL, ADONAI ELOHENU, ADONAI EHAD!
Hear, O Israel, the Eternal our God, the Eternal is One!

REFERENCES

Altman, Erwin (1987) 'Excerpts from *Reflections on this Thing* and *No-Thing called Life and Death*', *Journal of Psychology and Judaism* 11 (2), ed. L. Meier.

—— (1988) 'Excerpts from *Reflections on this Thing* and *No-Thing called Life and Death*', reprinted in L. Meier (ed.), *Jewish Values in Psychotherapy: Essays on Vital Issues on the Search for Meaning*, Lanham, Md.: University Press of America.

Altmann, Adolf (Avraham) (1928) 'Sinn und Seele des "Höre Israel."' ('The meaning and soul of "Hear, O Israel"'). Berlin: *Jeschurun* (ed. Joseph Wohlgemuth), 11/12.

—— (1991) 'The meaning and soul of "Hear, O Israel"', translated from the German by Barbara R. Algin and edited by Levi Meier. In Meier 1991b.

The Holy Scriptures (1917) 2 vols., Philadelphia: Jewish Publication Society.

Maimonides, M. (1974) *The Guide of the Perplexed*, Chicago: The University of Chicago Press.

Meier, L. (1986) *Jewish Values in Bioethics*, New York: Human Sciences Press.

—— (1988) *Jewish Values in Psychotherapy*, New York and London: University Press of America.

—— (1991a) *Jewish Values in Health and Medicine*, New York and London: University Press of America.

—— (1991b) *Jewish Values in Jungian Psychology*, New York and London: University Press of America.

Midrash (1961) Ed. H. Freedman and M. Simons, 10 vols., London: Soncino Press.

The Talmud (1961) Ed. I. Epstein, 18 vols., London: Soncino Press.

Throughout this work, I quote extensively from the writings of both Rabbi Dr Adolf (Avraham) Altmann and one of his sons, Dr Erwin (Morenu Shlomo Bunim) Altman. I wish to express my heartfelt gratitude to Dr Manfred Altman of London for granting me permission to quote from the published writings of his late father and brother.

Part III

CHRISTIANITY

EDITOR'S PREFACE

Judaeo-Christianity was the result of a split in Judaism in beliefs about theology, institutions and observances. Jesus founded Christianity as a Jew and Paul was to articulate most of Christian theology and its ethical practice. Solomon Nigosian, in his book *Judaism – the Way of Holiness* (Wellingborough: Thorsons, 1986), pp. 198–9, points out that

> the Jesus of history (whatever other characteristics are attributed to Him) was a devout adherent of Judaism who became the founder of a Judaic sectarian movement called Christianity in very much the same way that Martin Luther (1483–1546) was a devout adherent of Roman Catholicism who became the founder of a Christian sectarian movement called Lutheranism which, in turn, spawned protestantism.

Christians are, in this sense, non-conforming Jews. Paul believed that when Jews refused to accept God's plan of redemption through Christ, this was a temporary step which then required the redemption of the entire Gentile world before the Jews themselves could be saved.

Christians believe Jesus to be the Messiah (*Christos* in Greek, abbreviated to *Christ*). Christians believe God made a new covenant with them and that they then became the sole interpreters of God's will. But Christians retain important elements of Judaism such as the Mosaic Decalogue (Ten Commandments); a day of rest each week, baptism, the sanctity of marriage and the order of burial are Christian beliefs and practices derived from Judaic legacy. The official statement of the Roman Catholic Church at Vatican II Council (1962–4) affirms this:

> As this sacred Synod searches into the mystery of the Church, it recalls the spiritual bond linking the people of the New Covenant with Abraham's stock. For the Church of Christ acknowledges that, according to the mystery of God's saving design, the beginnings of her faith and her election are already found among the patriarchs, Moses, and the prophets. ... The Church, therefore, cannot forget that she received the revelation of the Old Testament through the

people with whom God in His inexpressible mercy deigned to establish the Ancient Covenant. . . . The Church recalls too that from the Jewish people sprang the apostles, her foundation stones and pillars, as well as most of the early disciples who proclaimed Christ to the world.

C. G. Jung, in two of his most important Christian papers, 'A psychological approach to the dogma of the Trinity' and 'Transformation symbolism in the mass' (*Collected Works*, vol. 11 (London: Routledge & Kegan Paul, 1958), pp. 107 and 201 respectively), reveals a psychological understanding of the profound dogmatic meanings *in psyche* to which the Christian beliefs testify that is unparalleled *in essence* by any other psychologist of the twentieth century. In breaking barriers between theology and psychology, Jung inestimably enlarges psychological understanding for the continued practice and support of Christian virtues and Christian mysticism. In his total Self theory of oneness and wholeness within psyche, Jung affirms an analogy to the comprehension of Oneness in God or monotheistic revelation. Jung always believes in the *unus mundus*, an eventual understanding of the unitary mirroring of the microcosm in the macrocosm and vice versa, which enables man's psyche to carry a monotheistic religious belief. Jungian psychology is behind monotheism. This empirical fact has yet to be comprehended by all of Judaism, Christianity and Islam.

8

JUNG AND PRAYER

Ann Belford Ulanov

The interrelationship of religion and the psyche, and particularly in prayer, is complex and primordial in its roots. Prayer touches us all so deeply and intimately that it is harder to talk about than our sex life or our bank balance. This is our experience of prayer when we wake in the night full of anxiety – the wolf hour; it is what spills out of us in gratitude in moments of joy. Prayer expresses what we fear, and often reduces us to utter silence, held in awe by its ministrations. It is with us when we die, or even begin to approach death, in the images we have of bridges to the other side.

It is this set of religious and psychological connections that is at the centre of Jung's special work with the psyche: he is concerned with the numinous, not in the abstract, but in all its concretions, wherever it touches us intimately. The abstract God 'beyond all human experience leaves me cold', says Jung. We do not affect each other. 'But if I know that he is a powerful impulse of my soul, at once I must concern myself with him' (Jung 1929: para. 74; see also Jung 1971: paras 412–13).

No, nothing general, abstract or distant here – Jung brings the issue right home to us where we live. He wants to know more and more about what his and our immediate experiences of God amount to. There is no substitute for this understanding, this experience, this knowledge. Our community, our environment, our society cannot give it to us (Jung 1956: paras 536–7). In this reading, dogma and our shared religious traditions are at their best a collective dreaming of such experiences of spiritual immediacy as prayer. Like a great river, dogma runs beneath our societies, watering and nourishing them. Hans Urs Von Balthasaar says something similar about contemplatives: 'Contemplatives are like great rivers which, on occasion, break out into springs at unexpected points, or reveal their presence only by the plants they feed from below' (Balthasaar 1961: 72). Despite our 'fear of primordial experience', Jung says, 'I consider it my task and duty to educate my patients and pupils to the point where they can accept the direct demand that is made upon them from within.' From his study of early Christian writings, Jung continues, 'I have gained a deep and indelible impression of how dreadfully

91

serious an experience of God is. It will be no different today' (Jung 1973, 26 May 1945: 41).

What is no different today is the placing of ourselves in prayer under the authority of the transcendent. In a curious way, the theologian Karl Barth and the psychiatrist Jung are brothers here. Barth starts his theology from God's side, so to speak, saying we cannot even know who we are without first looking to God. Only by seeing God's judgement and mercy do we realize we are sinners, for really we see our sins only when they are forgiven by God in Christ. Jung uses a different language, but the movement of soul is the same. Jung places the ego under the authority of the Self. Only looking there, in the Self's demands, do we find all the ego-life we are to live here: 'If that voice is listened to, one will have a chance of a more complete life, because one lives then almost as if one were two people, not one alone, and there will be a whole sphere of knowledge and experience in which all functions, all ideas, will enter besides our ordinary consciousness' (Jung 1984: 516).

We discover that trying to become ourselves, consciously to enter the process of individuation means to be on the receiving end of a conversation with an Other who addresses us. In and through the various psychic complexes that address us from within – shadow, anima, or animus – this greater centre of the whole psyche that Jung calls the Self puts us into relationship with itself. We may find, further, that in conversation with the Self we enter a discourse that transcends the Self. We thought we were one person only to discover that we are two – conscious and unconscious, ego and Self, Jung's famous number one and number two personalities – only to discover further the stunning fact that what we thought was a two-way conversation is in fact a three-way discourse. The conversation going on all the time is between ego, Self, and that which the Self knows about, God.

Jung speaks from the concrete facts of his own experience. His kind of empiricism is fundamental in any discussion of prayer. See how *in fact* life is affecting us. Admit it, wherever it is, and pay close attention to it and everything in and around it: this is the only useful approach. Jung wants to understand in the most concrete terms the depth of our experience of the primordial and to identify the reality of what is touching us there. Thus Jung puts himself in the place of the ordinary receiver. He can be himself touching about prayer because he himself is touched and honest and aware of his limits. He begins, and always counsels us to begin, in the midst of life, in immediate experience (Jung 1956: paras 507, 512, 521).

Prayer is to religious life what dreaming is to psychic life: experience at the source, in its narrowness and breadth, its daily fare, its interior space. It reveals that what lives most privately, hidden inside us, opens us far outside ourselves to shared living with others and with life itself. What Jung says about dreams could as well be said about prayer: 'In the deepest sense we all dream not *out of ourselves* but out of what lies *between us and the other'* (Jung 1973, 9 September 1934: 172). When we pray we speak not only out of our truest self but also into and from a space we are surprised to discover is inhabited by an unmistakable Other, clearly there before us. In the language of Judaeo-Christian tradition, it is the Holy Spirit moving in us that moves us to pray in the first place. What we thought was all in us is also the Other and many others like us too who are similarly moved to bow their heads and bend their knees.

RELIGIOUS INSTINCT

Jung stands out from other depth psychologists in his positing the existence of a religious instinct. Operating in us, independent of our will, this instinct is a capacity for and urge towards conscious relationship to transpersonal deity (Jung 1953: para. 11). We can fall just as ill from disorder in our relationship to this instinct as we can to any other. Repression of sexuality leads to all sorts of outbreaks of complicated symptoms. The splitting off of our aggression leads to schizoid disorder and variations of a passive–aggressive character. Efforts to control our hunger instinct land us in eating disorders of all kinds. So too with the religious instinct: when frustrated or thwarted it has its own unmistakable pathology.

I have seen the disease of alcoholism contain a massive psychosomatic defence against facing the inner emptiness that stands behind the disease. One man poured all his energy into persona performance to flee from an engulfing sense of lack which he simply refused admittance. He knew meaning existed, but he could not house it in his own living. He needed more and more drink to keep his persona – the mask he showed to the world – intact and adequate to present his usually high level of performance. Meanwhile behind the mask, when he faced inward to his own private and unconscious life, it was as if another part of him that felt both like and unlike himself, and turned up in dreams and fantasy as a hated woman (his anima), were raising more and more hell. Sometimes he dreamt of various women who were standing up in public to expose his drinking. Other times he dreamt of a female wanting to trap him into lifelong dreary servitude. Another dream theme presented women in various stages of illness, hysteria, or maudlin moping. He put it poignantly: 'Drink is my fuel to perform and my reward when alone, but it does not allow me to do two necessary things – to pray and to do this analytical work.' He might have added, 'dangerous analytical work'. The analysis was dangerous. When we worked successfully, we inevitably came to the mangled and dreaded woman-part that enraged the man. His psyche would use me in the transference to carry it. He would say, 'I love you as an analyst, but I don't want you to be a woman. Whenever I think of you as a woman I want to slap you!' When we reached his pivotal point, this point of breakthrough, where we could look at and talk with this anima, the drinking defence overcame him and interrupted therapy, sometimes for as long as three months. All the work seemed to wash away in alcohol.

We can repress the religious instinct, and the power of the primordial can fall on to drink and make it an idol that enslaves us in addiction. It can get identified with other things, too, and then we find our usual idolatries – money, work, food, drugs, family, love relationship. Or we can fall into identification with this power of the primordial and see ourselves as gurus, wise beyond telling, inflated beyond our small human size. We can always spot an idol because it apes the ways of God. Everything in us revolves around, say, food, or an inferiority complex, or identity crisis. We think of it all the time, in every situation, devote enormous amounts of energy to it. We are distracted from listening to others because of our thinking and fantasizing all the time about what we can eat and when, or how the other sees us and why. Inside our compulsion hides the religious instinct, bending us to masochistic enslavement, which is the shadow side of veneration (Gordon 1984).

We can also dodge the religious instinct by substituting our map of it for the territory it describes. Then we use our theories as convenient places in which to hide; Jung's map of the numinous, for example, becomes our pseudo-religion. Revelling in it, we avoid our own immediate experience of the religious territory, living at a great remove from our creative centre. Our unreceived primordial power puffs up our interest in Jung; we become fanatical – and boring!

We can also put another person in place of our religious instinct. A woman whose love and money were entangled with a man who had been central in her life for three decades, though it was essential to separate her life from his, found this extraordinarily difficult to do, to the point where she lost hundreds of thousands of dollars because she could not move quickly or decisively to make the break. She felt both homicidal and suicidal. Disentangling her connection to him involved identifying and separating many strands – giving up her idealization of him, ending her long practice of denying the bad in him and between them, withdrawing from all the demands and displacements and projections to claim in herself the power she had put on to him. The crucial piece was her projection of the religious instinct so fully on to him that she then identified him as the authority in her life. What made her feel conscious of her capacity for relating to a centre that gave her hope and a sense of living creatively and unified within herself was all caught up with him. God came in a wrapper made up of this man's parts. Her belief was not too clearly expressed, but was deeply felt. She hated official religions and traditional religious process and saw them as coercive and controlling. The values she held she had discovered with this man when younger, and these too she identified with him. She believed in humanness and humaneness, in the rock-bottom goodness of people, in their simple acts of kindness and respect. As she struggled to express all of this,

I asked her about what had surfaced: 'You believe in this, don't you? This is your value, isn't it?' She saw for a moment how she had wrapped her sense of value round this man like a coat that now would not come off. She saw then why she had felt that if she separated from him she would be separating herself from all she had ever believed made life worth while. She saw she could not leave him, because that meant living away from the primordial. To see that this sense of value was like indispensable protective clothing, like his raincoat around him, but was not the man himself and was not carried only by him, but was really her own coat of values, became a little epiphany for her. It was an immensely moving moment for both of us, a little bit of numinous fire suddenly flaming up in the office on an otherwise average Wednesday morning.

Jung writes early on that the soul 'is a function of relation between the subject and the inaccessible depths of the unconscious. The determining force (God) operating from these depths is reflected by the soul, that is, it creates symbols and images.' The soul is then 'both receiver and transmitter', perceives unconscious contents and conveys them to consciousness by means of these symbols (Jung 1971: para. 424). The soul lives, as it were, midway between the ego and the primordial unconscious, which expresses itself through the archetypal images that the soul receives, creates and transmits. Jung continues, 'when God is in the soul, i.e., when the soul becomes a vessel for the unconscious and makes itself an image or symbol for it, this is truly a happy state . . . [which] is a *creative* state' (Jung 1971: para. 424). The soul gives birth to images – like the wrapper, like the overcoat which really is removable from the man and must be acknowledged and donned by the woman herself – but we can lose these images in licentious behaviour, aesthetic indulgence, quasi-religious enthusiasm and addictive compulsion, where we project them into various substances where they soon lose their identity and disappear. To realize these images consciously and relate to them is to be free to adapt to reality and promote our happiness and well-being.

Depth psychologists other than Jung aim towards this same under-standing. It is interesting to see how this one-hundred-year-old discipline, as it advances towards the end of our century and millennium, increasingly takes up religious questions, even if only implicitly. For example, in our therapeutic theorizing, we reach further and further back in a child's life for the origin of being, for signs of the existence of any self at all. We seek that intra-subjective space where we feel alive, real, in a creative living of life that sustains hope and joy and makes for some sense of meaning even in the most wretched of circumstances. This is the space Winnicott calls transitional, from which our symbols spring (Winnicott 1970: 1–26, 65–72); the space that Freud finds between the free-associating ego and the observing-ego which allows us freedom from instinct at the same time that we channel it into life projects (Freud 1949: 33–6, 45, 108–14; see also Loewald 1978:

13–19). In this space Kohut locates the cohesive self, so elusive of definition, but also central to living (Kohut 1970: 134–5). Bion talks about this space as the ultimate O, the truth of the moment (Bion 1970: 26); Klein finds in it the mysterious triggering of our reparative efforts to make things better and to express gratitude (Klein 1957: 187–9). Such moments spring from facing the ambiguous mixture in us and in those we love of good and bad, love and hate. Christopher Bollas writes of this as an evocative space where we receive news from within, and Masud Khan of our lying fallow and finding the self from which to live (Bollas 1991: 202; Khan 1983: 183–9).

All workers in analysis aim for this space, but Jung speaks of it explicitly as our religious instinct – a force archaic and immediate, insistent and commanding. We may turn away from the instinct, put it to wrong use, deflect it, or fall into identification with it, but we cannot escape it. Jung brings the primordial right into the consulting room this way, and asks of every symptom or depression, or even trauma: what is the Self engineering? What is being made manifest here to which we must pay close attention?

For example, the woman who could not free herself or her money from the man she used to love discovered a radically different way of looking at her entrapment. She still saw her unsuccessful struggle over several decades to liberate herself in terms of her accusations against herself – as a product of illness, of fragmentation, of excessive projection of power on to him, of her tendency to be cowardly and too easily bullied. But now she also saw that she had equated leaving him with abandoning what she believed in, with perjuring the good as she knew it (Ulanov 1988: 37). She saw now that her getting free from this man manifested not just her sickness but also her faithfulness to the good where it had found her. Her addictive attachment to him did indeed reflect her woundedness – the result of never knowing a container, of having a mother afflicted with psychotic episodes and a step-father who tyrannized and molested her. It was not easy to give up the home-base she had established with this man. But this relationship also contained serious and ugly abuses of many different kinds, all mixed in with the goodness she and he had created together, and the goodness in which she believed and which she had identified with him as if it originated there.

The epiphany of the image of the wrapper – of the coat draped on this man – was no less for her than a discovery that God is portable. The good was not grafted on to this man, but removable. She could see it itself between them, between her and other people, on its own, existing in its own right. Like Yahweh's priests who carry the Ark and know it is not identified with just one particular place, or like Yahweh's words of self-revelation – I am who is, I am who is with you – she now saw that her responsibility and devotion were to goodness, not to the man upon whom she had grafted it. It lived. For her, this was where Being was and is.

Such seeing redeems suffering as it did in this case, not by denying the woman's fragmentation or woundedness, but by revealing that hiding in her illness was also a determination to stay close to goodness, to the transcendent, and not desert or abandon it. This may sound like a mere shift of accent, or even a verbal sleight of hand. But not to the person involved: to him or to her, it makes all the difference in the world, for here, found for us, is the deeper meaning of suffering, and that makes it bearable and forgivable. Redeemed, the woman's suffering opened a future to her.

Jung, it is clear from these examples, works to reconnect religion to its archaic instinctive roots, from which the symbols of theology and ritual spring. When we reach and link ourselves to the primordial religious impulse deep within us, we fashion a formidable hermeneutic for ourselves. We can now interpret religious doctrines, symbols and rituals in terms of their analogies in our own psychological experiences and those of the collective human psyche. Religion ceases to be merely an intellectual activity or a systematic exploration of abstract principles of being. Instead, it reaches right into our hearts, our souls, our bowels. It helps uncover the meaning hiding in our experiences. This hermeneutic does not replace such interpretative methods as literary-form criticism, historical criticism or sociological analysis, but rather adds to them the psychological. We ask, for example, about the psychological equivalent of the visions of Ezekiel, or of the parable of the sheep and goats (Jung 1932: para. 520; see also Ulanov 1986a).

To address the psychological meaning of symbols, both for ourselves and in the history of symbology, does not equate the psyche, or any of its parts, and especially not the unconscious, with the deity. The unconscious is not God, but it is another medium through which God speaks to us (Jung 1956: para. 565). God addresses us through images that arise from the deep unconscious just as much as God addresses us through national events, historical moments, other people, a sermon, another's pain or generosity, and especially through the witness of Scripture and the believing community. Jung reminds us with great force of God's freedom. He also reminds us that we tend to ignore the human psyche as another central way through which God touches us – in dreams, visions, symbols, even in symptom and complex. It behooves us to keep all this in mind when working with the unconscious. We have in hand an empirical method for studying living religion (Jung 1956: paras 565–6; Ulanov 1986a; Ulanov and Ulanov 1975: 35–9).

PRAYER

Prayer opens a psychological and religious reality to us. We must look at the ways prayer functions in the psyche, whether for illness or health, and we must look at whether or not prayer points to real transcendence. Jung devotes most of his attention to prayer as it functions psychologically. He says, for example, that the God-image is an archetypal idea which is everywhere, which 'I observe but I do not invent' (Jung 1984: 511). God is a 'psychic fact of immediate experience . . . God has general validity in as much as almost everyone knows approximately what is meant by the term "experience of God"' (Jung 1926: para. 625).

Our image of God is thrown up spontaneously from the unconscious like 'a being that exists in its own right and therefore confronts its ostensible creator autonomously' (Jung 1976: para. 95). We have a dialectical relationship with this figure. In naive moments we experience it as existing in and for itself and feel that we did not fashion it; it fashioned itself in us. We cannot really decide 'whether the God-image is created or whether it creates itself' (Jung 1967: para. 95). In religious language, this paradox is to be found in the creed, where in referring to Jesus, the God-image that God gives us, he is defined as 'begotten not made'. We put this dialectical and paradoxical relationship to practical use when we pray.

We call upon the 'divine presence in all difficult or dangerous situations, for the purpose of loading all . . . [our] unbearable difficulties upon the Almighty and expecting help. . . . In the psychological sense this means that complexes weighing on the soul are *consciously* transferred to the God-image' (Jung 1967: para. 95). Such praying benefits us because we can then carry our complexes consciously. Repression enacts an inversion of this prayer, a sort of dumping into the unconscious of all that we want to forget about. Here, instead, in prayer, we carry what belongs to us, and are able to do so because we are not all alone.

Jung goes further. He recognizes that any discipline undertaken for religious reasons not only aids us in remaining conscious of our difficulties, but also enables us to confess our sins; for it 'effectively prevents . . . [us] from becoming unconscious' (Jung 1967: para. 95). Confession brings us into a new community, because it is an enlarging enterprise, undertaken 'for the sake of collectivity, for a social purpose. . . . Through sin and secrecy one is excluded and when one confesses one is included again.' This builds up a new society: 'The idea of confession being a collective duty is an attempt on the part of the unconscious to create the basis of a new collectivity' (Jung 1984: 23).

By such a fullness of confession as we find in prayer, where we prevent 'a known suffering from turning into an unknown one', we join with others, both in keeping the conflicts of opposites within us conscious and in recognizing a superior power which lightens our burdens because we surrender them 'to God to whom all solutions are known' (Jung 1967: para. 95). It is crucial to note that all this enlarging and joining and recognizing occurs where we are most wounded and divided in our nature, just where we are 'weakest and lowest; there intercession takes place' (Jung 1984: 506). Could this be the stable in us where Christ gets born? Where the soul comes alive? Where we need and desire the most and wish most strongly, because we are so poor in our own resources? There God arrives.

One man, for example, long practised in the skills of analysis, none the less felt powerless in the grip of a compulsion. He put its power in psychological terms: the ego is not in control of everything in life; therefore my compulsion is a defeat for my ego. He knew that with certainty, he felt. But in the middle of the night he woke and could not return to sleep. Thinking on these things, he said: 'For the first time in years I earnestly got down on my knees to pray to the Self or to God for help. This I experienced as an act of humility and admission that something besides my ego was running the show. Maybe my compulsion is *its* way of letting me know of *its* presence and my tendency to think my ego can run my life.' Yielding to the impulse to get at the primordial root of his compulsion gave this man a glimpse of what purpose the compulsion might be hiding (Jung 1926: para. 525; Jung 1966: paras 68, 132). This is a risky business. As Jung puts it:

> Surrender to God is a formidable adventure. . . . He who can risk himself wholly to it finds himself directly in the hands of God, and is there confronted with a situation which makes 'simple faith' a vital necessity . . . the situation is so full of risk . . . that the deepest instincts are aroused. An experience of this kind is always numinous, for it unites all aspects of totality. . . . Christian faith insists on the deadly danger of the adventure.
>
> (Jung 1954a: para. 1539)

We begin a conversation, or continue one in the open, when we pray. From a psychological point of view, we concentrate libido on the God-image. By emptying our conscious mind and transferring its energy and expectation to this primordial image, we allow it to activate, to change us. Jung describes it thus: 'the libido . . . is immersed in introversion and is allegorized as God's kingdom. This amounts to . . . living in his kingdom, in that state where a preponderance of libido lies in the unconscious and determines conscious life' (Jung 1971: para. 424; Jung 1973, 23 May 1950: 558; Jung 1967: para. 178). What happens as a result is that we know a precious 'childlikeness' where we feel 'borne along by the current of life, where what was dammed up can flow off without restraint . . . "things go of themselves"'. This is 'that unique inner condition on which blissfulness depends . . . [it] means to possess a treasury of accumulated libido which can constantly stream forth' (Jung 1971: para. 422).

When we pray, we give over and we invoke. We surrender our ego control and enter into conversation with a power greater than ourselves that none the less inhabits us and strongly influences our lives. We grow more conscious and less repressed; our energy flows unblocked, and we confess – that is, become aware of – our weakest places, where our fabric has worn the thinnest and our wounds still bleed. There God meets us, binds up our wounds and unites us with others in new community. In psychological terms, we describe all this as our giving over to the primordial, opening to the power of archetypal images that come from the deep unconscious, and seeing through them to the transcendent they point to.

To do this opening and seeing, Jung says we need the 'concrete reality of religious figures', for they assist in 'the canalisation of libido into the equivalent symbols provided that the worship of them does not get stuck in the outward object' (Jung 1967: para. 259). Here we see Jung looking at prayer from a religious point of view: 'It is not a matter of indifference whether one calls something a "mania" or a "god". . . . When the god is not acknowledged, ego mania develops and out of this mania comes sickness' (Jung 1929: para. 55). We cannot pray to a concept or a psychological term. We pray to a Subject, an 'I' for whom we are the 'thou'. We pray from our weakest places, for there we stay most open and accessible. But we can only show our weakest place to One who knows us and holds us in that knowing. Jung writes:

> Only on the basis of such an attitude which tries with charity and forebearance to accept even the humblest things in one's own nature, will a higher level of consciousness and culture become possible. This attitude is religious in the truest sense and therefore therapeutic, for all religions are therapies for the sorrows and disorders of the soul.
>
> (Jung 1929: para. 71)

JUNG'S PRAYERS

Scattered through his letters and autobiography, we find Jung's own prayers. They give us a sense of his relationship to God and the questions in him that reached down to his weakest places. He writes: 'I thank God everyday that I have been permitted to experience the reality of the *imago dei* in me. Had that not been so, I would have been a bitter enemy of Christianity and of the Church. . . . Thanks to this *actus gratiae* my life has meaning, and my inner eye was opened to the beauty and grandeur of dogma' (Jung 1973, 13 January 1948: 487).

Prayer is getting down to basics. We stop before the fact that Being is. We experience the primordial as fact. Jung found prayer necessary 'because it makes the Beyond we conjecture and think about an immediate reality'. We enter a dialogue, a 'duality of the ego and the dark Other'. This changes us; we cannot doubt the reality of the 'That' whom we address. But, says Jung, 'The question then arises: What will become of Thee and of Me? of the transcendental Thou and the immanent I?' (Jung 1973, 10 September 1943: 338).

This relationship between the Thee and the me preoccupied Jung from his earliest years to the end of his days. He knew from his early experience of grace after his intense fantasy about the destruction of the Basle Cathedral 'that one's duty was to explore daily the will of God' (Jung 1963: 46). But, like most of us, Jung did not do this. Everyday concerns, duties, problems – all that makes up the life of what he called our 'Personality No. 1', the ordinary self – took up too much time. Nevertheless, Jung asked of these experiences: who makes me do this? Who makes me think these thoughts? Who poses this problem to me? And he responded: 'I knew I had to find the answer out of my deepest self, that I was alone before God, and God alone had asked me these terrible things' (Jung 1963: 47).

Out of that deep aloneness Jung discovered that 'The Divine Presence is more than anything else. . . . This is the only thing that really matters. . . . I wanted the proof of a living Spirit and I got it. Don't ask me at what price' (Jung 1973, 30 January 1948: 492). For what confronted Jung in that space between the transcendent Thou and the immanent I was the 'beatific vision', and with it a God who sometimes 'kicks us, as with Jacob, and you punch back', a God who might, as with Job, slay our firstborn, cause all our cattle to die and dump us in a heap of suffering among the potsherds (Jung 1975, 17 February 1954: 156). This other side of the deity Jung called 'the dark side' of God. He meant it concretely, giving voice that way to a great many of the questions of others: why does our child die in such pain from disease? Why does a hurricane wipe out everything families have worked for all their lives? Why do some of us know endless, repeated suffering and very little joy? What could this mean, this dreadful catastrophe falling on us? Why do the innocent suffer? How can God be good and loving when there is so much hurt and hate in the world?

What Jung calls the dark side of God refers to the hard, painful experiences which break apart the frames of our lives so that we cannot hold together any more. It might be war, the loss of our ideology or its exposure as bogus after we have given our whole life to uphold it. It might be the destructive impact of climate and environment so that for all our days we live with dust in our mouths and noses, unable to survive decently and yet unable to leave where we are. It might be the brutal impact of another's psychic disturbance that maims us before we have achieved secure connection to our body and a sense of self. These experiences engulf a child born into prison or crack addiction, a citizen left to starve in a barren land, the holocaust victim left to die alone a horrible death. These examples, alas, are countless; the questions, persistent: how? Why? What can this mean?

I would suggest that the dark side of God experiences are those that fall outside the light of our God-images, that exceed the grasp of our understanding, that confound our images of God. If we pray and keep on praying, this kind of experience always comes. The more our converse with God grows, changes, the closer we come upon the God who surpasses all images of God. The holy refuses to stay put in a box. Inevitably we will be led to experiences of God that are bigger than our pictures of the divine (Jung 1954a: para. 1536; Ulanov 1986b: 180; Ulanov and Ulanov 1991: 61–4). Such events come out from the shadows, beyond the light of our God-images. They break in, steal into us like a thief in the night, and they fall upon us. These meetings with God well beyond our images of God comprise great religious moments which can smash us, or open us further to the transcendent, or both. Mystics write of these moments. In Jung's terms, these are the moments that comprise the mysterious exchange between ego and Self. If we really want God as God is, then a God who is so much bigger than any of our concepts or imaginings about God will cast everything into the darkness the nearer God comes.

MYSTERY

To be brought to glimpse something of this God, so different from our pictures of God, leaves us breathless with surprise, fear, awe, gratitude. Jung knows such encounters: 'The deity is always preceded by terror, fear, or a feeling of divine presence, a special atmosphere' (Jung 1984: 179). Archaic emotion grasps Jung, leaving him ambivalent about the exact nature of the divine presence. We must always keep a sharp eye on God, pay close attention and observe who this is: 'There is no prejudice, there is supreme submission. God can appear in any form he chooses . . . to prescribe to that phenomenon which it ought to be, and not accept what it is, is not submission' (Jung 1984: 513). Or, to put it more boldly: 'The real Christ is the God of freedom' (Jung 1984: 519).

In our littleness, we feel this freedom as dread. Prayer becomes a risky business. The problem is not that we receive no answer, but that we might get what we prayed for. Worse, we may pray for the wrong thing, instead of trusting God to give what matches the real need deep in our soul or in our world. For Jung, such trust brings its own ambivalence: 'Can we address . . . the good God to the exclusion of the demon. . . . Can we really put on one side the God who is dangerous to us? . . . can we ignore the *absconditus*?' (Jung 1954a: para. 1537).

Jung calls us back time and again to our immediate experiences of God. He focuses not on refined formulations, but upon the instinctive gut encounters, primordial ones, mixed with dread as well as thankfulness, bad as well as good. We need to dig down to the primitive in us to reach a new experience of God, he counsels (Jung 1973, 26 May 1923: 40). There we find not just a God whom we must punch and kick back, but one of unspeakable bliss. Our fear is matched by trust:

> In his trial of courage God refuses to abide by traditions, no matter how sacred. In his omnipotence He will see to it that nothing really evil comes of such tests of courage. If one fulfills the will of God one can be sure of going the right way.
>
> (Jung 1963: 40)

These opposites, contained in God's radical freedom, and our utter submission connect and come alive in our experience of the mysterious exchanges between ego and Self. On the one hand, Jung speaks of the radical transcendence of God. He says, 'I know that my way has been prescribed to me by a hand far above my reach' (Jung 1973, 30 January 1948: 492). Or, 'I do not for a moment deny that the deep emotion of a true prayer may reach transcendence, but it is above our heads' (Jung 1954a: para. 1536). Or, 'There is only one divine spirit – an immediate prsence, often terrifying and in no degree subject to our choice' (Jung 1954a: para. 1538). On the other hand, Jung recognizes that God comes towards us, addresses us, speaks to us in the intimacy of our own psyche. He says, 'God has never spoken to man except in and through the psyche, and the psyche understands it and we experience it as something psychic' (Jung 1973, 15 August 1938: 98). The unutterably large enters the life of the infinitesimally small. The radically Other addresses us through the images of our own particular psyche, through coinciding events that strike us as full of meaning, as a telling synchronicity that opens a window for us on to an eternal wholeness of being – the *unus mundus* (Aziz 1990: 192–3).

From Jung's remarks, we might sketch a structure undergirding the conversation of ego and Self in us. We can think of this structure as the grammar of our conversation, moving from the ground of our being upward to consciousness. At the deepest level, at our core, dwells the radically free God, unfathomable and ever present. At the next level, the archetypes exist as contents of the collective unconscious; Jung calls them 'God's tools' (Jung 1975, 1 October 1953: 130). Above the archetypes, so to speak, the soul exists as the function of relation between our conscious ego and the inaccessible depths of the unconscious (Jung 1971: para. 426). Our souls reflect up to consciousness the images of the archetypes and bring to bear down into us the effects of consciousness on those images. The result is the construction of symbols. The soul is thus like a two-way mirror, reflecting unconscious to ego and ego to unconscious. Always, we must remember, above the soul exists the ego, the centre of our consciousness.

The energy of the ego–Self conversation constantly circulates between the great unfathomable depths of God acting in us and on us through the instrumentation of the archetypes. Our soul registers all of this action and spontaneously creates symbols that express 'something that is little known or completely unknown' (Jung 1967: para. 329). A symbol of this kind does not arise in the form of allegory or sign, but as an 'image that describes in the best possible way the dimly discerned nature of the spirit. A symbol does not define or explain; it points beyond itself to a meaning that is darkly divined yet still beyond our grasp, and cannot be adequately expressed in the familiar words of our language' (Jung 1926: para. 644). Such symbols are 'inexhaustible' because they are not 'objects of the mind, but categories of the imagination which we can formulate in ten thousand different ways . . . they are *before* the mind, the basis of everything mental' (Jung 1984: 330). Jung cites prayer as one such symbolic action and cites a dramatic example from the Elgonyi tribe of Africa. Its members offered 'the livingness from the inside of their bodies, held in their hands and presented to the rising sun. To us it would mean "I offer my soul to thee, O God"' (Jung 1984: 331).

Our souls' reception of the archetypes is one way God speaks to us, and in a way in which we 'know' being. We know archetypes in the concrete experiences of our life, not in the abstract. Our soul creates symbols which themselves express both archetypal influence and the life we live with our neighbours in our time in history, in our particular cultures. The symbols act as 'transformers', converting libido from a 'lower' to a 'higher' form (Jung 1967: para. 344; see also para. 99). In analysis or the disciplines of religion we try to understand these symbols and thus to absorb and respond to 'the unconscious, compensatory striving for an attitude that reflects the totality of the psyche' (Jung 1967: para. 346).

Religious experience has its own momentum, as if looming out of us, demanding both our awareness and its own communication. It 'strives for expression', Jung says, and 'can be expressed only "symbolically" because it transcends understanding. It *must* be expressed one way or another, for therein is revealed its immanent vital force. It wants to step over . . . into visible life, to take concrete shape' (Jung 1973, 10 January 1929: 59; see also Ulanov 1992: 37).

We can see, then, how dangerous it is to pray. For in prayer we stir up the archetypal background through which God touches us and symbols spontaneously appear which will press us to realize them in action in the world. When contents cross over from unconscious to conscious realms, they impose ethical obligations on us to respond, to realize them, to make them concrete. Otherwise we must lose them, or permit them to let loose something in us too big to contain. It may be even more dangerous not to pray!

THE MASS

Where does this leave us? In Jungian language, we are plunged into the mysterious exchange that occurs between ego and Self. In prayer, our ego and the Self enter into conversation, a mutual exchange that is ultimately mysterious, as anything must be that exists in the realm of primordial and archetypal being, as Jung makes clear in his examination of the Eucharist, the central sacrament in Christianity.

Before coming to the communion table, we collect ourselves in the prayer of confession. Here our ego recognizes all the things it puts in place of God. Confession means admitting into consciousness those things we have chosen to revolve around in place of God at the centre of our being. These may be our problems or our strengths, our faults, our needs, our worst acts, or our best values. Thus it was with the man who wrestled with his drinking: it became the centre of his thoughts. When he could, he drank; sometimes he avoided giving into its temptation; at other moments, he felt remorse at having once again succumbed. In each instance the fixation acted in him like a little god, an idol, around which his whole life turned.

In confession we become conscious of just what idols we live in thrall to – getting a job, for example, or trying to understand our neurosis, or working for a better environment, or a political cause, or a determined devotion to our child's welfare. In each case we can identify something that acts as a centre for us in place of God; with others we come to recognize that we all do this, all put the best of human values, the most vexing of human problems, everything that besets or gratifies us, in place of the God we are commanded to love first. Thus it is in common that we make our confession.

We collect into consciousness, both in shared and individual confession, what we have identified as our God in place of the true God. Our ego grows bigger this way as it becomes more conscious: in such awareness we gain ourselves. We see where our ego lives and in what it consists, with what or with whom we identify, where we invest our passion. Confession returns a fuller sense of ourselves to us, tells us much more about what we are, and who, and what matters to us. It gives us back to ourselves, enlarged in psyche and spirit. We have collected ourselves into one place, so to speak. Our awareness has been made full of just where it is that life blazes for us, where it feels negative, as with problems, or compulsions, and where it feels positive, as with affection or dedication to something, for someone well outside us, though the feeling is deeply within us.

Having thus possessed our ego, we can bring this as offering and sacrifice to the table of the Eucharist, in the shared human symbols, says Jung, of the bread and wine (Jung 1954a: paras 382–4). The wine represents the best of human spirit, its capacity to soar and create. The bread represents the human body with all its hunger and labour to satisfy its need. Through the bringing of the bread and wine, we offer our ego up to God. We give up and give over what we hold most dear, what we dread most deeply. We sacrifice our identification with whatever we have put in place of God. Because we feel identified with it, we know now that *we* are this problem, this love, this need, this cause. So we feel that we are sacrificing our very selves. This enlarged sense of self that confession returns to us comprises our offering to God. This can be understood as the 'broken and contrite heart' that Yahweh asks of Israel – not a burnt offering, but a living, loving spirit that comes home again, to first things put first.

To offer up what we identify with feels as if we are losing it. This is not a kind of magic, says Jung, in which we wheedle with God, secretly believing that what we offer will be returned to us a hundredfold. Such manipulation, such bargaining, we renounce. The mass revolves around sacrifice and open exchange. It is a great wrenching of our being to uncover what we have centred upon and bring it to the real centre, the great and true centre. It feels like a casting into fire, where we must be burnt up for ever with what we most prize, or what has most ruled us.

Why should we bother? Who in their right mind would want to sacrifice their highest hopes and best ideals? What moves us to such acts? The answer is the Self: it is what moves us here. At the same time we possess our egos more fully as we become conscious of all the ego-identifications, both good and bad, with things of this world. We feel moved to surrender all our ego concerns to the greater centre. We feel relativized. What once we experienced as the centre of ourselves – this ego at the centre of consciousness – we now experience as being moved by the bigger centre. We know ourselves now as object of a greater subject. Out of this inner experience, we surrender all our ego claims. Something mysterious compels us to do so: 'The ego must make itself conscious of its claim and the Self must cause the ego to renounce it' (Jung 1954a: para. 392).

If we just go through the motions of the ritual of confession and its accompanying offering, without feeling any inner compulsion, all we are doing is simply obeying a collective moral code. The Self appears to us, then, identified with the collective super-ego, that is, with the mores and customs of our religious culture. We want to live in full accord with what our group considers good behaviour; we fear the consequences of not doing so. But feeling this new inner compulsion means we have become conscious of the Self that addresses our ego, the Self that moves us to bring our gifts, our sacrifices and our ego-identifications to the altar as symbolized in the bread and wine (Jung 1954a: para. 394). We experience the Self moving us from within. It no longer exists in projected form, but now directly engages us. It calls us, as Abraham was called, to renounce our ego and to follow after it. Jung says we know it as a 'yea and nay' operating within us, like a union of opposites: this 'constitutes the most immediate experience of the Divine which is psychologically possible to imagine' (Jung 1954a: para. 396). As a result, our human ego experiences nothing less than transformation. It moves into direct conversation with the Self and begins to live from there.

The Self matches our sacrifice with its own surrender, yielding its all-powerfulness and infiniteness as it fits into the small confines of space and time in the incarnation of Jesus Christ. The Self, as Jung sees it, calls on the ego to sacrifice its ego-centredness, acting like a father to a son. By making ourselves conscious of our unconscious identifications and then surrendering them to a greater centre, we call the Self into being, in human terms. In this way, the ego becomes father to the Self as son. So, for Jung, God becoming man in Christ shows God's transformation. The mass, carried out by God, through the figure of the Christ, and returned through Jesus to God, manifests the Self to humankind, redeeming it from the narrow confines of ego-centricity.

We must remember that in offering this psychological interpretation of the mass, Jung does not substitute his terms 'ego' and 'Self' for 'human' and 'divine'. Instead he hopes to reconnect us to the mass by drawing analogies to our psychological experience (Jung 1953: para. 14). It is useful here, I think, to repeat my own understanding of the Self, not as God within us, but as that which knows about God, through which we know God knows us. For Jung, the Christ manifests the most complete Self-figure; for the Christian, the Self-concept offers a good, an appropriate, symbol for the Christ (Jung 1959: para. 70).

The incarnation of God shows us God's love for us. For God in Christ empties the infinite fullness of being – in the abasement of *kenosis* – to take on the struggles and darknesses of human life. In a sense, the dark side of God meets the dark side of the human, for as Jesus the Christ God takes on and suffers all our shadow bits, submits to all their lethal effects. The two sacrifices meet and converse in the mass. We become one in Christ, where he dwells in us and we in him. A momentous exchange occurs, the darkest mystery of all in the conversation of prayer.

What happens next in the Eucharist occurs to some extent in every prayer: we feel thanksgiving and joy. In Jung's terms, the Self, centre of the whole psyche, meets the ego, centre of consciousness, and a conversation ensues in the space between the big Subject, the Self, and the little subject, us. An intersubjective space forms. People who pray regularly know this space in themselves and somehow convey it to others. We can even hear a humming sound of their inner conversation if we pay close enough attention. Prayer puts us in an evocative state of mind whereby we receive bulletins from the Self, news from the large to the small self. This becomes a process whereby 'new internal objects are created' (Bollas 1991: 13). The core of unconscious psychic life seeks expression; it wants to unfold in relation to others. The process of attending to the core or source-point of our being – that level of the unfathomable mystery of God at our centre – yields images that feed the soul and prompt us to apposite action in the world. Jung says that the soul is happy when it makes itself a vessel for the unconscious and becomes an image or symbol for it: 'The happy state is the creative state' (Jung 1971: para. 426). Jung quotes Blake, saying that we feel bliss, ecstasy, 'energy as eternal delight' (Jung 1971: para. 422). This gives rise to a 'feeling of intense vitality, a new potential'. For God, 'life at its most intense, resides in the soul' (Jung 1971: para. 421). Here we feel alive, real, and living creatively (Winnicott 1970). One woman dreamt this state in a short blunt image: 'The Grail Cup sings!'

Attention to this sense of being at the core of our being leads us to recognize the uniqueness of what it is that resides in ourselves, and what its presence is in everyone of us. Violence is what happens when we foreshorten this inner conversation, interrupting it, forbidding it, even acting to prevent it. We refuse being this way. Conversely, attending to the source and centre given each of us feels like joy (Lacan's *jouissance*), wherein our true Self can unfold in experience with others and with the world. Being is manifested beyond argument. This is what is meant by the glory of God, as Irenaeus put it so long ago: the glory of God consists of human beings truly alive!

Because we are finite, so must our Self be and the access we have to it. What Jung calls the dark side of God is what falls outside what our Self knows, or what we as ego have learnt from Self. But still the Self persists, acting in us as link between the God we know and the 'unimaginable transcendence' beyond, joining inner and outer God (Jung 1959: para. 1536). It connects our inner conversation and the God we must first meet outside ourselves so that we recognize and deal with this holy presence when we go back inside ourselves. The one we converse with, and who initiates conversation with us, arranges all this through the Self in our psyche. It is extraordinarily like a little radio set forced to meet frequencies beyond its capacity to receive. If we pay attention, its power will grow and our skills in tuning will match the growth. We will find our equipment better and better suited to pick up the waves of communication of the One addressing us.

We learn from this inner conversation that God does not want to blast into us; but simply wants to be received. The smallest accord with the movement coming towards us acts like the butterfly effect in chaos theory. Chaos theory says that a butterfly lifting its wing in Chicago changes the atmosphere as far away as China because that delicate individual motion affects everything, all of creation, in a sense. As Jung puts it, 'I go together with it, [God's will] an immensely weighty milligram without which God had made his world in vain' (Jung 1973, 10 September 1943: 33). We do not know that we matter unless we engage in such conversation.

In this engagement, a theological revolution occurs. Earlier, we had prayed to God for the things we wanted and needed, for relief from pain and suffering, for forgiveness, health, peace, justice, love. Now we concern ourselves with taking care of the God we have found within us. The old prayer of the alchemists, spoken by the lapis stone, sums it up: 'Protect me, I will protect you' (Jung 1975, 3 August 1953: 120). Our need now is quite outside our own pain and suffering, our own urge to forgiveness, for health, for love. Now we want to make a little stable in which God can be born, a little hut in which God can live. In this reversal, conscious and unconscious come together in a feeling of oneness of being (Jung 1971: para. 421). Although this approach to wholeness means a great awareness of bearing our own weight, our own cross, we feel held in greater unity than ever before, both within ourselves and with the whole world. Augustine's commentary on the Gospel of John 26:10 sums it up: 'He that believes in me goes into me; He that goes into me, has me' (Ulanov 1983: 13).

REFERENCES

Aziz, R. (1990) C. G. Jung's Psychology of Religion and Synchronicity, Albany: State University of New York Press.

Balthasaar, H. U. von (1961) *On Prayer*, New York: Sheed & Ward.

Bion, W. R. (1970) *Attention and Interpretation*, London: Tavistock.

Bollas, C. (1991) *Forces of Destiny, Psychoanalysis and Human Idiom*, London: Free Association Press.

Freud, S. (1949) *An Outline of Psychoanalysis*, New York: Norton.

Gordon, R. (1984) 'Masochism: the shadow side of the archetypal need to venerate and worship', *Journal of Analytical Psychology* 32(3): 227–46.

Jung, C. G. (1926) 'Spirit and life', *The Structure and Dynamics of the Psyche*, *Collected Works*, vol. 8, New York: Pantheon, 1960.

—— (1929) 'Commentary on the secret of the golden flower', *Alchemical Studies*, *Collected Works*, vol. 13, Princeton: Princeton University Press, 1967.

—— (1932) 'Psychotherapists or the clergy', *Psychology and Religion: West and East*, *Collected Works*, vol. 11, New York: Pantheon, 1958.

—— (1953) *Psychology and Alchemy*, *Collected Works*, vol. 12, New York: Pantheon, 1966.

—— (1954a) 'Transformation symbolism in the mass', *Psychology and Religion: West and East*, *Collected Works*, vol. 11, New York: Pantheon, 1958.

—— (1954b) 'Letter to Père Lachat', *The Symbolic Life*, *Collected Works*, vol. 18, Princeton: Princeton University Press, 1976.

—— (1956) 'The undiscovered self', *Civilization in Transition*, *Collected Works*, vol. 10, New York: Pantheon, 1964.

—— (1959) *Aion*, *Collected Works*, vol. 9(1), New York: Pantheon, 1966.

—— (1963) *Memories, Dreams, Reflections*, New York: Pantheon, 1966.

—— (1966) *Two Essays on Analytical Psychology*, *Collected Works*, vol. 7, New York: Pantheon.

—— (1967) *Symbols of Transformation*, *Collected Works*, vol. 5, Princeton: Princeton University Press.

—— (1971) *Psychological Types*, *Collected Works*, vol. 6, Princeton: Princeton University Press.

—— (1973) *Letters*, vol. 1, ed. G. Adler, Princeton: Princeton University Press.

—— (1975) *Letters*, vol. 2, ed. G. Adler, Princeton: Princeton University Press.

—— (1984) *Dream Analysis: Notes of the Seminar given in 1928–30 by C. G. Jung*, ed. W. McGuire, London: Routledge & Kegan Paul.

Khan, M. R. (1983) 'Lying fallow', in *Hidden Selves, Between Theory and Practice in Psychoanalysis*, New York: International Universities Press.

Klein, M. (1957) *Envy and Gratitude and Other Works 1946–1963*, New York: Delacorte Press/Seymour Lawrence.

Kohut, H. (1970) 'On courage', in *The Search for Self, Selected Writings of Heinz Kohut 1978–1981*, ed. P. H. Ornstein, vol. 3 of 4, Madison: International Universities Press, 1990.

Loewald, H. (1978) *Psychoanalysis and the History of the Individual*, New Haven: Yale University Press.

Ulanov, A. B. (1986a) 'From image to imago: Jung and the study of religion', in *Jung and the Study of Religion*, ed. L. H. Martin and J. Goss, Washington: University Press of America.

—— (1986b) *Picturing God*, Cambridge, Mass.: Cowley.

—— (1988) *The Wisdom of the Psyche*, Cambridge, Mass.: Cowley.

—— (1992) 'The holding self: Jung and the desire for being', *The Fires of Desire: Erotic Energies and the Spiritual Quest*, ed. F. Halligan and J. Shea, New York: Crossroads.

Ulanov, A. B. and Ulanov, B. (1975) *Religion and the Unconscious*, Louisville: Westminster.

—— (1982) *Primary Speech, A Psychology of Prayer*, Louisville: Westminster.

—— (1991) *The Healing Imagination*, Mahwah: Paulist.

Ulanov, B. (1983) *The Prayers of St Augustine*, New York: Seabury.
Winnicott, D. W. (1970) 'Living creatively', in *Home is Where We Start From*, New York: Norton, 1986.
—— (1971) *Playing and Reality*, London: Tavistock.

9

JUNG'S *ANSWER TO JOB* IN THE LIGHT OF THE MONOTHEISMS

Joel Ryce-Menuhin

THE PROBLEM OF JOB

Dealing with religious contents meant for Jung moving about in a world of images that point to the ineffable. Our reason manipulates ideas and images, but is dependent on our immediate human imagination. The idea of the holy is therefore constantly changing in our psyches, which are based on temporal psychological awareness – and the deeper base of numinous archetypes.

Statements of the soul as in the biblical book Job, written between 800 and 300 BC and based on Sumerian manuscripts from 2000 BC, point to realities that transcend consciousness. Coming to terms with the religious ideas around the Job–Yahweh (God) story demands a balance of mind and emotion. This is because the contradictions of Yahweh as an immoderate God who makes pacts with Satan is an enormous challenge to humanity's concepts of Godhead. Often people think of God as all-good and like an anthropomorphic helpful father.

Yahweh's cruelty and creative power seem to have gone hand-in-glove; Yahweh's rage and jealousy seem to make Him amoral in the Job story from a merely human viewpoint. Yahweh is *totality* – whether of darkness or of light. Job, a God-fearing faithful man, learns that he can be struck down like a worm grovelling in the dust because Yahweh is an *antinomy*, a totality of inner opposites whose forces may be used omnipotently, striking any man or woman at any time.

All we know of Yahweh's origin is that He created the world from which all history began. He had fashioned Adam in His own image as Anthropos, or the original man. He had made a special covenant with the Jews and particularly with Noah, whose family survived the Flood. At one point Yahweh decided to make a bet with Satan that Job, his most faithful servant, must have some evil up his sleeve.

Yahweh robbed Job of his herds, had his sons and daughters killed by a whirlwind, and arranged that his servants were murdered; He also

111

premeditatedly made Job sick to the point of death. Then his wife and best friends were turned against him. So Yahweh has committed murder, robbery and injury and has denied Job a fair trial, as Job's voice is at first disregarded.

But Job rises to this occasion with a 'god-like' heightened behaviour. He senses God's inner antinomy and remains optimistic that he can appeal to divine justice. Job still apparently thinks of God as a moral being. Yahweh thunders back about His might and power, showing no compunction about Job's broken human situation. Job's loyalty is unshakeable – thus Satan has lost his bet with God. Job is not disloyal or secretly ridden with sin.

Yahweh's dual dark and light nature is revealed in the Job episode. A relativization of the God-concept has occurred. Yahweh behaves cruelly and inconstantly towards man. Yahweh has projected his own unfaithful tendencies on to a faithful scapegoat, Job. Job, for his part, has held firm; he has seen God's face and the unconscious split in His nature. God had repeatedly forgotten to 'take his absolute knowledge into account as a counterbalance to the dynamism of omnipotence' (Jung 1952: 65).

After the Job trials a transformation in Yahweh's attitude is achieved. Yahweh must begin to reflect because Job has morally surpassed God in his behaviour. Therefore God must become human to catch up and regenerate Himself. In this idea, Jung challenges holy thought radically. Christ, as half God and half man, must be born. Archetypally the life of Christ is seen as a *symbolism* which brings together a divine and a human nature almost as if Yahweh and Job were put together into one nature. For Yahweh's desire to become man had resulted from his collision with Job's loyal and shrewdly 'true' human nature. God wants to become fulfilled through Christ's life and suffering as, in Christian belief, a Redemption for all mankind.

From the text of Exodus 22:29 it is clear that Yahweh allows the firstborn sons of many to die in a savage display of will in spite of the fact that His omniscience and omnipotence are well known to every believer. God therefore knows everything about these people's faith already anyway. This example of violent destructiveness has shown every national ruler of the earth a way of savage barbarism that continues to be used politically to this very day.

Jung insists throughout *Answer to Job* (1952: xiv) that

> although our whole world of religious ideas consists of anthro-pomorphic images which could never stand up to rational criticism, we should never forget that they are based on numinous archetypes, i.e. on an emotional foundation which is unassailable by reason.

We can view Job in a symbolic way as an *archetype of the suffering innocent*. What has Job learnt from his terrible trial? From Jung's point of view Job's chance to see and speak with God is only mentioned parenthetically. But in a philosopher's need to make more reasonable that which Jung finds completely unreasonable, we have Maimonides' thirteenth-century account of 'what Job really learnt' from his experience. This is found in *Moreh* Nevukheim III:22 (translated from the Arabic in Goodman 1977). Maimonides understands the reference to Job sitting in ashes not as an outcast reduced to sitting amidst dust but as a reference to the ashes of mourning. Maimonides believes Job mourns his whole former, prosperous condition of life and that all objects of his previous desire became dust and ashes compared to the ultimate *felicity* of direct knowledge of God. Here Maimonides is arguing for a most profound interpretation of evil. He is saying that even the apparently 'good' Job would have the primordial evil contained in the very inadequacies of his own material nature. This is neither Job's nor one's 'fault'; nevertheless it is one's responsibility to resist, alleviate or overcome this 'fallen state' by, for example, the therapy of body and soul. Moral faults which even Job would contain in his righteousness, like physical flaws, are *privations*. Both kinds of faults, moral and physical, are symbolized by Satan, who comes in 'the throng of the angels' as there isn't any finite goodness without privation.

If man's task is to make an approach to God as closely as is humanly possible, I would want to argue with Maimonides, and slightly differently from Jung here, that *being in individuation* will involve some identification and assimilation to God which then inherently brings some alienation and difference between God and man, their viewpoints being so remote yet so close to one another. Job, as apparently a good man, is given the possibility of enlightenment – the knowledge of God – which virtue had opened to him not as a reward but as a part of continuing revelation towards wisdom and further individuation.

Maimonides argues that the justice of God and the justice of man are co-eternally different and separate:

> Thus, providential care, for Him, is not what it is for us; and what it means for Him to govern the objects of His creation is not what it is for us to govern what we govern. There is no single definition common to divine and human care, as is supposed by all who are perplexed and confused on this subject. Nor is there anything in common between divine and human governance and concern beyond the bare name. Just as there is no resemblance between our works and His and they have no single common definition, just as there is a gulf that separates natural from artificial events, so there is a gulf between divine governance, divine providence and care, divine purpose and intention for these natural things, and human governance, human care, human purpose and intention for what we govern, care for, and intend. This is the message of the whole Book of Job, to lay down his fundamental basis of belief and to awaken you to this evidence from natural things, so that you will not err by seeking in your imagination to make His knowledge like ours or His purpose, providence, or governance like

ours. Once a man understands this, all hardships are easily borne by him, and misfortunes do not add to his doubts about the Deity and whether He knows or does not know, whether He cares for or neglects creation. Rather, hardships will only increase his love, as is said at the close of Job's revelation: '*Therefore* do I abhor and repent of dust and ashes' (42:5–6). As the sages say, 'The pious act out of love and rejoice in sufferings' (Shabbat 88b).

(Goodman 1977: 363)

The numinosity of this material brings mythological motifs, philosophy and theology together in a nexus of archetypal assertions *that belong to analytical psychology*. All of these views point to man's desire for a closer union and understanding of God. Jung's courageous criticism of Yahweh and daring in claiming Yahweh learnt from Job and therefore began wanting the incarnation and planning for it in order to become man show the outcry of a psychiatrist's and analyst's heart at the condition of the suffering of the innocent, for example, in our mental hospitals, psychiatric prisons and geriatric wards. Maimonides maintains a reverential position towards God, as in the older traditions of the Torah, within which his voice is one of brilliant clarity.

YAHWEH, SATAN AND JOB IN THE CONSULTING ROOM

The contrasting psychological position in analysing the Yahweh–Job dialogue is nowhere more consciously and unconsciously lived out as in the consulting rooms where analytical psychologists meet their patients. This occurs in the quality and in the affects within the transferences involved between the analyst and patient. One of the most prevalent dangers to an analyst is the danger of playing God or Yahweh towards the patient, who can then be reduced to a Job. A personal example from my own analysis many years ago will illustrate the way this God–Job dyad can occur.

After two years of analysis at three sessions a week I tentatively asked my analyst if the time were far off when two sessions a week might be sufficient. The turn of Yahweh overtook my analyst. 'You just try surviving without me' were the searing words of contempt towards me, a mere patient! I answered back meekly, 'Oh, I'm sure you are right!' to the God-possessed analyst. I was reduced to a broken ego-heap and felt attacked for expressing any thought about my future in therapy.

Here the analyst fell into (or was taken over by) ego-centred power complexes that stopped further listening to resonances from the Self which would have softened and taken away such defences in answering my inquiry. It also made one wonder what was being invested on the analyst's part in my analysis that could so attack and anger her ego.

What is dangerous here for the patient is the vulnerability of his or her own ego-damage, which has always occurred at some level for a person to have to seek analysis. So a Yahweh-like attack is the last rejoinder that would be helpful to ego repair, reconstruction or the patient's security.

Patients themselves can also be infused with Yahweh-affect and attack the analyst for not curing him or her more quickly or showing more emotion towards him or her at certain times or for not being more like a father-God to them. Here patients will idealize the analyst to a delusional degree, wanting unconsciously to find a union with God through these feelings. The de-fusing of these powerful archetypal delusory transferences in patients is something few analytic trainings are sufficiently stressing in their training programmes for analysts.

I once asked a very senior analyst why all his patients behaved as children towards him. He replied that they had all had strong transferences to him before they had come to the first session. When I then asked why he didn't defuse these exaggerated transferences 'in order to be able to work from a more neutral ground in the analysis', he became furious at the thought of the power he would have to lose as their 'God-father'. He was taken over by Yahweh. The patients, in order to keep him as their patriarchal 'God', had to suffer idealization, splitting of ego needs and much reality repression to keep the delusion alive.

The 'Yahweh-need' can take over the analyst or the patient. It always brings unrelatedness into the analyst/patient dyad, the one situation that should never occur because it forces defensive ego positions that block the development of further self-initiation on either side.

Wherever analysts are stuck into an 'ego-Yahweh trip' the wager with Satan comes into play as the analyst's negative shadow emerges towards the patient. In analytical trainings I have sometimes observed in teachers and in trainees the ego-orientated concept that if an analyst doesn't 'like' a patient during one or two sessions, the analyst shouldn't consider working with the person. What an admission that a negative Yahweh is just hidden beneath the surface of such a judgement of the patient by the analyst on so little evidence! Why should the spectrum like/dislike be a factor when the analysis should proceed from a less affect-laden ground than personal emotive feelings, when so much is at stake for the patient? And what a Satan-like negative shadow analysts can have if they judge a personality before they have any grasp of the complexes, neuroses and pathologies to be overturned in the process of therapy!

Satan, a trickster, sets up these negativities in the Yahweh-inflation that many teachers assume unconsciously. Many trainees also take these barbaric attitudes into their consulting rooms. Patients are then assaulted like Job with unrelated assumptions, preordained non-analytic opinions and judgments, cheap counselling and false-self atmospheres in their analytic sessions. Where masochism exists in patients, they can waste many years in such an unproductive analysis, unable to escape the analyst's negative shadow persecution.

Another negative Satanic situation occurs when the analyst wants to become like the patient who is exaggeratedly admired, and therefore holds him or her in a stasis of non-movement within the process. The analytic atmosphere becomes a pretended 'paradise'. The patient, like Job, is all the good things the analyst-God may not be in his own view. Superior in character, education, financial and social position, the patient – like Job – seems to be a superior person. So then the analyst idealizes the patient and misses the cues and symptoms of where the therapist's work should be placed. It is almost as if the therapist has decided that this patient will 'incarnate' as his 'best' patient. This leads to projective identifications and illusions that interfere with the analyst's reality-sense, and such analytical mistakes usually cause the bemused patient to depart to try another therapy. Here the analyst has planned an 'incarnation', forgetting that only the actual Yahweh could 'plan' the birth of Christ, or of the Self. It's not so easy for a therapist with feet of clay to activate an ultimate birth of a patient's Self. It will depend very much on many forces analysts cannot control. Had the analyst seen the dark side of the 'perfect patient', he could have used this shadow and the opposing will necessary to deal with it to actualize an analytical process that would have felt real to the patient and that would have kept the analytic relationship well grounded. Had the analyst reflected more from his own anima, his self-worth would not have suffered such a lowering of presence in comparing himself with his patient.

The situation may also occur where the patient assumes a constant Yahweh-like attack on every aspect of analysis as a mode and upon the analyst, who is reduced to a 'Job'. Clinging to every limit of his or her own background, the patient will omnipotently try and 'run' if not 'ruin' the analysis. Regressing to extremes of infantilism to try to gain minute-by-minute nurturance from the analyst, the patient will make murderous verbal attacks on the style of the analyst's presence. Threats are made to tear apart the physical womb of the analytic setting, the consulting room. The patient secretly starts other therapies without telling the analyst, the work of trickster Satan who stayed so close to Yahweh for so long in the Old Testament Job story. The patient's own persecutory anxieties are projected on to the analyst, who has to be all bad, second-rate, too expensive, too different, too old or too young, not political enough or more interested in the other patients. The angry 'Yahweh-patient' finally decides to leave, refusing terminal sessions and sometimes not paying for the last sessions after pretending to compliment the analyst before not returning at all.

The 'Job-analyst' has lost effort, time, a chance to help and money, and has little to remember but the aggression against a relatively innocent practitioner, himself. This is the reality of such an experience of a patient's fits of cruelty, fury, unjustified arrogance and unreliability towards the therapist.

116

In summing up the Yahweh–Job position, whether in analyst or patient, I would like to quote D. W. Winnicott (1971). When reading this I have interposed that the *subject* is Yahweh speaking and the *object* is Job speaking.

> The subject [Yahweh] says to the object [Job]: 'I destroyed you' and the object [Job] is there to receive the communication. From now on the subject [Yahweh] says:
> 'Hello object [Job].' 'I [Yahweh] destroyed you.'
> 'I [Job] love you.'
> 'You [Job] have value for me [Yahweh] because of your survival of my destruction of you.'
> 'While I [Job] am loving you [Yahweh] I am all the time destroying you in unconscious *fantasy*.'
>
> (Winnicott 1971)

And how many people fantasize that there is no God!

Surviving numinous energies that hurt one's ego position becomes the great challenge of Jungian psychology. Ego survival is achieved by developing and manifesting the Self or totality of personality's dynamic resonance, both conscious and unconscious, which leads to the continuing relativization (especially in the second half of life) of the ego towards more of the immanent self. This process of individuation requires enormous spirit – a spirit that the holy seems allied with and a part of – in its numinous personal influence upon our experience.

Jung believed that the 'unconscious mind of man sees correctly even when conscious reason is blind and impotent' (1952: 386; also in *Collected Works*, vol. 2: 355–470). It was this belief that has transformed analytical psychology away from all other psychologies, for it includes the serious interpretation symbolically, mythologically or literally of transcendent visionary and numinous material from the unconscious. These psychological experiences often have profound religious and metaphysical connotations for the Self. The restorative effect that analytical respect for patients' autonomous holy experiences has on patients themselves is an outstanding contribution that analytical psychologists can make to the path of healing.

THE BIRTH OF UNITY

In *Answer to Job* Jung gives an example of the luminosity of visionary experience by way of an extraordinary interpretation of the apocalyptic predictions of Revelation, the last book of the New Testament, attributed to St John. I want to look briefly at the central aspects of the Jungian psychotherapeutic approach to such psychic contents by choosing examples from this rich material that illustrate the method of analytical psychology.

Jung points out that it *would* happen to someone like St John, who held a very one-sided and perfect view of God as perfect light and perfect love in whom there is no darkness at all, to become *dissociated* and then overwhelmed with conflicting material from the unconscious. Jungians believe the shadow of perfectionist attitudes often brings, as compensation, vengeful revelations to balance the conscious position. For St John, his fearless belief concerning Christ's perfect advocacy with God turns upon him in his first vision, where a changed Christ appears; the Son of Man is merged with an average man out of whose mouth a two-edged sword appears. St John reports that he fell as though dead in fear when he saw this form of Christ and was commanded by Him to write seven epistles to the Asian churches, five of which were admonished with devastatingly bad reports and the other two firmly chastened. This visionary 'double-image Christ' is power-conscious and bad-tempered, resembling the shadow of the perfect Christ St John had tried to imitate in life. This Christ is reminiscent of Yahweh.

Then a vision of inorganic stone, glass and crystal surrounds the deity, who became like jasper and cornelian. Here Jung is reminded of seventeen centuries of the alchemists' work with inorganic matter looking for 'the Man' or *homo altus* who was 'the stone that is no stone'.

Next comes the great vision of the Lamb, a horrendous theriomorphic seven-eyed and seven-horned ram-like thing who stands as if slain. He then comes and opens the Seven Seals of the Book. The first four seals reveal the frightening apocalyptic horsemen. The fifth seal unleashes the wailing of the martyrs crying for vengeance upon their earthly slaughters. The sixth seal brings the wrath of this horn-ram, and there is a cosmic catastrophe.

Jung suggests that years of preaching Christianity by St John had repressed negative insights in him until they burst forth in a brutal picture of hatred, wrath, fury and destructiveness. Blood and fire abound in these visions, bringing terror everywhere.

But is this material, this outburst from St John, psychotic? Is Jung saying that this much compensation for a conscious position of brotherly love has made St John sick? No, Jung maintains persuasively that the apocalyptic visions are so clear, consistent and unconfused as to rule out a severe psychosis. But St John *is* at the borderline. Jung points out, 'the really religious person, in whom the capacity for an unusual extension of conscious-ness is inborn, must be prepared for such dangers' (1952: 145).

The visions culminate in the opening of the seventh seal. The seventh angel trumpets in the vision of the *sun-woman* with the moon under her feet who is giving birth to a male child threatened by a red dragon. Jerusalem has been destroyed and the temple has been opened in Heaven. A heavenly *hieros gamos* between an 'unknown father' and an 'ordinary' woman clothed with the sun has occurred. She is an anima of the primordial Anthropos, the cosmic man.

The son of such a union is a uniting symbol, a totality, a *complexio oppositorum*. This duplication of characteristic events similar to Christ's birth led to beliefs that a second Messiah is to come at the end of the world.

Here Jung points out that we are getting from St John's unconscious everything rejected by consciousness, so the rather heathenish birth is envisioned. But St John is swept away himself by the archetype of the divine child, so for him God is born again in his own partly pagan unconscious. This *tremendum* of the divine child's birth when it happens in psyche is indistinguishable from the manifestation of the Self of St John just as it is in Jungian psychotherapeutic process, when the Self symbolically constellates as a birth of a child in dream material. The relationship of the Self to the ego of men and women reminds one of the symbolic relationship, for Christians, of Christ to man. As ego by definition represents only consciousness, so the totality of Self or *atman* in Indian philosophy consists of everything conscious and unconscious in human personality.

This representation of an inner rebirth in St John's psyche reveals the parallel between visionary experience and dream experience, for, as Jung remarks, 'If the vision were a modern dream one would not hesitate to interpret the birth of the divine child as the coming to consciousness of the self.'

The Self is a *complexio oppositorum*. If ego insists on perfectionism and morality, the Self will more strongly hold on to the shadow of darkness. St John's 'all-white' Christ held up by ego in his *imitatio Christi* has turned in vision into a very ferocious avenger who is unrecognizable as a saviour. The premonitions involved in the visions come from St John's collective unconscious. They point to an enantiodromia within the Christian aeon (the age of Pisces in astrology) so that after the first thousand years of Christ's influence (when Satan is locked up in a bottomless pit) the Antichrist will reign until the age of Aquarius (from AD 2000). And so it seems to have been in the reality of history!

In St John's vision, the devil, after roaming free again, is thrown into a lake of fire for ever. Then comes a sequence describing a mandala, so often the image that further manifests the self. The Lamb (ram) is to marry his Bride, the new Jerusalem. She is as radiant as jasper, as clear as crystal. The city is foursquare and built of clear, pure gold. The Lord God and the Lamb are in its temple enthroned. The four rivers of life and the tree of life are next to the throne. Here we have quarternity, in the city image and the four rivers of Paradise. The circle is the roundness of Heaven making a mandala shape.

Jerusalem is interpreted by Jung to relate to Sophia, who was with God before time began in the myth, and who at the end of time will be reunited with God through the sacred marriage. Yahweh is to be reunited with Sophia, with whom he had been in the original pleromatic state before the creation. They are originally one, *the archetype of the hermaphroditic being*.

In Jungian analysis we see again and again that when a patient is living through an insoluble conflict, no matter what empirical insights have been gained in the therapeutic work, it is often necessary to see whether in a dream, in active imagination, in sandplay or painting an unexpected third thing will turn up as a solution. The motif of the divine child, the child-hero and the mandala (squaring of the circle) signify very often a profound union of opposites which helps constellate the self, the essence of the individuation process.

God includes every ultimate idea and its opposite. In that realization one then is not surprised that a great Christian like St John came to compensatory visionary experience of great psychological significance for every man and woman.

The dominant elements of our lives involve the spirit of the holy, and, for Christians, the Holy Spirit is constantly working in and through selfhood. Man is divided with many opposing influences pressing his conscious mind from the unconscious. We know the unconscious frustrates, blocks and threatens the conscious mind. Prayer, as one practice of the spirit, tends to reinforce the unconscious in its potential and can have startling effects on consciousness. Meditation creates a psychic atmosphere in which clarifying conscious developments may occur. But it is the archetypal images of anima for man and animus for woman in which mankind reflects the need for a divine consort. Every man wants to unite with Sophia, the wisest woman. He may even wish to be born of Sophia and be the *puer aeternus*, the man-boy of changing consciousness, both black and white. The opposites lie close together in a child.

At the end of the Apocalypse the son marries the mother-bride. This symbolic *hieros gamos* is like individuation where a young man, the son of an adult man, unites with his anima (or images of bride and mother) as inspiration, union of soul and carrier of love.

This incarnation of every man and every woman is what Jungian analysis strives to enable, whenever possible. The holy often enters the psychological materials of an analysis, and its ideas can become the fulcrum of the Jungian way of spirit within psychotherapy. It is to Jung that we owe this transformation of depth psychology into a possible healing place for release and revelation of the holy within the psychological process.

This was previewed in Holy Scripture by St John's revelations hundreds of years ago. Those revelations are often lived through in a unique way by those patients who take the courageous journey of a long and full Jungian analysis.

I would like to close with a quote from Jung:

[Religious] dogma expresses a renewed hope for the fulfilment of that yearning for peace which stirs deep down in the soul, and for a resolution of the threatening tension between the opposites. Everyone shares this tension and everyone experiences it in his individual form of unrest, the more so the less he sees any possibility of getting rid of it by rational means. It is no wonder, therefore, that the hope, indeed the expectation of divine intervention arises in the collective unconscious and at the same time in the masses.

(1952: 17c)

JUNG, JOB AND ISLAM

If *Answer to Job* brings Judaeo-Christianity into a life focus through God's need to create the historicity of Jesus as a Prophet, who became Judaism's greatest spiritual gift to the outside religious world as a whole, it also brings issues and concepts forward of comparative interest to Islam.

Jung demonstrates throughout *Answer to Job* a Protestant Christian position in that Job sees and faces God alone without a mediator or priest. Islamic learned men in religious matters, the *ulama*, have an advisory position associated particularly with religious law which they have earned in their community, but they do not act as a direct intermediary between those who worship and their God, Allah. However fierce their religious law-making may become within certain Muslim groupings, they are not like intermediary priests. Like Protestant Christians, Muslims are their own priests using faith, loyalty to religion and its service in the community as essential precepts.

Islam, however, does not recognize a secular world as does Christianity, but considers all areas of life sacred and a part of the divine. Allah is *Al-Muhit*, the All-Embracing, a name God has given Himself.

Man's centrality is essential in Islam. The human heart is asserted to reflect the names and attributes of God.

> Man alone of all created beings and things is situated directly beneath the Divine Axis. It is for this reason and only for this reason that he can be said to reflect totality in the mirror of his innermost heart, and it is for this reason and only for this reason that he qualifies as the viceroy of God on earth and according to a *hadith* [a saying directly attributed to the Prophet Muhammad, blessings and peace be upon Him], 'Allah and His angels, together with the inhabitants of the heavens and the earth – even the ant in its hole, even the fish – invoke blessings upon whomsoever teaches what is good.'
>
> (Eaton 1985: 369)

Islam sees man as both vicegerent and slave to Allah, however. Man may be vicegerent in that he has a gift of knowledge sufficient to know aspects of the Reality, and with the power of speech man stands alone as Allah's interlocutor. Thus Islam believes man to be a synthesis from which no element is excluded; man is a mirror of God.

But where Islam understands so well the position of Job during his

121

extreme difficulties is that for the Muslim he is not only Allah's potential viceroy but also his submitting slave, and here, with the latter attribute, Islam teaches the other side of man's condition.

> Islam sees man as a creature of dust or clay, a nothingness before the overwhelming splendour of the Real – impotent before Omnipotence, a little thing (brother to the ant) who walks briefly upon the earth from which he was moulded, vulnerable to a pinprick and destined soon to be seized upon and taken to Judgment. He is a slave whose highest achievement is to obey without question his Master's Will or (in more esoteric terms) to rid himself of everything that might appear to be 'his', so that the Divine Will may operate through him without impediment. Any good that he may do comes from elsewhere. He can take no credit for it since it did not originate with him. Only the evil that he does is his to claim and possess as his own. Knowledge and virtue, if they are reflected in his being, are a loan from his Creator. So too are the senses, through which he perceives the theatre of his experience but which may be taken from him at any moment.
>
> (Eaton 1985: 359)

These two sides of man interpenetrate in the Muslim view. Mastery is dependent on the clear mirror of the slave. The theologian al-Ghazzālī (d. 1111) believed that everything, including the human being, has 'a face of its own and a face of its Lord; in respect of its own face it is nothingness, and in respect of the face of its Lord it is Being' (al-Ghazzālī 1983: 64–5).

This two-sided way of human seeing makes man a bridge as meeting-point. The human heart is seen by Islam as the *barzakh* (isthmus) which both unites and separates the divine and the earthly, the 'two seas'.

Job learns through his destiny that any good he has done has come from a Higher Source. Everything is on loan from his Creator. Job's example teaches the Jews this lesson in the Old Testament and makes Christ as Prophet an essential historical happening, to bring God to man again, the task each prophet carries for God. If Job presages a *logos* between God and man that demands a Christ, so, too, the earlier prophets beginning with Adam were to give divine guidance to mankind on its journey, as was Muhammad, blessings and peace be upon Him, to culminate, seal and complete as Final Messenger the circle of historical prophets in the Islamic view.

In Jung's theory of the collective unconscious, each person carries primordial and archaic pre-structural psychological potentials which when raised to ego consciousness connect the primordial image of ancient man to the whole of selfhood in contemporary man. So, too, in Islamic belief there is a similar awareness and importance given to the primordial. In discussing the particular way Islam sees its Prophet, Muhammad, blessings and peace be upon Him, Schuon (1979: 102) explains this with mastery:

The Prophet as Norm is not only the Whole man (*al-insan al-kamil*) but also the Ancient Man (*al-insan al-gadim*). Here there is a sort of combination of a spatial with a temporal symbolism; to realize the 'Whole' or 'Universal' man means to come out from oneself, to project one's will into the absolutely 'Other', to extend oneself into the universal life which is that of all things; while to realize the 'Ancient' or 'Primordial' man means to return to the origin which we bear within us; it means to return to eternal childhood, to rest in our archetype, in our primordial and normative form, or in our theomorphic substance.

There is an interesting comparative realization when considering the Prophet of Islam and the Prophet of Christianity. Islam *submits* to its Prophet, while Christians *believe* in their Prophet. In Islam it is the submission of Muhammad, blessings and peace be upon Him, as he was unlettered and without education that guarantees he added nothing to the authenticity of the Holy Qur'ān in terms of human knowledge. 'But the perfect scribe, who misses no syllable of what is dictated to him and who is, so to speak, all ear, is also *habib Allah* (the beloved of God), just as Adam was most dear to God' (Eaton 1985: 362). Muhammad, blessings and peace be upon Him, is thus a perfect receptacle and also a model of perfect receptivity to Allah.

The imitation of the Prophet of Islam is different from the spiritual imitation of Christ. This is because Muhammad's life is known in great detail and is humanized by every archetypal experience natural man may encounter. Christians must imagine what Jesus might have done in certain circumstances, as the historical record of His life is so sparse. With Muhammad, blessings and peace be upon Him, often a description of a similar situation to the believer's will exist in Muhammad's life which can be imitated more or less directly. If Islam exhibits a passivity or 'slavehood' to what is above, the complement to this is full activity within the world below as each can receive it. This implies effort and struggle (*jihad*) wherever the obligation is perceived to require this.

Both Christianity and Islam agree that in the imitation of the Prophets, it is the *inner incorporation* within a person's central religious concept of man that achieves the sacred as seen in the Prophet's mould of personality. There is here a potential understanding of deep complementary consistencies within aspects of the Christ and of Muhammad, widely contrasting but historically related as models of perfection in Prophethood.

In Islam to attempt to enter into the mould of the Prophet is to enter the very essence of the Holy Qur'ān; the Prophet's nature was the nature of the Holy Qur'ān. It could not be stated that all of the New Testament of the Holy Bible directly describes or reveals the exact nature of the Christ. Therefore piety in the face of 'unknowingness' of Christ's actual nature is the choice of many Christians.

123

In Jung's Protestant Christianity, as in Muslim Islamic belief, man and woman represent God in the dimension of the world even as they show the world before God to be partly as human beings *are*. In the sense of one example, Job fulfilled this task of speaking to God, revealing himself honestly in carrying the worship of one God to a fullness of heart and of intention. With suffering, Job became a prototype of the God-fearing, God-serving, God-loving man and a model for every person.

In Islam, the heart and the intellect become divinized in the love of Allah and potentially one in Unity.

> When we speak of the Heart-Intellect we mean the universal faculty which has the human heart for its symbolical seat but which, while being 'crystallised' according to different planes of reflection, is none the less 'divine' in its single essence.
>
> (Schuon 1959: 95)

The single essence of monotheism is the final and only Essence of God. To aspire towards God with fervent intent is to become what one is in Reality. *'Wa ma tawfigi illa bi' Llah'* – our success comes only through God. This is the essence of Job's experience, and it harmonizes profoundly with Jung's concept of the Self as the unknowable totality of the unconscious as it gradually becomes more conscious to man, to woman and to child.

REFERENCES

Eaton, C. G. (1985) 'Man', in *Islamic Spirituality* ed. S. H. Nasr, London: SCM Press Ltd.

al-Ghazzālī, Abū Hāmid (1983) *The Jewels of the Quran*, trans. M. Abul Quasem, London and Boston: Kegan Paul International.

Goodman, L. E. (trans.) (1977) *Rambam – Readings in the Philosophy of Moses Maimonides*, New York: Schocken Books.

Jung, C. G. (1952) *Answer to Job*, London: Ark Paperbacks.

Schuon, F. (1959) *Gnosis: Divine Wisdom*, London: John Murray.

—— (1979) *Understanding Islam*, London: Allen & Unwin.

Winnicott, D. W. (1971) *Playing and Reality*, London: Tavistock.

10

IN THE SHADOW OF THE MONOTHEISMS: JUNG'S CONVERSATIONS WITH BUBER AND WHITE

John P. Dourley

In his late autobiography *Memories, Dreams and Reflections*,[1] Jung draws a compelling picture of his early experience of institutional religion in his own life and in that of his father as nearly totally negative. From the perspective of his later years the son retrospectively indicts his minister father's faith in the monotheistic and transcendent God of Swiss Calvinism with his father's effective removal from life's supporting and balancing vitalities. The consequences of such removal took the form of the lifelong frustration of his personal potential and an endemic depressive condition, a condition, suggests Jung, which may have contributed to his father's untimely demise.[2]

From the recall of old age Jung contends that even as a youth he had already experienced the living reality of God in what he was later to call the collective unconscious.[3] In his living commerce with the unconscious then and throughout his life he found life's energies so much more readily and fully available in an unmediated and experiential access to their source within. Hence the religious import of his recall of his lifelong relation with his father is Jung's contention that he found within himself the energies and life-giving experience which a functioning religion should mediate and which his father sought in vain in a monotheistic deity somehow beyond the psyche. Sadly he recalls that he could not convey such experience to his father or minister uncles, whose faith and theology had impaired or destroyed their natural religious sensibilities and so capacity for such experience.[4]

Nevertheless, Jung's interest in religion continued throughout his lifetime. It did so, in large part, because he could not deny the religious content of so many of the expressions of the psyche with which he was confronted as a doctor and psychiatrist. From such unlikely origins as his experience of his father's monotheistic faith, Jung's own mature paradigm of the psyche came eventually to identify in the psyche as residual to it what he was to call 'an authentic religious function'.[5] Effectively this authentic religious function was the basis of Jung's understanding of humanity as the 'image of God' in so far as this function worked for the making whole or total of those lives open to its impress on their consciousness.[6] Viewed from this perspective, Jung's psychology may be understood as one in which humanity, naturally an 'image of God' in the wholeness its seeks, is moved by the psyche itself into ever sharper delineations of this image through greater appropriation and approximation of personal integration and universal relatedness.

In this manner Jung came to equate without residue psychological maturity and authentic religious experience. Their identity rests on the natural teleology of the psyche towards wholeness, a teleology which works to unify the many powers that constitute the individual even as it breeds in the individual an empathic identity with the totality. For Jung these qualities of life became the hall-mark of true religion and, indeed, especially of mystical experience. However, the process that led him to his own paradigm of the psyche eventually forced him to place the power that works these patterns of totality, the natural goal of psychic and religious life, within rather than beyond the psyche. The shift to this radical interiority became the ultimate counter to that transcendent monotheism that had so sapped his father's life energies. Thus Jung, again from the perspective of age, came to look back on the meaning of his life's work as the effort to heal the wound that monotheistic Christianity had inflicted on his father as a microcosmic instance of the wound it had inflicted on the wider Christian culture.[7]

Jung's psychology has thus attracted the widespread attention of religionists because of its claim to have identified the origins of religious experience in the human psyche itself.[8] This claim can be viewed as favourable to religion and to its study. For it supports the contention that human consciousness is in and of itself incorrigibly religious. Yet others have attacked Jung's claim as undermining religion itself. This response is particularly evident with those who identify true religion with its concretion in one or other preferred revelation, taken, at least in religion's monotheistic variant, as a definitive historical incursion by a wholly transcendent, self-sufficient and perfect God into human affairs. Such unforced forays of monotheistic deities into human history usually culminate in the formation of a privileged community, the chosen, bearing what some theologians sometimes and, from the viewpoint of their faith commitment, accurately, call 'the final revelation'.[9] The phrase itself and its associated psycho-theological dynamic bear critical scrutiny in the twentieth century, when there is historically warranted suspicion that the final revelation and the final solution may not be unrelated.

Jung's mature psychology came to provide humanity at least potentially with one of its more effective protections against monotheistic faith. For as it moved into its later and most sophisticated formulations it progressively undermined the religious and moral credibility of monotheistic faiths by showing their presiding divinities to be creations of the psyche itself. In his final paradigm of the psyche Jung was to conclude that the projections of the truth and power of the Self beyond the psyche created both the divinities themselves and their respective communities who worshipped in their disparate One and only Gods the truth of the Self in projections powerful enough to cluster competing communities of belief around them.

Sustained reflection on Jung's understanding of the psychogenesis of the various One and only Gods, a contradiction in itself which would be humorous if its historical effects were not so tragic, reveals transcendental monotheisms and their accompanying faiths to be currently serious threats to human life both personal and societal. At the personal level the removal of the energies of the Self through their projection on to a divinity beyond the psyche debilitates the psyche thus victimized. For the experience of the Self in projection can be but a pallid counterfeit of the immediate experience of the energies of the Self undiluted by collective symbolism and by the sometimes lifeless ecclesial means for the distribution of the graces of the one presiding God. The foregoing is but another way of describing more psychologically the processes of belief which so victimized Jung's father.

Yet a paradox remains in evaluating the psychological consequences of the psychogenesis of the One and only Gods. For the intensity of the experience of the divinity of the Self is both impaired by monotheistic projection even while the experience of the Self in projection can become burdensome to the individual member of a believing monotheistic community. Projected divinity can become a psychic weight on the soul of the believer for at least two compelling reasons. The moral imperative of the Self in projection creates a conscience which terrorizes the consciousness of the individual and, as Freud would argue, drives it into paroxysms of Self- or other hatred.[10] Since, from Jung's perspective, the source of this terror is the consequence of the betrayal of the inner Self, its power is easily understood but would be lessened if the believer could turn inward to the conscious service of that native divinity which cannot be indefinitely offended without the destruction of the natural image of God within the individual.

But the Self in projection is also destructive to the 'believing' mind, which must violate itself in offering intellectual assent to the 'sacrosanct unintelligibility'[11] of the monotheistic 'revelations' and their now culturally meaningless theological elaboration. This is particularly the case where the monotheisms take themselves literally and historically, as they usually do, and in so doing contribute to the loss of the symbolic and so religious sense in the individual and culture whose consciousness they inform. Religion thus becomes the self-defeating effort to read poetry as prose.

Here Jung's questioning is more perceptive than Freud's, it might be argued: he challenges the theologians of his day to come up with a more compelling reason for religion and its expression in and of themselves. This question would entail facing the question of why humanity cannot seem to divest itself of the unlikely and literally meaningless kind of statements that symbolic and primordial religious discourse seem always to express. For Jung such a facing of the deeper question 'Not why this or that God but why religion at all' seemed unlikely to be asked by the religious or theological community. 'Theology regards our efforts in this respect with mistrustful mein, while pointedly declining to tackle this very necessary task itself. It proclaims doctrines which nobody understands, and demands a faith which nobody can manufacture.'[12]

The realization that Jung's mature psychology is corrosive of monotheistic faiths surfaces with particular clarity in two of the many dialogues Jung carried out with theologians and religious thinkers of various types. The perceptive monotheist's well-founded fear, across denominational lines, of the full implications of the commerce between the divine and the human in Jung's paradigm of the psyche is nowhere more evident than in his interchanges with Martin Buber, the Jewish religious thinker, and with Victor White, OP, a Dominican and Thomist, and so a representative of the then presiding Roman Catholic theological tradition. These conversations are themselves classical instances of Jung's dialogue first with his father and then, throughout his life, with representatives of monotheistic religiosities and theologies. The conversations with Buber and White dramatically exemplify the threat Jung's psychology represented to their transcendentalist, monotheistic and so dualistic theologies. Yet, paradoxically, a sustained examination of the reasons for the failed dialogues with Buber and White contributes to the understanding of the religious and metaphysical import of Jung's own psychology and why it remains in the end incompatible with transcendental monotheism in any of its variants.

A sustained examination of his dialogue with Buber and White reveals that the latent foundational incompatibilities of Jung's psychology with their monotheistic transcendentalism, supernatural dualism and sophisticated fundamentalism aborted a successful outcome of the dialogues in principle and from the outset. Yet even as the dialogues themselves served to make the foundational incompatibilities between Jung's psychology and the unqualified monotheisms of his conversants blatantly apparent, they also helped or forced Jung towards the more radical formulations of his later major works as they touched on the relation of religion to psychology. Without the dialogues, especially with White, Jung would not so readily have come to the radical conclusions reached in his work on Job.[13] In this work Jung unfolds almost poetically the vision of a divinity unable to resolve its own self-contradiction in eternity and so forced to create human consciousness as the only locus in which such contradiction could first be perceived and then, with the help of its conflicted source, resolved. This manner of imagining the divine–human relation implies a mutuality of being and real need between the divine and the human with which a truly transcendent monotheistic faith can never be fully comfortable. Let us turn, then, to the conversations with Buber and White to give substance to what has been said.

Buber initiated the discussion with Jung without prior personal dialogue in an article entitled 'Religion and modern thinking' in a German journal, *Merkur*, in February 1952.[14] In the article Buber points back to 'a very early writing'[15] in which Jung first expressed his Gnostic leanings, which, in Buber's opinion, permeated Jung's psychology thenceforth. In 1916 Jung had indeed written a piece of Gnostic poetry entitled *Septem Sermones ad Mortuos*, or *Seven Sermons to the Dead*.[16] In his later reply to Buber, Jung was to describe this piece of poetry as 'a sin of my youth'.[17] This was hardly a very candid or courageous statement on Jung's part if by it he meant to imply that after his youth he moved away from a Gnostic sensitivity. To anyone who reads primary Jung, it is simply undeniable that Jung's appreciation of Gnostic religiosity, understood as an unmediated experience of the unconscious and its religion-making powers, remained firmly in place throughout his mature writings. For Buber the unmediated intercourse between divinity and humanity foundational to Jung's psychology was simply unacceptable and abrasive to his monotheistic mind. In his view Jung's psychology served only to corrode modernity's sense of the true transcendent and monotheistic God. It is not surprising, then, that in this initial article Buber linked Jung with Sartre and Heidegger as contributing to the modern *Eclipse of God*,[18] the title of a later book of essays containing Buber's initial attack on Jung and his reply to Jung's reply.

Buber's case against Jung in his opening attack thus centres on the charge that Jung's psychology was a sophisticated form of that reductionism known as psychologism and was imbued with a profoundly Gnostic spirit which too intimately related the divine and the human. Such gnosis allegedly vested the human with an illegitimate knowledge of the religious mystery beyond the competence of the human noetic capacity. Buber's was a well-stated variant of a charge made in more than one form against Jung's psychology. Indeed, the charge was, on one occasion, lodged in desperation by Jung against his own psychology when he admitted his difficulties with the contemporary monotheistic mind, especially Christian. The difficulties centred around his own prolonged efforts to author an understanding of the psyche which would serve to recall the projections that create the monotheistic deities and so reroot humanity in its own psychic soil and in its native sense of divinity. Jung is obviously referring to charges such as Buber's when he writes that anyone engaged in such a task is inevitably accused of '"psychologism" or suspected of morbid "mysticism"'.[19]

At this point it should be noted that Buber's charges of Gnosticism and reductionism imply that Buber himself clearly knew where the legitimate boundaries of human knowledge of the divine lay and how the divine and human interrelate in their experience of each other. Indeed his description of what divinity is and how it relates to humanity is frankly laid out in this article. Buber, in phrases reminiscent of Barth's formulations, variously describes this divine being as 'that absolute Other, the absolute over against me'[20] and 'One who is experienced or believed in as being absolutely over against one'.[21] In his later reply to Jung's response, Buber further describes this absolute other as a 'super-psychic Being'[22] and 'an extra-psychical Being'.[23] His central concern is to affirm that such a Being exists independently of the psyche or of what he calls 'the human subject'.[24] His fear is the classical monotheist's fear that Jung's psychology denies such transcendent independence of the One and only Divine Other. Buber's obvious uneasiness with radical human subjectivity forces his conclusion, in fact a correct one if properly understood, that Jung's psychology supports a religion 'of pure psychic immanence'.[25] In these passages Buber's presupposition, indeed his faith, is that true monotheism and true transcendence imply a divinity which exists or can exist independently of the human psyche which such divinity creates. Jung's suggestion that the psyche creates such divinity remained profoundly disturbing to him.

In a second distinct line of argument both in his original charge and in his rejoinder to Jung's reply, Buber argues that Jung's conception of the Self as made up of the unity of opposites, including good and evil, is the basis for a form of moral libertinism. To support his charge he cites Jung's usage of Carpocrates, a Gnostic, identified as such by no less an authority than Irenaeus himself.[26] Jung does indeed cite Carpocrates three times throughout his Collected Works[27] to point to the necessity of the assimilation of the shadow, the less acceptable sides of one's humanity, in the process of individuation.[28]

For Jung the conscious assimilation of the shadow is hardly libertine. It is a process of psychological suffering which always entails the painful and steadfast staring at the potential for evil in one's personal being, and, more, at the personal tendency to project such evil on to the other. Such confrontation with one's personal evil and the tendency to flee it through identifying it with another is the first step in the transformation of shadow through its appropriation. Such appropriation can work the change of shadow from an enemy into an ally in an expanded and safer consciousness less susceptible to projecting personal or collective evil in the demonization of the other as individual or as community.

Understood within the context of Jung's psychology, such rigorous honesty is a far cry from any moral irresponsibility. On the contrary the moral demand to confront one's shadow grounds a harrowing, lifelong Self-examination under the scrutiny of the Self's critique of one's conscious position made most tellingly through the dream. Such a process demands a far more prolonged, deeper and extensive examination of conscience and an accompanying penitential sensitivity than collective religions can provide with their lists of general sins. These lists of sins do, indeed, document the truly dehumanizing, but because of their general nature fall short of identifying the specific evil of an individual life as do dreams. Jung is explicit in his statement that such morally rigorous, often humiliating, shadow work is the work of a lifetime.[29]

The process is even more demanding when shadow reclamation takes the form of withdrawing a negative projection cast upon a community, especially upon a community bonded by a system of counter-beliefs presided over by a competing monotheistic God. Such collective demonization may be systemic to monotheistic consciousness, which to date has tended to relate to other and competing monotheistic communities as embodying, if not evil itself, at least an intransigent heart hardened against the preferred version of the One true God. This projection, to date apparently unavoidable in monotheistic collective consciousness, targets the competing community for conversion, genocidal extermination or, at best, a rejective tolerance in the ghetto. If the psychological dynamism operative in the discomfort with variant or contradicting forms and communities of monotheism shown by monotheistic communities to each other could be identified, such identification would contribute to the uncovering of the connection between communal monotheism and violence. Jung's psychology casts some considerable light on the historically and so empirically evident connection between monotheistic faith and death. For Jung's psychology strongly implies that monotheistic communities may need to project their shadow and so to demonize their variants as endemic to the process of their self-making or bonding under the One true God.

This type of analysis is not to deny that the monotheist's withdrawal of the projected collective shadow from other monotheistic communities would be any easier for the monotheist than it would be for any other individual engaged in shadow recall. In fact it could be more difficult. For it would force the individual devotee to realize that what was projected on to the other community and its members belongs to one's own communal shadow. In the light of this insight the shadow epithets projected on the Jewish community by traditional Christian anti-Semitism, as a historically verifiable instance of the process of projecting the communal shadow, would be helpful in surfacing what the Christian finds most repulsive about the Christian tradition. The substance of Christian anti-Semitism could then be used to identify what the Christian tradition unconsciously knows it lacks in itself or has forbidden to itself or, on the contrary, to identify the nature of its peculiar evil, which it cannot acknowledge in itself and so projects on to its Jewish co-monotheistic community as specifically Jewish.

At a deeper level yet, the recovery of the projection of the monotheistic shadow would implicate a relativism which would effectively corrode the faith of the monotheist of any persuasion. For such a recovery of the shadow would imply that the monotheisms and their shadows have a common origin in the psyche. Their owning of their shadows, currently perceived in mutual projection, would convince them that they are relative expressions of a stage in the development of the religious psyche in which interior libidinal urgencies could only be perceived in projection. Conscious awareness of the origin of the monotheisms and of their shadows would thus both depotentiate monotheistic shadow projection as well as dissolve monotheism itself towards a societally safer recognition that humanity's religious impulse originates within it and is not imposed upon it from some transcendental position with which it is not natively continuous. Moreover, following Jung's suggestion, each monotheistic expression could be valued as variant expression of the Self seeking ever fuller ingression in consciousness, again as a prelude in projection to a more immediate conversation with the source of deity within the psyche.

Jung replied to Buber in the May issue of the same journal in which Buber had launched his attack. His reply took three major thrusts. First he fell back on a position he frequently took in other discussions with theologians, namely that he was first and foremost an empiricist and not a metaphysician.[30] In evaluating Jung's first line of response one must try to make some sense of what he meant by the terms 'metaphysics' and 'metaphysician' and what he meant by his frequent claims that he was not a metaphysician but an empiricist.

Let us first examine his claim to be an empiricist. Jung stretched the term 'empiricism' to include more than those archetypal statements made by the mythologies, religions and folklore of the world. This material is usually accepted as empirical if for no more compelling reason than that it can be catalogued and usually forgotten in dictionaries of folklore, symbolism or religion. But Jung extends the meaning of 'empirical' to include psychological material drawn from dreams, hallucinations and fantasies of his contemporaries and clients. Frequently this material bore an amazing and empirical, that is, demonstrable likeness to themes in religions and folklore of the past, often no longer living and not previously known to the dreamers in whose dream they appeared.

Thus the data base, if one is to use so crude a term, of Jung's empiricism would include both the world religions and such current expressions of the psyche as the nightly dream or waking hallucination. The theoretical construction of the psyche's nature and dynamic that such a data base came to support was Jung's mature conviction that both personal dream and collective revelation are expressions of the same generative source, the collective unconscious. If one can thus extend the meaning of the term 'empiricism', Jung was indeed an empiricist, and his approach, both theoretically and therapeutically, was, indeed, empirical. In the discussion of monotheisms it is crucial to note that Jung's empiricism implies that the source not only of all religions but of the present dream is the collective ground of collective humanity. Thus Jung's empiricism, because it points to the intra-psychic genesis of all religion including the various monotheisms, is in itself a relativization of the monotheisms and so constitutes their undermining in principle.

Jung's discussion of metaphysics is more complex. His use of the term yields, at least, three senses throughout his work. Occasionally he will argue that metaphysics, as philosophy, is simply a systematized expression of the dominant complex in the philosopher's psyche. Depicting metaphysics as an unconscious expression of the unconscious would explain the apparent permanence of the practice of metaphysics in the face of its consistent failure to achieve any substantial agreement among its practitioners. The failure of a metaphysical consensus is thus due to the fact that metaphysicians remain implacably unconscious of the fact that their metaphysics is a rationalized expression of their dominant unconscious complex. The subtle irony of this position is evident when Jung endorses Nietzsche's suggestion that meta-physics for the modern should become the 'ancilla psychologiae',[31] the handmaiden of psychology. By these remarks Jung means that, just as certain medieval theologians would understand philosophy as the hand-maiden of theology which alone, informed with the gift of supernatural and infused faith, could explain philosophy's or reason's full meaning to it, so modern depth psychology could explain to today's metaphysician or theologian what complex informed the metaphysician's metaphysics or what complex funded the faith behind the theologian's theology.[32]

In the second sense he gives the term, Jung will occasionally refer to his own metaphysical aspirations and to himself as a *philosopher manqué*[33] in thinly disguised recognition, never fully acknowledged, of the philosophical implications of his own psychology. In so far as metaphysics can be understood as concerned with what is and how it is known, his psychology does indeed include a latent metaphysic, and Jung could have shown more candour in admitting it. Indeed it was Buber's clear perception of the metaphysical implications of Jung's psychology and the threat it posed to Buber's monotheistic cosmology which so threatened him and drove him to his initial attack.

But in its third and most frequently used sense, which grounds his denials of dabbling in metaphysics in his discussions with theologians, Jung means by metaphysics a body of knowledge for which there is neither compelling internal or subjective evidence nor external or objective evidence, that is, a body of knowledge for which there is no evidence at all. In no small measure he derived this meaning of metaphysics from his youthful observations that his clerical father and uncles, when discussing matters theological and dogmatic, had absolutely no experiential sense of what they were talking about.[34] In this sense metaphysics can be related to what he later called the 'preposterous nonsense'[35] of religious dogma, the sacred meaninglessness of statements that once bore the energies of the unconscious but now are dead, killed by a theological reasoning severed from the experience of the unconscious which created the myth on which theology reflects. By metaphysics in this third sense Jung means a blind faith divested of any experiential basis in humanity. Thus the term applies to those, among whom he includes Buber, 'who for one reason or another think they know about unknowable things in the Beyond'.[36] Thus when Jung denies that he is a metaphysician in his response to Buber, Jung is arguing that monotheistic faith imagines its object as a power beyond the human and so beyond the psyche when its referent is, in fact, the powers of the psyche which create both the experience of the monotheistic Gods and unmovable faith in them. The conclusion follows that the stronger the faith of the monotheist in the Wholly Other, the greater the degree of accompanying unconsciousness.

In discussing the Buber interchange in a later letter, Jung likens the metaphysical capacity, which, in this context, he closely relates to the monotheist's faith consciousness, to 'an organ' enabling the believer thus vested to 'tune in the transcendent'.[37] But he denies, and here he appeals to Kant, that such knowledge can ever be a public possession. Rather, wherever operative, such metaphysical, in this case monotheistic faith, is grounded in archetypal experience verging on possession of which the believer usually remains unconscious. For Jung such archetypal experience bears both the imaginal content of the so-called metaphysical faith and the energies that compel belief in it, though the origin of both usually remains unknown to the 'believing' individual. It is in this sense that Jung claims he is possessed of no such organ and so is not a metaphysician while implying that Buber's faith conviction and sense of a monotheistic God are based on archetypal possession of which Buber remained largely unaware.

Jung's second line of response to Buber rests on foundational elements of his own psychology of religion. It identifies in the power of the archetypes, here termed 'immanent-transcendent',[38] and in their imagery projected beyond the psyche, those energies which create the Gods, including the all male *monotheoi*, as well as the Goddesses and all of the deities' disparate revelations. Thus dialogue with the divine Thou, revealed through his interchange with Jung to be for Buber the absolute and transcendent Other, becomes for Jung dialogue with the unconscious and its archetypal powers as the source of 'everything one could wish for in the psychic Thou'.[39] It is on this foundational issue of the location, so to speak, of the transcendent 'One' or 'Other' that the views of the two are most incompatible. Jung locates the 'Other' in those dimensions of the psyche which infinitely transcend the ego but with which the ego remains organically continuous in the life of the psyche. For Buber the 'Other' dwells in a Heaven beyond the psyche.

The final line of Jung's response, again a wider theme in his work, centred on the difficulty of distinguishing which of the monotheistic divine contenders was in fact the true Objective One whom Buber insisted existed beyond the psyche. Here Jung touches somewhat sardonically on a problem which is obvious to all, but still defiant of any significant religious or theological solution. He writes:

> Consequently I do not permit myself the least judgment as to whether and to what extent it has pleased a metaphysical deity to reveal himself to the devout Jew as he was before the Incarnation, to the Church Fathers as the Trinity, to the Protestants as the one and only Saviour without co-redemptrix and to the present Pope as a saviour with co-redemptrix.[40]

In this citation Jung simply points to the obvious and embarrassing fact that Jew, Catholic Christian and Reformer each have their own variant of the true monotheistic deity whose monotheistic claims would be impaired or eclipsed should truth be granted to any of the competing alternatives. It should also be noted here that in these passages Jung goes on to wonder where the deities of the eastern religions fit into the divine squabble for exclusive ultimacy. In the context of his wider work he strongly insinuates that an eastern sense of radical interiority would complement the spiritually debilitating externalism, literalism and historicism foundational to mainstream western transcendental monotheism, Roman or Reformed.[41]

The recovery of such a living interiority remained for Jung among the more pressing spiritual needs in the West currently supported, even demanded, by the western unconscious. However, he was convinced that the West would legitimately recover such a living spirituality only through its reappropriation of those traditions of radical immanence such as the Gnostic, alchemical and mystical which it had excluded as heretical or relegated to the periphery of mainstream theological reflection in the making of its now impoverished tradition. The western religious dilemma thus becomes one in which its spiritual vitality can only be recovered through the reappropriation of immanental modes of religious experience whose negation was necessary in the creation of its reigning transcendent monotheism.

The impatience, even pique, evidenced in the last citation is again all too apparent when Jung suggests in his reply to Buber that a trip through an asylum would illuminate both the origin of religious metaphysical ideas and the conviction with which they are held to any interested observers, among whom he obviously meant to include Buber himself:

> It should not be overlooked that what I am concerned with are psychic phenomena which can be proved empirically to be the bases of metaphysical concepts, and that when, for example, I speak of 'God' I am unable to refer to anything beyond these demonstrable psychic models which, we have to admit, have shown themselves to be devastatingly real. To anyone who finds their reality incredible I would recommend a reflective tour through a lunatic asylum.[42]

Given the irritable tone of Jung's reply there can be little doubt, in the face of Buber's evenness of writing and self-assurance, who won the debate in terms of literary style and suavity. Nor does the exchange leave much doubt that Jung, on his part, was deeply emotionally engaged in the issues at stake. Buber had touched a tender spot, especially in one who denied a metaphysical implication in such conceptions as the archetypes and the nature of their influence on consciousness as the basis of humanity's religious instinct and so of the religions. Buber had rightly perceived the threat to the credibility of transcendent and self-sufficient One and only Gods posed by the wider, and in this sense truly metaphysical, implications of Jung's psychology. Jung might have been more open in simply admitting that indeed such philosophical and theological implications were there and defending them against the onslaught of Buber's transcendentalist monotheism.

However, the interchange did bring out quite clearly what, in fact, Buber's conditions were for the divinity to whom the human related as an I to a Thou. Such a divinity was exposed in the light of the conversation with Jung to be the all too familiar, wholly transcendent, and monotheistic deity who would somehow be eclipsed, indeed endangered with extinction, if He were to be understood as grounded in the psyche as the basis of His creation and projection into the heavens. The exchange leaves it very clear that the divine Thou to whom Buber relates the human I is in no significant sense a native and necessary function of the depth of human subjectivity in the orders of being, knowing or morality. In the light of the conversation with Jung, Buber's suggestions of intimacy between the divine Thou and the human I are exposed as little more than religious poetry whose metaphysical implications Buber could neither face nor accept, a poetry functioning as a literary façade behind which lurked the traditional Wholly Other and monotheistic God of orthodox Jewish and Christian imagination.

An examination of Jung's relationship with Victor White reveals a final and emotionally charged parting of the ways for many of the same philosophical and theological reasons. Jung was to write in a letter after their interchange that his relation with Buber was free of 'the slightest personal friction' and always 'polite', by implication, even throughout their debate.[43] Yet the truth is that they had never enjoyed a close personal friendship. This was not the case with Victor White. Jung became a close friend of White's for some sixteen years, from his initial correspondence with him in 1945 till White's untimely death at the age of 58 in 1960. Their relationship began when White, then teaching dogmatic theology at Blackfriars, Oxford, sent Jung a series of articles that he had written and published on Jung's psychology and its theological implications.[44] From his early letters to White, Jung makes it evident that he felt that finally he had found a theologian who understood his psychology and the 'enormous implications'[45] of seriously relating depth psychology to theology in the modern epoch.

Over the course of the years of their conversation White frequently visited Jung in Zurich and in Bollingen, Jung's retreat on Lake Zurich where only the truly favoured were invited. It is obvious from their correspondence that Jung was analysing White's dreams and working with him in other processes of discernment concerning the direction White's life should take.[46] It is equally obvious from the correspondence that White was in fact conducting what today would be understood as an analytic practice in England.[47]

The first point of serious contention surfaced as early as 1949 over White's understanding of evil as a *privatio boni*, that is, over a traditional theological conception of evil as having no substance in itself but being, rather, a privation of the good.[48] For Jung the point was both academic and clinical. In a foreword to a book written by White, Jung describes a case in which 'a scholarly man' was using the denial of the reality of evil as simply the privation of good to ease his conscience in the face of his 'morally reprehensible practices'.[49] Thus the question of evil as privation of good soon became a living and major issue between the two. Their extended discussion of the reality or non-reality of evil forced Jung to his final considered position, namely that evil had its own reality and could no more be defined as the absence or privation of good than cold could be defined as the privation of heat or dark the privation of light.

The issue for Jung moved directly to the question of how seriously White and the Christian mind could take the reality of evil not only as it existed in creation but, if creation reflected its Creator, in that Creator too. In this manner the dialogue with White prompted Jung's initial insinuation, which was to become an affirmation in his work on Job, that the God who authored all of creation in including its evil was rather far removed from the Joannine God in whom there was no darkness. On the contrary the prevalence of evil in creation demanded its presence in the Creator. The question soon extended from the Creator and creation to Christology and to the total split between the Christ-figure, embodying absolute good, and Satan, embodying absolute evil.[50] Thus the dialogue with White was operative in the formation of Jung's classic and mature position that the good and evil grounded in the One God must be differentiated in conscious-ness and so in history and reunited consciously as history moved to its eschatological culmination. In terms of Christology this meant that the absolute split between the figures of Christ and Satan at the heart of the Christian myth depicts symbolically an essential conscious differentiation of conflicting absolutes present as contaminated or undifferentiated in the creator's life. The differentiation given to absolute good and evil by the Christian myth serves, then, as a prelude to the final embrace of the dark and light emanations or sons of the One God.

The debate thus helped to define Jung's emerging psychological perspective, with its cosmological and metaphysical implications. For the discussion with White forced Jung to envision the split between absolute good and evil as reflective of a contradiction in the divine ground itself. Jung came to imagine this conflicted ground giving rise both to creation, in which good and evil are undeniably present, and to the Christian myth, where the absolute contradiction between Christ as absolute good and his shadow brother, Satan, as absolute evil can no longer be evaded in themselves or in their common origin. Inasmuch as the Christian myth made the contradiction in Creator and creation obvious it was, for Jung, a significant religious differentiation and substantial contribution to the evolution of humanity's religious consciousness. But by the same psychological logic, the Christian myth as differentiating the absolute split in God personified in Christ and Satan could not be ultimate because it lacked the symbol to unite the absolute divinely grounded contradiction it so dramatically pushed to the surface. As such it remained a penultimate stage in humanity's religious development now pleading for its own supercession.

Thus through the prolonged exercise of these wider issues, the discussions with White contributed to Jung's formulations of the all-encompassing dynamic of the psyche in his later major statements. In these mature statements the psyche's movement to maturation is one of the conscious differentiation and then unification of conflictual absolute opposites – good and evil in the discussion with White – which are ultimately grounded in the monotheistic source or Creator of consciousness itself. Putting the implications of Jung's psychology into a religious idiom this meant that the one ground of consciousness and being, God as Creator, is necessitated to create in order to resolve in human consciousness a contradiction that defied resolution within the divine life itself. These psychic movements are foundational to the mythology endemic to Jung's psychology, and they are at least abrasive and probably contradictory to the foundational themes of classical monotheism. For they deny to the monotheistic divinity the character of self-sufficiency, omniscience and moral perfection that are usually attributed to the monotheistic Gods. In the place of such perfect, self-sufficient remove from humanity, Jung inserts the very modern theme of necessity attaching to creation, with its implication that the monotheistic divinity was forced to create in order to work in the consciousness of the creature a resolution of the antinomy it could not work in itself.

In the mature Jung this sought-for resolution became the meaning of both individual life and the life of humanity as a whole, that is, the meaning of history itself. To borrow from the twelfth-century mind of Joachim di Fiore,[51] to whom Jung likens himself in the White correspondence, this meant that all opposites latent in God as Creator were to be differentiated in the age of the Son in history and united in the future age of the Spirit. This reunification would, of course, include the two major unresolved opposites of good and evil differentiated so well in the figures of Christ and

Satan in the Christian myth. To sum up this position, the one but profoundly unconscious God creates human consciousness as the only agency in the universe capable of first differentiating the wealth of divine self-contradictions in its ground and then, with the help of the Self, moving to that conscious synthesis of the divine opposites towards which the psyche moves, indeed impels, history, which it creates with the creation of consciousness.

In this context Jung, in his dialogue with White, came clearly to align himself with the position of Origen and with the latter's vision of the eschatological recapitulation of all that is in a divinity from which nothing is excluded. This is Origen's idea of the *apocastastasis*, for which he was early on condemned. In the context of the discussion with White, when Jung quite consciously aligns himself with Origen on this issue, he is consistent in rejecting White's accusation that he, Jung, is a dualist or Manichean. Rather Jung turns the tables on White and on the Christian mind and accuses it of a dualism which argues on the one hand that evil is not real but on the other dogmatically insists on a final dualism between the good and the bad, the eternally saved and the damned. By implication Christianity is dualistic both in its denial of evil in God and in its eternalization of the split in the eternally damned and saved.[52] In Jung's counter-myth the history of human consciousness is the stage on which the divine self-contradictions are perceived and synthesized in human consciousness so that in the end nothing is lost.

As Jung's position on these matters took shape in their discussion, White saw clearly the implied contemporary inadequacy of the image of Christ as an image of the Self, because of its one-sided spiritual nature, its lack of all shadow.[53] When White pointed this out to Jung, the substance of Jung's reply to him was that the same Spirit that had constelled the one-sided perfection of the Christ-figure over against the Satanic was now moving to unite the two. But the mode of such union and the symbol needed to effect it – currently the prior urgency of the contemporary unconscious addressing the Christian individual and collectivity – were as yet to reach the surface. Again consistently with his wider psychology he also points out that the surfacing of such a surpassing myth was a task beyond the power of reason alone to achieve.[54]

The inefficacy of reason to produce a new mythology out of its own meagre resources is the basis of Jung's frequently repeated motto, *tertium non datur*. The phrase means for him that the third as the symbol which would work the union of conflicting but valid opposites was not given to reason and its working. The symbol or myth that could unite the absolute opposites differentiated so well in the Christian myth would, no doubt, abrogate the myth itself. However, in Jung's estimate, such a symbol to be authentic would surface legitimately only through faithfully suffering the now pathological one-sidedness of Christianity to a psychic death from which would rise the mythic consciousness capable of uniting Christ and Satan. In this process neither reason and its puny power nor a premature jettisoning of the presiding myth would be of any significant or long-lasting use.[55] The wider implications of this position for a discussion of monotheism is that victims of the various monotheistic traditions must suffer the truth of their traditions and their now obviously dangerous claims to mutually exclusive truth until a mythic or symbolic sense emerges capable of raising them beyond themselves to a consciousness which would surpass them even as it included in itself their relative religious value.

This position, central to Jung's mature psychology, is what contemporary Jungian scholars identify as his shift from a Trinitarian to a quaternitarian paradigm.[56] This paradigm of the psyche implicates a new cosmology, metaphysics and religiosity which belie Jung's claim that his psychology is free of such endeavour. Driven to this counter-myth and metaphysic by what he considered the psychologically demonstrable one-sidedness of the Christian myth unable to deal with the instinctual, the demonic or the feminine in either its Trinity or Messiah,[57] Jung, helped by his dialogue with White, came to the position that God as Creator must include at least potentially all that is manifest in creation. This would have to extend, therefore, to the demonic, to the material, bodily world and to the feminine. If the body, the feminine and the demonic were again to be truly divinized and acknowledged as powers whose presence must be included in authentic configurations of wholeness both current and eschatological, then they must be seen as present in both the Alpha and Omega, in the creator and in the culmination, of the human journey. In Jung's counter-myth only the individual, through immediate conversation with the One within, can perceive how the divine contradiction is operative in one's person and work to its resolution there as one's personal and most significant contribution to the emergence of a more embracing myth in history and so to the redemption of God in humanity.

Contrary to the notion of transcendent and self-sufficient monotheistic deities, Jung seeks to describe a process in which the ground of consciousness and consciousness itself are involved by their nature in a single organic process. There are no elective and arbitrary interventions from beyond. Rather there is the ever-present religious task of grappling with and suffering the divine self-contradiction as it appears in one's life. This constant struggle moves, it is hoped, to its resolution in a consciousness more extensive in its empathy for having suffered through the divine contradiction which seeks some relief in each life. The fourth, which for Jung is a symbol of the resolution of the divine contradiction in human life and history, completes and replaces the idea of a self-sufficient and shadowless Trinity. The fourth is humanity itself as that locus in which divinity through the war of its opposites is becoming progressively more conscious. Thus in the context of Jung's superseding myth and its intricate dialectic, human consciousness becomes the only container in which the divine self-contradiction, now imagined as divinity's necessitating compulsion in the creation of human consciousness, is historically or consciously perceived and, it is hoped, resolved with the help and at the insistence of the conflicted source itself. Though this imagination may have much in common with Hegel, a realization that Jung came to only late in life,[58] it remains questionably compatible with a monotheistic world-view.

All these issues are explicit in the White–Jung correspondence. When White saw them exposed methodically yet poetically in Jung's *Answer to Job*[59] he was, at first, enthusiastic.[60] However, his enthusiasm turned to rejection and led him to negative responses in print and in correspondence with Jung, questioning the latter's motives and the prudence of printing the work at that time.[61] In spite of the later heated exchanges, in the last few years there were expressions of good will. When White died in 1960 Jung was almost eighty-five, and a final reconciliatory meeting in England which Jung had hoped for proved impossible because of Jung's health. In the end Jung felt that White's monotheistic theology with the supernatural dualism it posits between the divine and the human made it impossible for him to grasp and move into the religious future with the more intimate paradigm of the divine–human relation Jung sought so consistently to articulate in his psychology. In some of the sadder, more poignant lines in his letters, Jung writes to a mutual acquaintance close to White at the time of his death of the meaning he saw in White's passing:

> I have now seen quite a number of people die in the time of a great transition, reaching as it were the end of the pilgrimage in sight of the Gates, where the way bifurcates to the land of Hereafter and to the future of mankind and its spiritual adventure.[62]

In these words Jung implies as clearly as propriety allows that the meaning of White's death was not unrelated to White's lengthy interior struggle with the clash between Jung's psychology and his own theology. White's theology was predicated on a supernatural, self-sufficient and perfect deity in no need of the world of nature nor in organic continuity with human consciousness as its experienceable depth. It is not surprising, then, that White could not make the transition to the sense of a more intimate relation of divinity to humanity which Jung, in this letter, contends is the face of the human religious future. To make such a transition would have cost White his faith. His failure to make it may have cost him his life.

In the end Jung's discussions with Buber and White unite the latter two across the differences of their traditions. Their conversation with Jung revealed that the monotheistic God in whom they commonly believed was a Wholly Other and transcendent, supernatural, self-sufficient being. Such a being is not organically, that is, ontologically and necessarily, linked with human consciousness as that agency needed by divinity in the process

141

of its becoming conscious. For neither Buber nor White could the depth meaning of human history, personal or collective, be understood as the process of God's becoming self-conscious in humanity's suffering the divine self-contradiction towards its resolution in the human in a process of mutual redemption. From Jung's perspective the discussions reveal that his psychology could not tolerate such a distant monotheistic God uninvolved by nature in the heart of human suffering. Nor could his psychology endorse the supernatural dualism and sophisticated fundamentalism so thinly concealed by such conceptions of deity.[63] Jung remains indebted to both Buber and White for making the incompatibility of his psychology with their monotheistic theologies so clear first to himself and then to those who follow and continue to be fascinated by the religious implications and alternatives of his understanding of the psyche.

By identifying the religious impulse in the psyche itself Jung makes of religious experience a universal necessity grounded in human interiority in such a way that religion's expressions cannot be denied, though every one of them is denied the right to claim finality for itself. Thus his psychology appreciates the inescapable nature of religious experience while making it safer for humanity through the necessary relativity of its expressions.

This newer metaphysic implies a new spirituality which would understand the Spirits to originate, not in distant monotheistic skies, but in the archetypal energies of the unconscious always asking and sometimes demanding fuller incarnation in human consciousness. Such a spirituality would in turn implicate a morality which demanded of humanity the recognition of its role in the always dangerous birthing of deity in history. Such a morality would involve an intensified appreciation of the psychologically subjective as the source from which the sense of divinity rises to consciousness and can so easily escape conscious containment as in the creation of the *monotheoi*.

In the light of this psychology, projections of divinity beyond the psyche might be morally tolerated as a stage through which humanity had to pass to understand its deeper interiority by seeing its archetypal power over against itself. But in the light of the impairment of personal potential and the divisiveness and death now so closely associated with monotheistic affirmation, the question arises in the light of Jung's psychology whether or not monotheistic faith can any longer be viewed as morally acceptable. Unfortunately the taking with radical seriousness of the depths of the subjective from which divinity approaches humanity seeking to become real in it remains largely unknown or muted in the core of orthodox monotheistic spiritualities and moralities. Worse, the valuing of radical subjectivity remains impossible to spiritualities or moralities derived from disparate revelations from beyond the psyche.

To this now dangerous religiosity Jung's psychology proffers a real alternative. Whether the modern temper has the inclination or the time to turn towards a serious conversation with the deity within remains problematic. Jung may have gone to his death wondering whether humanity had a realistic hope of being saved from its own faiths, especially from the kind of exclusive or exhaustive claims to bear a saving truth made by the monotheisms in either their explicitly religious or more modern political forms. Though the outcome remained in doubt for Jung and for us, it should not be denied that he has left us with some considerable hope, as when he writes, 'The afternoon of humanity, in a distant future, may yet evolve a different ideal. In time, even conquest will cease to be the dream.'[64] Visions of such an afternoon more than suggest that humanity can and will survive the high noon of monotheistic conflict.

NOTES

1 *Memories, Dreams, Reflections*, ed. A. Jaffé, 2nd edn (New York: Vintage Books, 1965).
2 ibid., p. 95. Here Jung writes of his father's uncharacteristic enjoyment at a student reunion shortly before his death, 'The speech he delivered that evening was the last chance he had to live out his memories of the time when he was what he should have been. Soon after his condition deteriorated. In the late autumn of 1895 he became bedridden, and early in 1896 he died.'
3 cf. ibid., p. 62, 'Suddenly I understood that God was, for me at least, the most certain and immediate of experiences', and p. 92, where he expresses surprise that his father 'should not have had experience of God, to me the most evident of all experiences'.
4 See ibid., p. 93 for this typical comment about his father's ecclesiastical spirituality: 'he was entrapped by the Church and its theological thinking. They had blocked all avenues by which he might have reached God directly, and then faithlessly abandoned him.' (London: Routledge & Kegan Paul, 1958).
5 'Psychology and religion', *Collected Works* (henceforth *CW*), 11, para. 3, p. 6.
6 'Christ, a symbol of the self', *CW* 9ii, para. 74, p. 41.
7 cf. *Memories, Dreams, Reflections*, op. cit., pp. 212f., where Jung depicts his father as the fisher king suffering from the wound of Christianity, and pp. 218f., where he implies that his father's faith betrayed him, making of him a modern Uriah. Both images of his father and his faith were dream-inspired.
8 'Introduction to the religious and psychological problems of alchemy', *CW* 12, para. 9, p. 10. Here Jung refers to 'my demonstration of the psychic origin of religious experience'. That his demonstration is compelling can be questioned. That he thought it was cannot in the light of this typical affirmation.
9 See Paul Tillich, *Systematic Theology*, vol. 1 (Chicago: Chicago University Press, 1951), part 1, 11, B, 5, 6 and C.
10 See, for instance, S. Freud, *Civilization and its Discontents*, trans. J. Rivière, ed. J. Strachey (London: the Hogarth Press, 1969), sections VI, VII, pp. 54–70.
11 'A psychological approach to the doctrine of the Trinity', *CW* 11, para. 170, p. 109.
12 ibid., para. 285, p. 192.
13 *Answer to Job*, *CW* 11, pp. 357f.
14 See the documentation of the Jung–Buber correspondence in 'Religion and psychology: a reply to Martin Buber', *CW* 18, para. 1501, p. 663, n. 1.

15 Martin Buber, 'Religion and modern thinking', in *Eclipse of God* (New York: Harper & Row, 1952), p. 85.
16 *Memories, Dreams, Reflections*, ed. A. Jaffé, 1st edn (New York: Vintage Books, 1963), appendix 5, pp. 378f.
17 Jung, 'A reply to Martin Buber', op. cit., para. 1501, p. 663. Elsewhere he describes the piece as 'a poem in Gnostic style I made 44 years ago for a friend's birthday celebration (a private print!), a poetic paraphrase of the psychology of the unconscious', *C. G. Jung, Letters*, vol. 2, ed. G. Adler, trans. R. F. C. Hull (Princeton: Princeton University Press, 1975), p. 571, letter to Robert C. Smith, 19 June 1960.
18 Buber, 'Religion and modern thinking', op. cit., pp. 63f.
19 C. G. Jung, 'Psychological commentary on "The Tibetan Book of the Great Liberation"', *CW* 11, para. 771, p. 482.
20 Buber, 'Religion and modern thinking', op. cit., p. 68.
21 ibid., p. 78.
22 'Reply to C. G. Jung', in *Eclipse of God*, op. cit., p. 134.
23 ibid., p. 135.
24 ibid., p. 133.
25 Buber, 'Religion and modern thinking', op. cit., p. 84.
26 Buber, 'Reply to C. G. Jung', op. cit., p. 137.
27 'Woman in Europe', *CW* 10, para. 271, p. 131; 'Psychology and religion', *CW* 11, para. 133, p. 77; *Mysterium Coniunctionis*, *CW* 14, para. 284, p. 215.
28 'Psychology and religion', *CW* 11, para. 133, p. 77.
29 *Mysterium Coniunctionis*, *CW* 14, para. 759, pp. 553, 554. Jung writes typically, 'Always we shall have to begin again from the beginning.'
30 'Reply to Martin Buber', op. cit., para. 1503, p. 664.
31 'On the nature of the psyche', *CW* 8, para. 344, p. 160.
32 ibid., para. 346, p. 162. See also 'Basic postulates of analytical psychology', *CW* 8, para. 659, p. 343.
33 *C. G. Jung, Letters*, vol. 1, ed. G. Adler, trans. R. F. C. Hull (Princeton: Princeton University Press, 1973), p. 194, letter to F. Seifert, 31 July 1935.
34 *Memories, Dreams, Reflections*, op. cit., pp. 73f.
35 'Psychological approach to the Trinity', op. cit., para. 170, p. 110.
36 'Reply to Martin Buber', op. cit., para. 1503, p. 664.
37 *C. G. Jung, Letters*, vol. 2, op. cit., letter to Bernhard Lang, June 1957, p. 375.
38 'Reply to Martin Buber', op. cit., para. 1505, p. 665.
39 ibid., para. 1504, p. 665.
40 ibid., para. 1507, pp. 666–7.
41 This is the thrust of his two essays on the Tibetan Books of the Dead and the Great Liberation, *CW* 11, VII, pp. 475f.
42 ibid., para. 1506, p. 666.
43 *C. G. Jung, Letters*, vol. 2, op. cit., p. 101. Letter to Mitchel Bedford, 31 December 1952.
44 *C. G. Jung, Letters*, vol. 1, op. cit., p. 381, 16 September 1945.
45 ibid., letter of 4 October 1945.
46 See, for instance, *C. G. Jung, Letters*, vol. 1, op. cit., p. 448, n. 1 and p. 490, n. 2; see also the letter of 10 April 1954, pp. 169, 170.
47 See *C. G. Jung, Letters*, vol. 2, op. cit., letter of 10 April 1954, p. 171. Jung writes, 'Being an analyst, you know how little you can say, and sometimes it is quite enough when only the analyst knows.'
48 ibid., 31 December 1949, p. 539.
49 C. G. Jung, foreword to White's 'God and the unconscious', *CW* 11, para. 457, pp. 304, 305.

50 C. G. Jung, Letters, vol. 2, op. cit., 24 November 1953, pp. 133–8.
51 ibid., p. 138, in letter of 24 November 1953.
52 Though this issue is exercised a number of times in their correspondence, it is made explicit in 'Christ a symbol of the Self', CW 9ii, p. 61, n. 74.
53 C. G. Jung, Letters, vol. 2, op. cit., p. 134, n. 1, and p. 163, n. 1.
54 See ibid., the key letter of 10 April 1954, pp. 163f.
55 ibid. This is the thrust of the key letter, 24 November 1953, pp. 133–8.
56 See Murray Stein, Jung's Treatment of Christianity (Wilmette: Chiron, 1985), ch. 4, pp. 115f., 'The argument of the Trinity essay'. The basis of the argument in Jung's work is in his key essay on the trinity, 'Psychological approach to the Trinity', op. cit., pp. 109f. Cf. Stein's concluding ch. 5, 'On the patient's prospects', pp. 179f., where he argues that the unconscious currently seeks a myth which would surpass and contain Christianity as Christianity claims to have surpassed and yet contain previous dispensations.
57 See John P. Dourley, The Illness that We Are (Toronto: Inner City Books), ch. 5, 'Theopathology and Christopathology', pp. 51f.
58 C. G. Jung, Letters, vol. 2, op. cit., letter to Joseph F. Rychlak, 27 April 1959, p. 502. After a lengthy denial that Hegel had any conscious effect on his psychology Jung concludes, 'There is, of course, a remarkable coincidence between certain tenets of Hegelian philosophy and my findings concerning the collective unconscious.'
59 Currently in CW 11, pp. 355f.
60 C. G. Jung, Letters, vol. 2, op. cit., p. 238, n. 1. Here reference is made to a favourable review by White of the Answer to Job in Spring, no. 6 (1952).
61 C. G. Jung, Letters, vol. 2, op. cit., p. 238, n. 1.
62 ibid., p. 604, to the Mother Prioress of a contemplative order, 19 October 1960.
63 For an elaboration of the conception of fundamentalism used here see my article 'The challenge of Jung's psychology for the study of religion', Studies in Religion, 18(3) (1989), 311. 'In the field of religion this normative aspect of Jung's hermeneutic could lead to a new understanding of fundamentalism and of fundamentalist theology. Fundamentalism would be seen as that form of unconsciousness which is induced in the mind of the believer grasped and imprisoned by the archetypal power of the cherished myth. That theology could then be identified as fundamentalist in which the believing mind reflecting on its myth in the doing of theology remained unaware of the origin in the unconscious of both the myth itself and of the faith in the myth which prompts theological reflection upon it.' In the precise sense described in this passage Buber and White share, from the perspective of a Jungian hermeneutic, a common unconsciousness regarding the origin of their respective myths and of their faiths in them, and so engage in theological fundamentalism.
64 C. G. Jung, 'Psychological commentary on "The Tibetan Book of the Great Liberation"', op. cit., para. 787, p. 493.

Part IV
ISLAM

EDITOR'S PREFACE

The first and second *Shahadat* (Testimonies) of the faith in Islamic doctrine are *La ilaha illa 'Llah* ('There is no divinity outside the only divinity') and *Muhammadun Rasulu 'Llah* ('Muhammad is the Envoy of the Divinity'). These two levels or certitudes of reality represent certitude (Allah) and equilibrium (Muhammad), being and manifestation. In his book *Understanding Islam*, Frithjof Schuon states,

> If Islam merely sought to teach that there is only one God and not two or more, it would have no persuasive force. In fact it is characterized by persuasive ardour and this comes from the fact that at root it teaches the reality of the Absolute and the dependence of all things on the Absolute. Islam is the religion of the Absolute as Christianity is the religion of love and of miracle; but love and miracle also pertain to the Absolute and express nothing other than an attitude It assumes in relation to us.[1]

The uncompromising monotheism of Islam brings charges of polytheism to Christianity, with its belief in the Trinity. Muhammad, blessings and peace be upon Him, in the Holy Qur'ān 17:10 asserts: 'Praise belongs to God who has not taken to Him a son, and who has not any associate in the Kingdom.' The Christian concept of 'original sin' (inherited from Adam) is disagreed with by both Islamic and Judaic doctrines. Sin is not seen as hereditary, communal or transferable by Muslims or Jews. Sinners in Islam can seek God's forgiveness by submission to the law, theology and piety prescribed in the Holy Qur'ān. Islam gives Allah the divine prerogative of creation, preservation, revelation and predestination. The paradox of free will operating within predestination has concerned Muslim thinkers from early times. Today Muslims of orthodox faith maintain that *iktisah* (acquired action) explains that God foreordains human actions. Then human action, acquired from God, includes values, attributes and circumstances as identification with God's decreed actions. In this the Muslim tries to resign himself completely to the will of God.

God as absolute has an *essence* beyond human description, but devotional terms are assumed towards God. Ninety-nine *asma al-husna* (most beautiful names) of God are allowable. Solomon Nigosian sums this up in his book *Islam: The Way of Submission* in this way:

> The purpose of reciting the whole sequence of names is to make Muslims constantly aware of God's sovereignty over all affairs. It is not intended as an intellectual exercise or test. It reminds them that God is the *rab al-'alamin* (Lord of all spheres and realms). He exists from all eternity to all eternity. Everything comes into existence by His command. He alone grants life and death. Although He is regarded as the Majestic, the Terrible, and the Stern who punishes all offenders, yet He is also the Merciful, the Compassionate and the Forgiving towards penitents. Thus God is, in Islamic theology, 'nearer to man than his neck-vein', yet at no time revealed within the circumscribed orbit of human knowledge and understanding. He is unknowable, except insofar as He chooses to reveal Himself. Humans are called only to believe and to submit.[2]

In Jung's psychological concept of the God-image as present in the collective unconscious of every human being, we have an absolute psychological realization of an extraordinarily tight 'fit' with Islamic absolutism. The sense of a Reality-Totality in Jung's theory of unconscious archetypal potential of Self in persons agrees completely with Islamic metaphysics in principle, although not in empirical descriptive method. This, unfortunately, has not yet been comprehended by any of the leading Islamic writers, who have tended to be out of sympathy with Jung's archetypal model as it is expressed in empirical science, not in metaphysical assertion.

The images of Jesus in Islam and in Christianity vary widely and irrevocably. In these cursory notes I hope to clarify important points for the lay reader. Although the Holy Qur'ān repeatedly mentions Jesus as the Messiah (*almasih*), this merely indicates the Messiah to be a proper name for Jesus in general usage. The Holy Qur'ān (9:30) absolutely bars the New Testament's understanding of the word Messiah: 'the Christians say the Messiah is the son of God . . . . God confound them! How perverse they are!' Jesus is 'no more than a mortal whom We [Allah] favoured' (43:59).

Islamic tradition does believe Jesus to be the prophet proclaimed through God's word as a concrete fulfilment of the annunciation that Allah voiced at his birth. The Islamic belief is that Jesus is the son of Mary, not the son of Allah. The Holy Qur'ān states this thirty-three times, while in the Holy Bible it is stated only once (Mark 6:3). Jesus appears as blessed by Allah (19:31) and as elevated or favoured by God (3:45). Where his gifts as an intercessor are emphasized the Holy Qur'ān describes Jesus as 'strengthened with the holy spirit' (5:110). However, the Holy Qur'ān says this about all ordinary believers (58:22) and is not referring to the Holy Spirit of the Christian Trinity.

In denying the divinity of Jesus, Islam retains its understanding of a strict monotheism, as to Islam the Holy Trinity of Christian belief implies a belief in three Gods. It is subtly important to remember that the polemic of the Holy Qur'ān is not against Christ but more aimed at Christians who honour him as a God:

> People of the Book [Christian], do not transgress the bounds of your religion. Speak nothing but the truth about God. The Messiah, Jesus the son of Mary, was no more than God's apostle and His word which He cast to Mary; a spirit from Him. So believe in God and His apostles and do not say: 'Three'. Forbear, and it shall be better for you. God is but one God. God forbid that He should have a son! His is all that the heavens and the earth contain. God is the all-sufficient protector.
>
> (4:171)

Allah's omnipotence is seen as that of One who views Christ and Mary as very extraordinary people and apostles. The Holy Qur'ān only *indirectly* discards Jesus as God's son and therefore only indirectly discards his divinity while always proclaiming Jesus as a prophet (*nabi*: 19:30). This puts Jesus on a level with Noah, Abraham and Moses (33:7).

It is not clear how Muhammad, blessings and peace be upon Him, misunderstood the Christian teaching of the Trinity as not indicating a Oneness or Unity. It may be that the Marian cults of Christian sects in Abyssinia and Arabia were seen as separate religious services. In the contemporary world the doctrine of the Trinity for Christians does not allow a relinquishing of a belief in One God, but only the deepening of a monotheistic belief that reigns above its tripartite designation of *aspects* of God, namely Father, Son and Holy Ghost or Spirit.

For Muslims the Holy Qur'ān is the absolute word of Allah passed through the Angel Gabriel to Muhammad, blessings and peace be upon Him. At Jesus' death, the Holy Qur'ān does not ascribe to Jesus the redemption of mankind. In explicit directives (6:164) it is stated that no one should carry another's burden (sins) in the Holy Qur'ān.

As a prophet, Jesus is an apostle of Allah (4:157, 171) and 'only an apostle' (5:75). This enables Jesus to draw upon previous revelation, and the Holy Qur'ān praises Jesus, who is 'strengthened with the Holy Spirit' (5:110) for 'threatening the unbeliever and fractious with punishment' (43:65).

The Holy Qur'ān quotes Jesus as announcing the coming of Muhammad, blessings and peace be upon Him: 'And Jesus the son of Mary said to the Israelite: "I am sent forth to you from God to confirm the Torah already revealed, and to give news of an apostle that will come after me whose name is Ahmad"' (6:61). Ahmad is the meaning of the name Muhammad, the Praised One.

In *Islam and the Perennial Philosophy*, Frithjof Schuon clarifies the problem concerning the Trinity and the paradox of spiritual expression

151

for Islam in these words: 'Allah doeth what He will' and 'He is without associate.'[3]

These two key phrases explain the negation by Islam of the necessary succession of temporal phases, on the one hand, and of second or horizontal causes on the other. That is to say that for Muslim thought God alone is the cause, not natural law, and God creates each new thing anew at each instant, not because the existence of a tree – or its possibility or archetype – demands its continuance as a tree throughout time, but because 'God wills' ever anew that the thing existing should be a tree and nothing else, for motives known to Him alone; time is hence reversible, the physical causes being no more than apparent; the world is a chaos which only an incomprehensible and unforeseeable divine 'willing' holds together, not *a priori*, but by creative or causal acts forever renewed out of a perpetually resurgent nothingness. To believe the contrary would be – in the judgement of these thinkers – to deny that God 'doeth what He will' and to affirm that he has 'associates' who come to his aid and whom he cannot do without.

This doctrine, which is typically theological in its stubborn attachment to a single dimension of the Real – and in its consequent refusal to combine divergent but complementary aspects – is founded on a consideration of 'vertical radii' to the exclusion of 'concentric circles', to put it in geometrical terms: for this species of thought, the 'vertical' relationship precludes the 'horizontal' one, exactly as in trinitarian theology the divinity of the hypostasis precludes the non-hypostatic aspect of the Divinity, the Trinity being conceived of as the Absolute itself. In theology, aspects and points of view – objective and subjective situations – are pinned down in order to make them of spiritual value to a particular mental predisposition; only in pure metaphysics does the Real reveal various aspects – each variously divergent – and the intelligence change position to conform to these divergencies. Only metaphysics can reconcile the 'vertical' dimension of causality with the horizontal dimension, or the Absoluteness of the Divine Principle with its aspects of relativity.

In *The Essential Writings of Frithjof Schuon*, we are lifted above the divergence between Islamic and Christian dogmatic beliefs in these words:

St. Thomas Aquinas said that it was impossible to prove the Divine Being, *not because it was unclear*, but on the contrary, because of its 'excess of clarity'. Nothing is more foolish than the question as to whether the supra-sensory can be provided: for, on the one hand, one can prove everything to the one who is spiritually gifted and, on the other, the one who is not so gifted is blind to the best of proofs. Thought is not there in order to exhaust reality in words – if it could do this, it would itself be reality, a self-contradictory supposition – but its role can only consist in providing keys to Reality; the key is not Reality, nor can it wish to be so, but it is a way to it for those than can and will tread that way; and in the way there is already something of the end, just as in the effect there is something of the cause.[4]

I am indebted to the book of Josef Imbach, *Wem gehört Jesus? Seine Bedeutung für Juden, Christen und Moslems*,[5] in confirming references to the Holy Qur'ān and to all the published works of Frithjof Schuon in shaping these brief cursory ideas concerning Muslim and Christian differences of conception within monotheism.

NOTES

1 Frithjof Schuon, *Understanding Islam* (London: George Allen & Unwin, 1963), p. 18.
2 Solomon Nigosian, *Islam: The Way of Submission* (Wellingborough: Thorsons, 1987), p. 144.
3 Frithjof Schuon, *Islam and the Perennial Philosophy* (London: World of Islam Festival Publishing Company, 1976), pp. 75–6.
4 Seyyed Hossein Nasir (ed.), *The Essential Writings of Frithjof Schuon* (Amity, New York: Amity House, 1986), pp. 538–9.
5 Josef Imbach, *Wem gehört Jesus? Seine Bedeutung für Juden, Christen und Moslems* (Munich: Kosel Verlag, 1989).

11

THE ISLAMIC CONCEPT OF HUMAN PERFECTION*

William C. Chittick

The name 'Islam' refers to the religion and civilization based upon the
Qur'ān, a Scripture revealed to the Prophet Muhammad in the years AD
610–32. About one billion human beings are at least nominally Muslim, or
followers of the religion of Islam. The modern West, for a wide variety of
historical and cultural reasons, has usually been far less interested in the
religious dimension of Islamic civilization than in, for example, that of
Buddhism or Hinduism. Recent political events have brought Islam into
contemporary consciousness, but more as a demon to be feared than a
religion to be respected for its sophisticated understanding of the human
predicament.

Those few Westerners who have looked beyond the political situation of
the countries where Islam is dominant have usually devoted most of their
attention to Islamic legal and social teachings. They quickly discover that
Islam, like Judaism, is based upon a Revealed Law, called in Arabic the
Shari'a or wide road. Observance of this Law – which covers such domains
as ritual practices, marriage relationships, inheritance, diet and commerce –
is incumbent upon every Muslim. But western scholars have shown far less
interest in two other, more inward and hidden dimensions of the Islamic
religion, mainly because these have had few repercussions on the contemporary scene. Even in past centuries, when Islam was a healthy and
flourishing civilization, only a relatively small number of Muslims made
these dimensions their central concern.

The more hidden dimensions of Islam can be called 'intellectuality' and
'spirituality'. The first deals mainly with the conceptual understanding of
the human situation and the second with the practical means whereby a full
flowering of human potentialities can be achieved. They are important in
the present context because they provide clear descriptions of human
perfection and set down detailed guidelines for reaching it. If we want to
discover how Islam has understood the concept of perfection without

* This article appeared in the February 1991 issue and is reprinted with permission from *The
World & I*, a publication of The Washington Times Corporation, copyright © 1991.

reading our own theories into the Qur'ān or imposing alien categories on the beliefs and practices of traditional Muslims, we have to pose our question to the intellectual and spiritual traditions of Islam itself.

Muslims look back to the Qur'ān and the sayings of the Prophet Muhammad as the primary sources for everything authentically their own. These sources provide a number of teachings concerning the nature of reality, which are accepted by all Muslims and, as it were, instil the myth of Islam into the Muslim consciousness. The most succinct expression of these teachings is found in the Islamic testimony of faith: 'There is no god but God, and Muhammad is the Messenger of God.' All Muslims have faith in God and in the Qur'ān, the divine word brought by God's Messenger. More generally, according to the Qur'ānic formulation, Muslims believe in God, the angels, the Scriptures, the prophets, the Last Days and predestination. From these basic objects of faith, the later authorities derive three principles that form the core of all Islamic intellectuality: the declaration of God's unity (*tawhid*), prophecy, and eschatology, or the return to God. In theory all Muslims agree on these concepts, but in practice they have interpreted their meanings in a wide variety of ways. Naturally, the majority of Muslims have not been concerned with anything more than the basic catechism. The interpretation and exposition of the principles of faith have been left to those with an intellectual bent, and it is these learned classes of society who founded the various schools of thought in Islamic civilization.

Most of the vast literary output of the Islamic intellectual and spiritual traditions over the centuries has dealt directly or indirectly with the question of human perfection and the manner in which it can be achieved. Nothing is more central to the concerns of the religion. But the Islamic world-view differs profoundly from that of the modern West; before we can even begin to ask what constitutes a perfect human being a few general trends in Islamic thinking need to be brought out. Three of these are of particular interest: Islam's theocentric view of reality, its cosmological presuppositions, and its idea of hierarchy.

THE UNDERPINNINGS OF ISLAMIC THOUGHT

Islam begins with the statement 'There is no god but God', and all thinking that has an Islamic element to it takes this 'declaration of God's unity' – the first principle of faith – as its point of reference. In brief, God, the ultimate reality, is one, and everything other than God comes from God and is related to Him. No true understanding of anything is possible unless the object in view is defined in relationship to the divine. All things are centred on God.

Theocentrism gives Islamic cosmology its peculiar contours and differentiates it sharply from everything that goes by the same name in the modern

West. In the Islamic view, cosmology serves to describe the existential situation of human beings in relationship to God and the universe, thus allowing people to understand the purpose of life in the context of the world around them. Interestingly, those traditional Muslims who still study and understand Islamic cosmological teachings feel in no way threatened by contemporary cosmology or the findings of modern science, since these pertain only to one of the several worlds with which Islamic cosmology concerns itself.

Muslim thinkers look upon the world with a view towards the symbolic significance of phenomena. All things are – to use the Qur'ānic expression – signs (ayat) of God, pointing towards invisible realities lying beyond outward appearances. In contrast, modern cosmology deals strictly with what the Muslims call the visible realm (shahada), so it has nothing whatsoever to say about the most significant dimensions of the universe, the unseen (ghayb) realities that are hidden from ordinary sense perception. It might be suggested that modern physics deals largely with unseen phenomena, but this would be to ignore their inherent qualities as discussed in Islamic thought: everything unseen is alive and aware. The invisible realm is not found in the outward world of quantity and dispersion, but in the inward world of quality and unification. It lies in that dimension of reality that stands beyond the inanimate realm on a curve ascending from life, to consciousness, to enlightenment, and beyond.

The cosmos as a whole – often defined as 'everything other than God' – derives from God and manifests His signs. Its invisible and visible dimensions can be viewed either synchronistically or temporally. From the first point of view, the universe might be compared to a vast globe, whose surface is the sensory world and whose centre is God's own Spirit, to which all the angels and other invisible beings are subordinate.

Invisible things stand closer to ultimate reality than visible things. Hence they are more real. They manifest God's signs more intensely than the objects of sense perception. Since angels are made out of the light of self-awareness, they are direct manifestations of God, who is 'the light of the heavens and the earth' (Qur'ān 24:35). They possess the divine attributes – such as life, knowledge, will, power, speech, generosity and justice – with an intensity not found in the creatures of the lower worlds. At the opposite end of the ontological spectrum, inanimate objects fail to manifest any of these qualities, except in a dim and indirect fashion.

Those creatures that have both visible and invisible dimensions – such as plants, animals and humans – possess the divine qualities in various degrees of intensity. Hence, for example, the divine attribute of awareness is only weakly present in a plant (and even then in a rather metaphorical manner), while it shows itself clearly in the higher animals, and may reach intense degrees of actualization in human beings.

It is important to note the special place of human beings in this picture of the cosmos. The Qur'ān expresses the peculiar human situation in its own mythic language when it says that God created Adam by kneading a handful of clay and breathing into it from his own Spirit. Hence human beings represent a mixture of clay and spirit, darkness and light, ignorance and knowledge, activity and passivity. In fact, all the divine attributes are present in man, but they are obscured by those dimensions of existence that manifest a lack of the same divine attributes. The most invisible dimension of the human being reflects the divine light directly, while the bodily or visible dimension reflects it only dimly or not at all. Between the divine Spirit and the body stand many degrees of relatively invisible existence where the divine attributes manifest themselves in all sorts of mixtures and permutations. This whole intermediate domain of the human microcosm is often called the soul or imagination.

When we take the temporal dimension of existence into account in describing the Islamic cosmos, we perceive immediately that things have a beginning and an end. At present we find ourselves situated within a visible domain, but in the future we will enter into a realm known as the 'next world' that is now wholly invisible to us. There human beings will face reward and punishment for their activities in this world, or, as the intellectual tradition prefers to put it, they will possess modes of existence totally appropriate to their own true natures. Those who have followed a course in life that has strengthened their inner participation in the luminous ontological attributes of God will manifest openly and with great intensity the qualities of existence that they have acquired, such as life, knowledge, will, power, speech, generosity and justice. But those who have dispersed their spiritual light and failed to orientate their lives towards the divine unity will remain in a world of multiplicity and dispersion, far from the luminous qualities which bring about happiness and wholeness.

A final guiding idea of the Islamic world-view is hierarchy. The cosmos just described is ranked in degrees. Thus the angels, in respect to the intensity of the divine attributes manifest within them, stand at a higher level than other creatures, and the creatures whose bodily forms are present in the visible world – human beings, animals, plants and inanimate objects – are also ranked according to the same qualities. This ranking in degrees is especially important in the human domain, where no two individuals possess the same qualities and characteristics. Though all human beings are created by God and are commanded to serve Him, nevertheless, 'God charges no soul, save to its capacity' (Qur'ān 2:286). Each person has a unique capacity to receive God's charges. This capacity goes back to a number of factors. The intellectual tradition often describes these factors in terms of the degree to which a person acts as a mirror for the attributes of God, and this in turn is determined by a host of secondary causes related to factors such as heredity, physical constitution, individual aptitude and environment.

Perhaps the most important of the divine attributes that human beings manifest are knowledge and understanding. Certainly, as Franz Rosenthal has shown in *Knowledge Triumphant*, no religious tradition places more emphasis upon the importance of knowledge than Islam. The Qur'ān and the Islamic tradition recognize that no two people have the same degree of knowledge, since the divine attributes have been distributed unequally among creatures. 'God has preferred some of you over others in provision' (16:71). That is why the Qur'ān can say, 'Above everyone who knows is a knower' (12:76). The excellence of knowledge is stressed repeatedly. 'Are they equal', asks the Qur'ān, 'those who know and those who know not?' (39:9).

This recognition of differing human capacities has had profound practical repercussions throughout Islamic history. For example, it has meant that Islamic societies have never tried to coerce the masses into striving for the highest ideals of the religion. Rather, Islam has set down the path of perfection for those who have the interest and aptitude to undertake the arduous journey themselves. At the same time, there has never been any suggestion that knowledge has limits that might define an educated person. On the contrary, the quest for knowledge is never-ending, and those with the necessary preparedness must pay close attention to the advice which God addresses to the most perfect and knowledgeable (in the Islamic view) of all human beings, the Prophet Muhammad: 'Say: "My Lord, increase me in knowledge"' (Qur'ān 20:114).

THE ROAD TO PERFECTION

With these general presuppositions of Islamic thought, we can turn to the specific question of human perfection. Islam's three principles demand the interrelationship of all things in a manner that is intimately connected to human becoming. First, the declaration of divine unity demands that all things come from God and return to Him. Hence, human perfection needs to be understood as a harmonious relationship with all things established on the basis of the underlying unity of reality. The second principle of Islam – prophecy – sets down the path whereby perfection can be actualized. The Qur'ān and other Scriptures are God's guidance, sent to mankind in order to show the way to the perfect human state. On their own – that is, without divine guidance – human beings remain ignorant of the nature of their own selves, since human nature derives from the divine nature, and God in Himself is unknowable. He is only known to the extent He chooses to make Himself known. 'God knows what is before them and what is after them, but they comprehend nothing of His knowledge save such as He wills' (Qur'ān 2:255). God makes Himself known through the prophets, setting down the proper human relationship with Himself and the cosmos.

The third principle of Islam, eschatology, deals with the actual mode of the return to God. The prophets bring guidance in order that human beings might attain to perfection and realize ultimate happiness, which depends upon their being fully themselves – or fully human, which is the same thing. A foretaste of ultimate happiness may be found in this world to some degree, but for the most part it is stored away for the next world, where each individual's true nature will be made manifest.

The question of how the divine guidance revealed in the Qur'ān should be understood marks the point where the different perspectives within the religion begin to diverge. But until very recent times, all Muslims have agreed that the Prophet Muhammad embodies the divine guidance perfectly. To follow the Prophet is to follow God. In the words of the Qur'ān, 'Say (O Muhammad!) "If you love God, follow me, and God will love you"' (3:31). The codification of the prophetic model is known as the *Sunna*, the wont or custom of the Prophet.

The *Sunna* can be viewed on a number of levels. To begin with, it lays down the model for correct activity. The *Shari'a*, or Revealed Law, represents those elements of the *Sunna* that are incumbent upon all followers of the religion. Every believer must perform the five daily prayers, fast during the month of Ramadan, pay the alms tax, and so forth. These activities were legislated by the Qur'ān in general form, while the Prophet, through his specific activities during his lifetime, set down the details of how these rules and regulations must be put into practice. This is not to deny a certain divergence of views as to what the Prophet actually said and did. The five major 'schools of Law' codify the traditional range of this divergence.

One of the many concrete results of the Islamic conception of hierarchy has to do with the esoteric orientation of much of Islamic learning. The sciences were not concealed from people, but it was recognized that not everyone would be able to make full use of the available resources. Learning was viewed as one of the chief means by which the way to human perfection could be clarified and pursued. But few individuals have the interest or aptitude even to come to an understanding of the full reality of human perfection, much less to undertake the disciplined training that leads to it. At the same time it was recognized that not all seekers would attain to the same state of perfection, since each human being represents a unique capacity for knowing and understanding, and God expects from each person only 'to the extent of his capacity' (Qur'ān 2:286).

In broad outline, this hierarchical view of knowledge and learning meant that all Muslims were expected to follow the Revealed Law, since only a minimal understanding of Islamic teachings, accessible to any sane person, was necessary in order to put the basic injunctions of the Law into practice. Hence Islamic Law defines an adult simply as a person who has reached physical maturity in control of his or her rational faculties. All who become adults are required to observe the injunctions of the Law, whereas before adulthood they are not answerable to God for the Qur'ānic commandments.

From the point of view of the Revealed Law, 'human perfection' can mean no more than careful observance of the Qur'ānic legal injunctions and imitation of the Prophet's *Sunna*. The Law deals only with activity and does not ask about intentions or the moral and spiritual dimensions of the person who performs the activity. As far as the Law is concerned, the right and wrong ways of doing things are at issue, not love for God and neighbour or the moral attitudes and spiritual realization that are the inward complements of correct action.

Islam's intellectual and spiritual dimensions take the legalistic concept of adulthood as the first step in a process of realizing the fullness of humanity, a process that will occupy a person until the end of his or her life. The Prophet had intellectual, moral and spiritual qualities that are more central to human perfection than activity. Activity, after all, while answering to certain outward circumstances, must be grounded in those inward and unseen dimensions of the human being which precisely set human beings apart from other creatures. But most human beings are hardly aware that these invisible dimensions exist, and it does little good to tell them unless they have the capacity to understand. And then they must discover the practical significance of these dimensions for themselves.

The Law provides the framework within which the moral and spiritual attributes potentially present in human nature can be protected and nurtured, but it cannot guarantee their continued growth; nor will all people have the capacity to devote themselves to developing and strengthening these qualities. The Law stipulates the minimum requirements for living up to the divine standards for mankind and for fulfilling the goal of human existence. If the Law is observed 'to the extent of one's capacity', God will see to it that the person ends up in a happy state of existence after death. But capacities are diverse. What is sufficient for salvation for one person may be insufficient for another, since God demands 'to the extent of capacity'. People may observe the Law but nevertheless live below their capacities. In other words, they may have the aptitude for developing their intellectual and spiritual dimensions but fail to do so, being distracted by affairs of 'this world', that is, anything that turns them away from activity for God's sake and understanding with a view towards God.

THE GOAL OF HUMAN LIFE

Those dimensions of Islam dedicated to providing the guidelines for the development of the full possibilities of human nature came to be institutionalized in various forms. Many of these can be grouped under the name 'Sufism', while others can better be designated by names such as 'philosophy' or 'Shiite gnosis'. In general, these schools of thought and practice share certain teachings about human perfection, though they also differ on many points. Here we can suggest a few of the ideas that can be found in most of these approaches.

1   Human beings are God's vicegerents (*Khalifa*) or representatives in this world. The cosmos as a whole represents an infinitely vast display of the signs of God. All the divine attributes are reflected in unfathomable diversity through the myriad worlds and the creatures scattered therein. But human beings are microcosms. Just as the universe reflects all the divine attributes in an infinitely vast display, so also human beings reflect all the divine attributes in a concentrated unity. Man is the mirror image of both God and the cosmos. Since man finds all things within his own being and awareness, he is able to rule the outside world. He recognizes all things within himself, and, knowing them, is able to control them. This provides him with the necessary qualities to be God's vicegerent. But by the same token, he is responsible for the manner in which he interacts with the creatures under his power.

2   The model for attaining to human perfection, also called the 'vicegerency of God', is set down in the divine word, that is – in the Islamic sense – the Qur'ān. Without following the guidance set down in the Scriptures, human beings will fall short of their full humanity and fail to reach ultimate happiness, which depends upon being true to their own nature. The divine guidance revealed in the Qur'ān is embodied in the Prophet Muhammad. Thus his wife A'isha remarked that those who wanted to remember the Prophet should read the Qur'ān, since 'his character is the Qur'ān'. But emulating the Prophetic model does not mean simply conforming to the Prophet's outward activity: it demands assimilation of his moral and spiritual traits as well. In other words, the Qur'ān and the *Sunna* represent God's guidance for the full actualization of human perfection on every level, from the outward levels – those of activity and social concerns – to the more inward levels, such as knowledge, morality, love, spirituality and every human virtue.

3   All human attributes are in truth divine attributes. Just as the cosmos and everything within it are nothing but the signs of God, so also man and everything within him are God's signs. Every positive trait displayed by a human being derives from God. All human knowledge represents a dim reflection of the divine knowledge, just as all virtues – generosity, justice, patience, compassion, gratitude, love – are manifestations of divine qualities. A human being possesses nothing positive which he can claim as his own, since everything belongs to God. This holds for other creatures as well, but human beings, because of their peculiar synthetic configuration embracing all the divine attributes, are held responsible for their own choices and activities. The fact that most of them dwell in heedlessness (*ghafla*) of what they owe to God will not excuse them from being called to account. (This concept of heedlessness, it should be noted, is as close as Islam comes to the concept of original sin.)

4   People are profoundly mistaken when they identify anything positive as their own. This holds not only for outward possessions, which are on loan

from God, but also for inward possessions, such as the positive attributes and characteristics that go to make up their own specific identities. The only thing human beings may rightfully claim as their own are those attributes that define the distance that separates them from God. Existence and everything that goes along with it – such as life, knowledge, will and power – belong strictly to God, whilst non-existence and its concomitant qualities – such as ignorance, need, death and weakness – belong specifically to the creature.

5 Human beings on their own are nothing, but as representatives of God they are everything, since they manifest all the divine names and attributes. However, the fundamental nature of this 'everything' is itself indefinable, since it is modelled upon God, who is ultimately unknowable. Full human perfection involves the actualization of all the divine attributes present in the human configuration, and hence it involves entrance into indefinability. When human beings identify the positive contents of their persons with any specific attribute or definition, they have failed to grasp their own true nature. Perfection demands the shedding of all attributes and definitions, since these are limitations. Perfect human beings manifest all divine attributes, so they are defined by none of them. They employ each divine attribute in the appropriate circumstances, recognize all things for what they are, and interact with all creatures in accordance with the creatures' realities.

6 Though in theory any human being can achieve the fullness of human perfection, in practice only a tiny minority will reach it. Nevertheless, the majority will benefit from the human state if they observe the Law and strive to the extent of their own capacities, and they will benefit from all those who achieve human perfection, since it is the vicegerents who act as intermediaries between God and the cosmos, serving as channels for the divine replenishment that sustains the world.

7 The purpose of the social order is to provide a stable framework within which human perfection can be achieved, and all other goals are secondary. The more a society forgets the purpose of human existence, the further it moves from legitimacy. It is the duty of the learned to preserve to the fullest extent possible the teachings and practices of religion in order that the greatest number may attain ultimate happiness and the door to human perfection may always remain open.

The contemporary situation

The past two hundred years have witnessed profound changes in the social and political situation of Islamic countries. For a great variety of reasons, not the least being the pressures of western political intervention and cultural colonialism, the Islamic intellectual and spiritual traditions have become peripheral if not extraneous to the events taking place in the Islamic world. The traditional educational system was structured in a manner which encouraged a never-ending search for knowledge and established close personal relationships between teacher and student, or better, master and disciple. Education was viewed as a lifelong process of developing the human personality in the fullest sense, especially its moral and spiritual dimensions. The most gifted students were led by their innate desire for learning and a system that emphasized praxis as much as theory to a personal quest for *tawhid*, or the right relationship between themselves and God on the deepest levels of awareness and existence.

As a result of the vast changes that have overcome the Islamic world, the nature and goals of education have been radically altered. In order to meet the challenge of the western powers, the political authorities have exerted all their efforts towards training young people according to the norms of western education. The great desire for 'development' has pushed most traditional concerns into the background. Gifted students are attracted to fields like engineering and medicine, while only a small minority follow the traditional path of education. Even in former times, only a relatively small number of the learned had the proper qualifications and aspirations to come to an understanding of the nature of human perfection and enter into the path of achieving it. Now practically all the young are drawn into fields that yield quick and concrete results, and the possessors of the traditional learning are hard pressed to transmit even the basics of the *Shari'a*. It has become more and more difficult to find students prepared to receive the far more sophisticated intellectual and spiritual teachings.

It is true that not all intellectually gifted young Muslims study modern western disciplines, but even most of those who study their own traditions do so in accordance with western norms of learning. 'Critical editions of texts' are frequently published, but all too often the contents of these texts are not understood, and certainly not perceived as a programme for human life. To the extent that 'objectivity' in the western academic mode has become established, the living spiritual tradition has been strangled.

Education is no longer an end in itself, a road leading towards the personal actualization of the highest ideals of a religion. On the contrary, it has become a matter of developmental policy. National and social goals take precedence, and the very idea that there might be an individual road to human perfection is ridiculed. Islam is no longer a wide road aiming at bringing about ultimate happiness for the greatest number of people and human perfection of the gifted few, but an ideological tool, subservient to the goals of political factions. To the extent that any idea of human perfection is discussed in Islamic terms, it is now orientated towards social and political objectives – objectives inspired by those dominant currents in the modern world which see material gain as the highest good.

Some western observers tell us that the highly visible movements found in Islamic countries today represent a return to Islamic ideals. But those more sensitive to the intellectual and spiritual dimensions of Islam know that most of the visible activity represents an intensified destruction of Islamic values. The Islamic concept of human perfection has been banished from the stage, to be replaced by various types of outwardly orientated human endeavour borrowed from contemporary ideologies. The traditional Muslim quietly set out on a personal quest, while the modern zealot shouts slogans from the pulpits with the aim of reforming everyone but himself.

The modernizing movements in Islam have been especially concerned with reformulating the concept of human perfection. In order to 'bring Islam into the modern world', it was necessary to provide a new portrayal of the human ideal, the Prophet Muhammad. The Islamic tradition as a whole, and the spiritual tradition in particular, had always recognized the supra-mundane dimensions of the Prophet's personality, dimensions that follow from the very definition of human perfection. The early Muslim modernists, in their zeal to set up a goal for human life commensurate with the idea of 'reform' in the western mode, set out from the beginning to 'demythologize' the Prophet's person. The tradition had long interpreted the Qur'ānic verse 'Say: "I am only a human being like you"' (18:110) to be a denial of Christian-style incarnationism and a confirmation of the idea that all human beings are made on the divine model and should aspire to full perfection. For the modernists, this statement was taken to mean that the Prophet's aspirations went no higher than their own. When he was commanded to say, 'My Lord, increase me in knowledge', he had chemistry and engineering in mind. In short, by rejecting the sublime dimension of the Prophetic personality, the modernists were able to turn attention away from the possibility of perfection in any mode but that defined by social and political categories derived from the West.

More recently, certain modernist groups – including some perceived in the West as fundamentalist – have attempted to overthrow the Prophetic model completely, claiming that 'the Qur'ān is enough for us'. Without the guidance of the Prophet and the traditional authorities, Islam becomes a weapon that can be wielded by anyone for any purpose whatsoever. Human perfection is what you say it is, and your view is as good as anyone's.

In short, the entrance of Islam into the modern political scene has meant the eclipse of the highest and most sophisticated dimensions of the religion. An intellectual elite that had once, through teaching, writing and personal influence, been able to keep the goal of human spiritual perfection always in view has all but disappeared, to be replaced by ideologues with prescriptions for human betterment foreign to the tradition. The survival of Islam as a religion serving the highest human aspirations will depend largely upon the ability of Muslims to reclaim this eclipsed spiritual heritage.

REFERENCES

Danner, V. (1988) *The Islamic Tradition*, Warwick, N.Y.: Amity House.
Le Gai Eaton, Charles (1985) *Islam and the Destiny of Man*, Albany, N.Y.: State University of New York Press.
Murata, Sachiko (1992) *The Tao of Islam: A Sourcebook on Gender Relationships in Islamic Thought*, Albany, N.Y.: State University of New York Press.
Nasr, Seyyed Hossein (1975) *Islam and the Plight of Modern Man*, London: Longman.
Schuon, Frithjof (1963) *Understanding Islam*, London: George Allen & Unwin.

12

KHIDR IN THE OPUS OF JUNG: THE TEACHING OF SURRENDER

Nicholas Battye

The opus is a life, death, and rebirth mystery.

(Jung 1945, *CW* 13: 459)

The opus consists of three parts: insight, endurance, and action. Psychology is needed only in the first part, but in the second and third parts moral strength plays the predominant role.

(Jung 1945, *JL*: 375)

As an old man, C. G. Jung (1875–1961) professed: 'I am grateful to the particular genius – *vultu mutabilis, albus et ater* ("Of changeful countenance, both white and black") – that took it upon itself to weave the patterns of my fate, that he included the experience of Africa and its glory.'[1]

Jung (1952) remembers: 'When I was in Africa (1925–26) the headman of my safari, a Mohammedan Somali, told me what his Sheikh (an honorific which means "old man") had taught him about Khidr. He said: "He can appear to thee like light without flame and smoke, or like a man in the street, or like a blade of grass."'[2] Elsewhere Jung (1930) said:

> Everything that we reject as mere fantasy because it comes from the unconscious is of extraordinary importance for the primitive, perhaps more important than the evidence of his senses. He values the products of the unconscious – dreams, visions, fantasies, and so on – quite differently from us. His dreams are an extremely important source of information, and the fact that he has dreamt something is just as significant for him as what happens in reality, and sometimes very much more significant. My Somali boys, those of them that could read, had their Arabic dream books with them as their only reading matter on the journey. Ibrahim assiduously instructed me in what I ought to do if I dreamt of al Khidr, the Verdant One, for that was the first angel of Allah, who sometimes appeared in dreams.[3]

But , of his Somali porters, Jung (1959) says: 'If they were in doubt about an interpretation, they would actually come to me for advice. They termed

166

me a "man of the Book" because of my knowledge of the Koran. To their minds, I was a disguised Mohammedan."[4] Another time Jung (1939) told the story of his African safari he says simply that he was regarded as Muslim.[5]

The first mention of Khidr in Jung's writings is to be found in *Psychology of the Unconscious* (1912),[6] and though Jung makes frequent mention of Khidr thereafter, his most extensive treatment of the enigmatic prophet is to be found in *Concerning Rebirth* (1939),[7] Jung's exegesis of 'The cave' (*al-Kahf*), Surah 18 of the Qur'ān. The relevant verses Jung quotes in both works.[8] This is a summary of them.

Moses sets out on a journey with his servant Joshua ben Nun, in search of the place where the two seas meet. They stop at the place, without recognizing it, to rest. At their next stopping place, Moses asks Joshua ben Nun to serve him the fish he was carrying for their breakfast. Joshua ben Nun tells Moses he put the fish on a rock at their last stopping place, where, in a moment of forgetfulness inspired by the devil, the fish was returned to life, leapt into the stream, and swam to the sea. Moses then knows that rock to be the place where the two seas meet, and the two men make their way back to it. There they find a stranger, a man simply described in the Qur'ān by Allah as 'one of Our servants, whom We had endowed with Our Grace and Our Wisdom'. Moses asks Khidr to teach him Allah's grace and wisdom, but Khidr tells Moses he does not have the patience to experience things he does not understand. Moses denies this. Khidr acquiesces, and permits Moses to follow him on the sole condition he asks no questions. Khidr then does three things forbidden by the Law, and each time he does so Moses loses his patience and questions Khidr. The first two times he is questioned, Khidr merely silences Moses by reminding him of his promise; but when questioned the third time Khidr explains to Moses the grace and wisdom of his three crimes, and then dismisses Moses from his service. Moses thus proves Allah's opening remark, 'man is the most disputatious of things'.[9]

In *Concerning Rebirth* (1939), Jung comments:

> Khidr may well be a symbol of the self. . . . Moses accepts him as a higher consciousness and looks up to him for instruction. Then follow those incomprehensible deeds which show how ego-consciousness reacts to the superior guidance of the self through the twists and turns of fate. To the initiate who is capable of transformation it is a comforting tale; to the obedient believer, an exhortation not to murmur against Allah's incomprehensible omnipotence. Khidr symbolizes not only the higher wisdom but also a way of acting which is in accord with this wisdom and transcends reason.[10]

But, if Moses symbolizes the ego and Khidr the Self, Joshua ben Nun symbolizes the shadow. Jung explains that *ben Nun* means 'son of the Fish', and that thus the forgotten fish is 'the father of the shadow'.[11] Moreover, 'it is neither Moses nor Joshua who is transformed, but the forgotten fish. Where the fish disappears, there is the birthplace of Khidr.'[12]

Khidr is a protean figure, capable of appearing in any guise, as anything, but is usually paired with Elijah if not identified with him. The two prophets are imagined to sit beside the well of life or wander the earth, oases appearing wherever they stop to rest. Each prophet is known as the Stranger, and the two strangers are said to meet each year on the two days of sacrifice, in Jerusalem after the fast (*ramadan*), and in Mecca after the pilgrimage (*hajj*). Through his experience of Africa, his own wandering across north Africa in 1920 and through east Africa in 1925–6, where Jung was a stranger in a strange land, his genius or self may be identified with Khidr, the Stranger. But for Jung (1939), archetypes 'always remain strangers in the world of consciousness, unwelcome intruders saturating the atmosphere with uncanny forebodings or even the fear of madness'.[13]

Jung's only reference for his exegesis of Surah 18 is Karl Vollers' *Chidher* (1909),[14] which suggests Jung first met Khidr when he began his reading on 'archaeology or rather mythology' in 1909,[15] the same year Sigmund Freud (1856–1939) announced himself to Jung as *'the old man'*.[16] The year 1909 was also the year Jung saw himself freed from Freud's 'paternal authority',[17] or 'paternal dignity', as Freud corrected the phrase,[18] as it was the year Jung wrote *Significance of the Father in the Destiny of the Individual*, or *Father Destiny*, as Freud abbreviated the title.[19] Jung's essay ends with the same reference to the genius – *vultu mutabilis, albus et ater* – 'the demon who shapes our fate'.[20] In that essay Jung felt himself 'obliged to say that *in essence our life's fate is identical with the fate of our sexuality'*,[21] as in his experience 'it is usually the father who is the decisive and dangerous object of the child's fantasy'.[22] Two years before, after his first meeting with Freud in Vienna, Jung had written the old man: 'I dreamt that I saw you walking beside me a *very, very frail old man*. . . . The dream sets my mind at rest about your – dangerousness!'[23] Khidr appears as an old man, but as a man who has never suffered the frailty of age, and his changeful countenance, though both white and black, is always that of youth. In commenting on the dream of a man whose father led him to the *aqua nostra non vulgi*, the 'special water' of alchemy, Jung (1935) says that in the dreams of modern man the personal father appears instead of the archetypal wise old man.[24] Perhaps this was the service Freud performed for Jung as a substitute father, evoking in him the archetype of the wise old man, of Khidr.

We do know Jung's personal father, Johann Paul Achilles Jung (1842–96), performed that role in his son's dreams, especially in that of early 1948 known by the setting of its last part, the council hall (*divan-i-kaas*) of Akbar the Great (1542–1605), a Mogul Sultan who promoted a personal religion similar in its universality to analytical psychology.[25] In Jung's dreams his father is often featured with fish, and this dream is no exception. It opens in his father's study, where his father interprets some verses from a *Bible* 'bound in shiny fishskin'.[26] Jung fails to understand his father's interpretation though he knows it to be intelligent and learned, and so, as so often happens in dreams, Jung is then shown rather than told his father's meaning. Jung's father takes him into the council hall, the same as Jung saw on his visit to India in 1937–8, and then:

> In the dream I suddenly saw that from the centre a steep flight of stairs ascended to a spot high up on the wall – which no longer corresponded to reality. At the top of the stairs was a small door, and my father said, 'Now I will lead you into the highest presence.' Then he knelt down and touched his forehead to the floor. I imitated him, likewise kneeling, with great emotion. For some reason I could not bring my forehead quite down to the floor – there was perhaps a millimetre to spare. But at least I had made the gesture with him. Suddenly I knew – perhaps my father had told me – that the upper door led to a solitary chamber where lived Uriah, King David's general, whom David had shamefully betrayed for the sake of his wife Bathsheba, by commanding his soldiers to abandon Uriah in the face of the enemy.[27]

Jung could not prostrate himself in the direction of 'the guiltless victim'[28] because he was 'defiant and determined not to be a dumb fish'.[29] This was so in 1948, even though in 1939 Jung had written: 'Where the fish disappears, there is the birthplace of Khidr.'[30]

Jung's father 'graduated as an Orientalist, in Arabic',[31] having written his thesis 'On the Karaite Jephet: an Arabic interpretation of the Song of Songs', which in the German subtitle also reads as 'the highest poetry', a phrase Jung (1943) uses to describe the psychology of the transference.[32] It is possible that Jephet ben Eli (AD 915–20) was a Muslim convert to Judaism, having changed his name from Alm'allim abu Ali Hassan ben Ali Allevi Albacri. If so, he converted to a sect whose name is derived from the Hebrew root meaning 'to read', and specifically means 'readers of Law', that is, of the Torah and not the Talmud. This is just what Jung's father was doing in his dream. In refusing the oral tradition of the Talmud and insisting on a literal interpretation of the Torah, the Karaites were strict legists: 'an eye for an eye' meant 'an eye for an eye'.[33] And yet, when it came to reading the Song of Songs, 'Let him kiss me with the kisses of his mouth' did not mean 'Let him kiss me with the kisses of his mouth.'[34] The Karaites opposed the Rabbinates, and yet both agreed with Rabbi Akiva ben Joseph (c. AD 50–135) when he said: 'For in all the world there is nothing to equal the day on which the Song of Songs was given to Israel, for all the writings are Holy, but the Song of Songs is the Holy of Holies.' But he warned: 'He who, for the sake of entertainment, sings the Song as though it were a profane song, will have no place in the next world.'[35]

Jung could not have read Jephet's interpretation of the Song of Songs, for that was in Arabic and Jung could not read the language, even admitting he could not learn it because his father spoke it. Jung did, however, interpret the Song of Songs himself, making constant reference to it throughout his work on alchemy. Thus, Jung's 'defiant and determined' answer to his father's interpretation of the Torah may be summed up in a sentence, that of the alchemist George Ripley (1415–90): 'I'll be reborn, I know not by what love.'[36] Jung (1944) interpreted the *Cantilena Riplaei* ('Ripley's song') with regard to 'the motif of the king's birth in alchemy'.[37] Ripley called the king the *antiquus dierum* ('Ancient of Days'), which Jung translated into the *senex–puer* symbolism of analytical psychology: the king's birth in alchemy meant, as it did in Goethe's *Faust*, 'the transformation of the old man into a boy'.[38]

Jung's hostility to the Law finds expression in *Concerning Rebirth* (1939), when he explains why he does not interpret the story of the present life, the story of two men, one defiant and the other surrendered, a story so similar to that of Job. For Jung, its 'moral observations', its 'edifying comments are just what are needed by those who cannot be reborn themselves and have to be content with moral conduct, that is to say with adherence to the law. Very often behaviour prescribed by rule is a substitute for spiritual transformation.'[39] In his seminar on dream analysis, Jung (1929) was more outspoken: 'There is no development under the law of conventional morality.'[40]

The story of Khidr, that which follows the story of pseudo-Job with its 'conventional morality', is a story of 'spiritual transformation'. In that story Khidr holes a fishing boat, kills a youth, and rebuilds a wall without asking for payment. These are the three crimes Moses could not tolerate, and which Jung did not interpret in either *Psychology of the Unconscious* (1912) or *Concerning Rebirth* (1939). However, in interpreting the dream-image of an Arab boy who beats the dreamer with a rod and whom the dreamer then tries to bind with a rope, Jung (1929) comments:

> I am pretty much convinced that if this man were a real criminal, meant to commit murder, his unconscious would say, 'You must commit that murder, or you evade your own problem.' The East knows this, so the East can say, 'The perfect one will play the role of the king, beggar, criminal, or murderer, being aware of the Gods.' The East knows a murderer must commit a murder, or he is immoral. This means that the man who is meant to be a criminal, or murderer, must do it, or he does not fulfil the role given to him in this life.[41]

Though Jung is thinking of reincarnation as taught in Hinduism and Buddhism here, similar teaching is to be found in Islam: 'whomsoever God guides, he is rightly guided, and whomsoever He leads astray, thou wilt not find for him a protector to direct'.[42] This is said of the sleepers in the cave, a story identified with the Seven Sleepers of Ephesus of the Christian tradition, which is told in Surah 18 of the Qur'ān before that of the pseudo-Job. In Pickthall's translation, that used by Jung, the phrase 'a protector to direct' is translated 'a guiding friend', and in *Concerning Rebirth* (1939) Jung speaks of Khidr as both 'guide' and 'friend'.[43]

What Jung says about Freud and religion is even more provocative, for it makes of his substitute father, a Jew, a Muslim convert. Jung (1957) thought any serious attempt to understand Freud 'would carry us beyond Jewish orthodoxy into the subterranean workings of Hasidism (e.g., the sects of Sabbatai Zwi), and then into the intricacies of the Kabbalah, which still remains unexplored psychologically'.[44] Sabbatai Zwi or Zevi (1625–76) of Anatolia claimed to be the Messiah, but was forced to convert to Islam in 1666 to save his life. Jung would have been familiar with S. Hurwitz's essay on Sabbati Zwi published in 1955, if not with G. Scholem's essay on him published in 1957, the same year Jung made his comment. Both Hurwitz and Scholem present Sabbatai Zwi as manic-depressive and antinomian. The manic-depression is betrayed by Sabbatai Zwi's game of hide-and-seek with God, while his antinomianism is made possible by his identification with God. Sabbatai Zwi spoke of either God or himself as 'Him who allows the forbidden'.[45] For Jung, Freud played a similar role, allowing the forbidden.

Jung himself could easily have identified with Nathan of Gaza (c. 1643–80), a Kabbalist who had married the daughter of a wealthy merchant. It was Nathan who, after two visions of Elijah, persuaded Sabbatai Zwi he was the Messiah, and then acted as his prophet. Nathan's Kabbala was that of Isaac ben Solomon Luria (1534–72), rather than that of Moses Cordovero (1522–70). Cordovero's thesis 'No evil descends from heaven' was that of Jewish mysticism up to the sixteenth century, while Luria's thesis that it does, Jung's thesis in *Answer to Job* (1952), was that of Jewish mysticism from the seventeenth century.[46] Nathan adapted with great ingenuity his prophetic writings about the Messiah to absorb first Sabbati Zwi's conversion in Constantinople, then his exile to Albania, and finally his death. Nathan, however, never could do what Sabbatai Zwi permitted himself: for example, take the Torah in his arms and sing a Spanish love-song.[47] Similarly Jung's interpretations of the Song of Songs always heed the warning of Rabbi Akiva: a kiss is not a kiss. At its best a kiss is 'the highest poetry', and at its worst a 'provocative stimulus word'.[48]

The followers of Sabbatai Zwi who converted to Islam are known as the *dönme*, and since the seventeenth century have had close connections with the Sufi orders and used their poetry in their own meetings.[49] Freud's close connection with Islam is more obvious than Jung's reference to Sabbatai Zwi and the history of the *dönme* would suggest. In *The Psychopathology of Everyday Life* (1901), Freud writes of 'the customs of the Turks living in Bosnia and Herzegovina' in his analysis of why he forgot the name of a painter in a conversation with a stranger when on holiday there in 1898:

171

These Turks place a higher value on sexual enjoyment than on anything else, and in the event of sexual disorders they are plunged in a despair which contrasts strangely with their resignation towards the threat of death. One of my colleague's patients once said to him: '*Herr*, you must know that if *that* comes to an end then life is of no value!' I suppressed my account of this characteristic trait, since I did not want to allude to the delicate topic in a conversation with a stranger. But I did more: I also diverted my attention from pursuing thoughts which might have arisen in my mind from the topic of 'death and sexuality'.

Freud did so, because 'A patient over whom I had taken a great deal of trouble had put an end to his life on account of an incurable sexual disorder.'[50] Freud's anecdote may stand as a summary of psychoanalysis, and in its telling Freud identifies 'the topic of death and sexuality' as 'the repressed topic' for the European, whether Jewish or Christian.

Jung (1958–9) himself thought 'the modern psychology of the unconscious . . . had been inaugurated by Freud, who had introduced along with it the classical Gnostic motifs of sexuality and the wicked paternal authority'.[51] Those Gnostic motifs are often encountered in 'dream wanderings' as a meeting with 'an old man who is accompanied by a young girl. . . . Thus, according to Gnostic tradition, Simon Magus went about with a young girl whom he had picked up in a brothel. Her name was Helen, and she was regarded as the reincarnation of the Trojan Helen.'[52] Sabbatai Zwi is another example, for his third marriage was to a virgin-whore called Sarah, as a projected fourth marriage was to be with Rebecca, the resurrected 13-year-old daughter of Moses. Jung associates his example of the Gnostic couple with Elijah and Salome who appeared to him in a series of dreams in 1913–14.[53] Jung dismisses the possibility that his father, 'a clergyman', may have evoked the religious imagery. Rather: 'Salome is an anima figure. She is blind because she does not see the meaning of things. Elijah is the figure of the wise old prophet and represents the factor of intelligence and knowledge; Salome, the erotic element.'[54] In a previous interpretation of the dreams, Jung (1925) said simply, 'Salome is the anima and Elijah the wise old man'.[55]

What is repressed for the European is more than death and sexuality, more than gnosis, but surrender (*islam*) itself; that is religion, for as it is said in the Qur'ān: 'There is only one religion and that is surrender.'[56] It is just this Jung could not quite do in the *divan-i-kaas* of Akbar the Great, or more precisely, it was his Muslim dream ego, which reflected the 'splendid ambition'[57] of Akbar 'the Great', *al-Akbar* in Arabic, that could not surrender. But what, or to whom?

In his 1948 dream it is David's adulterous love for Bathsheba which makes Uriah 'the innocent victim'.[58] I suggest that behind the figures of David and Bathsheba, as behind the figures of Elijah and Salome in Jung's 1913 dream, are those of Freud and Sabina Spielrein (1885–1941), who was taken from the son Jung by his substitute father. Jung (1953) himself provides the personal association when he writes: 'The "professor and his daughter" is a well-known modern image for the archetype of the old man and his daughter in gnosis: Bythos and Sophia.'[59] Moreover, in the same letter, Jung associates the 'professor' with Elijah when he interprets the dream-image of an eagle circling above a concentration camp. Jung (1952) writes of the eagle:

> It is *all-seeing*, spying out its prey from above with a telescopic eye which nothing escapes. Understandably enough, this invigilation is particularly disagreeable to the rationalistic and atheistic Jew as it reminds him of the *eyes of Yahweh*, which 'run to and fro through the whole earth' (mentioned in my *Job*!) and from which nothing remains hidden.[60]

In the Midrashim, it is the prophet Elijah 'who soars like an eagle over the earth and spies out the secrets of the human heart'.[61]

By October 1911 Freud was an all-seeing eye, spying into the secrets of Jung's heart; for it was then that Spielrein unexpectedly moved to Vienna and joined the Vienna Psychoanalytic Society, as it was then that Emma Jung (1882–1955) began writing in secret to Freud. By November 1911 Jung knew; for Freud had written Jung his criticism of Spielrein's 'On transformation', as Jung had discovered one of Freud's letters to his wife. At the same time, Jung was writing part 2 of *Psychology of the Unconscious* (1912), with its interpretation of the story of Khidr.

Freud's 'Psychoanalytic notes on a case of paranoia (dementia paranoides)', better known as Schreber's case, and whose *Memoirs* (1903) Jung brought to Freud's attention in *The Psychology of Dementia Praecox* (1907), was published in the *Jahrbuch* of August 1911. Schreber's case is Freud's answer to Jung's *Dementia*, as Jung wrote part 2 of *Psychology of the Unconscious* (1912) to answer Freud's *Schreber*.[62] Schreber's relationship with God is interpreted in terms of the father–son relationship. Freud writes of Schreber's 'reverent submission and mutinous insubordination',[63] as he does of Schreber's 'abject submission and deferred obedience'.[64] Such ambivalence describes Jung's relationship with Freud, even that which survived Freud's death. Jung's *Answer to Job* (1952) is anticipated in a single sentence of Schreber's: 'From this apparently unequal struggle between one weak man and God himself, I have emerged as the victor – though not without undergoing much bitter suffering and privation – because the order of things stands upon my side.'[65] Freud argues that Schreber is in the grip of his infantile sexuality, and it is this which explains his paranoid or schizophrenic relation to the father. Jung answered Freud by reinterpreting infantile sexuality, which for Freud is polymorphous perverse, in terms of the dwarf *cabiri*, of whom Khidr is one.[66] In 'Aspects of the libido', the first chapter of part 2, Jung writes: 'The phallus is this hero dwarf, who performs great deeds; he, this ugly god in homely form, who is the great doer of wonders, since he is the visible expression of the creative strength incarnate in man.'[67] Moreover, 'The dwarf form leads to the figure of the divine boy, the *puer eternus*';[68] while 'in the Mohammedan legend Moses and Joshua lose the fish, and in his place Chidher, the teacher of wisdom appears (like the boy Jesus in the Temple)'.[69]

If reading the galleys of Schreber's case in March 1911 prompted Jung to begin writing part 2, I suggest it was the submission of Spielrein's manuscript, 'Destruction as the cause of coming into being', in January 1912, which prompted Jung to write 'The sacrifice', its last chapter, the following month. The importance of Spielrein to Jung is obvious from his strategic quotation of Spielrein's dissertation, 'Concerning the psychological content of a case of schizophrenia (*dementia praecox*)', which he supervised for her medical studies and published at Freud's insistence in the August 1911 issue of the *Jahrbuch*: with Spielrein resident in Vienna, Jung claims her for the Zurich school.[70] What then, was so provocative about Spielrein's 'Destruction' that it forced Jung to 'sacrifice' his friendship with Freud?

In *Beyond the Pleasure Principle* (1920), Freud acknowledges Spielrein to have anticipated his theory of the death-instinct,[71] which Jung in his *Symbols of Transformation* (1952) says Freud misunderstood: 'In my opinion it is not so much a question of a death-instinct as of that "other" instinct (Goethe) which signifies spiritual life.'[72] This 'footnote' debate is well known,[73] but I suggest it is a screen for a more personal and vehement argument. Jung added not only the footnote to his 1950 revision of *Psychology of the Unconscious*, but also the accompanying paragraph. This paragraph, one of six new paragraphs on the Terrible Mother, Jung could only have written after reading the manuscript of Erich Neumann's *The Origins and History of Consciousness* (1949). What was to be overcome in 1912 was just the father, or 'instead of the father, it may be a fearful animal'.[74] In his rewriting of the 1912 text the 'fearful animal' became a 'magic animal', and, Jung added, the father 'can equally well be represented by a giant or a magician or a wicked tyrant'.[75]

In August 1912, Freud wrote to Spielrein with regard to her love for Jung: 'My wish is for you to be cured completely. . . . We had agreed that you would let me know before October 1, whether you still wanted to drive out the tyrant by psychoanalysis with me.'[76] It is Jung's addition of the 'tyrant' to his list of symbols for the father in his 1950 rewriting of the 1912 text, like Freud's description of Jung as a 'tyrant' in his 1912 letter, which provides the textual clue for what Freud and Spielrein as contributors to the *Jahrbuch* were telling Jung as its editor.

In her abstract of the second part of 'Destruction', Spielrein quotes without acknowledgment the Sufi Maulana Jalaluddin Rumi al-Balkhi (d. 1273): 'Where love rules the dark despot of the I dies.'[77] Freud quotes with acknowledgment the same lines from Rumi in Schreber's case. In Ruckert's translation, that used by Freud, the lines read: 'For when the flames of love arise, then Self, the gloomy tyrant dies.'[78] Though both Freud and Spielrein thought of Jung as a 'tyrant', the relationship of each to him was different. Freud quotes Rumi to support the assertion: 'Similarly, an individual's megalomania is never so vehemently suppressed as when he is in the grip of an overpowering love.'[79] Spielrein, by contrast, quotes Rumi to support the assertion: 'Then the image of one's psychology or physiology being altered under the impact of a strange, alien power – as in the sexual act – is a destruction or death image.' Spielrein's thesis is simple: love destroys as it transforms or 'resurrects' the lover's self-image: 'No change can happen without destruction of the old statues.'[80]

Spielrein's 'On transformation', read to the Vienna Psychoanalytic Society in November 1911, was rewritten to become 'Life and death in mythology', part 3 of her 'Destruction'. Since Freud had used Spielrein's paper to criticize Jung's use of mythology in December 1911, and, presumably, having read between the lines of Spielrein's 'Destruction' in January 1912, Jung was in March curious to learn if Freud had read Spielrein's manuscript.[81] He had not,[82] though Jung took his revenge in the editing of it, as he did in writing Freud his caveat criticism on April Fool's Day.[83] Freud, a master of understatement, wrote back that he did not mention Jung's criticism to Spielrein, though they 'discussed certain intimate matters',[84] presumably their wish 'to drive out the tyrant by psychoanalysis'. That was the last mention of Spielrein in the correspondence of the two men; she was introduced into it, anonymously, in Jung's first confidence in October 1906.[85] Then Jung was forced to abreact his experience of Spielrein in analysis, the experience that was to become the case Jung described in *The Freudian Theory of Hysteria* (1907).[86] Late in life, Jung (1955) called his defence of Freud his 'first great indiscretion'.[87]

In 1912 Jung was less sanguine, and it seems he is addressing Spielrein and Freud respectively when he writes:

> How many profligates are there who inwardly preserve a mawkish virtue and moral megalomania? Both categories of men turn out to be snobs when they come in contact with analytic psychology, because the moral man has imagined an objective and cheap verdict of sexuality and the unmoral man is entirely unaware of the vulgarity of his sexuality and of his incapacity for an unselfish love. One completely forgets that one can most miserably be carried away, not only by a vice, but also by a virtue. There is a fanatic orgiastic self-righteousness which is just as base and which entails just as much injustice and violence as a vice.[88]

Ostensibly this is a passage from a four-page diatribe against the Christian repression of sexuality, a diatribe edited from Jung's 1950 revision of the text, a diatribe which ends with reference to Khidr: 'Much is said of pious people who remain unshaken in their trust in God and wander unswervingly safe and blessed through the world. I have never seen this Chidher yet. It is probably a wish figure.'[89]

Part 2 of *Psychology of the Unconscious* was published in the *Jahrbuch* September 1912 by Jung, who as editor placed it immediately before Spielrein's 'Destruction', thus giving it a sort of priority. In November, having read part 2, Freud signed a letter to Jung, 'Your untransformed Freud'.[90] He had not been persuaded by Jung's argument, a transformation of the libido which meant in essence that resistance against sexuality, the 'purely sexual', to use Jung's phrase,[91] was overcome through religious ritual, through an indulgence. With reference to masturbation, Jung had written:

> The fact alone that something is mysterious means the same as something done in concealment; that which must remain secret, which one may not see nor do; also something which is surrounded by severe punishment of body and soul; therefore, presumably, *something forbidden* which has received a licence as a religious rite.[92]

Freud had already accused Jung in February 1912 of hiding behind a 'religious libidinal cloud', as in December Freud was rumoured to have said Jung's libido theory was 'the product of anal erotism'.[93] Though Jung thought the accusation unwarranted and the rumour nonsensical, there were warrant and sense in both. Spielrein's case, as abreacted to Freud in 1906 and as used to justify Freud's sexual theory in 1907, is noted for its anal erotism. In 'The unconscious origin of the hero', the chapter that follows 'The transformation of the libido', Jung devotes four pages to a discussion of anal imagery, a discussion which includes the sentence, 'The birth from the anus also reminds us of the motive of "throwing behind oneself"', a sentence evocative of Jung's later definition of the shadow as *synopados*, the Greek for 'He who follows behind'.[94] It is only after Jung throws behind himself the anal erotism which becomes his shadow, the anal erotism of Freud's *Notes upon a Case of Obsessional Neurosis* (1909), the case-history of the Ratman written at exactly the same time as Freud mediates between Jung and Spielrein in June–July 1909, that he, Jung, introduces the story of Khidr with the sentence: 'While the previous materials betrayed to us something of the infantile theory of creation, this phantasy opens up a vista into the dynamics of the unconscious creation of personality.'[95] In Freud's 'telescopic eye which nothing escapes', it is with this sentence Jung enters his 'religious libidinal cloud'.

According to Spielrein (1910), Jung had 'the drive to liberate himself from the paternal edicts through an unbelieving Jewess'.[96] That Jewess Jung saw first in his cousin Helene Preiswerk (1881–1911), the medium S.W. of his doctoral thesis, 'On the psychology and pathology of so-called occult phenomena' (1902), whose seances he attended in 1895–1900; then Freud's daughter Mathilde in 1907; before Spielrein herself was displaced by Toni Wolff (1881–1953) in 1911.[97] When Spielrein attempted to describe her relationship with Jung to Freud in 1909, she wrote that Jung was first 'my doctor, then he became my friend and finally my "poet", i.e., my beloved. Eventually he came to me and things went as they usually do with "poetry". He preached polygamy, his wife was supposed to have no objection, etc. etc.'[98] That to which Jung would not surrender was his Jewish anima, the 'talented psychopath' who told Jung his psychology was art, and to whom Jung would not listen.[99]

When Jung attempted to explain his relationship with Spielrein to Freud in 1909, Jung referred back to his first visit with Freud in Vienna in 1907, after which he and his wife Emma went to Budapest, Fiume and Abbazia, an Adriatic resort, for a holiday:

> my first visit to Vienna had a *very* long unconscious aftermath, first the compulsive infatuation in Abbazia, then the Jewess popped up in another form, in the shape of my patient. . . . To none of my patients have I extended so much friendship and from none have I reaped so much sorrow.[100]

For Jung (1941), Jewesses were '*pagan* in their eroticism' as they enjoyed 'heightened consciousness'.[101] In her second letter to Freud, Spielrein writes of Jung as being torn between two women, his wife Emma and herself. She suggests Jung may have to 'flee' to America or, since he calls her the Egyptian, to Africa![102]

When writing to Freud a few months before of the scandal caused by Spielrein in Zurich, Jung had written that 'before the bar of my rather too sensitive conscience I nevertheless don't feel clean'. 'But you know how it is', Jung demurs, 'the devil can use even the best of things for the fabrication of filth. Meanwhile I have learnt an unspeakable amount of marital wisdom, for until now I had a totally inadequate idea of my polygamous components despite all self-analysis.' Then, Jung analyses Ernest Jones, better known as Freud's biographer than the friend on to whom Jung projected his shadow:

> To be sure, he is very nervous about the emphasis placed on sexuality in our propaganda. . . . By nature he is not a prophet, nor a herald of truth, but a compromiser with occasional bendings of conscience that can put off his friends. Whether he is any worse than that I don't know but hardly think so, though the interior of Africa is better known to me than his sexuality.[103]

If the 'talented psychopath' of Jung's autobiography is Spielrein, then what she would have meant by art is different from what Jung thought she meant. Spielrein wrote of transformation as the sublimation of the sexual drive into collective imagery. The transformation took place in the unconscious, and was made possible by a regression of the ego. The sexual drive with which it was cathected could only be transformed in the interval between its death and rebirth. Thus, in his Black and Red Books, Jung had undertaken an 'aesthetic transformation', rather than the 'spiritual transformation' he imagined.[104]

Jung never agreed with what he called 'the insinuations of the anima',[105] but through them he came to see that in putting down all this material for analysis, 'I was in effect writing letters to the anima, that is, to a part of myself with a different viewpoint from my conscious one.'[106] In one of his last letters to Spielrein, and possibly to his anima, Jung (1919) wrote:

> The love of S. for J. made the latter aware of something he had previously only vaguely suspected, that is, of a power in the unconscious that shapes one's destiny, a power which later led him to things of the greatest importance. The relationship had to be 'sublimated' because otherwise it would have led him to delusion and madness (the concretization of the unconscious). Occasionally one must be unworthy, simply in order to be able to continue living.[107]

It was through the agency of the black snake that 'travelled' with Elijah and Salome that Jung (1913) was transformed into Aion, the Leontocephalus of the Mithraic mysteries,[108] a statue of which Jung reproduced as the frontispiece of *Aion* (1951). The snake had squeezed Jung's heart, and in 'the agony and the struggle', Salome regained her sight and Jung's head was turned into that of a lion. 'The lion ... is the symbol of *concupiscentia effrenata*, "frenzied desire"', says Jung (1950).[109]

In 1909 Jung 'fled' to America with old man Freud to talk of 'sexuality and the wicked paternal authority' a few months after his imbroglio with Spielrein reached a tentative denouement, though it was not till 1920, a few months after Jung wrote his last letter to Spielrein, that he 'fled' to North Africa, al-Maghreb, meaning 'the west' or 'the sunset' in Arabic. From the oasis of Sousse, Jung wrote Emma a long letter which begins: '*This Africa is incredible*'; it ends: 'This is all nothing but miserable stammering; I do not know what Africa is really saying to me, but it speaks.'[110] Within days of writing this letter Jung dreamt of an Arab prince, a dream of such significance he remembered it and reflected on it when writing about his travels for his autobiobraphy in 1959: in that dream the Arab had tried to kill Jung by pushing him under water, and he in turn forced the Arab, 'with a sort of paternal kindness and patience', to read a book he, Jung, had written.[111]

Muhammad is reported to have said, 'A true dream is a fortieth of revelation', and for Jung Khidr was the prophet of dreams.[112] He appeared in Jung's own, first as Elijah (1913–14), then as Philemon (1914), again as Elijah (1916–17), and then as the Arab (1920), as Mercurius (1942), and finally as the Old Man (1947).[113] Of the last dream, Jung (1947–48) wrote: 'The bed was very clean, white, and fresh and he was a most venerable looking, very old man with white locks and a long flowing white beard. He offered me graciously one half of the bed and I woke up when I was just slipping into it.'[114]

> While I stood before the bed of the Old Man, I thought and felt: *Indignus sum Domine* ('I am not worthy, Lord'). I know him very well: He was my 'guru' more than 30 years ago, a real ghostly guru – but that is a long and – I am afraid – exceedingly strange story. It has been since confirmed to me by an old Hindu. You see, something has taken me out of Europe and the Occident and has opened for me the gates of the East as well, so that I should understand something of the *human* mind.[115]

The 'ghostly guru' to which Jung refers is Philemon, of whom he says: 'Psychologically, Philemon represented superior insight. He was a mysterious figure to me. At times he seemed to me quite real, as if he were a living personality. I went walking up and down the garden with him, and to me he was what the Indians call a guru.'[116] Moreover, 'It was he who taught me psychic objectivity, the reality of the psyche. Through him the distinction was clarified between myself and the object of my thought that there is something in me which can say things that I do not know and do not intend, things which may even be directed against me.'[117] This, Jung thought, was the lesson the Arab taught him: 'The Arab's dusky complexion marks him as a "shadow", but not the personal shadow, rather an ethnic one associated not with my persona but with the totality of my personality, that is, with the self.' In short, the Arab was 'the shadow of the self'.[118]

In his 1928–30 seminar on dream analysis, Jung says:

> Everybody has his *synopados*, the one who follows with and after, the shadow, understood as the individual daimon. The very word I would have used – demon – would not have suggested anything mysterious and evil any more than divine. But divine did not have the connotation that we give to it. It was the daimon, something tremendous, intensive, powerful, neither good nor bad necessarily; it simply did not enter the category of good and evil, it was a power.

Jung identifies the *synopados* with the *genius* of Horace (65–8 BC), as he names Khidr such a figure.

The lines of Horace to which Jung referred he knew by heart:

> scit Genius, natale comes qui temperat astrum
> naturae deus humanae, mortalis in unum
> quodque caput, voltu mutabilis, albus et ater.

(Why so, the Genius alone knows – that companion who rules our star of birth, the god of human nature, though mortal for each single life, and changing in countenance, white or black.)[119]

Jung had already quoted these lines to end his essay on the father in 1909, and will quote them again when remembering his 1920 and 1925–6 travels to Africa. Jung will also quote Horace in *Answer to Job* (1952), but there the genius is neither the shadow nor the shadow of the Self, but the Self proper. Moreover, the confrontation with the shadow is not enough, for

> we also need the Wisdom that Job was seeking. But at that time she was still hidden in Yahweh, or rather, she was not yet remembered by him. That higher and 'complete' . . . man is begotten by the 'unknown' father and born from Wisdom, and it is he who, in the figure of the *puer aeternus* – 'vultu mutabilis, albus et ater' – represents our totality, which transcends consciousness. It was this boy into whom Faust had to change, abandoning his inflated one-sidedness which saw the devil only outside.[120]

In this passage Jung assimilates the Bythos and Sophia of gnosis to the Yahweh and Shekinah of Lurianic Kabbala, as he does to the wise old man and anima of analytical psychology.

Not only is the Jewish Elijah or the Greek Philemon the figure or *albus* of the Self, and the nameless Arab, presumably Muslim, the shadow or *ater* of the Self, but the shadow of the Self is to be distinguished from the Self, the Arabic Khidr or the *puer aeternus* of analytical psychology, which is *albus et ater*. Similarly, these archetypal shadows are to be distinguished from the personal, those of Johann Paul Achilles Jung or Freud, which mediate them. In Jung's opus these various shadows are confused.

Though Jung repeatedly names Khidr as an image of the Self, he says very little about Joshua ben Nun, the image of the personal shadow. In *Aion* (1951), Jung gives the etymology of the 'redemptory name' Joshua: the Hebrew *yeshua* means 'Yahweh is salvation'. Moreover, it is the Jewish name of the Christian Jesus, *Iesous* in Greek.[121] Jung does not mention, however, either in *Aion* (1951), *Concerning Rebirth* (1939) or *Psychology of the Unconscious* (1912), that Joshua ben Nun is the name of the Jewish and not only the Muslim Joshua.[122] Perhaps Jung does not, for at the beginning of that fateful year, January 1909, Freud wrote to Jung: 'We are certainly getting ahead; if I am Moses, then you are Joshua and will take possession of the promised land of psychiatry, which I shall only be able to glimpse from afar.'[123] Joshua ben Nun is the personal shadow in the story of Khidr, as Moses is the ego. Freud identified himself with Moses throughout his works, and thus Jung may be identified with Joshua ben Nun. This identification means that Jung's 'poetry' with Spielrein may be associated with Joshua's forgetting of the fish: it led to things of 'the greatest importance', the appearance of Khidr.

Jung's interpretation of Surah 18 in *Concerning Rebirth* (1939) focuses on the forgetting of the fish, but even so Jung makes no mention of the fact that the forgetting was prompted by the devil. In *Answer to Job* (1952), however,

Jung argues that salvation comes through the devil, the image of the archetypal shadow, that is, the shadow of the Self. The difference between the two arguments is the difference between the Book of Job and the Song of Songs, the first exemplifying the fear of God and the second the love of God. Job is not only smitten 'with sore boils from the sole of his foot unto his crown',[124] but he is asked by Yahweh, 'Have the gates of death been opened unto thee? or hast thou seen the doors of the shadow of death?'[125] In contrast, the Shulamite who authors the Song of Songs says of herself, 'I am sick of love',[126] and asks of her beloved, a goatherd, 'Set me a seal upon thine heart, as a seal upon thine arm: for love is strong as death; jealousy is cruel as the grave: the coals thereof are coals of fire, which hath a most vehement flame.'[127] Here again, we find the topic of psychoanalysis, death and sexuality, or the wicked paternal authority and sexuality, as Jung preferred to think of them. Jung discusses both the fear and the love of God in *Answer to Job* (1952),[128] though he imagines them in terms of the wise old man and anima of analytical psychology. Though Jung does not consider the Song of Songs a profane song, his imagery subordinates it to the Book of Job, and makes of it a father's daughter. Moreover, towards the end of *Aion* (1951), Jung makes this claim for his psychology of religion: 'The anima/animus stage is correlated with polytheism, the self with monotheism.'[129]

Both *Aion* (1951) and *Answer to Job* (1952) were written by Jung after he had finished writing most of his works on alchemy, works in which the Song of Songs is often quoted. Over the same years Jung was working on *Aion* (1951) and *Answer to Job* (1952), he revised *Concerning Rebirth* (1939) and *Psychology of the Unconscious* (1912), published in 1950 and 1951 respectively. There is no anima-figure in the story of Khidr, and Jung's return to it suggests a return to the father–son relationship, that of ego and shadow and Self. The theoretical development of Jung's psychology following his loss of Spielrein to the break with Freud, 1909–13, and his confrontation with the unconscious through such figures as Elijah and Salome, 1913–28, meant substituting the father–daughter relationship, that of the wise old man and anima, for that of father and son. *The Significance of the Father in the Destiny of the Individual* (1909) was written for Freud and psychoanalysis, as his interpretation of the story of Khidr in *Psychology of the Unconscious* (1912) was written against both. However, the father to which Jung returned in 1950–1 was not personal, but resolutely archetypal. In *Symbols of Transformation* (1951), the past has been rewritten.

Despite Jung's stressing of the anima, I suggest that Jung's opus assumes that 'salvation' comes through a double process: integration of the personal shadow into ego consciousness, and the individuation of the Self, which as an archetype cannot be integrated. It is the shadow of the Self which is the driving force behind this double process, returning to consciousness that which was repressed as a consequence of flights *from* and *to* the world, to use Freud's terms.[130] Though Jung's opus suggests as much, this double process is never expressed as neatly as it is in the story of Khidr. It is the devil, the shadow of the Self, who makes Joshua ben Nun, the personal shadow which in men is so often confused with their father, forget the fish, the self *in potentia* which is realized *in actu* in Khidr.

Jung's treatment of the Christ in *Aion* (1951), as the prefigurement of that incarnation in *Answer to Job* (1952), may be thought of as Jung's treatment of Joshua ben Nun. However, in Job we see a man as 'defiant and determined' as Jung, unlike the surrendered Joshua ben Nun. We may say Jung's personal shadow is an Arabist like his father and would have surrendered to the Arab in his dream of 1920; where it is Jung's dream ego in both that dream of 1920 and that of 1948 that refuses to surrender.[131] Jung's refusal in both dreams is little different from that of Moses with Khidr. Though the object of that resistance is very different, the shadow of the Self for each was opposite: Jung resisted the Jewish Law, as he resisted the death and sexuality of Freud's psychology, just as the Jews are said to resist Christian love, a spiritual rebirth *which means freedom from the Law*, death and sexuality.

Given Jung's humanism and idealism, as exemplified by his interest in the alchemy of Paracelsus (1493–1541) and the philosophy of Immanuel Kant (1724–1804) respectively, such a rebirth was only possible through a more modest incarnation than that taught by Christianity, the individuation of the Self into consciousness. If Jung's psychology approaches any Christology, it is that of docetism, the Christian heresy on which he comments in *Transformation Symbolism in the Mass* (1940–1), for example. There Jung interprets The Acts of John, in which John sees Jesus 'standing in the midst of the cave and illuminating it'.[132] The Jesus who talks with John, in a cave on the Mount of Olives, is at the same time being crucified at Golgotha. Henry Corbin (1903–1978) introduced his 1954 Eranos lecture *Divine Epiphany and Spiritual Birth in Ismailian Gnosis* with a discussion of a similar vision taken from the Acts of Peter. Corbin refers to Jung's interpretation of the Acts of John, and then states 'the Christology professed by the Koran' is 'expressly Docetic'.[133] Yet, in *Concerning Rebirth* (1939), Jung does not mention the denial of the incarnation, for the Muslim 'a monstrous word', which opens and closes Surah 18.[134]

The incarnation is often defined in words taken from the Gospel of John: 'the Word was made flesh'. St John 'beheld his glory . . . full of grace and truth'. Moreover, 'In him was life; and the life was the light of men. And the light shineth in darkness; and the darkness comprehended it not.'[135] St John's phrase 'full of grace and truth' is evocative of the grace and wisdom with which Khidr is attributed in the Qur'ān, as life and light are his attributes according to tradition. What is monstrous for the Muslim is that St John should speak of 'the glory as of the only begotten of the Father'.[136] Khidr is a servant, not a son. Both images are anthropomorphic, and are reconciled in a docetic theology that sees 'the flesh' of which St John speaks as a glorious body, a subtle body, an angel. Both Khidr and Christ are spoken of as angels of God, as each is in some sense the unique Angel. For Jung this means that both Khidr and Christ are images of the Self, as they are the life and light of nature, which he defines as spirit.

Jung also spoke of the Self as the *spiritus rector* in man. Thanking Corbin for his favourable review of *Answer to Job* (1952), Jung (1953) says, 'It was an extraordinary joy to me, and not only the rarest of experiences but even a unique experience, to be fully understood.'[137] Jung then confides to Corbin that the theologian Friedrich Schleiermacher (1768–1834), who converted and baptized Jung's grandfather, was just such a *spiritus rector*: 'The vast, esoteric, and individual spirit of Schleiermacher was a part of the intellectual atmosphere of my father's family. I never studied him, but unconsciously he was for me a *spiritus rector*.'[138] The theologian Lülmann spoke of Schleiermacher as a 'priest and prophet in one person and a king in the realm of the mind'; as Karl Barth (1886–1968) says he gave 'a liberating word, an answering word' to his generation, a word which inaugurated modern theology.[139] In essence, Schleiermacher substituted two words in the verse of St John already quoted with two words of his own, but that substitution made a world of difference: it turned theology upside down, inside out. Where St John says, 'the Word was made flesh, and dwelt *among us*', Schleiermacher's theology says, 'the Word was made flesh, and dwelt *within him*'. With Schleiermacher it was the self-consciousness of Jesus that became the subject of theology. Though Schleiermacher used St John as his authority, the modern theology he inaugurated neglected the Gnostic, possibly docetic fourth gospel in favour of the other three, in particular the second, that of St Mark, with its historical primacy. Modern theology sought for the moment of self-consciousness in the life of Jesus, and most theologians found that moment to be His baptism.

Jung (1912) condenses this theological history and gives it his own psychological twist in a single sentence: 'it happened that the death of Christ on the cross, which creates universal salvation, was understood as "baptism"; that is to say, as rebirth through the second mother, the mysterious tree of death'.[140] Moreover, for Jung, 'It was only in the power of the incest prohibition which created the self-conscious individual, who formerly had been thoughtlessly one with the tribe, and in this way alone did the idea of individual and final death become possible.'[141] It did so, because 'the libido which lies inactive in the incestuous bond repressed and in fear of the law can be led by sublimation through the symbol of baptism (birth from water) and of generation (spiritual birth) through the symbol of the descent of the Holy Ghost'.[142] For Jung, this descent is an ascent. Moses finds Khidr, 'wrapped in his mantle, sitting on the ground . . . on an island in the sea, or "in the wettest place on earth", that is, he was born from the maternal depths. Where the fish vanished Chidher, "the verdant one", was born as "son of the deep waters", his head veiled, a Cabir, a proclaimer of divine wisdom.'[143]

Jung associates the story of Dhulqarnein and Khidr, that which follows the story of Khidr and Moses in Surah 18, with that of Jesus 'baptized' or 'christened' by John. The Muslim commentators of the Qur'ān identify Dhulqarnein and Khidr with Alexander the Great and Aristotle, and thus Jung writes:

> Dhulqarnein led his friend Chidher to the 'source of life' in order to have him drink of immortality. Alexander also bathed in the stream of life and performed the ritual ablutions. . . . The analogous situation in the Christian legend is found in the scene by the Jordan where John leads Christ to the 'source of life'. Christ is there, the subordinate, John the superior, similar to Dhulqarnein and Chidher, or Chidher and Moses, also Elias.[144]

It was in March 1910 that Freud wrote to Jung: 'Just rest easy, dear son Alexander, I will leave you more to conquer than I myself have managed, all psychiatry and the approval of the civilized world, which regards me as a savage! That ought to lighten your heart.'[145] It was then that Freud followed Jung into the field of mythology, though he did not admit this to Jung till November 1911.[146] The importance of Surah 18 to Jung should now be obvious: just as the story of Khidr and Moses justifies Jung's relationship with Spielrein, that of Dhulqarnein and Khidr asserts that Jung is Freud's superior in the psychology of religion.

Let us now turn back to Jung's 1948 dream, which begins in the study of Johann Paul Achilles Jung and ends in the council hall of Akbar the Great, a dream in which Jung's father is his guide, and interpret it through the story of Khidr. Though comparative theology considers the Qur'ān to be the Muslim version of the incarnation, this comparison is misleading. Where Christianity is founded on a Christology which was defined in AD 325–451, Islam is founded on 'the science of the Balance' ('ilm al-Mizan), definitely so with the rise of shiism from AD 644. The law (shari'a) and the truth (haqiqa) of Muslim theology, terms which correspond to but do not equate with the flesh and the spirit respectively, are in the Balance.[147] Thus the Qur'ān speaks not only of the East and the West but of the two seas, law and truth, and thus of the two Easts and two Wests. Moreover, it speaks of a blessed tree, light on light, which is neither of the East nor the West.[148]

'Say: God is the Master of the East and the West. He guides whom He wishes on the right path'[149] was the epigraph of the first orientalist journal in Europe, Fundgruben des Orients (1809–18), founded by Josef von Hammer-Purgstall (1774–1856).[150] It is the angel Gabriel who tells Muhammad to 'say' just that to 'the fools' who question why God changed the direction of prayer (qibla) from Jerusalem to Mecca. The verse, of which von Hammer-Purgstall only quoted half, is the pivot of a long section which begins with the surrender of Abraham and his housing of the black stone (*ka'bah*) and ends with Muhammad urging all men to take that ancient house as their direction of prayer.[151]

Orientalism from its beginning regarded Islam as a curiosity to be studied, rather than a revelation to which they as Europeans surrendered, a call to prayer which they as Europeans needed to answer. Jung, who was called 'Father Abraham' as a schoolboy,[152] would have first heard the call to prayer (*adhan*) on his trip to north Africa in 1920, and then again in east Africa in 1925–6. What this meant to Jung in 1928–30, he expressed in interpreting the dreams of a European born in Africa. The man's twentieth dream is of a crocodile in an African hut, somewhere in upper Egypt. The hut is lit by lamps which the dreamer associates with mosques lit for the feast of sacrifice (*eid al-fittr*), the feast that ends the fast (*ramadan*), the very day Elijah and Khidr meet in Jerusalem: '*this house is a mosque*, a house of God', says Jung.[153] Speaking of the dreamer, Jung says:

> He was born among the Moslems. That is a very showy religion, and in Cairo and the coast towns one still sees very impressive sights, the afternoon prayer, for instance, when traffic stops, and long rows of kneeling people bow low to Mecca. Whole streets are filled with them. So it must have gone deep into him, particularly as his Christian education was so exceedingly pale and Protestant in comparison. The mosques are far more impressive than Christian churches, they are marvellous, as fine as the most beautiful Gothic cathedrals in the West. This religion has been misrepresented by prejudiced teachers; we have a funny idea of Islam through bad education. It is represented by our theologians as dry and empty, but there is tremendous life in it, particularly in Islamic mysticism, which is the secret backbone of Islam.[154]

Jung thought:

> To arrive again at a primordial religious phenomenon, men must return to a condition where that functioning is absolutely unprejudiced, where one cannot say that it is good or that it is evil, where one has to give up all bias as to the nature of religion; for as long as there is any kind of bias, there is no submission.

> My Somali friend in Africa gave me very good teaching in that respect. He belonged to a Mohammedan sect, and I asked him about Khidr, the god of that particular cult, about the ways in which he appears. He said: 'He may appear as an ordinary man, like myself or like that man there, but you know that he is Khidr, and then you must step right up to him, take both his hands and shake them, and say, "Peace be with thee", and he will say "Peace be with thee", and all your wishes will be granted. Or he may appear as a light, not the light

of a candle or a fire, but as a pure white light, and then you know this is Khidr.' Then, bending down, he picked up a blade of grass and said: 'Or he may appear like this.' There is no prejudice, there is supreme submission.[155]

The ritual prayer (*salat*) is the symbol of the Balance between the law and the truth, between the surrender and the presence that is Islam. In the simplest terms, to paraphrase Rumi, we stand in this world of the law, with its East and West; bow into the next, with its East and West; but prostrate into the highest presence, which is neither of the East nor the West. *Allahu Akbar*, 'Allah the most Great', are the first words the muezzin recites when he calls the prayer, as they are the first words said in the prayer itself. Both recitations are made standing, facing in the direction of the black stone, with hands touching the ears. In contrast, when the head touches the ground in prayer, *Subhana Rabbiya-l-a'la*, 'Glory to my Lord the most High', is quietly recited. It is in that gesture that the two seas meet, the forgotten fish is resurrected and Khidr, 'One of Our servants, whom We had endowed with Our Grace and Our Wisdom', appears.[156]

NOTES

Jung used J. M. Rodwell's translation of the Qur'ān, which was first published in 1861, and then republished in Everyman's Library in 1909. Rodwell's *Koran* attempts to put the suras in chronological order, and perhaps this is why N. J. Dawood's translation of 1956 was used by the editors of *CW*, for he attempted the same. Jung also consulted Marmaduke Pickthall's 1930 translation, *The Meaning of the Glorious Qur'ān*, whose numbering of the ayats is used here.

1 26 December 1954, *C. G. Jung Letters*, ed. Gerhard Adler in collaboration with Aniela Jaffe, trans. R. F. C. Hull (London: Routledge & Kegan Paul, 1973) (henceforth *JL*), 2: 201.

2 9 February 1952, *JL*2: 40.

3 19 January 1930, *The Collected Works of C. G. Jung*, ed. Herbert Read, Michael Fordham and Gerhard Adler (London: Routledge & Kegan Paul, 1959) (henceforth *CW*), 18: 1290.

4 Summer 1959 (MS), C. G. Jung, *Memories, Dreams, Reflections*, recorded and edited by Aniela Jaffe, trans. Richard and Clara Winston (London: Collins and Routledge & Kegan Paul, 1963) (henceforth *MDR*), 294.

5 August 1939, *CW*9i: 250–1.

6 September 1912, *Psychology of the Unconscious: A Study of the Transformations and Symbolisms of the Libido*, trans. Beatrice M. Hinkle (London: Kegan Paul, Trench, Trubner & Co., 1919) (henceforth *PU*), 119–24. The 1912 edition was revised in 1950 and republished as *Symbols of Transformation* in 1951. The two editions are effectively two different works.

7 August 1939, *CW*9i: 240–58. Jung's revised *Concerning Rebirth* was republished in 1950, the same year he revised *Psychology of the Unconscious*.

8 *The Koran Interpreted*, trans. A. J. Arberry (London: George Allen & Unwin, 1955) (henceforth *Q*), 18: 54–82; quoted September 1912, *PU*: 120; August 1939, *CW*9i: 243; September 1950 (MS), *CW*5: 282.

9 Q18: 54.

10 August 1939, *CW9i*: 247.
11 August 1939, *CW9i*: 244.
12 August 1939, *CW9i*: 248.
13 1939, *CW9i*: 517.
14 September 1912, *PU*: 121, n. 31; or September 1950 (MS), *CW5*: 285, n. 33. See Karl Vollers, 'Chidher', *Archiv für Religionswissenschaft* (Freiburg i.Br. 8), XII (1909), 234–84.
15 14 October 1909, *The Freud/Jung Letters: The Correspondence between Sigmund Freud and C. G. Jung* (Princeton: Princeton University Press, 1974) (henceforth *FJL*), 251.
16 7 July 1909, *FJL*: 239.
17 2 April 1909, *FJL*: 217.
18 6 April 1909, *FJL*: 218.
19 21 November 1909, *FJL*: 266.
20 March 1909, *CW4*: 744, n. 26, p. 302, n. 3.
21 March 1909, *CW4*: 738, n. 21.
22 March 1909, *CW4*: 744.
23 2 November 1907, *FJL*: 96. The three crosses, which Jung would have seen chalked by peasants on the inside of their outer doors, are apotropaic. Jung, however, refers to Freud's ' — sexuality'. See 1 January 1907, *FJL*: 19, n. 7.
24 August 1935, *CW12*: 159.
25 January 1959 (MS), *MDR*: 244–7.
26 January 1959 (MS), *MDR*: 244.
27 January 1959 (MS), *MDR*: 245–6.
28 January 1959 (MS), *MDR*: 246.
29 January 1959 (MS), *MDR*: 247.
30 August 1939, *CW9i*: 248.
31 29 September 1953, *JL2*: 129.
32 1943 (MS), *CW16*: 460.
33 Leviticus 24: 20. Authorized Version. All the biblical quotations below are from the AV.
34 Song of Solomon 1: 2.
35 Paul Johnson, *A History of the Jews* (London: Weidenfeld & Nicolson, 1987), 90.
36 November 1944 (MS), *CW14*: 380.
37 20 November 1944, *JL1*: 354.
38 November 1944 (MS), *CW14*: 463.
39 August 1939, *CW9i*: 243.
40 22 May 1929, *SP1*: 214.
41 19 June 1929, *SP1*: 279–80.
42 Q18: 17.
43 August 1939, *CW9i*: 238.
44 April 1957, *JL2*: 359.
45 Johnson, *A History of the Jews*, 268, 270; Aharon Wiener, *The Prophet Elijah in the Development of Judaism: A Depth-Psychological Study* (London: Routledge & Kegan Paul, 1978), 113.
46 Joseph Dan, '"No Evil Descends from Heaven": Sixteenth Century Jewish Concepts of Evil', in *Jewish Thoughts in the Sixteenth-Century*, ed. Bernard Dov Cooperman (Cambridge, Mass.: Harvard University Press, 1983), 89–105.
47 Johnson, *A History of the Jews*, 270.
48 1904, *CW2*: 345.
49 Annemarie Schimmel, *Mystical Dimensions of Islam* (Chapel Hill, N.C.: University of North Carolina Press, 1975), 337.

50 July 1901, *The Standard Edition of the Complete Psychological Works of Sigmund Freud*, ed. James Strachey (London: Hogarth Press) (henceforth *SE*), 6: 3–4.
51 January 1959 (MS), *MDR*: 227.
52 January 1959 (MS), *MDR*: 206.
53 11 May 1925, *SP3*: 63–4; 1–8 June 1925, *SP3*: 88–99.
54 January 1959 (MS), *MDR*: 206.
55 8 June 1925, *SP3*: 92.
56 Q3: 19.
57 Spring 1939, *CW*10: 983.
58 2 Samuel 11: 1–27.
59 18 November 1953, *JL2*: 132. Bythos means 'abyss' and Sophia 'wisdom'.
60 8 December 1952, *JL2*: 100. Jung quotes Zechariah 4: 10.
61 18 November 1953, *JL2*: 132. The dream and its interpretation were added to the 1954 edition of *The Philosophical Tree*, *CW*13: 463–81.
62 19 March 1911, *FJL*: 407; 11 December 1911, *FJL*: 471.
63 August 1911, *SE*12: 52.
64 August 1911, *SE*12: 55.
65 August 1911, *SE*12: 19.
66 September 1912, *PU*: 73 and 123.
67 September 1912, *PU*: 72.
68 September 1912, *PU*: 74.
69 September 1912, *PU*: 208.
70 September 1912, *PU*: 85; edited from Jung's 1950 revision, *CW*5: 200.
71 September 1920, *SE*18: 55, n. 1.
72 September 1950 (MS), *CW*5: 504, n. 38.
73 See John Kerr, 'Beyond the Pleasure Principle and Back Again: Freud, Jung and Sabina Spielrein', in *Freud: Appraisals and Reappraisals*, ed. Paul E. Stepansky (Hillsdale, NJ: The Analytic Press, 1986), 3–79.
74 September 1912, *PU*: 200.
75 September 1950 (MS), *CW*5: 504.
76 August 1912, Aldo Corotenuto, *A Secret Symmetry: Sabina Spielrein between Jung and Freud*, trans. Arno Pomerans, John Shepley and Krishna Winston (London: Routledge & Kegan Paul, 1984) (henceforth *SS*), 116–17.
77 Kerr, op. cit., 27.
78 August 1911, *SE*12: 65.
79 August 1911, *SE*12: 65.
80 Kerr, op. cit., 28.
81 10 March 1912, *FJL*: 494.
82 21 March 1912, *FJL*: 494.
83 1 April 1912, *FJL*: 498.
84 21 April 1912, *FJL*: 499.
85 23 October 1906, *FJL*: 7.
86 4 September 1907, *CW*4: 53–8.
87 2 April 1955, *JL2*: 242.
88 September 1912, *PU*: 142; edited from Jung's 1950 revision, *CW*5: 336–9.
89 September 1912, *PU*: 144.
90 29 November 1912, *FJL*: 524–5.
91 September 1912, *PU*: 103; edited from Jung's 1950 revision, *CW*5: 248.
92 September 1912, *PU*: 91.
93 18 February 1912, *FJL*: 485.
94 September 1912, *PU*: 118.

95 September 1912, *PU*: 119.
96 19 October 1910, *SS*: 30.
97 20 June 1909, *SS*: 104–7; 4 June 1909, *FJL*: 229.
98 11 June 1909, *SS*: 93.
99 January 1959 (MS), *MDR*: 210–12.
100 4 June 1909, *FJL*: 229.
101 31 December 1941, *JL*1: 308.
102 12 June 1909, *SS*: 95.
103 7 March 1909, *FJL*: 207–8.
104 Cf. September 1912, *PU*: 85–6 or September 1950 (MS), *CW*5: 201–2, where Jung conforms Spielrein's theory to his own.
105 January 1959 (MS), *MDR*: 212.
106 January 1959 (MS), *MDR*: 211.
107 1 September 1919, *SS*: 190. Jung's last letter to Spielrein is dated 30 October 1919, *SS*: 181.
108 8 June 1925, *SP*3: 95–9.
109 September 1950 (MS), *CW*5: 425.
110 15 March 1920 (MS), *MDR*: 403–4.
111 Summer 1959 (MS), *MDR*: 270–4. The struggle between Jung and the Arab takes place under water.
112 19 January 1930, *CW*18: 1290; August 1939, *CW*9i: 238, 250–1; 9 February 1952, *JL*2: 40; Summer 1959 (MS), *MDR*: 294.
113 11 May 1925, *SP*3: 63–4; 1–8 June 1925, *SP*3: 88–99; 20 July 1942, *JL*1: 319; 19 December 1947, *JL*1: 481; 30 January 1948, *JL*1: 491; January 1959 (MS), *MDR*: 205–9, 337.
114 19 December 1947, *JL*1: 481.
115 30 January 1948, *JL*1: 491.
116 January 1959 (MS), *MDR*: 208–9.
117 January 1959 (MS), *MDR*: 208.
118 January 1959 (MS), *MDR*: 273–4.
119 28 November 1928, *SP*1: 49. For references to *synopados* see *SP*1: 48, 508.
120 February 1954 (MS), *CW*11: 742. See n. 46 above.
121 August 1948, *CW*9ii: 173, n. 33.
122 Joshua 1: 1.
123 17 January 1909, *FJL*: 196–7.
124 Job 2: 7.
125 Job 38: 17.
126 Song of Solomon 2: 5.
127 Song of Solomon 8: 6.
128 May 1951 (MS), *CW*11: 732.
129 August 1948, *CW*9ii: 427.
130 1945, *CW*13: 437.
131 There is a subtext to Jung's telling of his 1948 dream in his autobiography, and that is a childhood memory from the ages of 4 to 6. Of all the paintings in the parsonage at Klein-Hüningen, Jung remembered 'an Italian painting of David and Goliath. It was a mirror copy from the workshop of Guido Reni; the original hangs in the Louvre.' Jung would sit for hours in front of this painting: 'It was the only beautiful thing I knew' (*MDR*: 31). David as a youth slew Goliath with his slingshot: 'the stone sunk into his forehead, and he fell upon his face to the earth' (1 Samuel 17:49). Goliath was not only a giant, but a Philistine (1 Samuel 17:4). Goliath could easily have been the father in the fantasy of the infant Jung, and we do know that as a youth Jung thought

his father a philistine: 'My father, too, was a PhD, but he was merely a philologist and linguist' (*MDR*: 95). At the beginning of Jung's 1948 dream, he was surprised at his father's understanding, where the other father present 'understood nothing at all', and his son 'began to laugh' (*MDR*: 244). The other father and son were 'both psychiatrists', and may well refer to Freud and Jung when they were the father and son of psychoanalysis in 1906–13. At the climax of the dream, it was Johann Paul Achilles Jung who was the first to pray, who knelt down and touched his forehead to the floor, and Jung who tried to imitate him (*MDR*: 245–6). Was it his personal father, a Goliath, who tried to lead Jung to his substitute, perhaps archetypal father Freud, a Uriah? In the shifting shadows of Jung's projective rapport with Freud, I suggest Freud was also Uriah, the 'innocent victim' of Jung's 'adulterous' relationship with Spielrein. If so, then Jung appears in his autobiography as both the young and the old David, goatherd and king.

132 August 1941, CW11: 428.
133 Henry Corbin, *Cyclical Time and Ismaili Gnosis*, trans. Ralph Manheim and James W. Morris (London: Kegan Paul International and Islamic Publications, 1983), 62, n. 9.
134 Q18: 1–8, 110.
135 John 1: 14, 4–5.
136 John 1: 14.
137 4 May 1953, *JL2*: 115.
138 4 May 1953, *JL2*: 115.
139 Karl Barth, *Protestant Theology in the Nineteenth Century: Its Background and History* (London: SCM Press, 1959), 426, 428; James D. G. Dunn, *Christology in the Making: An Inquiry into the Origins of the Doctrine of the Incarnation* (London: SCM Press, 1980), 22–3.
140 September 1912, *PU*: 196.
141 September 1912, *PU*: 162–6; edited from Jung's 1950 revision, CW5: 415f.
142 September 1912, *PU*: 140.
143 September 1912, *PU*: 123.
144 September 1912, *PU*: 121–2.
145 6 March 1910, *FJL*: 300.
146 12 November 1911, *FJL*: 459. Freud's first response to Jung's interest in mythology was to express his own interest in biography. Freud's interpretation of Leonardo's character on 17 October 1909, *FJL*: 255, he wrote up as *Leonardo da Vinci and a Memory of his Childhood* (1910) (*SE*11: 63–137). Jung refers to Freud's *Leonardo* in his introduction to *Psychology of the Unconscious*, as he alludes to Leonardo's vulture fantasy in his commentary of the dialogue between Jesus and Nicodemus. See *PU*: 3 and 139–42, or CW5: 332–46 respectively. Cf. George B. Hogenson, *Jung's Struggle with Freud* (Notre Dame, Ind.: University & Notre Dame Press, 1983), 26–30.
147 Q55: 1–8; Q57: 25. Cf. Henry Corbin, *Temple and Contemplation*, trans. Philip Sherrard with the assistance of Liadain Sherrard (London: Kegan Paul International and Islamic Publications, 1983), 55–125.
148 Q2: 142; Q55: 17–21; Q24: 35.
149 Q2: 142.
150 Maxime Rodinson, *Europe and the Mystique of Islam*, trans. Roger Veinus (London: I. B. Tauris & Co., 1988), 56, 141, n. 118.
151 Q2: 124–53.
152 April 1958 (MS), *MDR*: 85.
153 16 October 1929, *SP1*: 317–18.

154 30 October 1929, *SP*1: 335–6. In his interpretation of Samuel 1: 3, 'Speak, O Lord, for thy servant hears!' Jung defined 'prayer' (his quotes) in 1912 as 'a wish (libido) directed towards divinity (the unconscious complex)', and in 1950 as 'a wish addressed to God, a concentration of libido on the God-image'. See September 1912, *PU*: 109, and September 1950 (MS), *CW*5: 257 respectively.

155 5 March 1930, *SP*1: 513.

156 Q18: 65. Cf. Schimmel, *Mystical Dimensions of Islam*, 150.

13

THE *MYSTERIUM CONIUNCTIONIS* AND THE 'YO-YO SYNDROME': FROM POLARITY TO ONENESS IN SUFI PSYCHOLOGY

Sara Sviri

Sometimes He shows Himself in one way
Sometimes in the opposite way – the work
of religion is naught but bewilderment
(Rūmī)[1]

MYSTERY AND PARADOX

Separateness and affinity

From time immemorial human beings have longed to build a bridge over the abyss which separates their individual existences from the totality of Being. The moment one becomes awakened, even to a lesser degree, to this longing underlying one's existence, one has already taken the first step towards bridging over the abyss. Yet at the same time one has entered, perhaps with no way of retreat, into the realm of mysteries and paradoxes: a realm of mental and psychological impossibilities, which, on the one hand, intensify the longing, and with it also the quest-energy and the degree of wakefulness, but on the other hand, make the goal seem further and further away, more and more elusive and evanescent.

In the first instance one 'sees' the following paradox: the object of one's longing, in the particular 'form' by which It chooses to manifest Itself, has certain similarities with oneself – there is a certain affinity which allows one to recognize in It a superior aspect of oneself; yet at the same time It is wholly different. It is both akin to one's deepest experience of oneself and unlike any known experience.

In *The Conference of the Birds*, the great symbolic Sufi epic of the Quest, Attar, the twelfth-century Persian poet, describes how the Great Being, the

Simorgh (literally, *sim-murgh* = Silver Bird, Persian), first revealed Itself to the world:

> It was in China, late one moonless night,
> The Simorgh first appeared to mortal sight –
> He let a feather float down through the air,
> And rumours of its fame spread everywhere.[2]

This feather is recognized by the multitude of birds, who are the symbolic seekers, as 'a sign of Him', their Superior King, because they too are feathered creatures. And at the same time it is a feather so unlike any other feather, so magnificent, so undescribable, that the poet feels obliged to withdraw from his creative eloquence into a reverent silence:

> But since no words suffice, what use are mine
> To represent or to describe this sign?

> (p. 35)

It is the recognition of something deeply familiar yet totally other in its numinosity which ignites in the hearts of the 'birds' the aspiration to set off on a journey in quest of the Simorgh, their Higher Self. This is an archetypal longing which is echoed in many a tradition: Arjuna, the illustrious archer of the Hindu epic *The Mahabharata*, calls out to Krsna, his charioteer, who is none other than the earthly incarnation of Vishnu: 'I long to behold your Divine Form.'[3] And Moses on Mount Horeb, after being spoken to by God 'as a man speaketh unto his friend' (Exod. 33: 11), says: 'I beseech Thee, show me Thy Glory' (33: 18). In the Islamic tradition at large, and in Sufi tradition in particular, Moses has become the archetype of the prophet, a highly evolved aspirant, a mediator between God and man, who cannot content himself with the gift of conversing with God, but is driven by an unquenched thirst to 'see' eye to eye, to have a 'visual' encounter with the divine. Yet this encounter is a shattering experience. The fiery longing of the spirit cannot be matched by the frailty and density of the physical, emotional and mental vessels. Thus Arjuna, shocked and shaken by the 'vision of God in its Universal Form', cries:

> I have seen what no man ever saw before me:
> Deep is my delight, but still my dread is greater
> Show me now your other form, O Lord, be gracious . . . .
> Show me now the shape I knew of old.[4]

And Moses, in Midrashic elaborations of the biblical story, when confronted with the heavenly host, with thousands upon thousands of angels – the angels of storms, and the angels of hail, and the angels of snow, and the angels of fire – all assailing him and attacking him for his human audacity – shouts at the end of his tether: enough! Let go of me! I relinquish my request!

The mystical journey, like indeed the journey towards individuation, when taken sincerely, alludes from the outset to this mystery: one seems to travel away from one's ordinary human self into the realm of the Numinous, the Extraordinary, the Ravishing, only to realize again and again that ultimately the journey is towards one's deepest sense of Selfhood.

At the end of a lifelong journey some of the 'birds' in Attar's poem arrive at the Simorgh's court. Not the multitude which had been so eager to set off, but only a small number – thirty birds, to be sure. After a long preparatory stage, which takes up most of the epic, in which their guide, the Hoopoe, initiates them into the knowledge of the obstacles and mysteries of the 'seven valleys of the Path',

> They saw the bow of this great enterprise
> Could not be drawn by weakness, sloth or lies,
> And some were so cast down that then and there
> They turned aside and perished in despair.
> The remnant rose up ready to depart.
> They travelled on for years; a lifetime passed
> Before the longed-for goal was reached at last.
> What happened as they flew I cannot say,
> But if you journey on the narrow Way,
> Then you will act as they once did and know
> The miseries they had to undergo.
> Of all the army that set out, how few
> Survived the Way; of that great retinue
> A handful lived until the voyage was done –
> Of every thousand there remained but one . . . .
> A world of birds set out, and there remained
> But thirty when the promised goal was gained,
> Thirty exhausted, wretched, broken things,
> With hopeless hearts and tattered, trailing wings
> Who saw that nameless Glory which the mind
> Acknowledges as ever-undefined.

(pp. 213–15)

And here, at last, when these 'thirty birds' (in Persian: *si-murgh*) are allowed entry into the innermost chamber of the Simurgh, the mystery of Oneness and Separateness unfolds:

> Then, as by shame their spirits were refined
> Of all the world's weight, they began to find
> A new life flow towards them from that bright
> Celestial and ever-living Light . . . .
> Their life came from that close, insistent sun
> And in its vivid rays they shone as one.

There in the Simorgh's radiant face they saw
Themselves, the Simorgh of the world – with awe
They gazed, and dared at last to comprehend
THEY WERE THE SIMORGH AND THE JOURNEY'S END.
They see the Simorgh – at themselves they stare,
And see a second Simorgh standing there;
They look at both and see the two are one,
That this is that, that this, the goal is won.
They ask . . . how is it true
That 'we' is not distinguished here from 'you'?
And silently their shining Lord replies:
'I AM A MIRROR SET BEFORE YOUR EYES,
AND ALL WHO COME BEFORE MY SPLENDOUR SEE
THEMSELVES, THEIR OWN REALITY.'

(pp. 218–19)

We shall return to the image of the mirror and the reflection later on.

Time, space and Timeless Time

Before one arrives at the mystery of the reflection of one's Essence on the mirror of total Being, one is confronted with yet another paradox: the mystery of time and space. Time and space imply movement; movement implies change; change implies growth. This is the linear, the progressive aspect of the journey, and it is essential for the 'progress' one expects to make on the path of transformation. In the quest for wholeness one acts and moves within the boundaries of time, place and circumstances; and yet one becomes aware that Wholeness, of which one can occasionally have glimpses, is beyond the boundaries of time, place and circumstances.

Sufi tradition is keenly interested in the progressive aspect of the journey, and therefore has elaborated emphatically the spatial image of the 'journey' (sayr, sulūk) or the path (tarīqa). Sufis are often nicknamed 'wayfarers' (sā'irūn, sā'ihūn, sālikūn), and their journey is carefully mapped in the Sufi manuals according to its various stages and stations (maqāmāt). The seeker moves progressively from one 'station' to the other. Each station is a halting place in which the wayfarer has to 'work' on a certain aspect of himself in order to be able to move on to the next. In fact, each station designates a certain ethical obstacle, or a psychological block, related to blindspots and unresolved needs. These have to be overcome in order to achieve the ethical stature and the psychological maturity which is prerequisite for genuine spiritual life. The Sufi masters have recognized, of course, that within the structured outline of the journey, room should be allowed for flexibility and variations in order to accommodate different types and individualities – after all, this is a journey 'of the alone to the alone', and it varies from one

195

wayfarer to another. Hence the well-known saying, attributed to al-Hallaj, a Sufi martyr of the ninth to tenth century: 'The Paths are as many as the souls of men and women on the surface of the earth.' And yet, from the early compilations of the tenth century to later poetic illustrations such as *The Conference of the Birds*, Sufi authors deemed it necessary to include in their works a detailed, albeit variegated, mapping of the journey's stations, to be used as a guideline and as a means for orientation.

Observing the nature of these 'stations' an eleventh-century Persian compiler writes:

> 'Station' (*maqām*) denotes anyone's 'standing' in the Way of God, and his fulfilment of the obligations appertaining to that 'station' and his keeping it until he comprehends its perfection as far as lies in a man's power. . . . Thus, the first 'station' is repentance (*tawba*), then comes conversion [of the heart] (*ināba*), then renunciation (*zuhd*), then trust in God (*tawakkul*) and so on.[5]

The 'stations' are traversed in time, and are indicators of the progress achieved through practices and effort (*mujāhada*).

Alongside this temporal–spatial aspect of the inner journey, however, Sufis realize another type of psychological occurrence: they call it *ḥāl* (sing.)/*aḥwāl* (pl.), which means changing, or fluctuating 'states', and they describe it as 'flashes of lightning' which 'vanish almost as soon as they descend on the heart'.[6] The brevity of these inner happenings corresponds directly to their intensity, and it is the intensity, not the amount of effort, by which their effect is measured. 'States' constitute a polar-complementary aspect of 'stations'. In his *Kashf al-Maḥjūb* al-Hujwīrī writes:

> 'State' [*ḥāl*] . . . is something that descends from God into the heart, without the recipient of it having any control within his power to either repel it when it comes or attract it when it goes away. Therefore, whereas *maqām* denotes the seeker's journey, and the progress he has been making on the level of efforts, and hence the stage he takes before God accordingly, *ḥal* denotes God's grace which He bestows upon His servants, regardless of any effort on their part. *Maqāmāt* belong to the realm of activities [= practices]; *aḥwāl* belong to the realm of boons.
>
> (p. 181)

The *aḥwāl*, which are likened to lightning, descend suddenly and unexpectedly upon the heart with violence and vigour, sweeping away all perception of time. 'When the *aḥwāl* descend upon the heart they cease to exist in time', writes Al-Qushairī, one of the main Sufi compilers of the eleventh century in his *Epistle on Sufism* (= *al-Risāla fī 'ilm al-taṣawwuf*).[7] And Najm al-Dīn Kubrā, a great visionary of the thirteenth century, describes in these words the emotional intensity and complexity of a visual *ḥāl*, experienced probably in a state of deep meditation:

196

When the 'well' [= the symbol of multi-dimensional existence] reveals itself to you in the state of 'absence' [*ghaiba* – loss of waking consciousness], you will experience such awe, fear and trembling, that the spirit of life will seem to be departing from you. . . . From the 'well' wondrous images and visions will arise in front of you; visions you will never be able to forget because of the intensity of suffering they will cause you to experience. . . . Then you will rejoice in them and be terrified by them and be attracted to them, and you will taste opposing 'states' in one state.[8]

Sufi psychology thus differentiates between two polar modes of the mystical journey: the ethical and the ecstatic; the wilful, disciplined, ego-controlled, physically orientated, time- and earth-bound efforts; and the fluid, ethereal, affective, archetypal, spontaneous, numinous, timeless peak-experiences. Some later Sufis related the former to 'horizontal time' (*zamān aāfāqī*) and the latter to 'psychic time' (*zamān anfosī*).[9] Both modes are indispensable: they balance each other. The two are complementary to the extent that when the ego has reached a breaking point in the field of discipline and 'work' and its efforts cease (as we shall see further on), a 'state' takes over; when the intensity of the 'state' wanes and evaporates, activity and practices are called for. Seeker-disciples who have over-developed one mode are instructed by their masters to 'work' on its opposite, in order to correct their over-indulgence.

Yet in spite of this complementarity, Sufi mystical psychology is definitely coloured by *aḥwāl*, by the intense fluctuations of the heart from state to state. 'For the heart fluctuates from state to state' writes Ibn 'Arabi, the well-known Andalusian mystic of the early thirteenth century, 'just as God – the Beloved – is "each day upon some task" (Qur. 55: 29)'.[10]

A subtle semantics links the mystical state (*ḥāl*) with ecstasy (*wajd*) and with the mystical sense of time (*waqt*). In Sufi lists of technical terms (*iṣṭilaḥāt*) and their definitions, *wajd* is described as 'an unexpected stumbling of the heart upon the remembrance of something lost'.[11] By this term Sufis point to the overwhelmingly intensified emotions encountered on the journey. *Wajd* is sometimes associated with drunkenness (*sukr*) or amorous rapture (*walah*). Etymologically, *wajd* derives from W J D, an Arabic root which means 'to find' or 'to exist'. *Wujūd*, the infinitive, means 'existence', 'being', or also – especially in Sufi vocabulary – 'to find oneself in a mystical space' which transcends sequential time. Ecstasy is thus conceived of as a psychic state which is experienced as a sheer state of 'being', a state of 'presence' in a timeless moment. Hence, in Sufi vocabulary, 'time' (*waqt*), as a technical term, means 'present', 'moment', 'now'. The Sufi is said to be 'the child of the moment'. Al-Qushairī, the eleventh-century author of the *Epistle* (= *Risāla*), a compilation which became the classical manual of most Sufi circles, writes:

Time (*waqt*) is that in which you are. . . . If you are in [a state] of joy, your time is joy; if you are in [a state] of sadness, your time is sadness . . . . 'Time' means the 'moment' in which one is. . . . Thus it is said: The Sufi is the child of the 'time' [*al-ṣūfī ibn al-waqt*], namely the Sufi is occupied with that which is most appropriate for that moment. . . . [He] is not occupied by his past or by his future; he is totally occupied by the 'time' in which he is.[12]

'Time is precious', says Junaid, the great ninth-century Sufi teacher of the Baghdadi centre; 'once it has passed it cannot be captured.' And Abu Naṣr al-Sarrāj, the tenth-century compiler in whose *Book of Shimmering Lights* (*Kitāb al-Lumaʿ*) Junaid's dictum is quoted, adds a commentary: 'he means your breath, and the time which passes between past breath and future breath: if it passes and you are forgetful of the remembrance of God you will never catch it again'.[13]

What is this 'time' whose duration lasts between one breath and another? What is the high value which is attached to the conscious remembering of the divine at every passing breath? What is that which is lost for ever when the desired state of presence and consciousness gives way to an unconscious, heedless state of forgetfulness (*ghafla*)? This is one manner – significant for capturing the 'existential' flavour of mysticism in the Sufi tradition – by which Sufi teachers have alluded to the mystery of the eternal 'now', of a timeless time.

Let me present this perception from yet another perspective, much pondered in Sufi literature. The mystical tradition to which one is affiliated is by definition a historical phenomenon; and yet its time-bound lineage, its chain-of-transmission (*silsila* in Arabic), through which the esoteric teaching unfolds in time, and which is passed on from teacher to disciple generation by generation, always points to a 'mythical event' beyond time and space, at which the link between man and God was established once and for all, and at which the seed of longing was planted for ever. In the Sufi tradition this 'primordial event' is known as 'the Day of the Covenant' (*yawm al-mīthāq*). It is based on a Qur'ānic verse which reads:

> And when thy Lord took from the children of Adam, from their loins, their seed, and made them testify touching themselves, 'Am I not your Lord?' They said, 'Yes, we testify.'
>
> (7: 172)[14]

According to Sufi commentaries, this Primordial Covenant in which the 'Children of Adam', i.e. humanity as a whole, testify and accept God's Lordship represents a 'time before time', 'an existence before existence'. It relates to an undifferentiated state of human existence, in which the individual existences of men and women are potentialities only.

Junaid, the main Sheikh of Baghdad in the ninth century makes the

'Covenant' a central theme in his teaching. His understanding of Unity (*tawḥīd*) and mystical knowledge (*ma'rifa*) is the outcome of his meditations on this verse. In one of his Epistles he writes:

> In this verse God tells you that He spoke to them at a time when they did not exist, except so far as they existed in Him. This existence is not the same type of existence as is usually attributed to God's creatures; it is a type of existence which only God knows ... embracing them he sees them in the beginning when they are non-existent and unaware of their future existence in the world. The existence of these is timeless.[15]

The Primordial Covenant is understood also as an intimation of the ultimate proximity between human beings and God at this Timeless Time. It alludes to the primordial 'union' between human beings and the divine. It is this state of nearness (*qurb*) and intimacy (*'uns*) that the mystic longs for during his lifetime. The journey in this respect is nothing but a 'return to the beginning', or more precisely: 'return to the "Source of Being"' (in Arabic – *al-ma'ād ilā al-mabda'*). The ultimate goal, the arrival (*wuṣūl*) at a state of Oneness with the Beloved, is the return to the state in which one was before one was. Here is Junaid again:

> What is the Unity (*tawḥīd*) of the mystics? that the servant [= human being] be as a lifeless body in front of God ... in a state of annihilation (*fanā'*) from the [lower-] self (*nafs*) and from people's expectations ... devoid of sense perception and bodily movement, so that Truth [= *al-Ḥaqq*, one of God's names] may fulfil what It had willed for him, namely: that HIS END WILL RETURN TO HIS BEGINNING, AND THAT HE BE AS HE WAS BEFORE HE WAS .... Unity means to come out of the confinement of temporality into the spaciousness and expanses of Timelessness (*sarmadīyya*).[16]

But now, if the 'Day of Covenant' (can we not see in it an archetype of a universal initiation into the mystery of the One and the many?) and the primordial state of being in Oneness are indeed timeless, then the longed-for state of intimate proximity belongs to an eternal NOW!

Here Sufi psychology challenges our deeply engrained temporal-causal perception, which insists on understanding the 'Day of Covenant' as belonging to some remote past, and on envisaging the end of the quest as an evanescent goal hidden in some distant future. It takes a Rūmī to address this paradox from the intuitive vantage point of poets-lovers-mystics. Far simpler than any speculation, his words go straight into the heart:

> Lovers don't finally meet somewhere,
> They're in each other all along.[17]

Unconscious knowledge

The act of testifying, the explicit acceptance by humanity of God's Lordship, contains yet another paradox: the mystery of knowledge which is innate, but does not necessarily become conscious, the paradox of unconscious 'remembrance'. Deep in the unconscious all human beings carry an 'imprint' of the 'Yes' with which they responded to God's question: 'Am I not your Lord?' Yet this imprint, the 'memory' of this act of acknowledgement – a Gnostic act par excellence – is bound to remain buried, dormant and unconscious during their wakeful life. Ibn 'Arabi, whose teaching became one of the central theosophical systems within the Sufi tradition from the thirteenth century onwards, writes:

> God deposited within man knowledge of all things, then prevented him from perceiving what He had deposited within him . . . . This is one of the divine mysteries which reason denies and considers totally impossible. The nearness of this mystery to those ignorant of it is like God's nearness to His servant, as mentioned in His words, 'We are nearer to him than you, but you do not see' (Qur. 56: 85), and His words 'We are nearer to him than the jugular vein' (50: 16). In spite of this nearness, the person does not perceive and does not know . . . . No one knows what is within himself until it is unveiled to him instant by instant.[18]

In the Sufi tradition the hidden knowledge unfolds in the state of mystic recollection, which is brought about by the practice of *dhikr*. *Dhikr* means remembrance, recollection, and it has become the technical term for Sufi meditation. Practically it entails focusing one's attention on God by repeating – orally or silently – God's names, in particular the most sacred name, ALLAH. This is an absorbing practice in which one's consciousness transcends the cognitive boundaries of time and space and one's temporal attributes are obliterated. In the practice of *dhikr* the Sufi becomes absorbed within an undifferentiated totality. This state is said to be a re-enactment of the primordial state of Unity. In the total absorption of all one's faculties one's ego consciousness becomes diffused. The ego rests in a suspended state of non-being, annihilation, for which the Sufi term is *fanā'*. Yet simultaneously something else takes over, a different state of consciousness on a level which transcends the mind and the sensory perceptions. Since this type of consciousness is beyond any temporal or spatial points of reference, the Sufi is said to be in a state of 'permanent existence', for which Sufi terminology assigns the term *baqā'*.

Through this stripping-off of one's individual existence in time, the Sufi returns to 'the state he was before he was', and through this experience the dormant memory of his participation in the collective 'Yes' is revived. He 'remembers' and knows that which had been 'deposited within' his innermost being. This is the knowledge of the heart, since it is the heart which Sufis see as the treasure-house of the divine mysteries, and as the locus of the mystical journey.[19] 'God placed the heart within the cavity of the chest', writes al-Ḥakīm al-Tirmidhī, the ninth-century sage of Khurasan in north-east Iran, 'and it belongs to God alone. . . . Within the heart God placed the knowledge of Him and He lit it with the divine light . . . . By this light He gave the heart eyes to see.'[20]

The mystical knowledge, the knowledge of the heart, is true Gnosis. It cannot be acquired through books and theoretical formulations. It is primarily experiential. It cannot come from without, because it has been stored all along in the innermost recesses of one's heart. When it emerges from the depths, stirred by the energy of the 'journey', or more precisely: stirred by the energy of the 'guide' (murshid, pīr, sheikh), it does not come up as abstract notions, but as tender insights, or as an expansion of one's horizons, or as all-encompassing experiences which both include and transcend body, mind and psyche.

Here is Rūmī again, with poetic imagery:

> Those who have attained union have nothing
> but the inward eye and the divine lamp –
> they have been delivered of signs and roads.[21]

The path of efforts and the effortless path

Earlier on we observed the polarity and complementarity of maqāmāt and aḥwāl. Let us look closer at the dialectics between these two poles of the mystical journey in relation to the dynamics of the ego, the lower-self (nafs) in Sufi psychology.

The maqāmāt, as we have seen, reflect the arduous process by which human strength and perseverance are put to the test. The journey, from this angle, calls for tremendous will power. It is associated with pain, suffering and sacrifice. On the path of sincerity and purification the wayfarer has to give up most, if not all, of what he possesses – not only material possessions, but most importantly, mental and psychological conditionings. So much does he invest in it, that a certain amount of expectation and self-appraisal – a kind of 'bargaining' – creeps in: I have given up so much that I desire to see progress . . . ; indeed, I can see in myself a tremendous change, therefore. . . . These ego-centred calculations are unavoidable partners to any enterprise achieved by ego-will. Hence, sooner or later, inflation comes in via the efforts. The more ascetic the path of efforts is, the graver the risk of an inflated ego. This is a law to be reckoned with on the path of transformation; an extremely subtle law which creates a paradoxical vicious circle: one cannot progress without making efforts; the results of the efforts are the indication of the progress; when one becomes conscious of the extent of one's progress, one falls into the trap set up by the 'calculating' ego.

In Sufi psychology the ego – *nafs* – is the psychic component which ascribes everything to itself. It is the centre from which one perceives oneself as a separate entity. This is the seat of the I-consciousness. From this psychic centre one is aware of one's needs – instinctual, sexual, emotional or spiritual; hence – it is through the ego that one feels frustrated or gratified, failing or successful. When ego consciousness is directed towards a certain object or goal, and the object or goal is won, the ego is gratified. Even when the object is self-mortification, one of the stations on the path, perhaps especially then, the ego is gratified when this has been achieved. The identification of the ego with the object of the quest is particularly strong in the arena of spiritual experiences. No experience, lofty as it may be, is immune from being possessed by the *nafs* which always ascribes it to itself: my visions, my dreams, my intuition, my perseverance, my surrender . . .

Sufi terminology has developed subtle differentiations between various psychological obstacles which are bound up with the ego: *'ujb* = inflation, conceit, auto-eroticism; *riyā'* = being aware of one's merits and achievements; *iddi'ā'* = arrogance, presumption. These terms are seldom used in a moralistic context, but rather in candid psychological observations of how the sly, power-driven *nafs* functions in many a cunning and deceptive way, in order to undermine the process of the quest; simply because the object of the quest always transcends the ego, while the ego, by definition, is always self-centred.

The point at which the sincere seeker encounters the full consequence of this vicious circle becomes a crucial turning point: he encounters the impossibility of extracting himself from the ego. In other words: he sees that it is impossible to achieve the object of his quest through his own will and efforts. Disillusionment, bewilderment and humility replace the former inflatory elation. This is the point when his sincerity makes him see the futility of his efforts, because whether he likes it or not, it is at this point that he must face his human limitations, those in the limelight and those in the shadow . . . Here is the main psychological paradox encountered by countless Sufis in their various centres: the mystic wayfarer goes in search of the loftiest object imaginable, yet his sincere efforts, if they are truly sincere, lead him right into the lowliest components of his personality.

'Man is clay', writes al-Hujwīrī in *Kashf al-Maḥjūb*, 'and clay involves impurity. Therefore purity bears no likeness to acts, nor can human nature be destroyed by means of efforts.'[22]

The following is an authentic description, most probably carved out of first-hand experiences, of this psychological impasse, written by al-Ḥakīm al-Tirmidhī, a ninth-century mystic known for his astute analysis of the psychology of the mystical journey:

> And when the seeker has exhausted all his sincere efforts, and has found that his lower self (*nafs*) and all its features are still alive and well, he falls into bewilderment, and his genuine efforts cease.

He says: how can I prevent my lower self from [being gratified] by the sweetness of these spiritual experiences? He realizes that he can do it no more than white hair can turn black.

He says: I have harnessed my lower self with my true submission to God, but it has broken off and gone loose. How shall I capture it again?

And so he falls into the wilderness of confusion. There he strays alone, lonely and desolate. No longer is he close to himself ... nor is he as yet close to God. He becomes constrained (*muḍṭarr*) and bewildered. He does not know whether to go forward or backward.

Despairing of his sincerity he cries out to God, empty-handed, his heart empty of any effort, and thus he says in his heart's communication: You who know all the hidden things, You know that there is not even one step in the arena of true efforts left for me; You know that it is not possible for me to wipe out the lusts and desires from my self and from my heart. You rescue me!

Then Compassion (*raḥma*) reaches him and he is spared. From the place where his sincere efforts stopped his heart is lifted up in a flash to the platform of proximity at the divine throne ... and in the spaces of Unity he expands. This is the meaning of God's speech (Qur. 27:62): 'He who answers the constrained (*al-muḍṭarr*) when he calls unto Him, and removes the evil, and appoints you to be successors in the earth; is there a god with God?'

This verse informs you that the passion of your heart for sincere self-exertion will not remove the evil from you and will not answer what you call for, until your call and the passion of your heart be directed utterly towards God, who made the hearts passionately constrained and reliant on Him.[23]

The Sufi term which I have rendered here as 'constraint' (*idṭirār*) or 'constrained' (*muḍṭarr*) describes the state in which the confused and helpless seeker is taken over by a benevolent transcendent power. It is a state of total surrender, except that this surrender is not by choice, since choice (*ikhtiyār*) is related to the ego. When the surrender to the divine will is thus complete, the path changes direction. It is not trodden any more by the wilful I, but by the Higher Self. Then it becomes effortless, and the wayfarer is moved by a transcendent energy. The *maqām* has become a *ḥāl*.

Of all Sufi masters it was al-Ḥakīm al-Tirmidhī who, at a very early stage in the development of Sufi psychology, analysed minutely this turning point on the path. He laid the foundation for later elaborations on the theme of 'constraint' and 'choice' (*idṭirār wa-ikhtiyār*). 'The "constrained" whose provisions and supplies have expired', he writes in his *The Journey of the Friends of God* [=*Sīrat al-awliyā*'],

and who has stopped bewildered in the wilderness, not knowing which way to go, is spared [by compassion] and is delivered [by divine help]

203

... He who wanders constrained in the wastelands of the road to Him is the one who truly merits divine compassion and relief .... He is spared [by compassion] because his call is truly sincere. IT CANNOT BE TRULY SINCERE UNTIL HE BECOMES CONSTRAINED, WITH NOTHING TO HOLD ON TO AND WITH NO ONE TO TURN TO. He who looks with one eye to God and with the other eye to his efforts is not truly constrained, and his call is not truly sincere. When the call of this constrained is answered, his heart is lifted in a flash to the abode of the free and noble.[24]

One can clearly see the delicate balance which is struck here between the path of efforts and the effortless, selfless path. In the historical experience of Sufi fraternities there has always lurked the danger of confusing the state of 'constraint' with a kind of apathetic passivity. The instructions to 'let go' 'surrender', 'put your trust in God alone' have been often misunderstood as advocating the relinquishing of efforts from the outset, and as a call for a quietistic attitude. Nothing can be more wide of the mark than this interpretation. The Sufi teachers have emphatically maintained that true surrender cannot be achieved before the path of efforts has been followed to the ultimate.

The understanding that at a certain point devotional acts may become effortless and transcendent is best illustrated by a divine saying, an extra-Qur'ānic saying attributed to God [= ḥadīth qudsī], which has become perhaps the most often quoted piece of tradition in Sufi literature:

My servant does not draw near to me by performing the obligatory commandments; he draws near to me by supererogatory acts of devotion, and then I love him. And when I love him I become his ears, his eyes, his tongue, his hands, his feet and his heart: he hears by Me, he sees by Me, he speaks by Me, he handles by Me, he walks by Me and he comprehends by Me.[25]

The deep implication of this ḥadīth from the viewpoint of mystical life is beyond the scope of this essay. It is alluded to, however, in the following passage from the Kashf al-maḥjūb, from which I quoted above.

The true Sufi is he who leaves impurity behind ... purity (ṣafā') is the characteristic of the lovers of God ... because purity is the attribute of those who love, and the lover is he who is dead to his attributes and living in the attributes of his Beloved.[26]

THE YO-YO SYNDROME

The 'Yo-Yo Syndrome' is a term coined in a modern Sufi group to describe the constant 'fluctuations of the heart from state to state'. This fluctuation – the Sufi term for it is talwīn (which means also 'variegation', changing colours) – is complemented by a state of poise and stillness – *tamkīn* – which may come as a temporary relief from the intensity of the psychic oscillation. In another sense *talwīn* denotes the dynamics of polarity itself, including the polarity between man and divine, whereas *tamkīn* may refer also to the 'ultimate' state of Unity and Oneness, in which the distinction between opposite states, or between 'lover' and 'Beloved', is obliterated.

Sufi psychology is visualized along the lines of polarity and complementarity. Polarity is the basic law of existence on any level taken. It can be amplified by the breathing process: everything breathes, breathing is unceasing, and the phases of IN-breath and OUT-breath exemplify polarity in an uncompromising way. Yet it is the ineffable pause between one breath and the other, or the elusive point between the IN-halation and the EX-halation, which symbolizes Oneness. The practice of *Dhikr*, Sufi meditation, mentioned above, is about living out consciously Polarity and Oneness by the breath.

The 'fluctuations of the heart from state to state' reflect in fact the polarity within the Divine Oneness. God is said to be 'the First and the Last, the Outward and the Inward' (Qur. 57: 3). To human beings God reveals Himself via two polar complementary aspects (called also 'measures' or 'powers'): beauty (*jamāl*) and majesty (*jalāl*). The vision of these polar attributes and the inner understanding of their nature awaken in the heart a corresponding polar response. 'Fear and Hope have overtaken [the] heart [of the seeker] because of his awakening to God's words', writes al-Muḥāsibī, one of the earliest Sufi teachers who died in Baghdad in 837.

> At times it is as if his heart would soar up with joy because of the hope and expectation stirred within him, that his Lord and Master may look upon him with contentment and favour; and at times it is as if his heart would melt of grief, and be shattered by terror, when fear, caution, anxiety and awe become agitated in him .... Thus is he thrown between these two states.[27]

Fear (*khauf*) and hope (*rajā'*) represent the two poles of the first, or lowest, rung on the ladder of devotional ascension. The journey is seen as ascension (*'urūj*) from the point of view of the escalation, the intensification, of the emotional energy which produces the inner states. The deeper one descends – or the higher one ascends – the more intense and more polarized the states become. Thus they have to become, since the dynamic process is envisaged as a reflection of the 'nearness' to (*qurb*) or the 'remoteness' from (*bu'd*) the Divine Presence. In the state of nearness one feels intoxicated and elated, life feels vibrant and full of possibilities, there is a sense of purpose and direction, hardships seem manageable, obstacles are easily overcome, synchronicities come in abundance, and one gets insights and revelations – sheer ecstasy. In Sufi terminology this state is known as 'expansion' (*bast*). Then one's inner state changes, sometimes with no apparent reason: a deep depression sets in, apathy and inertia, there is no light, no hope, no comfort, no security, no guidance, no God; an unexplained anxiety blocks the chest and the throat, and everything is dark and gloomy. Sufi terminology names this state 'contraction' (*qabḍ*).

The following is a vivid description of the state of *qabḍ* (contraction) experienced and recorded by Irina Tweedie, a modern woman who has gone through a complete Sufi training with an Indian Naqshbandi [= one of the Sufi fraternities] teacher:

> So much sorrow in me that there is no speech left to express it. Have no desire to speak to him. Go there in the morning and sit. About 10 a.m. he sends me home. I am sort of empty. Everything seems to be dead. No desires are left, only one. . . . Only this terrible, deadly longing. But there seems to be no hope. It is a sort of peace made of darkness.[28]

Qabḍ and *basṭ*, contraction and expansion, represent the polarity of the second rung on the ladder of ascension.

This rung, perhaps better than any other, is well attested in Sufi literature. Najm al-Din Kubrā (d. 1221), whose *Exhalations of Beauty and Revelations of Majesty* (*fawā'iḥ al-jamāl wa-fawātiḥ al-jalāl*) alludes in its title to the divine polarity, writes:

> Contraction and expansion come from the Primordial Might . . . . It is not bound with the wayfarer's choice, but with the choice of the One and Mighty. It is experienced (lit.: tasted) by both heart and body, whereas fear and hope are experienced by the heart without the body. It may be asked: it is well known that fear and hope can occur at one and the same state . . . is this also the case with expansion and contraction, albeit these are opposites which do not concur? This is our answer: at the first stages of the entrance into this arena the heart is at times expanded, and the face bears witness to it, and at times contracted, and the face bears witness to it. This is the stage of variegation (*talwīn*) . . . . But once one becomes established in it, he is expanded-contracted [concurrently]. To the ignorant he looks simply contracted, but the expert will read from his visage that he is a casket of contraction containing a gem of expansion, for he has arrived where he has arrived, and he has tasted what he has tasted.[29]

The mystical teaching cannot be complete without experiencing both *qabḍ* and *basṭ*, their alternations, their concurrence and their complementarity. It is only through experiences, what the Sufis would call 'tasting' (*dhauq*), that one can learn how to hold the opposites and ultimately to reconcile them. Sufi masters, who are nicknamed 'the spies of the hearts' (*jawāsīs al-qulūb*), have used their intuitive function in order to assess the less-developed pole in the psyche of their disciples, and teaching experiences would be given accordingly. Excess of 'expansion', which runs the risk of turning into uncontrolled ecstasy and inflation, is balanced by experiences which cause contraction and self-restraint. Excess contraction, on the other hand, may bring about stagnation, impotence and a continuing depression; therefore in types of the more depressive or 'melancholic' nature, expansive experiences are reckoned beneficent.

> Sometimes He makes you learn in the night of contraction what you have not learnt in the radiance of the day of expansion 'you do not know which of them is nearer to you in benefit'.[30]
>
> (Qur. 4: 11)

These verses were written by Ibn 'Aṭā'-allāh, a thirteenth-century Egyptian Sufi Sheikh of the Shādhiliyya fraternity. The psychological and didactic need for the fluctuation of the seeker from one pole to the other, and the ultimate reconciliation of the opposites and the transcendence of all polarity, are described by the same Sufi poet thus:

> He expanded you so as not to keep you in contraction;
> He contracted you so as not to keep you in expansion;
> And He took you out of both
> so that you not belong to anything apart from Him.[31]

Qabḍ is said to reflect divine severity, and basṭ, divine gentleness.

Rumi retells the biblical story of Joseph and Benjamin. Benjamin is arrested and detained in Egypt by order of Joseph, the powerful vizier whose identity is as yet veiled from his brothers. Joseph, in fact, plays a trick on Benjamin, his beloved younger brother: he has a valuable goblet sneaked into Benjamin's bag, so that he will be arrested as a thief. He does it out of his special love for Benjamin, and out of his wish to reveal his real identity to Benjamin alone, in private intimacy, before he reveals himself to all the other brothers. But Benjamin is anxious and bewildered. He cannot 'see' the true meaning behind these unnerving events. Rūmī puts these words in the mouth of Joseph:

> I have seized you as a thief and turned you to the guards,
> for the goblet of my treasury was found in your saddlebag.
> You are bewildered at my severity and have no chance to speak –
> though I am mightily severe,
> a thousand gentlenesses are hidden in my severity.[32]

In metaphoric descriptions of the reconciliation of the opposites a recurring image is that of THE BIRD: its two wings symbolize both the polarity of the states and the need for equilibrium and balance: 'Fear and hope are like the two wings of a bird: when they are balanced the bird can fly, but if one of them is weaker than the other the bird is in danger.'[33]

In Kubrā's *Exhalations* the balanced and poised bird symbolizes the teacher, the Sheikh [lit.: the Old Man], the guide who has reconciled the opposites within himself. This is also the symbol, or the reflection, of the disciple's Higher Self. A Sheikh is he who has attained, and gone beyond, the third rung on the ladder of ascension: above the rung of contraction and expansion – which represents the stage of 'the mature man' (*kahl, rajul*) – comes the rung of 'awe' (*haiba*) and 'intimacy' (*'uns*), the state of the Wise Old Man. The polarity here is between 'awe', the manifold intensified state of fear which derives from a direct numinous experience of the majestic aspect, and 'intimacy', which derives from a deep experience of God's nearness and benevolence. In Kubrā's description there are two more rungs to ascend:

> From the stage of awe and intimacy the Sheikh ascends the double-winged stage of love (*mahabba*) and mystic knowledge (*ma'rifa*), and from there to the double-winged stage of annihilation (*fanā'*) and permanence (*baqā'*).[34]

In these altitudes all differentiation ceases. The process of growth and transformation has reached its acme. Ladder, bird, wings, opposites and the reconciliation thereof disappear. What remains is Oneness of lover and Beloved in Pure Love:

> When the lover is annihilated in Love his love becomes one with the Love of the Beloved, and then there is no bird and no wings, and his flight and love to God are by God's love to him.[35]

THE *MYSTERIUM CONIUNCTIONIS*

The ultimate mystical experience is beyond perception, beyond visualization and beyond conceptualization. It is also beyond individuation. The mystic who is standing at the gate of the mystery of the Essence is stripped of all attributes and predicates. Anything that can be said about him as to his identity, qualities, origins or destination falls away. He becomes 'featureless' and 'colourless'. All distinctions between him and any 'other', any non-him, disappear. An experience such as this by definition cannot be described. It belongs to the realm of the unknowable, where all our reference points are lost. None the less, it is this experience which lies at the core of all mystical traditions. It is this very essence of the 'Hidden', the 'Veiled', the 'Secret of Secrets', the 'Mysterium', the 'Silence', the 'Nothingness', the 'Luminous Darkness', the 'Black Light', the 'Void', the 'Cloud of Unknowing' which is the object of mystical quest, whatever the tradition to which it adheres and from which it originates. Mystical traditions have the reputation of being esoteric and secretive. Yet this appearance is upheld not necessarily because of a law which forbids the disclosure of secrets to non-initiates, but simply and essentially because at the level of the Essence nothing can be said or disclosed. It is not only non-initiates who do not and cannot 'know'; the mystic himself, he who has dived into the depth and darkness of the Essence, cannot 'know', and in truth could tell nothing, even had he desired to do so. How can a state of being which is pure Essence, and therefore devoid of any descriptive elements, be described? Not even in similes and parables. When there is no distinction between seer, seen and seeing, between knower, known and knowing – what can be said and by whom?

None the less, mystical traditions have somehow found a way to allude through suggestive and evocative language to this 'total' experience. It is therefore an experience which is within human dimension and capacity. Whatever references to it exist, they are not meant as descriptions, but as allusions, as pointers, as stimulants. They may awaken in the inner perception of the susceptible reader or listener (in the case of a verbally transmitted tradition) a dim sense of recognition, an intuitive empathy, or even a strange feeling of being overtaken, overwhelmed, silenced, stupefied, by hints pointing to an 'experience' the magnitude of which the listener has never knowingly tasted. This is an indication that the Unknowable, Pure and Total Essence may lie at the core of our own depths, and therefore, in some ways and to some extent, can be communicable.

In the earliest extant compilation of Sufi traditions, compiled at the end of the tenth century by Abu Bakr al-Kalābādhī (d. c. 990), we read:

> Passing away (fanā' = annihilation) is a state in which all passions pass away, so that the mystic experiences no feelings towards anything whatsoever, and loses all sense of discrimination: he has passed away from all things, and is wholly absorbed with that through which he has passed away .... Persistence (baqā'), which follows passing-away, means that the mystic passes away from what belongs to himself, and persists through what is God's .... When a man persists all things become for him but one thing.[36]

In the same compilation al-Kalābādhī quotes a poem by an anonymous Negro, who, 'whenever he recollected God his colour changed to white':

> So we remembered – yet oblivion
> Was not our habit: but a radiance shone,
> A magical breeze breathed, and God was near.
> Then vanished selfhood utterly, and I
> Remained His only, Who with tidings clear
> Attests His Being, and is known thereby.[37]

The Sufi tradition is deeply committed to the 'state' of fanā', which points to the annihilation of all individual traits of the seeker within the totality of the indivisible Essence-of-All-Being. Many attempts to refer to it and 'describe' it have been recorded in the vast and many-layered Sufi literature. Unlike the state of paradisial bliss promised to the righteous in the after-life according to Islamic piety and eschatology, this deepest mystical state of merging with the Divine Essence is to be experienced in the midst of life. This is, in fact, one of the hallmarks of mysticism: the duality between this life and the after-life ultimately falls away, as well as the duality between 'creature' and 'Creator' (in Sufi terminology: *khalq* versus *Ḥaqq*; *nāsūt* versus *lāhūt*). Junaid, the teacher of 'sober' Sufism, says:

> [The third stage in the experience of *fanā'* is] the obliteration of the consciousness of having attained the vision of God at the final stage of ecstasy . . . . At this stage you are obliterated and have eternal life with God, and you exist only in the existence of God because you have been obliterated. YOUR PHYSICAL BEING CONTINUES BUT YOUR INDIVIDUALITY HAS DEPARTED.[38]

Before reaching this state the mystic has to go through successive experiences of symbolic 'deaths' and 'resurrections', since these, in different forms, and at all stages of the path, are part of the process of shedding the limiting traits of individuality in the quest of Oneness.

> I died as mineral and became a plant
> I died as plant and rose to animal,
> I died as animal and I was man.
> Why should I fear? When was I less by dying?
> Yet once more I shall die as man, to soar
> with angels blest: but even from angelhood
> I must pass on: all except God perish.
> When I have sacrificed my angel soul,
> I shall become what no mind ever conceived.
> Oh, let me not exist! for Non-existence
> Proclaims in organ tones, 'To him we shall return.'[39]

Abu Yazīd al-Bisṭāmī (d. 875) and Ḥusain ibn Manṣūr al-Ḥallāj (d. 922) have become two Sufi models for the non-compromising seeker. Perhaps this is so because the shattering impact of their inner realization – that ultimately, at the hidden core of Existence, all distinctions pass away – could not be contained by them and became explicit in most controversial utterances. In the case of Abu Yazīd it was expressed in his well-known ecstatic exclamation: 'Praise be to Me! How great is my Glory!' (*subḥānī! ma a'ẓama sha'nī!*). This, to be sure, was not easily swallowed by more 'sober' or restrained Sufis, let alone by Islamic orthodoxy. As for al-Ḥallāj, he was crucified as a heretic in Baghdad in front of cheering crowds because, among other paradoxical statements, he gave expression to his experience of Oneness by the shocking exclamation: 'I am Truth' (= *anā al-Ḥaqq*) (*al-Ḥaqq* is one of the divine names, most favoured by Sufis). However, Sufi tradition, albeit not without apologetics, has not obliterated these statements from its records, and both Bāyezīd (this is the Persian, more popular version of his name) and al-Ḥallāj became the archetypes of the intoxicated mystic who, in the face of Truth, is driven by ecstasy beyond inhibitions and boundaries. Here are some lines from Rūmī's *Mathnavī* [IV, 2102–48] describing Bāyezīd's divine ecstasy:

> That magnificent dervish, Bayazid Bestami
> came to his disciples and said, 'I am God' . . .
> Pure Spirit spoke through him.
> Bayazid was not there. The 'he' of his personality
> dissolved. Like the Turk who spoke fluent Arabic,
> then came to, and didn't know a word.
> The Light of God poured into the empty Bayazid and became words . . . .
> A selfless one
> disappears into Existence and is safe there.
> He becomes a mirror. If you spit at it,
> You spit at your own face . . . .
> Bayazid became nothing,
> that clear and that empty.[40]

In a 'sacred tradition' (*ḥadīth qudsī*, reported in the name of God) often quoted in Sufi literature, Allāh says:

> I was a hidden treasure, and I desired to be known, therefore
> I created creation.

Creation is thus seen as the mirror through which God becomes 'known' to Itself. In Attar's *Conference of the Birds*, with which this essay began, it is through the reflection in the mirror of the Simurgh that the seekers realize their own true identity. To quote again from Attar's imagery:

> If you would glimpse the beauty we revere
> look in your heart – its image will appear.
> Make of your heart a looking-glass and see
> reflected there the Friend's nobility . . . .
> Search for this king within your heart; His soul
> reveals itself in atoms of the Whole . . . .
> The Simorgh's shadow and Himself are one;
> seek them together, twinned in unison.[41]

In the experience of Oneness who, then, is whose mirror? Mirror reflecting mirror, mirror reflected in mirror, whilst there is NOTHING in between as either beholder or beheld – this is perhaps the subtlest and most mysterious image which the Sufi masters have used by way of 'allusion' (*ishāra*) in the attempt to 'reflect' the Essence of the *mysterium coniunctionis*.

Here, in conclusion, is another of Bayezid's sayings:

> For thirty years God Most High was my mirror, now I am my own
> mirror, and that which I was I am no more, for 'I' and 'God' represent

duality and polytheism, and this is a denial of His Oneness. Since I am no more, God most High is His own mirror. Behold, now I say that God is the mirror of myself, for with my tongue He speaks and I have passed away.[42]

NOTES

1 Jalāl al-Dīn Rūmī, *Mathnawī*, I, 312, trans. W. C. Chittick, *The Sufi Path of Love* (Albany: State University of New York Press, 1983), p. 227.
2 Farid ud-Din Attar, *The Conference of the Birds*, trans. A. Darbandi and D. Davis, Penguin Classics (Harmondsworth: Penguin, 1984), p. 34.
3 *The Bhagavad-Gita*, trans. Swami Prabhavananda and C. Isherwood (New York: New American Library, 1972), p. 91.
4 ibid., p. 96.
5 Al-Hujwīrī, *Kashf al-Maḥjūb* (= *The Unveiling of the Veiled, The Oldest Persian Treatise on Sufism*, trans. R. A. Nicholson (London: Luzac & Co., 1911 (revised 1936; reprint 1976)), p. 181).
6 ibid., p. 182.
7 See *al-Risāla fī 'ilm al-taṣawwuf* (= *Epistle on Sufism*) (Beirut: Dār al-Kitāb al-'Arabi, n.d.), p. 32; my translation.
8 *Fawā 'ih al-Jamāl wa-fawātih al-jalāl* (= *Exhalations of Beauty and Revelations of Majesty*), ed. F. Meier (Wiesbaden: Franz Steiner Verlag, 1957, p. 8, para. 17) (Arabic); my translation.
9 See H. Corbin, *The Man of Light in Iranian Sufism* (Boulder and London: Shambala, 1978), p. 106.
10 A. J. Arberry, *The Quran Interpreted* (Oxford: Oxford University Press, 1964), p. 164.
11 Abu Naṣr Al-Sarrāj, *K. al-Luma'* (Cairo: Dār al Kutub al-Hadītha, 1960), p. 418; my translation.
12 Al-Qushairī, *al-Risāla fī 'ilm al-taṣawwuf*, p. 31; my translation.
13 Al-Sarrāj, op. cit., p. 418; my translation.
14 Ibn 'Arabi, *al-Futūḥāt al-makīyya* (= *Meccan Openings*), vol. II, 113.33 (quoted and translated by W. C. Chittick, *The Sufi Path of Knowledge* (Albany: State University of New York Press, 1989), p. 109).
15 A. H. Abdel-Kader, *The Life, Personality and Writings of Al-Junayd* (London: Luzac & Co., 1976), p. 76.
16 Al-Sarrāj, op. cit., p. 49; my translation.
17 J. Moyne and C. Barks, *Open Secret, Versions of Rumi* (Putney, Vt: Threshold Books, 1984), p. 19 (1246).
18 Ibn 'Arabi, *al-Futūḥāt al-makīyya*, vol. II, 686.4 (quoted and translated by Chittick, *The Sufi Path of Knowledge*, pp. 154–5).
19 For more on the 'heart' as the seat of mystical knowledge, see my forthcoming paper: '*Daughter of Fire* by Irina Tweedie: documentation and experiences of a modern Naqshbandi Sufi', in *Women, Discipleship and Power*, ed. E. Puttick and P. Clarke (Aberystwyth and New York: Edwin Mellen Press, 1993), pp. 77–89.
20 al-Hakīm al-Tirmidhī, *Kitab al-riyaḍa wa-adab al-nafs* (= *The Book of Spiritual Training and the Ethics of the Self*) (Cairo, 1947), pp. 116–17; my translation.
21 Jalāl al-Dīn Rūmī, *Mathnawī*, II, 3313 (trans. Chittick, *The Sufi Path of Love*, p. 126).
22 Al-Hujwīrī, op. cit., p. 32.
23 al-Hakīm al-Tirmidhī, *Sīrat al-awliyā'*, ed. B. Radtke (Beirut and Stuttgart: Franz

Steiner Verlag, 1992), pp. 14–15, paras. 26–9 (all passages from this source translated by me).

24 ibid., pp. 15–17, paras. 30–2.

25 See ibid., p. 34, para. 49.

26 Al-Hujwīrī, op. cit., p. 32.

27 Al-Muḥāsibī, *Masā'il fī aʿmāl al-qulūb wal-jawāriḥ* (= *Questions concerning the Duties of the Hearts and the Limbs*) (Cairo: ʿĀlam al-Kutub, 1969), p. 112; my translation.

28 Irina Tweedie, *Daughter of Fire* (Nevada City, Calif.: Blue Dolphin Publishing, 1986), p. 170.

29 Najm al-Dīn Kubrā, op. cit., pp. 43–4, paras. 89–90.

30 Ibn Aṭā-ʿallāh, *The Book of Wisdom*, trans. V. Danner, The Classics of Western Spirituality (London: SPCK, 1979), p. 85, no. 150.

31 ibid., p. 68, no. 80.

32 Rūmī, *Divan-i Shams-i Tabrizi*, no. 1723 (trans. Chittick, *The Sufi Path of Love*, p. 345).

33 Al-Qushairī, *al-Risāla*, p. 63 (a saying attributed to Abū ʿAli al-Rudhabārī).

34 Najm al-Dīn Kubrā, op. cit., p. 46, para. 96.

35 ibid., p. 49, para. 101.

36 *The Doctrine of the Sufis*, trans. A. J. Arberry (Cambridge: Cambridge University Press, 1947), p. 120.

37 ibid., p. 97; also p. 125.

38 Abdel-Kader, op. cit., p. 81.

39 Rūmī, quoted from R. A. Nicholson, *The Mystics of Islam* (London: Routledge & Kegan Paul, reprinted 1975), p. 168.

40 Quoted from *Delicious Laughter*, versions (of the *Mathnavī*) by Coleman Barks (Athens, Ga.: Maypop Books, 1990), pp. 30–1.

41 Attar, p. 54.

42 Quoted in M. Smith, *Readings from the Mystics of Islam* (London: Luzac & Co., 1950), p. 27.

14

THE MIGRATION FACTOR: COMPARING THE EXPERIENCES OF THE MUSLIM AND JEWISH COMMUNITIES OF SOUTH ASIA

Sarah Ansari

Migration on a large scale, and the movement of large numbers of involuntary migrants or refugees in particular, has become a firmly established feature of the twentieth century. It has been triggered off by, among other things, political crisis, economic upheaval and religious conflict. Mass migration is also an experience which Jews and Muslims have shared. In both cases, their migration has been closely connected to the establishment of a state created, in the context of British decolonization, ostensibly to satisfy their demands as distinct religious communities: Pakistan for India's Muslims in 1947 and Israel for the Jewish Zionist movement in 1948.

The processes which led to the establishment of these two states were not identical. In the case of the former, the demand for Pakistan emerged relatively late in the day and substantial historical debate has centred on whether or not even the Indian Muslim politicians leading the movement envisaged or really desired a separate political state at independence.[1] Mass migration to the parts of British India which became Pakistan also followed rather than preceded the establishment of the new state, and took place on a scale which few contemporary observers had anticipated. In contrast, Jewish migration to what became Israel began in the nineteenth century, and it was the rolling process of migration itself which helped to lend weight to increasing demands for a Jewish state. Even so, for many Jewish communities including Indian Jews, migration to the Middle East became a realistic option only after Israel had been created, and the years since 1948 have consequently witnessed a continued albeit uneven stream of new arrivals from wherever Jewish communities are found in the world, including India. The two states can likewise be contrasted in terms of who migrated to them: while Pakistan attracted only Muslims from other parts of what had been British India, the new Israeli state served as a focus for all Jews. Again, the exodus of Jews has been so great that there were fewer than 6,000 remaining in India in 1981, compared with the 120 million Muslims found in India today. But, despite these differences, for those Muslims and Jews who actually migrated, there was much that was shared: the upheaval involved in uprooting themselves, and the stresses, strains and challenges associated with settling in a state that was still in the process of establishing itself.

These experiences can be contrasted and compared by looking, on the one hand, at Indian Muslim migration to Pakistan and, on the other hand, at Jewish migration to Israel from the Indian subcontinent. The two migrations took place at completely opposite ends of the scale in terms of the numbers involved – millions of Muslims moved to what had become Pakistan as opposed to a relative handful of Jews leaving India – yet both communities had the shared experience of being a minority which enjoyed a relatively protected position under British rule and which felt the need in the context of the changed political circumstances brought about by independence to pursue options which protected their communal identities: both perceived themselves to be a 'vulnerable minority group, without political power, and at the mercy of possible or threatened discriminatory practices'.[2]

Thus, in the context of Muslim–Jewish relations which have been badly affected by the relationship between the state of Israel and the Muslim world, this chapter acknowledges the similar experiences of members of both religions caught up in the process of migration. It looks at how Muslim and Jewish minorities in India reacted to being in a minority and then at how they responded to the idea of migrating to a state in which they would become part of the majority. The first stage in this comparison outlines the historical development of India's Muslim and Jewish communities. It goes on to investigate what the act of migration meant for these two groups, before finally examining what migration to what they believed would be their new homelands meant in practice.

Muslims have for long been the subcontinent's largest and most influential religious minority, representing by the beginning of the twentieth century over a quarter of the population of the region. The presence of Islam in India dates back to the Arab conquest of the western province of Sind by Muhammad bin Qasim during 711–12. This initial contact did not yield a great deal in terms of conversions of Indians to Islam, but did establish the legal status of non-Muslims in Indo-Muslim states through the application of a de facto status of *zimmi*, or protected peoples, to all Indian subjects as if they were 'People of the Book' like Christians and Jews. In short, 'the initial contact between Arabian Islam and the subcontinent was one in which the former yielded considerably to the realities of Indian religion and society'.[3] It was the establishment of the Delhi Sultanate (1206–1526) by Muslims of Turkic Central Asian origins which began the period of the political dominance of Islam in India. Under the Sultans of Delhi, Islam enjoyed official patronage and consequently conversions increased, albeit often as a result of contact between non-Muslims and individual saintly figures, which led in turn to the appearance of communities of Indian Muslims. Under the Mughals (1526–1858), this process was considerably advanced until Muslims became an actual majority in parts of north-western and north-eastern India. Often, these conversions were linked to the way in which the coming of Muslim rule was linked to the socio-economic transformation of rural society.[4] Where Muslim rule did not involve such change, as in the Deccan and South India, conversion to Islam remained much more limited.

The fact that Muslims enjoyed political power in much of India for several hundred years cushioned their community against the potential realities of being a religious minority. Generally pragmatic in their relations with Hindu society, Muslim rulers by and large adopted a conciliatory approach to Indian religions and non-Muslims. As long as Muslims retained political control, it was relatively easy to follow this policy, but once Muslim power was challenged, Indian Muslims were forced to reconsider their position. Muslims in India had always been 'aware of, and anxious about, their minority status', which had meant that 'to guard against becoming engulfed by India's non-Muslim majority, barriers, both mental and social' were more erected and maintained than they were dismantled.[5] With the decline of the Mughal empire and, in particular, the spread of British influence during the eighteenth century, these barriers became all the more important as Muslims increasingly had to come to terms and learn how to cope with their deteriorating power in the region. The suppression of the mutiny uprising in 1857–8 which resulted in the formal ending of Muslim rule and the transfer of power to the British crown finally brought home to many Muslims the need to work out how to be an Indian Muslim in a world where Indian Muslims no longer ruled.

It was in this context that the seeds of Muslim separatist politics were sown, which were to lead eventually to the creation of the separate Muslim state of Pakistan and the huge migration which accompanied it. As has already been pointed out, Muslims, although concentrated in the northern half of the Indian subcontinent, were not distributed evenly even there. There were regions where Muslims made up over 50 per cent of the population, such as western Panjab and eastern Bengal. Equally, though, there were places such as the United Provinces (UP) and Bihar, where Muslims only represented some 10–15 per cent. In addition, although they were united by the fact that they were all Muslims, and even then important sectarian differences between them existed, Indian Muslims still represented a very diverse group of people, belonging to different classes, speaking different languages, and participating in different regional cultures. A shared religion did not automatically mean that they had more in common politically with their co-religionists than with the non-Muslims amongst whom they lived. Muslims were to some extent absorbed as a distinct group in the day-to-day operation of the Hindu caste system, while aspects of the caste system rubbed off on them in the way that Muslims themselves interacted with each other. Muslims, for instance, used terms associated with 'caste' to define their own position within the hierarchy which operated within the Indian Muslim world. In other words, the realities of Indian society very much helped to shape the identity of its Muslim communities, which, although distinct, were by no means separated from the mainstream of Indian life.

As a result, the emergence of Muslim separatism during the late nineteenth and early twentieth centuries cannot be simply explained along the lines that 'they were all Muslims' and therefore automatically came together in a political movement. Rather, its development has to be seen as something which was closely related to the impact of a combination of social, economic, religious and political changes which were taking place during this period, particularly in northern India and in the position of the local Muslim service elite, who had enjoyed a local importance out of all proportion to their numbers or share of the population. Northern India had been the heartland of the Muslim Mughal empire, and Muslims living in rural towns known as qasbahs had consequently been heavily involved in local administration. Until the nineteenth century this world had continued to prosper, but with the consolidation of British power, the qasbahs began to decline and their Muslim service elites found that their skills were no longer in such demand. They feared that their locally strong position would be undermined by bureaucratic and educational reforms. In the western UP, many Muslims were also losing land to Hindu commercial men.[6] These factors seemed to confirm growing Muslim suspicions about the main all-India political organization, the Indian National Congress, which was founded in 1885, particularly as it often seemed to them that Congress's mainly Hindu supporters were benefiting at Muslim expense.

The way that Muslims in northern India viewed their political involvement was also affected by the fact that most of the various processes of Muslim religious revival and reform movements, which had been energized by retreating Muslim power in the region, originated in this region – the former heartland of Muslim state power – where the political decline of Muslims was felt most deeply. In addition, these circumstances worked in ways which reinforced the tendency of the north Indian Muslim elite to believe that religion and politics could not and should not be divided.[7] As many of these Muslims were likely to assume that only Muslims could truly represent Muslims, it was hard for many of them with this kind of outlook to contemplate joining the officially heterogeneous Indian nationalist movement led by the Indian National Congress, in which their communal identity would be totally absorbed.

Islam was not the only religion affected by the changing political realities of the time. Hindu revivalism and Hindu communalism also underwent an upsurge during the same period, and were similarly concentrated in northern India. So, in addition to their own reasons for emphasizing their Muslim identity in political terms, north Indian Muslims had to confront increasingly vigorous Hindu movements whose specific demands, such as the abandonment of cow-slaughter and the conversion of Muslims back to Hinduism, posed direct challenges to their position as a religious minority. Indeed, many north Indian Muslims were deterred from joining the Indian National Congress by its increasing association with Hindu revivalism in terms of the symbols and idioms which it came to employ.

Finally, there was the impact of British rule, which constructed the political framework within which all the other developments of the period took place. The British, largely for reasons of administrative effectiveness in what remained a fairly alien setting, saw Indian society and reponded to it as often as not in terms of stereotypical perceptions, especially in relation to its religious groupings. In northern India this meant that they tended to regard all Muslims as members of a disaffected displaced ruling class whose loyalty and co-operation had to be won in order to help to protect Britain's position both in India and elsewhere in the Muslim world. With the rise of the nationalist movement from the end of the nineteenth century, the British need for local collaborators increased. The authorities consequently helped to protect Muslim sensitivities. They welcomed moves such as those led by Saiyid Ahmad Khan, whom they later knighted for his political and educational services, to build bridges between the Muslim community and the government. Sir Saiyid urged Muslims to co-operate with the Raj rather than with the Indian National Congress, as he argued that the latter's hopes for representative legislatures would only place Muslims in a permanent political minority. In return the British gave support to his Aligarh College, founded in 1877 to bring western learning and aspects of a more traditional Islamic education together under the same roof.

The whole so-called Aligarh movement was dominated by the concerns of north Indian Muslims, and once it became clear that the British were going to concede constitutional reforms in the first decade of the twentieth century, it was Muslims from the UP who masterminded the creation of the All-India Muslim League to lead their campaign to protect the Muslim position in general and more specifically to secure separate electorates with special provision for Muslims in those provinces where they were a minority. These concessions were duly obtained in the Morley–Minto reforms of 1909, when the franchise for election to provincial legislative assemblies was extended. Thus, the British acceptance that Muslims, regardless of differences between them, deserved some kind of special treatment meant that a separate Muslim political identity was formally integrated into the development of India's modern political system at a relatively early stage in the process by which India moved towards self-government. This acknowledgement made it all the easier for the Muslim separatist movement to claim legitimacy once political circumstances in the late 1930s and early 1940s had enhanced the position of the Muslim League and drawn it into the negotiations which were taking place over when and how India would receive its independence. This legitimacy was crucial to the success of the Muslim League, for it was only during the final decade preceding independence in 1947 that it succeeded in winning over support in the all-important Muslim majority provinces of the north-west and the north-east. The combination of the Second World War, the British response, skilled leadership and Congress intransigence meant that by 1946 the Muslim League had extended the basis of its support from the Muslim minority provinces to the whole of Muslim India as Muslims everywhere in the subcontinent were confronted by the need to reassess their futures in a state not ruled by the British.[8]

All the same, as late as 1946, the British still hoped that it would be possible to get the Indians to agree on a single successor state. Failure to get agreement to the Cabinet Mission's scheme for an Indian Union in the summer of 1946, however, meant that some kind of partition was unavoidable. The problem was now about how to partition the country, and by the end of 1946 the situation was in total deadlock. The Muslim League leader, Jinnah, completely rejected the idea of partitioning the Muslim majority provinces themselves, but when the British announced in February 1947 that the transfer of power would take place not later than June 1948, this became the basis of the British plan of how to divide up India. Under pressure from Mountbatten, the new Viceroy, the League felt that it had to accept what Jinnah himself described as a truncated and moth-eaten state, a Pakistan without western Bengal or the eastern two-fifths of the Panjab because the alternative meant conceding power completely to the Congress – virtually impossible in view of the severe deterioration in communal relations by this stage. These same tremendous communal tensions and bitterness meant that when partition did take place, it was accompanied by enormous loss of life and bloodshed as an estimated million Muslims eventually migrated from India to Pakistan, with similar numbers of Hindus and Sikhs moving in the opposite direction. Despite warning signs, such as the Hindu attacks on Muslims in Bihar in October 1946, which had led many politicians to fear that there would be some loss of life as a result of partition, few contemporary observers envisaged that the creation of Pakistan would trigger off the extremely bitter communal reactions which provided much of the impetus for migration. The extent of the migration involved turned out to be almost as much of a surprise to British officials and the respective governments of India and Pakistan as it was to the bewildered refugees themselves.

Turning now to the development of India's Jewish community, the first point to make is that it was minute in comparison with its Muslim counterpart. Yet the prospect of independence also caused Indian Jews to reassess their position, with the result that a very large number in proportionate terms were prepared after 1948 to uproot themselves from a home in which they had been settled for hundreds of years. Like Indian Muslims, Jews were a varied group with extremely varied origins. Although Judaism was never a very widespread religion in India, and Jews were numerically very limited at only just over 25,000 in 1947, Jews had long been settled in the subcontinent. While some claimed to be descended from the lost Ten Tribes of Israel and to have reached India about two thousand years ago, there is definite evidence that they were settled in the country by the ninth century. Accounts by medieval travellers and geographers make it clear that by the thirteenth century there were small settlements of Jews strung along the south-western Malabar coast. There also developed small Jewish settlements on the Konkan coast near Bombay. From the late eighteenth century, India experienced the arrival of Jews from the Middle East who settled mainly in Bombay and Calcutta, while the last wave of immigration was of a limited number of European refugees from the Nazi genocide in the years before the Second World War.[9]

The scattered nature of Jewish settlement helped to isolate the various groups from one another so that each became distinctive in character. In addition, these groups were divided into endogamous sub-groups which further limited contact between them. For example, there were three groups of Cochin Jews: the Malabar or Black Jews, the Pardesi or White Jews and the Meshuararim or Brown Jews. The first were the earliest settlers, whose physical similarity to the indigenous population suggests earlier intermarriage with non-Jewish native inhabitants; the second were later arrivals who maintained a more separate Jewish identity; while the third were the 'offspring of slaves of the Pardesi Jews (who had been given their freedom by the Pardesis and had voluntarily converted to Judaism) or of unions between Pardesi men and native women'.[10] All three sub-groups had come to adopt some of the local Hindu customs and traditions but remained clearly differentiated from the local population by the strict observance of their Jewish faith and the regular contact which they maintained with other Diaspora communities.

In contrast, the Bene Israel, who, as their name suggests, in particular maintained that they were descendants of the members of the Ten Tribes of Israel who had found their way to India in the second century BC, had remained isolated from other Jewish settlements for hundreds of years and had experienced prolonged lapses of religious observance. As was often the case with groups of Indian Muslims, the Bene Israel were partly assimilated in the Hindu caste structure – as 'Saturday oil pressers' – but the religious observances which they retained helped to distinguish them from the majority community,[11] and led eventually to their 'rediscovery' by Cochin Jews in the eighteenth century. They, too, were divided into two groups (the Gora or White Jews and the Kala or Black Jews), which like the three categories of Cochin Jews did not intermarry. The Bene Israel also usually abstained from eating beef and discouraged widow remarriage in order not to offend the Hindus amongst whom they lived. Baghdadi Jews,[12] who had arrived in India from the end of the eighteenth century, tended to identify with the British and on the whole maintained a distance both from Indians themselves and other Jewish groups, apparently adopting 'castelike attitudes towards the Bene Israel because of their lack of ritual orthodoxy and supposed "ancestral impurity"'.[13] 'Stratification, factions and internal status divisions among Jews of a locality have long been common features of Jewish life', but in most places this has been a shifting gradation allowing movement along and up it. In India, however, this ranking was of a far more rigid order, maintained as it was, especially among the Cochin Jews, over centuries.[14] It was only after British rule had come to an end that Indian Jews were able to put these long-standing divisions far enough aside to participate in the shared communal experience of mass migration to Israel.

The ending of British rule, therefore, took on great significance for India's Jews. As a very tiny community, they had always tended to seek protection from the ruler of the day. Jews by the ninth century had already developed amicable relations with the local Hindu Raja of Cochin, no doubt aided by the fact that they were most probably extensively engaged in trade with the overseas contacts that were important for Kerala's own maritime trade. As a result they were granted valuable privileges, including financial advantages and symbolic prerogatives of high status, aspects of which, such as some of the tax privileges, were honoured by the Rajas of Cochin until their rule was ended with independence and the establishment of the Indian Republic.[15] Somewhat later on, the Bene Israel built up their own special links with local authority, in their case with the British. By the eighteenth century, Jews had become very prominent in all the trading posts of the European East India Companies, and it was at this time that a large group moved to Bombay, where many joined regiments of the British East India Company, while others became office clerks involved in the lower-level administration of the developing British Indian empire. Likewise, Baghdadi Jews included a proportion of very wealthy traders-cum-business entrepreneurs, and their adoption of British customs and life-styles bound them even more closely to the fortunes of the British *raj*.[16]

As the experiences of India's Muslims have already demonstrated, British rule favoured minorities, and Jewish groups, like their non-Jewish counterparts, tended to be given special educational and job opportunities which meant that, on the whole, Indian Jews maintained a distance from the nationalist movement, reluctant to antagonize the British. As demands for Indian independence developed, Indian Jews for their part were being introduced to ideas of Jewish nationalism via the activities of Zionist emissaries: the Bene Israel were invited to attend the First Zionist Congress in Basle in 1897. Five years later, the Cochin Jews founded their own Zionist organization, and in 1920 Baghdadi Jews established the Bombay Zionist Association.[17] Although different Jewish groups still tended to organize separately, it was clear that many had begun to realize that the ending of British rule would signal a clear break with the past: India's independence in 1947 was perceived as 'the end of a golden era'.

Independence plunged India into turmoil, with the influx of a massive number of Hindus from newly established Pakistan.

> The economic situation was precarious with serious inflation; there was an acute shortage of housing as well as intense competition for job vacancies. The Indian Jews ... now had to compete with the local non-Jewish population on no more than equal terms.[18]

In the aftermath of the communal tension which had preceded partition, and being hardened in the event, Hindus not surprisingly tended to favour fellow Hindus. Jews found it harder than before to obtain satisfactory employment because, as they felt, preference was given to Hindus. Many Jews whose main source of income had been land ownership were affected by new land laws and encountered severe financial difficulties:

> During the British rule, the Bene Israel had jobs ... in the Civil Service, army, postal and railway services. This changed with Independence .... The standard of living changed. So many of our people left for Israel with the help of the Jewish Agency. They thought they would get good job opportunities and better housing there – so they left.[19]

Politically, independence meant that Jews became almost completely invisible. The privileges and rewards enjoyed under the British authorities or local maharajahs were replaced by the introduction of an electoral system based on adult suffrage which rendered them as an insignificant minority politically ineffective. In addition, the increase in communal awareness which was produced by Hindu–Muslim hostility in the run-up to independence meant that the Bene Israel, who 'clearly had a non-Hindu identity and who lived in a primarily Muslim-dominated area in Maharashtra, felt doubly excluded'. As a Bene Israel who emigrated to Israel commented:

> The Shiva Sena [a fundamentalist Hindu political party] is very powerful in Bombay. They have control over everything and only want their people to have good positions.[20]

With the establishment of the state of Israel only one year after independence, and future prospects deteriorating in India, the first plans for migration there were made with the long-term result that by 1987, according to official sources, over 25,000 Jews from India had settled in Israel, leaving fewer than 6,000 in the subcontinent itself.[21]

The migration of Muslims and Jews away from independent India, there-fore, was intimately connected to the way in which Muslim and Jewish communities had evolved and to how they perceived their interests would suffer once the British presence was ended. For both, the closing years of British rule helped to create a strengthened if not a new sense of communal identity which, in the case of the former, gave impetus to the movement demanding the establishment of Pakistan, and, as far as the latter were concerned, helped to prepare them physically and mentally to look for alternatives to remaining in India. Migration became the option open to Muslims left behind in India after partition – in the minority provinces and in the halves of the two majority provinces of the Panjab and Bengal which were allocated to India. Migration to Israel was the most obvious choice for Jews, especially bearing in mind the assistance which they could expect from agencies connected to the new state of Israel itself. Migration on the scale which took place, however, was unexpected – neither the authorities nor the Muslim League had expected so many Muslims to leave, while few Indian Jews had migrated to what was Palestine, although the option had been available before 1948. But, in both cases, religious and historical precedents for migration existed which helped to justify migration on grounds other than changed political and material circumstances.

For Indian Muslims, the precedent was the obligation to migrate which had been established during the early years of Islam by the Prophet Muhammad's own hijrat (Arabic term meaning literally 'to abandon') from Mecca to Medina in AD 622. This first hijrat had been obligatory and involved almost the entire Muslim community. By the twentieth century, hijrat had come to mean the physical movement away from unbelief and was considered by some Muslims to be an essential expression of Muslim identity.[22] It relied to a large extent on the twin existences of *dar al-harb* (the land of war) and *dar al-Islam* (the land of Islam). Whereas in the former Muslims are unable to practise their religion freely, the latter represents the territory in which the law of Islam prevails, with the result that Muslims have not only tried to change the land in which they live from *dar al-harb* into *dar al-Islam*, but have also on occasion felt the need to migrate from the one to the other to preserve their faith.[23] Hence, in the political turmoil of the years following the First World War, during which opposition to British rule fused with opposition to the way in which the British had treated the Turkish Sultan, or Muslim Caliphate, large numbers of Indian Muslims, mostly from provinces in the north-west, performed hijrat and left British India for neighbouring Afghanistan, partly in response to declarations by Muslim leaders that this migration was religiously incumbent upon them.[24] What is often overlooked in this episode is the fact that economic circumstances also played a large part in motivating individuals to move. Religious factors alone did not explain their decision to migrate, even if this was the justification most widely offered at the time.

Muslims in 1947 could not claim that their migration was in response to religious injunction – many of the same Deobandi *ulama* who had sponsored the 1920 hijrat actually opposed the creation of a separate Muslim state in 1947. But, as fifty years earlier, a variety of different factors came into operation to determine why such a large number of people eventually moved from India to Pakistan, ranging from the purely religious to the really mundane need to protect life and limb. And even though talk of hijrat was muted before August 1947, the analogy was often made once partition had taken place and Pakistan was trying to cope with the millions of migrants who sought 'refuge' within its newly formed borders. The arrival of such huge numbers of people placed enormous burdens on the society which was receiving them. Consequently it did not take very long before resentment on the part of those already living in what had become Pakistan developed towards to what they perceived as the preferential treatment being given to the refugees. While the initial response to the refugees' arrival had been welcoming, as the number of migrants steadily climbed, the welcome wore thin in places and was often replaced by resentment. The practical difficulties of looking after so many people, competition for resources such as land, and the scramble for jobs in urban areas all combined to produce a gradual coolness towards the migrants on the part of certain sections of the 'host' population and disillusionment on the part of the refugees themselves. As early as January 1948, letters in local newspapers had begun to reflect the disappointment and even disillusionment with what the reality of Pakistan meant: in the words of one anonymous *muhajir*,

> I feel it is the struggle, suffering and sacrifices of people like us that went a long way towards the realisation of Pakistan. Or is is that we were cleverly duped and Pakistan was meant for the people of Panjab, Sind, Baluchistan and Bengal only and not for every Musalman of India?[25]

The authorities in efforts to promote greater harmony emphasized the comparison with the original hijrat. Hence the refugees became known as 'Muhajirs' as opposed to 'Ansars', a term which was applied to the people receiving them, ideally in the same way as the first Ansars had looked after the Prophet Muhammad and his companions upon their arrival in Medina. Newspaper articles and politicians' speeches repeatedly made the analogy in the hope of helping to reduce the tensions which were already apparent by the end of the 1940s.[26]

The situation was not helped by the fact that the *muhajirs* often actually did expect a degree of special treatment, regarding it as just compensation for what they had been forced to leave behind in India. Even their name – *muhajir* – contributed to creating this gap in perceptions. Whereas a refugee is pushed largely by circumstances, a *muhajir* is supposed to have made a positive decision to migrate, and hence might well consider it reasonable to receive respect, including material benefit, from the wider Muslim community.[27] In reality, the majority of *muhajirs* arriving in Pakistan were acute migrants – refugees who had seen little option but to leave India – however, once they were in their adopted homeland, it was possible for different interpretations of their flight to come into play.

The fact that well into the 1950s hundreds of thousands of refugees had not been resettled made their 'sacrifices' seem all the more extreme. Karachi, then the capital of Pakistan, was particularly bad, with some 250,000 people still living in improvised dwellings in 1953 and over 100,000 people in 1958. The government's inability or incapacity to deal effectively with these kinds of problems came in for harsh criticism. Refugee organizations sprang up to protect *muhajir* interests, and many were very critical of the administration. The hardships of this first decade following partition increased economic insecurity, unemployment rose and standards of living fell, resulting in a decade of disappointment for many *muhajirs* who watched the rich become richer as inflationary spirals forced down their own real incomes. Politically, *muhajirs* also felt frustrated for most of the time by a lack of adequate representation, even bearing in mind the general short-comings of Pakistan's political system during this period, which meant that no general election actually took place until 1970. Their own feelings of being distinct led them to consider themselves to be in a separate political category from other Pakistanis, and so throughout Pakistan there were demands for separate seats in provincial assemblies: in the Panjab, *muhajirs* obtained the places formerly filled by non-Muslims, but in Sind they did not.

The resulting bitterness felt by many *muhajirs* about the reception that had greeted them in their new homeland combined with disappointment with what their new lives meant in practice was great, and was reflected in the popularity of satirical poetry which emphasized their resentment 'at the powers that be', or those who were generally seen to have come to power with the creating of Pakistan. As in the following poem, 'Leadership allotted', by Majeed Lahori, they often targeted their criticism at the unfairness of the way in which resources and opportunity were being distributed:

> Land was allotted and factory was allotted,
> And along with it leadership was allotted to you.
>
> You are the one who has been allotted every happiness,
> And I am the one who has been allotted poverty.
>
> Those who were rich are owners of buildings,
> The poor citizen has been allotted vagrancy.
>
> My amazed eyes have also seen it happen,
> That those who were robbers were allotted leadership.
>
> Those who could not qualify as clerks before,
> By God's glory were allotted posts of officers.

During this era of allotment, O Majeed,
I could not get a house but was allotted poetry.

Rather than bringing the Muslims of India closer together, then, the process of migration seemed to be driving wedges between different groups of them. Language differences which had not been very important before independence took on a new significance in the years which followed it. Indeed, language became one of the main issues around which 'ethnic divisions' aligned themselves from the 1950s onwards. Apart from the conflict between Urdu and Bengali which resulted in riots in East Pakistan in 1952 and helped to fuel growing Bengali nationalism there, there was also a clash of interests in Sind: Sindhis regarded *muhajir* demands for the recognition of Urdu as symbolic of their determination to impose their dominance on the province, while *muhajirs* saw in the rejection of Urdu the negation of their identity and the sacrifices which they had made by migrating to Pakistan in the first place. Bearing in mind these early signs of the ethnic tension which has become one of the hallmarks of Pakistani political life, it is difficult not to conclude that partition and migration heightened rather than lessened the meaning of ethnicity for Muslims of the subcontinent, with the result that *muhajirs* who might once have explained their reason for moving to Pakistan in religious terms – such as the need to protect their religion – tended by the 1970s and 1980s to emphasize instead that they had been denied full access to what they had migrated for: full access to economic and political opportunity.

Parallels between the Indian Muslim experience and that of Indian Jews migrating to Israel can be drawn. First, the Jews also had a precedent to follow when it came to the act of migration. The idea of concentrating Jewish people from all around the world in the national home or state of Israel was well established in the minds of the Jewish Diaspora: hence, Jews throughout the Diaspora prayed for centuries for the return to the Holy Land, and 'next year in Jerusalem' became a basic principle of the Zionist movement at the end of the nineteenth century, when migration took on an increased political reality.[28] Then began the series of successive *aliyahs* (from the Hebrew meaning 'to go up', originally used to designate the honour accorded to a worshipper of being called up to read an assigned passage from the Torah) or waves of modern Jewish immigration to Palestine which began in the 1880s and carried on until after the Second World War.[29]

Like Muslims who migrated to Pakistan, Indian Jews had mixed views about why migration from India to Israel took place as well as experiencing a mixed reception upon their arrival in what they hoped would be their new homeland. A study of how Indian Jews perceived the factors which influenced them to emigrate to Israel revealed how most of 'the informants who had made *aliyah* stressed the importance of the religious factors in their own decision to emigrate' but 'put more emphasis on economic and political considerations when giving their opinions about the factors which would influence the *aliyah* of all the Jewish groups in India'.[30] Considering the emphasis traditionally placed on the religious imperative to live in the land of their ancestors, it is not surprising that Indian Jews should have stressed religious factors as the main motivation for their having gone on *aliyah*: 'to give more prominence to economic or political considerations would be to admit that, in their own case, materialistic values were more important than religious ideals'.[31] This, however, they were more prepared to do for others, in the process acknowledging that economic, political and social factors were important in the balance of motives which explained migration.

As far as experiencing a mixed reception in Israel was concerned, the example of the Bene Israel may be used to illustrate what happened to some Indian Jews upon their arrival there. Many Bene Israel hoped that migration to Israel would result in complete acceptance by other Jews. In reality, having settled in Israel, many complained that they were not accepted but regarded as inferior by European Jews. Indeed, these complaints dated from the very beginning of Bene Israel immigration.[32] Problems of discrimination in jobs and housing meant that a number of Bene Israel were repatriated to India at the expense of the government of Israel during the early 1950s. Migration to Israel and complaints in Israel against their treatment there, however, continued. The uncertainty of their position was reinforced by doubts about their religious status as full Jews in regard to marriage with other Jews which were first raised in the 1950s by some orthodox Jews

> who feared that their past ignorance of Jewish law relating to divorce and levirate marriage made them unacceptable. At that time ... the Sephadic chief rabbi ... refused to declare that the Bene Israel were acceptable as proper Jews ... [and] individual rabbis could ... refuse to perform marriages between Bene Israel and other Jews unless the Bene Israel party underwent ritual conversion.[33]

Special directives on the subject were promulgated in February 1962 which required an investigation 'as far back as possible' of the ancestry of Bene Israel contemplating marriage with members of other communities of Jews and resulted in further fury on the part of the Bene Israel, who responded with demonstrations and hunger strikes, forming an Action Committee in Israel and a Bene Israel Purity Justification Committee back in Bombay. Eventually, in August 1964 the Knesset affirmed that it viewed the Bene Israel as Jews in all respects and with the same rights as all other Jews, including matters of personal status. This official change of heart led increasing numbers of Bene Israel to emigrate to Israel with the active encouragement of the Jewish Agency.[34]

Both Pakistan and Israel have faced the twin problems of integration and assimilation in relation to the many Muslims and Jews who have migrated to them. Muslims and Jews alike uprooted themselves in the hopes of greater security – both spiritual and material – but for both the difficulties involved in putting down new roots were far greater than they had imagined. The outcome has been in both cases the evolution of societies in which different groups of migrants have retained huge chunks of their cultural ethnicity and consequently separateness. Pakistan and Israel have emerged as states in which powerful ethnic and cultural divisions persist in defying moves towards a more homogeneous and uniform society. Indian Muslims who moved to Pakistan and Indian Jews who settled in Israel are still identified and labelled in terms of their Indian origins despite the distance they have moved physically and psychologically in migrating to what they hoped would be their new homelands.

NOTES

1 For the latest entry in this debate see Ayesha Jalal, *The Sole Spokesman: Jinnah, the Muslim League and the Demand for Pakistan* (Cambridge, 1985).
2 Margaret Abraham, 'The normative and the factual: an analysis of emigration factors among the Jews of India', *Jewish Journal of Sociology*, 33(1) (June 1991), 12.
3 Entry on 'Islam' in *The Cambridge Encyclopaedia of India, Pakistan, Bangladesh, Sri Lanka, Nepal, Bhutan and the Maldives* (Cambridge: Cambridge University Press, 1989), p. 339.
4 For instance, see R. M. Eaton, 'The political and religious authority of the shrine of Baba Farid', in *Moral Conduct and Authority: The Place of Adab in South Asian Islam*, ed. Barbara Daly Metcalf (Berkeley, 1984) and Sarah F. D. Ansari, *Sufi Saints and State Power: The Pirs of Sind, 1843–1947* (Cambridge, 1992).
5 *The Cambridge Encyclopaedia of India*, p. 343.
6 Francis Robinson, *Separatism among Indian Muslims: The Politics of the United Provinces' Muslims, 1860–1923* (Cambridge, 1974).
7 Farzana Shaikh, *Community and Consensus in Islam: Muslim Representation in Colonial India* (Cambridge, 1989).
8 Ian Talbot, *Provincial Politics and the Pakistan Movement: The Growth of the Muslim League in North-West and North-East India, 1937–47* (Karachi, 1988).
9 *The Cambridge Encyclopaedia of India*, pp. 360–1.
10 Abraham, 'The normative and the factual', 6.
11 Such as circumcision, the observance of some dietary laws (*kashrut*) and of the Sabbath, and the recitation of the Shema (the Jewish confession of faith) on important occasions, Abraham, 'The normative and the factual', 6.
12 The description 'Baghdadi' referred to Jews not just from Baghdad but from various parts of the Middle East and west Asia such as Basra, Aleppo in Syria, Iran and Aden.
13 Joan G. Roland, *Jews in British India: Identity in a Colonial Era* (London, 1989), p. 157.
14 This rigidity endured despite formal condemnation by eminent rabbis in their responses to questions sent to them from Cochin. See David G. Mandelbaum, 'Social stratification among the Jews of Cochin in India and in Israel', *Jewish Journal of Sociology* 17(2), 166.
15 ibid., 167–8.
16 Abraham, 'The normative and the factual', 7.

17 Roland, *Jews in British India*, pp. 80–2, 151.
18 Abraham, 'The normative and the factual', 12.
19 ibid.
20 ibid., 15.
21 India's 1941 census enumerated 22,480 Jews; in 1951 the total had risen to 26,512. By 1961, this figure had declined to 18,553; in 1971, it was 5,825; and in 1981 it stood at 5,618. See S. B. Isenberg, *India's Bene Israel. A Comprehensive Inquiry and Sourcebook* (Bombay, 1988), pp. 293–5.
22 Md K. Masud, 'The obligation to migrate', in D. Eickelman and J. Piscatori (eds), *Muslim Travellers* (London, 1990), pp. 29–30.
23 *The Encyclopaedia of Islam* (Leiden) (new edition), vol. II, pp. 126, 127.
24 M. Naeem Qureshi, 'The "Ulama" of British India and the hijrat of 1920', *Modern Asian Studies* 1 (1984), 41–59.
25 *Dawn* (Karachi), 18 January 1948, 5.
26 For example, see *Dawn*, 17 June 1948, 4, and 30 August 1949, 8.
27 See the article on 'al-Muhadjirun' in *Encyclopaedia of Islam*, vol. VII, pp. 356–7.
28 Teodor Shanin, 'The Zionisms of Israel', in Halliday and Alavi (eds), *State and Ideology in the Middle East and Pakistan* (London, 1988), p. 223.
29 See D. J. Elazak, *Israel, Building a New Society*, (Indiana, 1987), pp. 11–12, for discussion of the tradition of *aliyot* in relation to immigration to what became Israel.
30 Abraham, 'The normative and the factual', 18.
31 ibid.
32 Schifra Strizower in 'The Bene Israel in Israel', *Middle Eastern Studies* 2(2) (1965), 123, includes the following quote from the *New York Times*, 22 November 1951: 'In Bombay we were told that there is no colour bar in Israel, but in a shop in Beer Sheba we were told that we should eat only black bread as we were black and the white bread was only for white Jews.'
33 Roland, *Jews in British India*, pp. 249–50.
34 Abraham, 'The normative and the factual', 16.

Part V
THE SONG OF SONGS

15

JUNG'S FATHER, PAUL ACHILLES JUNG, AND THE SONG OF SONGS: AN INTRODUCTION

Joel Ryce-Menuhin

It is not generally known to persons interested in C. G. Jung that his father, Dr Paul Achilles Jung, was an Arabist whose university thesis at Göttingen dealt with an early Karaite text by Japheth on The Song of Songs. This

Ueber

des Karäers Jephet

arabische Erklärung

des

Hohenliedes

von

Paul Jung

aus Basel.

Inaugural - Dissertation

zur

Erlangung der philosophischen Doctorwürde

der

Georgia Augusta.

Göttingen,
Druck der Dieterich'schen Univ.-Buchdruckerei.
(W. Fr. Kaestner).

reproduced with the permission of the Familien-Archiv Jung

inaugural dissertation was submitted to Georgia Augusta University at Göttingen for the Doctorate in Philosophy.

Karaism (from Hebrew *Qara*, to study the Scriptures) was a Jewish movement in Persia (eighth century) which rejected the oral tradition of the Talmudic rabbinites. The Muslim conquest of Persia (640) and the fact of the great Omazyad dynasty (750) brought a prophetic passion for an uncompromising monotheism among the Jews in Arab-style zeal, fervour and passion. This included a desire for social justice for the individual. The religious calender and marriage and Sabbath laws were changed. The Karaites were deeply influenced by the school of the Mu'tazilites, which developed a rational theology named *Ilm-al-Kalam* (Science of the Word) to protect monotheism in a unity of reason, conscience and revelation.

Benjamin ben Moses al-Nahawandi of Persia named the sect the 'Karaites'. Orthodox Jewry fought this developing group because the Karaites insisted upon the personal freedom of each individual to interpret the Torah as he or she saw fit. There were so many ritual privation laws involved in religious practice in Karaism that few could actually maintain such an extreme discipline, which included sexual privations, no fire on the Sabbath, an increase in dietary and ritual cleanliness laws and more extreme fasting and clothing rules than orthodox Jewry was then practising. Practical observances became more important for the Karaites than ethics or metaphysics.

In spite of frequent criticism and attack, the Karaites managed to produce important works in Arabic and Hebrew that involved biblical exegeses and polemics as well as Hebrew lexicography.

During the ninth to twelfth centuries Karaism spread from Babylonia to Palestine and on to Egypt, Syria and Spain. At the end of the seventeenth century even Swedish Protestant theologians became interested in the sect. Abraham Firkovich (1786–1874) brought together the largest collection of Karaite manuscripts, now in the St Petersburg Public library. He believed the Karaites were descended from the lost Ten Tribes of Israel who had settled in the Crimea in the sixth century.

Jung's father, in studying the Karaite movement, became concerned with a tenth-century commentary to the Song of Songs by the Karaite commentator Jepheth Ben Ali Ha-Levi. Because he lived in Jerusalem, a spiritual centre of Karaism during the second half of the tenth century, his biblical commentaries in Arabic and his translation of the entire Holy Bible into Arabic made Jepheth widely known. In the text under study in the thesis of Paul Achilles Jung, Japheth (the spelling in English) conveys literal meanings of the Song of Songs while interposing allegorical inter-pretations from time to time. He also comments on Hebrew grammar and lexicography. When his commentaries in Arabic were translated into Hebrew for the Karaites living in Byzantium who did not read or speak Arabic generally, his reputation became historically widened among the Karaites.

The Karaite sect

appears to have come into being as the result of a combination of factors; the amalgamation of various heterodox trends in Babylonian–Persian Jewry; the tremendous religious, political and economic fermentation in the entire East, resulting from the Arab conquests and the collision of Islam with world religions; and the social and economic grievances of the poorer classes of Jewry, particularly those who had left the populous centre of Babylonia and had migrated to the sparsely settled frontier provinces of the caliphate, where they were more or less independent of the Babylonian Jewish authorities. The Karaite sect absorbed both such Jewish sects as the Isawites (adherents of Abu Isa al-Isfahani) and Yudghanites, who were influenced by East-Islamic tendencies, and small remnants of pre-talmudic Sadducees and Boethusians and similar anti-traditional movements.

(Encyclopedia Judaica, vol. 9, p. 764)

Now I would like to quote a large section of Paul Jung's dissertation starting with section III, entitled 'Commentary on the Song of Songs':

Like all the others, this Commentary is written in Arabic with Hebrew quotations. His (Japheth's] hand written text of which we here give the first chapter without the preface, is complete except for the preface. In it Japheth briefly discusses the three texts relating to Solomon. Nevertheless what is missing would not amount to much. The actual script is in the possession of my highly esteemed teacher, Professor Ewald, through whose kindness it has been handed over for me to work on.

The explanations given in the text are of an allegorical kind. One example will suffice to show this. Let us take the two main characters of *The Song of Songs*, the Shulamite maiden and King Solomon. According to the explanation, the former represents now Yahweh, now the awaited Messiah, or, lastly the historical King Solomon.

The handwriting of the manuscript is Hebraic cursive script which is somewhat different from the present day script in its characters. I found it particularly difficult to render the Hebraic letters into Arabic as Japheth used to omit the dots which differentiate the Arabic consonants. For example, D in Hebrew is both D and DH in Arabic; TS in Hebrew for both Ṣ and Ḍ in Arabic.

Song of Songs
Verse I. [The first verse is translated directly from the Arabic and is omitted here. Ed.]

2. *'May he kiss me with the kisses of his mouth, for your delights are better and sweeter than those of wine.'*
Know that this song has four aspects. First of all it is what the spiritual

leaders of the people say before the Lord of the forefathers and themselves, and asking for the fulfilment of his promise. Secondly, it is what the daughters of Jerusalem say when they bemoan their lot and describe God's deeds to the people and exhort them to obey him and to seek what he has promised. Thirdly, it is what the people say to each other about their own affairs, as in the paragraph about '*a little sister*' (VIII, 8ff). Fourthly, it is the answer of the Creator (may He be powerful and great!) to the questions and requests from the spiritual leaders and also describes their beauty and grace during the time when they are obedient and obey their civil laws, as we will explain in each section. This is the general purpose of this song. But the words, '*He will kiss me*', is the word of the spiritual leaders of the people, who lead the many to righteousness, the Ternbithen of salvation (These three designations from Daniel XI, 33, Daniel XII, 3, Isaiah LXI, 3.) through which salvation and the kingdom of the offspring of the sons of David will appear. In this first section which contains three verses, they demand six things from God, of which the first is the cooling of His anger and the appearance of Eliahu, peace be to him! The second thing is the manifestation of the signs and wonders in the world which brings to an end the dominion of the heathen. And the third thing is the manifestation of His testimony which is the law of Moses for thereupon the peoples will enter into His religion. And the fourth thing is the coming together in the land of Israel from the four corners of the earth, of those who were driven out of Israel. And the fifth thing is the building of the temple and that Israel will reside within it. And the sixth thing is the reinstatement of the civil laws of the people and of the tribe of Levi. These six things are the central core of what God promised. Thus they begin first by begging Him to temper the fury of His anger and to make peace with them. And this is the meaning of '*He will kiss me.*' When someone is angry with his companion and then when he wants to make peace with him, the first thing that he should do is to embrace him and kiss him. Thus by saying, '*from the kisses of His mouth*', He shows that it has become His habit to be angered by their disobedience but when they show humility, then to be willing to come back to them and make peace with them. And with His words, 'from the kisses', He points to the time of Moses and Joshua and of the Judges and of the Kings of Israel and Judah just as indicated in the works of the prophet. And He adds, '*His mouth*' to show that His happiness in the past was due to the prophets Moses and Aaron and Samuel and the other prophets after them, but in the future will be due to Eliahu who with the greatest fervour will instruct them in those duties towards God which they should carry out and through which they will achieve salvation. With the words, '*Because your loving friendship is good*', He combines what is in the past and what is in the future. These *'references to love'* are God's mercy and good deeds which after the Peace of God continue ceaselessly one after the other. And He says that they are better than the delights of wine experienced during a drinking bout, since these do not last and are only linked to drinking the wine for they end too when the drinking bout ends.

3. *'The scent of your balm is marvellous. Balm which can be poured, is your name. That is why the virgins love you.'*
Know that the particle in *'for the aroma'* is superfluous and that *'good'* (plural) refers to *'oils'* not to *'aromas'*. That is because the people compare the fame of their loved one with the scent of the most delightful balm. It is also said to be the scent of nutmeg for various reasons. Partly because the fragrances incorporated in the balm do not lose their scent so soon. Partly because one can be certain that they do not spoil when they become old. Partly because the balm retains the strength of the fragrances and thus penetrates inside the body. And the purpose of it is to be the anointing oil with which priests and kings are anointed. The words *'maidens have loved Thee'* indicate Israel in the opinion of some.

4. *'Draw me after you. I will run. The king leads me into his chambers. Let us be happy and rejoice over you. We want to applaud your delights more than wine. They who conduct themselves properly love you.'*
It is explained in this verse that the Almighty (God) who is the one sought and the one searching has been cast down to the bed of the sea and into the deepest pit. This refers to those of Israel who angered the Lord Most High and so were cast out into exile comparable with the depths of the sea and the deepest pit, according to the words, *'I sank in the deepest mud'* (Psalms LXIX, 3) and further *'I called your name Yahweh out of the deepest pit'* (Thren. III, 55). And his words, *'drag me'* mean *'Bring us out of exile at the time when your signs and your solace appear in the world through which we will be liberated from exile.'* However the meaning of the words, *'behind you we shall run'*, is that when He brings them out of the pit and leads them into His chambers, then *'they will run after him'* meaning that they will make it their duty to render service to Yahweh with love and with their whole heart, just as He instructed them. *'You must follow Yahweh your God'* (Deut. XIII, 5). They took this upon themselves as an obligation according to their words *'We do not want to turn away from You, etc.'* (Psalms XXX, 19) and He said of them *'Do not turn back to foolish things!'* (Psalms LXXXV, 9). The words, *'the Kiss has brought me into His chambers'*, teach that when He brings them out of exile into His chambers, these chambers are the land of Israel and

the Holy Mountain. Thus they will be united with the servants of God, and this is the fulfilment of the union and the promise.

5. *I am dark and beautiful, O daughters of Jerusalem, and my darkness is like the darkness of the tents of the Arabs, and my beauty is like the beauty of the draperies of Solomon's tents.'*

Know that the first section is entirely a song, namely what was said between them and God. They clamoured and demanded. However it is not stated that He gave them an answer, but instead was thinking of the situation of all the people. The reason for this was the assembly of the spiritual leaders did not give any answer on God's behalf which they were otherwise able to do when they were obedient to God asking Him for the fulfilment of His promise. No answer was forthcoming when the people did not join in obeying God and when there was not complete obedience. When the spiritual leaders recognized this, they were forced to seek the cooperation of the people. And know that the daughters of Jerusalem are those who direct their prayers towards Jerusalem. That is the city of their dominion and power. That is why He calls them daughters of Jerusalem. There is a meaning in their complaint to them about their situation before they tried to act obediently towards God. This meaning is namely that one of the causes of the flight of the people from joining their spiritual leaders in acting obediently, is that they see the dire situation of the spiritual leaders and how they want to justify themselves and show that is not a result of their misdemeanours and sins but only a result of the sins of Israel and its time in captivity because God had been angered. For when this is firmly in the minds of the daughters of Jerusalem, they say to her, *'Where has your beloved gone? We want to help you look for Him'* (VI, 1). This is the sense that they indicate with their words, *'I am dark but do not look at me as if I am dark skinned!'* (I, 6). The superficial sense of the words is the darkness of colour. And she compares it with the darkness of the tents of hair which Kuraisch has. Thereupon she says, *'Yes, the shape of my face and my body are beautiful by being like the tents of Solomon.'* But the inner meaning is shameful if her situation is that of many countries and most of the people because it refers to all God's blows striking them, as they relate, *'Every day I go around in a daze, etc.'* (Psalms XXXVIII, 7), as a result of the other text *'For Your arrows have pierced me'* (Psalms XXXVIII, 3). With the words, *'and fair or beautiful'* (feminine), they mean the beauty of their obedience towards God which is natural in appearance because it is not like the colour which appears and then fades. And the meaning of comparing the colour with the tents of Kedar is because they stayed some time in Kedar's kingdom and they continually complained about their situation there. They said, '*Woe is me that I live in Meshech dwelling by the tents of Kedar!*' (Psalms CXX, 5). And this comes from the same place which indicates that they dwelt within the fourth kingdom (Daniel II, 40). As far as the previous kingdoms are concerned, it is quite clear that those who pursued righteousness and sought Yahweh did not dwell there. With the words, '*as the tent-cloths of Solomon*', they indicate the period of Solomon in which they were accustomed to obey God. Only after the death of Solomon did they split into factions.

6. '*Do not look at me who am dark and burnt by the sun. The sons of my mother were angry with me. They made me look after the vineyards and I have not looked after the vineyard which belongs to me.*'

After she said to them, '*I am dark*', she explains to them the reason for her darkness. She says to them, '*Do not look at me as a dark person as if you think that it is a natural darkness like the dark skin of the blackamoors which never ever changes. In my case it happened by chance. I went out of my chambers and the castle of my friend and while I was in the fields, the sun tormented me and burnt me so that my skin became dark.*' And then she explained to them what she had done in the fields so that she became dark. She said, '*After I had become the guardian of the vineyards, I had no place to rest and the sun tormented me.*' And then she explained to them that those who had assigned her to watch over the vineyards were her brothers not her husband. This is the outward meaning of the words. But the inner meaning is to teach them that these blows and this degradation which have befallen them, do not originate in the past but are something which befell them in exile. And the explanation about the sun refers to the dynasties of the peoples who subjugated them, namely the kings of Assyria and Aram and the four kingdoms, for they destroyed and burnt everything to the ground. The dynasties are being likened to the sun in the sense that this has power over the world. In the same way some of the dynasties are compared to the heavenly army according to His word. '*And up to the General, etc.*' (Daniel VIII, 11). But with the words, '*The sons of my mother were angry with me*', she is referring to the kings leading them astray and to false prophets and after them the priests of the exiled, who ruined Israel through their vile administration and lack of care. '*They made me guardian of the vineyards*' allow for one of two possible meanings. One is that she is thereby referring to a way of life which is contrary to Yahweh's laws. Thus she says, '*They forced me to pursue a way of life which they assigned me and prevented me from observing the law and His commandments.*' This was just like Jeroboam at first, who ordered

239

obeisance towards the calves and who changed the Kibla (order of prayers) and the feast days. And he was joined in this by the false prophets as shown in the verses, *'Your first father sinned'*, and, *'your spokesman was unfaithful to me'* (Isaiah XLIII, 27). They were followed by the priests of the exiled, who changed many of the prayers and forced their observance for they had the power to condemn those opposing them to death. As they said, *'Everyone who transgresses against the proclamations of the Elders, will be condemned to death.'* Or it may be that what was meant by the words, *'They made me guardian'* was that they served the people by being their artists, rhetoricians and writers, according to these words, *'And you serve your enemy in a land that you do not know'* (freely after Deut. 28, 36, 48). With the words, *'my vineyard'*, they mean *'I do not administer my realm as if I were in my own land and under the authority of my king whom I obey and whom I serve.'* This explanation may probably be derived from the words, *'Solomon had a vineyard in Baal Hamon'* (VIII, ii) as we will explain in the proper place. In this way they have explained in these two verses that it was the deeds of the kings and the priests which were the causes of their period in exile, according to the words beginning, *'You have scattered my sheep'* (Jeremiah XXIII, 2).

Paul Achilles Jung remarks at the end of this: 'We thought it necesary to translate Japheth's text up to this point for those readers who do not understand Arabic. The commentary on these first six verses is enough to allow an appreciation of the kind of spirit behind this form of commentary.' In founding his studies within Arabic, Judaic and Christian sources, C. G. Jung's father, Paul Achilles Jung, proves himself to be a true monotheist with a much broader range of comprehension of the sources of the Semitic religions than Jungians have realized. I believe this atmosphere, in the household of a Swiss Protestant minister, would have been unique in Switzerland at the time in which C. G. Jung grew up, and that in this sense, Jung's repeatedly disappointed remarks about his father, for example, in the autobiography, need to be taken with a grain of salt by contemporary Jungians. Sons often do not appreciate the gifts of their fathers and lack compassion in their description of their fathers.

16

EROS AND MYSTICISM
Early Christian interpretation of the Song of Songs
Andrew Louth

'Eros and mysticism' – such a title suggests, I suppose, *one* side of the phenomenon of religion, and to many a side that they find congenial. Eros – a force that arises from deep within ourselves, not wholly understood by ourselves but reaching through the whole of the human person, all that it is to be human, sometimes creatively, healingly, sometimes with a shattering and destructive force. Eros – opposed to *logos*, the rational discriminating faculty that tends to look outside for signs of order, that seeks to rule the realm within, to impose structure on it, to subdue it and control it. Eros, then – in a religious sense – stands for the hidden mysterious depths, interpreted by symbol, as opposed to a rational system, supported by an institution, the religion of dogma. And mysticism suggests something of the same contrast: mysticism being a quest into the unknown, shocking and upsetting to the representatives of traditional religious structures: by its emphasis on the unknowable reality of God, the Infinite, it calls in question the tidy rationalizations of dogma. The mystic is feared – and often persecuted – by the representatives of dogmatic religion: one thinks of the great Sufi mystic, al-Hallaj, or within Christianity of the condemnation at Avignon in the early fourteenth century of Meister Eckhart, or the persecution faced by St John of the Cross in sixteenth-century Spain. Eros and mysticism, then – as opposed to *logos* and dogma. It is a contrast that strikes a chord of understanding with most of us living in the West in the late twentieth century, and we can trace an awareness of such a contrast well back into the last century and beyond.

What I want to do here, however, is to look back behind this contrast: I want to look at some strands in early Christianity and suggest that these contrasts – between eros and *logos*, between mysticism and dogma – are really complementary parts of a greater whole, and that we catch at least glimpses of such a vision of wholeness in some of the early Christian writers, some of the Fathers, as they are called. I want to do this by selecting – from among a great mass of writings – just one genre, and that is commentaries on the Song of Songs.

The Song of Songs is one of the shortest books in the Hebrew Bible. It belongs to the third part of the Hebrew Canon, the Writings, and within that is usually classed as part of what is called Wisdom literature, though it is in many respects rather different from the rest of the Wisdom literature. These books of Wisdom – which include the Book of Proverbs and the Book of Ecclesiastes, or the Preacher (*Qoheleth*) – were ascribed to King Solomon, the son of David. Consequently, the Song of Songs was taken to be a collection of love songs, perhaps an epithalamion or wedding song, composed by Solomon for one of his (many) wives, a Shulamite (see S. of S. 6:13). It is clearly a piece of oriental love poetry, and bears comparison with other examples of the genre: in particular, in its evident and unashamed delight in the sensuousness of human love-making. In this poem (or poems) the man describes the hair, the neck, the breasts of his beloved, while the woman longs for the kisses and the caresses of her lover. There are different voices in the Song, so that it can be regarded either as a dramatic poem in dialogue, or as a collection of love songs loosely strung together: on the one hand, there is the voice of the bridegroom speaking to his beloved or to his companions, while on the other there is the voice of the bride responding to her lover, or musing to herself or to her maids. The Song contains an account of their courtship, their snatched meetings, her longing for him during his absence, and doubts as to whether he will return, provoking an agonized search for him, and his calling to her and coming to her at night. Some texts of the Bible – the New English Bible, for instance – print the Song out as a dialogue, specifying the parts for the bride and the bride-groom, but this is unusual; it is usually left to the wit of the reader.[1]

It is, as I have said, a very sensuous poem. Many readers will know Eric Gill's illustrations for various editions of the Song; the sensuousness of his etchings – especially those he did in white line on black to illustrate an edition of the Latin Vulgate text of the Song – match the poem itself very well.[2]

For all the obviousness of the celebration of human love between man and woman in the Song of Songs, however, the Song of Songs was never interpreted in such a way by Christians. Perhaps that ought to be put more precisely: it is not that any denied that, on the surface, it was a human love song; it is rather that they felt that its sacred meaning did not lie on the surface (it is true that one early Christian writer, Theodore, Bishop of Mopsuestia, who died in 428, did think that the Song of Songs was nothing but a human love song, but he argued that for this reason it should not be regarded as a sacred book for Christians at all. His was a lone voice). Christians felt that it was an *allegory*, pointing to some higher truth. There are two points that need to be emphasized about this. First, Christians – and not only Christians – thought that the real meaning of any sacred, inspired writing (for Christians, the Bible) could not simply be its surface meaning: the real meaning was a deeper meaning, and allegory was the key that unlocked this hidden meaning. What Christians applied to the Song of Songs they applied generally to the Scriptures. Second, however Christians interpreted the Song of Songs, they always regarded it as fundamentally a *love* song: the allegory was an allegory of love.

In fact, it was very easy to interpret the Song of Songs allegorically, as the Bible itself had already interpreted the relationship between God and humanity as a love-relationship. The prophets had shown the way: Hosea represented God as deeply in love with Israel, for all her faithlessness,[3] and the prophet Ezekiel takes up the same theme.[4] Following this lead, already in early Christian times the Jewish rabbis had interpreted the Song of Songs as referring to the love between God and Israel. The New Testament develops the idea of God's love very strikingly: a patient, self-sacrificing love, of which the crucifixion of the Son of God is the culminating expression. Bridal imagery, marriage imagery, is also used. In Ephesians (5:32) the relationship between Christ and the Church is compared to the love between husband and wife; in the Apocalypse the apostle John sees the New Jerusalem, coming down from heaven, like a bride adorned for her husband (Apoc. 21:2). All this made it very easy and natural for Christians to interpret the Song of Songs as referring to the relationship of love between Christ and the Church. Such an interpretation is first found in a commentary ascribed to Hippolytus, the first antipope (died 235), belonging to the beginning of the third century. Soon after, this interpretation was taken up by the great early Christian theologian Origen, about whom I shall have more to say. With Origen the idea that the Song refers to the relationship between Christ and the Church is supplemented by another: that it refers to the love between Christ and the soul of the individual Christian. It is this that opens the door to the later mystical interpretation of the Song of Songs which became very popular – there are several dozen commentaries on the Song of Songs surviving from the early Middle Ages[5] – an interpretation that culminates in the poems of St John of the Cross and their mystical interpretation, for all the poems that form the basis of his mystical treatises are based on the Song of Songs.

Let us now look in somewhat more detail at some of these commentaries on the Song of Songs. I want to concentrate on the works of two early Christian theologians: Origen and St Gregory of Nyssa. Origen belongs to the third century, to the period when Christians still faced persecution by the authorities of the Roman empire. At the beginning of the third century Origen's father, Leonides, was martyred and, the story goes, Origen was only saved from accompanying his father by his mother's hiding his clothes, so that he could not go out.[6] Origen himself was to die as a result of the great persecution that took place under the Emperor Decius in 251: he was tortured – they wanted his recantation, not his death – and he died some years later of the injuries he had sustained. In between, the Church in the parts where Origen was seems to have enjoyed relative peace, and Origen's fame as a Christian thinker was such that Julia Mamaea, the mother of the Emperor Alexander, invited him to visit her in Antioch to talk to her about Christianity.

For the first part of his life, Origen lived where he had been born, in Alexandria, and taught and studied there; but in the late 230s he set up a Christian academy in Caesarea, on the Palestinian coast, having fallen out with his bishop back in Alexandria. Three centuries after his death, at the fifth Ecumenical Council called by the Emperor Justinian at Constantinople in 553, Origen was condemned as a heretic: as a result most of his works were destroyed. What survives is very considerable, but it is only a small part of his immense output. His works on the Song of Songs survive only in part, in a Latin translation: three books (out of ten) of his *Commentary on the Song*, translated by Rufinus, and two *Homilies* (out of an uncertain number) translated by Jerome.[7] They represent the two kinds of biblical interpretation that Origen engaged in. His *Commentaries* were intended for those who were studying with him; on the one hand, they sometimes contain quite a technical discussion of the text; on the other, they are intended for people who are already well grounded in theological studies (which included the study of philosophy) and expound the deeper mysteries of the Christian faith. His *Homilies* are rather different: they are sermons that Origen gave at the celebration of the Christian liturgy in Caesarea; they were intended for Christians in general, not just for his students, and may have been heard by pagans and Jews interested in Christianity who were allowed to attend the first part of the Christian liturgy, which consisted of readings from Scripture, prayers and a sermon. The contrast between Origen's *Commentaries* and *Homilies* is very suggestive: they seem to represent an esoteric and an exoteric teaching. In fact, the contrast is not usually that great: Origen was prepared to draw even quite simple Christians towards deep matters. In the case of the Song of Songs, however, there is a very palpable contrast: the *Homilies* are concerned almost exclusively with interpreting the Song in terms of the relationship between Christ and the Church; in the *Commentary* such an ecclesial interpretation, while still there, lies in the background and the interpretation that focuses on the love between Christ and the individual soul comes to the fore.

How does Origen interpret the Song? I think this can be answered at a number of different levels. In the course of his commentary on the Song of Songs, Origen actually sets out some principles for the interpretation of Scripture as a whole:

> All the things in the visible category can be related to the invisible, the corporeal to the incorporeal, and the manifest to those that are hidden; so that the creation of the world itself, fashioned in this wise as it is, can be understood through the divine wisdom, which from actual things and copies teaches us things unseen by means of those that are

seen, and carries us over from earthly things to heavenly. But this relationship does not obtain only with creatures; the Divine Scripture itself is written with wisdom of a rather similar sort.[8]

The idea that the world – the cosmos – and Scripture are, as it were, parallel to each other and point beyond themselves to a deeper reality is the key to Origen's understanding of everything. The one who reads Scripture, like the one who seeks to understand nature, is not just finding out things, but is being led to a deeper understanding, a deeper harmony. So with the Song of Songs, the mystery of human love points beyond itself – to the 'love that moves the sun and other stars', to the love that calls us to union with the cause of all.

But so far as the Song of Songs is concerned, Origen offers two approaches to understanding it, both of them concerned with *placing* it within what for him, as a Christian, is the Old Testament. The first way turns on the title, the Song of Songs: in Hebrew (*Shir ha-Shirim*) this is a superlative, he notes. The Song of Songs is, then, the most sublime song, the highest of all songs. In both the first *Homily* and the *Commentary*, he spells this out by saying that the Song is the summit of all the songs sung in the Old Testament: more precisely he sees it as the seventh, and thus most sublime, of a sequence of songs (though the sequence he gives is not the same in the *Homily* and the *Commentary*), and to sing it one must have progressed through each of the six earlier songs. In the first *Homily* he puts it like this:

You must come out of Egypt and, when the land of Egypt lies behind you, you must cross the Red Sea if you are to sing the first song, saying: Let us sing unto the Lord, for He is gloriously magnified (*Song of Moses*: Exod. 15). But though you have uttered this first song, you are still a long way from the *Song of Songs*. Pursue your spiritual journey through the wilderness until you come to the well which the kings dug so that there you may sing the second song (Numbers 21:17–20). After that, come to the threshold of the holy land that, standing on the bank of Jordan, you may sing another song of Moses, saying: Hear, O heaven, and I will speak, and let the earth give ear to the words of my mouth (Deut. 32). Again you must fight under Joshua and possess the holy land as your inheritance; and a bee must prophesy for you and judge you – Deborah, you understand, means 'bee' – in order that you may take that song also on your lips, which is found in the *Book of Judges* (Judges 5: *The Song of Deborah*). Mount up hence to the *Book of Kings*, and come to the *Song of David*, when he fled out of the hand of all his enemies and out of the hand of Saul, and said: The Lord is my stay and my strength and my refuge and my saviour (2 Sam. 22:2–51, *The Song of David*). You must go on next to Isaiah, so that with him you may say: I will sing to the Beloved the song of my vineyard (Isa. 5). And when you have been through all the songs, then set your course for greater heights, so that as a fair soul with her spouse you may sing this *Song of Songs* too.[9]

It is, I think, worth noting a few points about this way of 'locating' the Song of Songs. First, this series of songs begins with the Song of the crossing of the Red Sea, the Song of the Exodus (this is true of the sequence of songs given in the prologue to his commentary to the Song of Songs, too). For the early Christians the crossing of the Red Sea was seen as a type or figure of baptism: as God saved Israel by water at the Exodus, so in baptism, through water, the Christian shares in the Paschal mystery of Christ's death and resurrection. The Song of Moses, for Christians, is the song of their being called by God through baptism: it is the Song of the second exodus, as it were. For Origen the soul's quest for God begins by the soul's being called by God through baptism: the mystic is no esoteric, pursuing his or her own peculiar way, but a Christian realizing more and more deeply the meaning of the life to which he or she is called in baptism. Second, these songs are the songs of a journey, a journey through deserts and battles, a journey in which the soul suffers want and privation, and needs to learn to find its sustenance in wells (cf. Ps. 84:6). It is no comfortable way, but a hard and often discouraging way, in which the soul learns to rely more and more on God and His grace. But third, from beginning to end, the Christian *sings*: however hard the way, it is still, for the Christian, a *joyful* way.

That is one approach to the Song of Songs. It is, in a way, especially characteristic of Origen: it is not much picked up by later commentators on the Song, though for Origen himself it is sufficiently important to find a place both in his *Homilies* and his *Commentary* on the Song. Origen's other way of placing the Song of Songs, however, caught on and made a profound impression on the whole of the subsequent Christian mystical tradition. This is based on the fact that in the Christian ordering of the books of the Old Testament the Song of Songs is the third of the books of Wisdom, after Proverbs and Ecclesiastes. Origen is fond of triads, and fond of pointing out parallels between triads. Here he points out a parallel between the triad of Wisdom books and a triad of branches of philosophy: ethics, physics and 'epoptics'. Ethics is the study of moral behaviour, especially the study of virtue: this corresponds to the Book of Proverbs. Physics is the study of nature (in Greek: *physis*), the study of the cosmos as God created it: this corresponds to the book of Ecclesiastes. 'Epoptics' – the word comes from the Greek *epopteia*, and means mystic contemplation – corresponds to the Song of Songs. These three branches of philosophy, these three books of wisdom, correspond to the three stages of the Christian life, leading to union with God. The first stage is concerned with restoring balance within the human person by the learning of virtue; the second stage is concerned with a true contemplation of the nature of things, a seeing the world in God, or a contemplation of the cosmos with detachment and delight; this second stage leads us to the source of all, and in the third stage, the soul comes to contemplate God Himself in a union of love. These three stages are called by Evagrius, one of the Desert Fathers of the end of the fourth century who was a careful student of Origen, *praktike, physike, theologia*: an active (practical in that sense) struggle against temptations in the pursuit of virtue, leading to natural contemplation, and then finally to *theology*, meaning not what academics do in studies but what we do in prayer – a prayerful communing with God that leads to a union of love. It was the same Evagrius who said, 'If you are a theologian, you pray truly: if you pray truly, you are a theologian.'[10] Evagrius' three stages of *praktike, physike* and *theologia* – clearly derived from Origen – became the standard vocabulary of Greek and Byzantine ascetical theology. But in the West, the so-called 'three ways' – or purgation, illumination and union – are clearly a variant of Origen's three ways based on the three books of Wisdom.

But these three ways are also based on three branches of philosophy: more is going on here than a development of themes from the Bible; Origen is drawing on philosophy, too. Origen thought that a study of ancient philosophy was essential for the Christian theologian. He himself, as a young Christian, sat at the feet of the Alexandrian philosopher Ammonius Saccas, one of whose other disciples was the great pagan philosopher Plotinus, and in his Christian academy at Caesarea he insisted that his pupils drank deeply of the wisdom of ancient Greek philosophy. In fact, Origen was immensely learned in Greek philosophy, and certainly knew far more than we ever shall: his citations from, and comments on, Greek philosophers, especially in his lengthy reply to the Greek critic of Christianity Celsus,[11] are often enough indispensable for our understanding of some of the less-known Greek philosophers. So far as his interpretation of the Song of Songs is concerned, the main thing to notice is that Origen knew and valued Plato's dialogues devoted to the nature of eros, the *Banquet* or *Symposium* and the *Phaedrus*. In the prologue to his *Commentary* he makes use of the distinction Plato has Pausanius introduce in his speech in the *Symposium* between heavenly love and earthly love – *eros ouranios* and *eros pandemos*. But more importantly, like Plato, Origen presents the purification and spiritualizing of love as a process in which love retains all its passion, indeed becomes more and more deeply passionate. Just as in Diotima's speech, love, as it is abstracted from the physical and the particular, becomes more and more intense, so the spiritual love with which the soul responds to the word, the Logos, of God is something deeply passionate:

> The soul is moved by heavenly love and longing when, having clearly beheld the beauty and fairness of the Word of God, it falls deeply in love with His loveliness and receives from the Word Himself a certain dart and wound of love. For this Word is the image and splendour of

the invisible God . . . . If, then, a man can so extend his thinking as to ponder and consider the beauty and grace of all the things that have been created in the Word, the very charm of them will so smite him, the grandeur of their brightness will so pierce him as with a chosen dart – as says the prophet (Isa. 49.2) – that he will suffer from the dart Himself a saving wound, and will be kindled with the blessed fire of His Love.[12]

There is another theme Origen introduces that is especially important for his interpretation of the Song of Songs. This contrast just mentioned between heavenly love and earthly love parallels, for Origen, a much deeper contrast between the inner and the outer man. It is the inner man that is created in the image of God: it is the inner man that has an affinity with God Himself and so can know union with Him in love. The outer man is the human being turned outwards, outwards towards the world perceived through the senses; the inner man is the human being turned inwards, inwards towards the world perceived through . . . well, how? Origen continues the contrast in the simplest way: turned inwards towards the world perceived through the *spiritual senses*. Through these spiritual senses we perceive the spiritual world: the realm of God, the angels and souls that have woken up to spiritual reality. But most human beings are so turned outwards – turned inside out, really – have poured so much of themselves into the external world, which is not so much the physical world as a world valued in terms of the external – a world of reputation and ambition, a world of possessions and consumption – most human beings are so committed to that world that the world of spiritual reality is dead to them – or rather, they are dead to it. But if we will turn inwards, if we will allow ourselves to hear the call of the word of God, then we will begin to wake up *within*, so to speak, to the spiritual world. From then on, it is a matter of becoming accustomed to this inner world of spiritual reality, and as we become used to it our spiritual senses will quicken, will come to life. The Song of Songs invites the development of such a doctrine of the spiritual senses, precisely because it is so sensuous in its imagery. It is not just a matter of seeing and hearing, but of touching and smelling and tasting. As Origen draws out his doctrine of the spiritual senses, he builds up a picture of someone inwardly aware, able to respond to the smallest sign of the divine presence with a delicate, loving sensitivity. Later writers (not Origen himself) will interpret this as a state of *apatheia* – a state not of insensitivity, as the word has often been misunderstood in the West, but of inner calm that makes possible a kind of acute attentiveness – to God, to the spiritual world, and so to the souls of others. So Origen says 'that soul only is perfect who has her sense of smell so pure and purged that she can catch the fragrance of the spikenard and myrrh and cypress that proceed from the Word of God, and can inhale the grace of the divine odour'.[13]

I want to leave Origen now, not that I have done any more than barely scratch the surface of his interpretation of the Song, but because I want to move on to say a little about St Gregory of Nyssa. St Gregory of Nyssa lived more than a century later than Origen: he was born in about 330 into a Roman empire governed by a Christian Emperor, Constantine. He is regarded as one of the Cappadocian Fathers – along with his elder brother, Basil, and the friend of his brother, also called Gregory, Gregory of Nazianzus – together they played an important part in the victory of orthodox Christianity in the Byzantine world. He is called 'of Nyssa' because in the early 370s he was made bishop of that small town in Cappadocia (the eastern province in Asia Minor that stretches to the Euphrates): one of several 'reliable' bishops, appointed by Basil, bishop of Caesarea, the metropolis of Cappadocia, so as to create an orthodox power-base in Asia Minor. He played a prominent role at the Second Ecumenical Council held at Constantinople in 381, which set the standard of orthodoxy for the Emperor Theodosius' state Church. From about 386 onwards he lost influence at court and spent his final years (he died shortly after 394) back in Nyssa as its bishop. It is to this last period that his *Homilies on the Song of Songs* belong.[14] They are homilies – sermons preached to a congregation. But although they are dedicated to a famous (aristocratic and wealthy) deaconess, Olympias, renowned for her asceticism, there is no reason to suppose that they were delivered anywhere else than in his cathedral church in Nyssa to his ordinary congregation during Lent. There is, then, quite a contrast between Origen's academic setting in a Church under persecution and Gregory's setting in a small town in Cappadocia in a period when any persecution was mounted by the state Church to which he belonged. But there is another contrast too – it is really part of the same contrast – in Origen's day orthodoxy was ill-defined, and Origen was able to pursue quite daring speculations without the fear of ecclesiastics' breathing down his neck; in Gregory's day, orthodoxy was much more clearly defined – the Council of Constantinople had condemned Arianism, Apollinarianism, Manichaeism and Macedonianism, to mention but a few of the heresies named – and Gregory was closely identified with those who had thus defined orthodoxy. Underlying many of the controversies that had clarified orthodoxy and outlawed the several heresies was the problem of Platonism. Origen, we have seen, was influenced by Platonism and sympathetic to it: in particular, he endorsed the Platonic belief that the soul was akin to God, and that the realization of this kinship in all its fullness was the essential task of the soul. Gregory, on the other hand, felt that any kinship between the soul and God had to be qualified by the fact that God had created the universe out of nothing: this meant that there was a great gulf between God and all else, so that (as he put it) there was much greater affinity between the most glorious archangel and a stone than between that archangel and God, because, however glorious, an archangel was, like a stone, created,

created out of nothing, and therefore utterly remote from the uncreated splendour of God. It is this emphasis on the gulf between the uncreated Trinity and the created cosmos (the 'all things visible and invisible' of the Nicene Creed), an emphasis felt even more acutely by Gregory after his controversy with the extreme Arian, Eunomius, that informs and lies behind the whole of his reflection on God and the cosmos, God and humanity – and in particular his understanding of the Song of Songs.

The most immediate way to illustrate this is to see how Gregory develops Origen's idea of the three stages of the spiritual life: the stage of active virtue, the stage of natural contemplation and, finally, the stage of loving union with God. Origen saw this as a process of ever-growing illumination: the darkness of the soul separated from God by its sin is gradually dispelled by the radiance of God so that finally the soul is penetrated by the divine light and contemplates God in a gaze of love. Gregory takes up this idea – he wrote commentaries on Ecclesiastes and the Song, which represent the second and third stages – but it is transformed by his sense of the gulf between the created soul and God. In his *Homilies on the Song*, he expresses this most clearly by introducing the theme of Moses' experience of God: something he will treat at length in his last work, the *Life of Moses*. He puts it like this:

> Moses' vision of God began with light: afterwards God spoke to him in a cloud. But when Moses rose higher and became more perfect he saw God in the darkness. Now the doctrine we are taught here is as follows. Our initial withdrawal from wrong and erroneous ideas of God is a transition from darkness to light. Next comes a closer aware-ness of hidden things, and by this the soul is guided through sense phenomena to the world of the invisible. And this awareness is a kind of cloud, which overshadows all appearances, and slowly guides and accustoms the soul to look towards what is hidden. Next the soul makes progress through all these stages and goes on higher, and as she leaves below all that human nature can attain, she enters within the secret chamber of the divine knowledge, and here she is cut off on all sides by the divine darkness. Now she leaves outside all that can be grasped by sense or by reason, and the only thing left for her contemplation is the invisible and the incomprehensible. And here God is, as the Scriptures tell us in connection with Moses: 'But Moses went into the dark cloud wherein God was' (Exod. 20:21).[15]

In contrast to Origen, Gregory's three stages are an advance into deeper and deeper darkness: only the first stage is experienced as illumination, as we abandon error for the truth. Thereafter, the closer we come to the truth that God is, the more the soul feels that it is entering a deeper and deeper darkness. So Moses passes from light (*phos* – the experience of the Burning Bush), into the cloud (*nephele* – as he begins the ascent of Mount Sinai) to thick darkness (*gnophos* – on top of the mountain). Even the very term contemplation (*theoria*) is abandoned by Gregory when he comes to speak of the third stage, union with God in love: sight is a misleading analogy or metaphor for the soul's experience of closeness to God. The sense of entering darkness, of going beyond one's own powers, is one that Gregory sometimes expresses as a kind of spiritual vertigo. For instance, in his commentary on Ecclesiastes, he says:

> And though the mind in its restlessness ranges through all that is knowable, it has never yet discovered a way of comprehending eternity in such wise that it might place itself outside of it, and go beyond the idea of eternity itself and that Being which is above all being. It is like someone who finds himself on a mountain ridge. Imagine a sheer, steep crag, of reddish appearance below, extending into eternity; on top there is this ridge which looks down over a projecting rim into a bottomless chasm. Now imagine what a person would probably experience if he put his foot on the edge of this ridge which overlooks the chasm and found no solid footing nor anything to hold on to. This is what I think the soul experiences when it goes beyond its footing in material things, in its quest for that which has no dimension and which exists from all eternity. For here there is nothing it can take hold of, neither place nor time, neither measure nor anything else; it does not allow our minds to approach. And thus the soul, slipping at every point from what cannot be grasped, becomes dizzy and perplexed and returns once again to what is connatural to it, content now to know merely this about the Transcendent, that it is completely different from the nature of the things that the soul knows.[16]

In his *Homilies* on the Song Gregory, then, sees the union between the soul and God as a union in which the soul lets go of all that can make sense and ventures on an infinite quest of love that can never be satisfied: it is a continual reaching forward into the Infinite that God is:

> The soul, having gone out at the word of her Beloved, looks for Him but does not find Him. She calls on Him, though He cannot be reached by any verbal symbol, and she is told by the watchman that she is in love with the unattainable, and that the object of her longing cannot be apprehended. In this way she is, in a certain sense, wounded and beaten because of the frustration of what she desires, now that she thinks that her yearning for the Other cannot be fulfilled or satisfied. But the veil of her grief is removed when she learns that the true satisfaction of her desire consists in constantly going on with her quest and never ceasing in her ascent, seeing that every fulfilment of her desire continually generates further desire for the Transcendent. Thus the veil of her despair is torn away and the bride realizes that she will

always discover more and more of the incomprehensible and unhoped-
for beauty of her Spouse throughout all eternity. Then she is torn by
an even more urgent longing, and through the daughters of Jerusalem
she communicates to her Beloved the dispositions of her heart. For
she has received within her God's special dart, she has been wounded
in the heart by the point of faith, she has been mortally wounded by
the arrow of love. And 'God is love.'[17]

Here, it seems to me, Gregory develops Origen's doctrine of the spiritual
senses in an extraordinarily interesting way. Origen, we have seen, develops
this doctrine as a kind of 'psychology of the doctrine of *theologia* conceived
as the highest degree of the spiritual life', as Karl Rahner once put it.[18]
Gregory's development of this doctrine amounts to a reflection on the very
notion of perception. For the Greeks, sight – for Plato the 'keenest of the
senses'[19] – is the paradigm of all the senses: seeing is the real way of
perceiving; the other senses are imperfect ways of seeing, so to speak.
Consequently understanding – intellectual perception – is regarded as a kind
of intellectual 'seeing'. It is not difficult to deduce what is going on behind
all this. Sight is the sense that gives the greatest sense of objectivity in what
is perceived, and gives us the greatest sense of control: we see things at a
distance; we can control our encounter with them. Understanding, as
intellectual 'sight', takes over these characteristics: it is objective; what we
understand we can begin to control. But for Gregory, intellectual 'seeing' –
theoria – is no longer possible in the darkness, *gnophos*, where God is
encountered, and so, with every encouragement from the Song of Songs, he
turns to the other senses, smell, taste, touch (not hearing, especially)
to characterize the experience that takes place in the darkness. It is
an experience of immediacy and presence, which is undeniable but
very difficult to objectify (just as smells and tastes are very hard to
objectify):

> [The Soul] is encompassed by a divine night, during which her Spouse
> approaches, but does not reveal Himself. But how can that which is
> invisible reveal itself in the night? By the fact that He gives the soul some
> sense of His presence, even while He eludes her clear apprehension,
> concealed as He is by the invisibility of His nature.[20]

For Gregory, the Song of Songs is about the soul's quest of love for the
invisible and unknowable God, who reveals Himself by His presence and
by transforming the soul into Himself in a quite unobjectifiable way. God
becomes known to the soul not as He is in Himself – something that is
literally unknowable – but in the power of His presence, which transforms
the soul into what He is through grace and virtue. So Gregory speaks of
the bridegroom in the Song smelling the spikenard that the bride wears
between her breasts and says:

I think that the Word teaches us that by His very nature He transcends the entire order and structure of the created universe, that He is inaccessible, intangible and incomprehensible. But in His stead we have this perfume within us distilled from the perfection of our virtues; and this imitates in its purity His essential incorruptibility, in its stability His immutability, and in all the virtues we possess we represent His true virtue, which as the prophet Habacuc says, covers all the heavens (Hab. 3:3).[21]

In these two brief sketches I hope to have shown something of the way in which the themes of eros and mysticism are developed by the early Christian Fathers by means of meditation on the Bible's allegory of love: the Song of Songs. But I hope I have shown, too, how *logos* and dogma are part of eros and mysticism for the Fathers, how, if eros is a striving beyond what can be understood – *logos*, so to speak – it is a striving that accepts and transcends what can be understood, what has been revealed, rather than something detached from understanding altogether. But perhaps what is most striking is the way in which dogma and mysticism interrelate: how it is dogma itself – the dogmas of the Trinity and creating out of nothing, together with, as we would discover if we had time to go into Gregory's mysticism in more detail, the dogma of the incarnation – how it is dogma itself that lends to Gregory's mysticism a greater tentativeness, a greater sense of a mystery transcending human understanding, than we seem to find in Origen. But in both Origen and St Gregory we find an attempt to develop the allegory of love that makes love and its purification the very heart of the Christian understanding of God.

NOTES

1 There is a translation into English verse of the Song of Songs by Peter Jay, with an introduction by David Goldstein and illustrations by Nikos Stavroulakis (London: Anvil Press Poetry, 1975). But I am not sure that the older translations – in the Authorized Version of the Bible and especially in Jerome's Latin Vulgate – do not capture more of the strange beauty of the Song of Songs. I am not enough of a Hebraist to say anything about the original.

2 In *Eric Gill: The Engravings* (London: The Herbert Press, 1990; originally published in a limited edition by Christopher Skelton, 1983), plates 618, 662–70.

3 See Hosea, chapters 2 and 3; also 6:4ff., 11:8ff. But it is a constant theme.

4 See, especially, the long allegory in Ezekiel, chapter 16.

5 See the list of Latin commentaries to 1200, printed as an appendix in E. Ann Matter, *The Voice of the Beloved. The Song of Songs in Western Medieval Christianity* (Philadelphia: University of Pennsylvania Press, 1990), pp. 203–10.

6 The story is told by Eusebius in his *History of the Church* 6.2.5 (in the Penguin Classics revised edition (Harmondsworth: Penguin, 1989), p. 180). Book 6 of the *History of the Church* is more or less a life of Origen.

7 There is an English translation by R. P. Lawson (Ancient Christian Writers 26 (Westminster, Md.: The Newman Press and London: Longmans, Green & Co., 1957).

8 *Comm.* III.12; p. 223 in Lawson's translation.
9 *Hom.* 1.1; pp. 266f. (Lawson).
10 In his *On Prayer* 61 (in English translation in *The Philokalia*, trans. G. E. H. Palmer, Philip Sherrard and Kallistos Ware, vol. 1 (London: Faber, 1979), p. 62).
11 See *Origen: Contra Celsum*, trans. Henry Chadwick (Cambridge: Cambridge University Press, 1953).
12 *Comm.*, prologue; pp. 29f. (Lawson).
13 *Comm.*, II,11; p. 168 (Lawson).
14 There appear to be two American translations, one published by Brill (Leiden, 1988), and one published by the Hellenic College Press (Brookline, Mass., 1987). Long extracts are translated in J. Daniélou, *From Glory to Glory*, trans. H. Musurillo (London: John Murray, 1962), from which my quotations come.
15 *Homily XI on the Song, From Glory to Glory*, p. 247.
16 *Comm. on Eccles. 7, From Glory to Glory*, pp. 127f.
17 *Homily XII on the Song, From Glory to Glory*, pp. 270f.
18 Quoted in my *Origins of the Christian Mystical Tradition: From Plato to Denys* (Oxford: Clarendon Press, 1981), pp. 68f.
19 *Phaedrus* 250D; cf. *Republic* VI: 508B.
20 *Homily XI on the Song, From Glory to Glory*, p. 248.
21 *Homily III on the Song, From Glory to Glory*, p. 164.

17

THE SONG OF SONGS

Gustav Dreifuss

INTRODUCTION

Shir ha'shirim, the Song of Songs, is a poem of rare beauty with metaphorical descriptions of the mystery of the male–female relationship. It talks about romantic love and passion. It is musical poetry, an expression of feelings, a mutual song of love between man and woman. It must have been written by a sensitive poet. One is moved, because the images of the poem stir the deepest layers of the soul. The partners describe each other in beautiful metaphors: landscapes and towns, like Gilead, Lebanon, Carmel, Jerusalem; flowers, like the rose of sharon, the lily of the valley; animals, like the gazelle, the young hart, the dove. The use of symbols to address each other points to the symbolic level of the relationship, to a reality beyond the conscious relationship of the partners. Something of the divine, of another realm, of the unspeakable mystery is hinted at and is felt. Love in its archetypal dimension is a fascinating secret, an enigma to all, and no psychological interpretation is sufficient to 'explain' the mystery of love. Should we not just leave it at that? Can an interpretation of any kind (religious, psychological) add anything? Yet we wonder why we are touched by the poem. To be touched belongs to the realm of feeling, of experiencing, and this experiencing is mystical. In a chapter entitled 'Erotic images for the ecstatic experience' Idel (1988: 179ff.) states that

> images portraying the spiritual connection between the lover and his beloved, i.e., descriptions of such emotions as longing, submission, etc. . . . are extremely common . . . these images appear alike in mystical literature and among philosophers, religious poets, and exegetes of the Song of Songs.

In quoting Abulafia, Idel (1988:186) continues:

> the Song of Songs is seen as a love song which describes the erotic contacts between bride and groom on the literal level, and the character of prophecy or mystical experience, on the esoteric level . . . . It is

worthy to note that the soul is understood as a woman, a very widespread image in mysticism.

To understand a traditional, orthodox Jewish interpretation of the narrative of the book, I want to quote Rabbi S. M. Lehrmann in his introduction to the Song of Songs in the Soncino Bible (in Cohen 1946:X, XI):

Despite problems of authorship and interpretation, the story is briefly told. It describes the trials of a beautiful peasant maiden from Shunem, or Shulem, who was employed by her mother and brothers as shepherdess to their flock of goats. She had fallen in love with a shepherd of the same village, but the brothers did not look with approval on the union. They, accordingly, transferred her services from the pasture to the vineyards, in the hope that her meetings with her lover would not be possible. One day, as she was tending the vines, she was seen by the servants of king Solomon, when he chanced to pass the village on his way to his summer resort in Lebanon. Impressed by her beauty, they try to persuade her to accompany them. She refuses and is finally led away as a captive to the king's chambers. No sooner does the king behold her, when he, too, falls violently in love with her. He sings her beauty and uses all his endeavours to induce her to abandon her shepherd for the love and wealth he can shower upon her. The ladies of the court also join in trying to dislodge her love for her humble swain. Her heart, however, belongs to him and she remains steadfast.

During her stay in the palace, she yearns for her lover and is tantalized by the taunts of the ladies of the court that he has rejected her. In her agitated state of mind she speaks to him as if he were in her presence, and even dreams that he has come back to rescue her and escort her back to her mother's home. Awaking from her dream, she rushes out of her chamber to seek him in the streets where she is roughly treated by the watchmen of the city, who misjudge her character.

When the king is finally convinced of the constancy of her love for the shepherd, he dismisses her from his presence and allows her to return home. She is now joined by her lover and, leaning on his arm, approaches Shunem where a warm welcome awaits her. They come upon the scenes so dear to them, and she recounts the vicissitudes through which she has lately passed. The story ends on a triumphant note. Not only could her love not be extinguished by the temptations offered by the king, but she also assures her brothers that their solicitude for her virtue was unwarranted. She has proved that love is capable of heroic endurance. The tale she tells to their assembled friends makes a strong protest against the luxury and vice of the court, and pays testimony to the beauty and dignity of pure love and fidelity.

It seems to me that this interpretation does harm to the book. It does not go into the depth of the love relationship and tries to make a story like the rabbis quoted below.

I shall discuss the different approaches to the Song of Songs. Is it a coherent story? Are there different love stories? Is it a song of King Solomon, or is the authorship just attributed to him? What is the attitude of normative Judaism, of Jewish mysticism? Of Christianity? What can a psychological Jungian understanding add to the understanding? What is the position of man and woman in the Song?

THE SONG OF SONGS IN ART

The Song of Songs has been a source of inspiration for artists: composers, like Bruckner, Buxtehude, Honegger, Palestrina and the contemporary Israeli composers Ben-Haim, Boskovitch, Lavry; painters like Chagall; poets like Goethe, and so on. The list could be endless! The fact that the Song of Songs inspired so many artists shows that the poem touches deep archetypal layers of the soul, which are reformulated and recreated time and again in works of art.

With regard to music I want to give two examples of the text on which the works of Palestrina and Lavry are based.

Palestrina (sixteenth century)

Palestrina's composition is called *Canticum Canticorum*, the Latin name of The Song of Songs. It consists of twenty-three motets and its complete title is *Motettorum Liber Quartus Quinque Vocibus ex Canticis Canticorum*. Turner (1986:8) writes that the composer wrote in his dedication of the work to Pope Gregory XIII that he blushes and is sad at having once belonged to those who wasted their musical art on love songs, which are alien to the Christian faith. He continues that therefore he now writes 'poems for the glorification of our Lord Jesus Christ and his most holy mother, the Virgin Mary'. These poems contain 'the Godly love between Christ and his spouse, the soul'.

Lavry and Brod (twentieth century)

The English text in the libretto for 'Song of Songs' – a cantata for soloists, mixed choir and orchestra by Marc Lavry (born 1903 in Riga; domiciled since 1935 in Israel), first performed in Tel-Aviv in 1940, is a setting of Max Brod's re-arrangement of the Song of Songs (Brod n.d.). Following this new sequence of verses, the work falls naturally into four scenes, each having its particular character. The first scene is pastoral in nature, the second festive with much ensemble work, the third – in the King's Palace – features women's voices and is therefore more lyrical, and the fourth – Shulamite's dream – is in the form of a ballad and finale. The composer has remained faithful to the patterns of the biblical text, but the work has no religious associations whatsoever: it is simply a tender and poetic love story, or as many think, a compilation of different love stories. Then follows a quotation from the poet Max Brod:

> It is, in my opinion, impossible to adapt (i.e. modify) the 'Song of Songs' as the wonderful beauty and power of the work would be diminished by any addition or alteration. I have taken an entirely different path: I have not added nor omitted a single line. I have merely changed the sequence of lines and in this respect I admit that I have been distinctly radical. But I believe that I have restored the original form of the poem. 'Song of Songs' is a poem of pastoral character which sings of the ardent and true love of a shepherd and shepherdess triumphing over all obstacles. The King and his court and his harem appear as disturbing elements in this tale of love. The shepherdess is abducted and taken into the King's harem. But she remains deaf to all his pleading and eventually flees from the royal palace. In this way a picture, very different from the traditional conception, is presented to us.

Then Brod refers to his book *Paganism, Christianity and Judaism* (vol. II), where he states in detail the reasons that induced him to come to this new interpretation of the text. He continues by saying that the biblical text as it has been handed down to us contains many 'lapses', even contradictions, and by his re-arrangement it is made into a complete poetical unit, a small-scale lyrical drama in four acts. One situation necessarily develops from the other, and the consequent unity of the artistic form indicates that we have before us the original shape of this poem.

The author Max Brod remodelled the text, and after his artistic revision, he presumptuously thinks that we now have the original form of the poem before us: Brod takes the artistic liberty of editing the biblical text!

Goethe

Goethe (1819) describes the Song of Songs as follows (my translation from the German):

> We now dwell with the Song of Songs for a moment, the most delicate and inimitable of what has been passed on to us as an expression of passionate, graceful love. Yet we regret that the fragmentation and disorder of the poems don't guarantee a full, pure enjoyment. Still we are delighted to imagine the bliss of the participants, the wafting of the mild air of the loveliest regions of Cana'an: an intimate country atmosphere, wine-, garden- and spice cultivation, something of townlike

limitation, and then a royal court, with its splendour in the background. The main theme, however, is the burning inclination of youthful hearts searching for each other, finding, repelling and even attracting in some of the simplest situations. Many times we tried to bring some order into this lovely entanglement; but the enigmatic, insoluble content gives charm and originality to the few pages. How often were non-reflecting and order-loving spirits attracted to put or find some understandable connection in the text, and yet the same task remains for another . . .

Goethe, so it seems to me, emphasizes the essential nature of the Song of Songs, namely the enigmatic, inimitable quality of it, something which is a mystery in every deep relationship. He expresses his unbounded admiration at the beauty of the imagery. In this context I wish to refer the reader to Goethe's translation of the Song of Songs of 1776 (quoted by S. M. Lehrmann in Cohen (1946: XII).

Chagall

Chagall (Chagall and Mayer 1990) painted five pictures, according to the following verses:

1 8:6 Set me as a seal upon thy heart,
2 5:2 I sleep, but my heart waketh,
3 3:11 In the day of his espousal,
4 1:4 Draw me, we will run after thee,
5 7:7 How fair and how pleasant art thou, o love, for delights!

The artist takes the liberty of choosing from the Song of Songs subjects he wants to deal with. He stresses the transpersonal mystical aspects of the relationship between the sexes, which expresses the love of God. According to Mayer (Chagall and Mayer 1990: 11) Chagall needed a principle of order for his cycle of five pictures. Mayer sees an intensification from picture to picture in the way the artist, with each picture, penetrates deeper into the mystery of love which is grounded in God. So he sees in the last picture the testimony that love evades the laws of time and transcends time; it is eternal. Psychologically speaking Chagall expresses the archetype of love, or in other words the transcendental aspects of love. In his pictures he circumambulates the mystery of love; he paints images of the secret of love which cannot be expressed rationally, but only symbolically. The dynamics of the figures and colours express the mystery, so to speak.

Modern poetic interpretation

The Song of Songs has inspired modern poets, who have translated or elaborated the text according to their own artistic feeling. I want to illustrate this with chapter 1, verses 5 and 6:

259

The traditional Soncino text:

> I am black, but comely,
> O ye daughters of Jerusalem,
> As the tents of Kedar,
> As the curtains of Solomon.
>
> Look not upon me, that I am swarthy,
> That the sun has tanned me;
> My mother's sons were incensed against me,
> They made me keeper of the vineyards;
> But my own vineyard have I not kept.

Marcia Falk's version

> Yes, I am black! and radiant –
> O city women watching me –
> As black as Kedar's goathair tents
> Or Solomon's tapestries.
>
> Will you disrobe me with your stares?
> The eyes of many morning suns
> Have pierced my skin, and now I shine
> Black as the light before the dawn.
>
> And I have faced the angry glare
> Of others, even my mother's sons
> Who sent me out to watch their vines
> While I neglected all my own.

THE SONG OF SONGS IN JUDAISM

In the biblical story man and woman freely express their mutual feelings of human love. This is extraordinary for a biblical text. If one considers the Bible as a religious text of patriarchal Judaism, the Song of Songs could be included only as a metaphor for the relationship of God to the people. Within the context of Judaism, the relationship to God is mainly through the people, through one's being a part of the people. The Jewish mystic, however, looks for a personal experience.

The Jewish and the Christian allegoric interpretations avoid seeing in the story the love-relationship between man and woman, which the biblical text so clearly deals with. Whereas in normative Judaism the Song of Songs is allegorically interpreted as the love between God and His people, in Christianity it expresses the love between Christ and the soul of man, or between Christ and the Church. Further, the woman is not mentioned because of the reinterpretation of woman as the soul of man (Christianity) or as the people (Judaism). Only in this way could the Song of Songs be incorporated into the biblical canon. This is in contrast to the mystical and depth psychological interpretations. Within the Jewish and Christian interpretation of the Bible, based on patriarchal collective consciousness, the love- and sexual relationship of man and woman had no place!

Two contemporary rabbis proposed structuring the biblical text in order to clarify its meaning. Carlebach (n.d.: 48–126) classifies the text into eighteen songs, giving to each song a title, as follows:

Song 1: I:2–8   The woman in disguise
Song 2: I:9–11: 3   The message of love
Song 3: II:4–8   The love-potion
Song 4: II:8–16   Betrothal
Song 5: II:17–18   Time not ripe
Song 6: III:1–5   Love-dream
Song 7: III:6–11   Wedding-procession
Song 8: IV:1–7   The delight of the bridegroom
Song 9: IV:8–15   Wedding poem on the day of entrance
Song 10: IV:16–V:1   Wedding feast
Song 11: V:2–VI:3   Love song after renewed separation
Song 12: VI:4–VII:13   New message as reward of love
Song 13: VII:1–6   Enticement
Song 14: VII:7–14   Mutual longing
Song 15: VIII:1–4   Last inhibition
Song 16: VIII:5–8   The lovers united for ever
Song 17: VIII:8–12   Once and now
Song 18: VIII:13–14   Finale

De Sola Pool (1945) sees in the poem 'a dramatic unity with an inherent consistency and progressive development of thought, feeling and purpose'. He constructs a dialogue between the following characters:

The Shulamite Maiden
Her Shepherd Lover
King Solomon
Chorus of Women from the Royal Court in Jerusalem
Chorus of Shepherds.

Neither of these attempts to bring order into the text is very convincing. As I will show later, the deeper meaning of the text lies for me in the interplay of feminine and masculine energies and archetypes, in the union of opposites.

Another rabbi, Malbim (abbreviation for Meir Loeb ben Jechiel Michel, 1809–79, rabbi in Germany), quoted by Carlebach (n.d.: 130) sees in the Song of Songs a fight between spirit and sensuality, between the soul-demands of the higher man and the desire of bodily lust. He further states that King Solomon learns to differentiate between worldly and celestial love.

It seems to me that Malbim projects his ethical conviction into the text in accordance with the Jewish faith. He remains stuck in the opposition of spirit and instinct. He lacks a symbolic attitude towards sexuality, and in consequence he has no feeling for the unity of body, soul and spirit.

In Jewish tradition, there are four ways of interpreting a text:

1 literal meaning, simple, superficial (*pshat*)
2 allegorical meaning, hinted, concealed (*remes*)
3 homiletic meaning, interpreted, learned (*drash*), metaphorical, philosophical, ethical, psychological
4 mystical meaning, esoteric, transpersonal (*sod*).

The attempt to construct a literal meaning of the Song of Songs is artificial and unsuccessful, as pointed out above.

Rashi explains *Shir ha'shirim* as *drasch*, i.e. allegorically. For instance, verse 1:2 says: 'Let him kiss me with the kisses of his mouth – for thy love is better than wine.' As *drash* this means: communicate your innermost wisdom again in loving closeness. It means further that the exiled Israel now says in her temporary widowhood: communicate directly, once again, mouth to mouth, as you did to the people on Mount Sinai, *Panim el panim* – face to face. Kissing is a *drash* referring back to Mount Sinai. Separated from God, Israel longs for Him. 'Show me affection again.' It is the nature of *drash* to be somewhere esoteric, hidden.

Remes is more difficult to explain. Sometimes there is no clear division between *remes* and *sod*. *Remes* is sometimes more the *sod*-aspect, sometimes more the *drash* aspect. 'Kiss me' on the level of *sod* refers to the holy union, *ha'sivug ha'kadosh*.

In Kabbalistic interpretation the drama or content of *Shir ha'shirim* is the interplay of the Sephiroth, on the branches of the tree of life. One takes every verse and interprets it. Then the verses don't have to be connected as on the *pschat*-level. One does not need to follow the story. Each verse is a formula. Yet there is a connection, but a hidden one. There is a story behind it: according to the *sod*-interpretation all verses circumambulate around the *ihud* (union) and *sivug* (copulation) of God and the Shekina.

The 'Ari', Isaac Luria, Safed, 1534–72, wrote a book on *Shir ha'shirim* which, together with the commentary of the Hagra, the Vilna Gaon, 1720–97, was republished in 1982. He comments that all words of the Song of Songs are code words which refer to the Sephiroth. Song, *shir*, for instance, is a code word for Tiferet. And the 'h' of *ha'shirim* is Malkhut. *Shirim* is Yesod and Da'at. 'Shir Ha'shirim asher (= Binah, Ima) le'shlomo (=Hokma, Aba)' ('The song of songs which is Solomon's'): this whole verse is itself a code language for all the Parzufim (the personified aspects of the Sephiroth). With Tiferet, one has to take into consideration the two branches, the left and the right side, Hesed and Gevurah, and this goes for the other Sephiroth of the middle column: Yesod with Hod and Netsah, and Keter with Binah and Hokmah. All the verses are referring to the interrelation of the seven lower Sephiroth.

THE SONG OF SONGS AND JUNGIAN PSYCHOLOGY

Each love-relationship has a personal and transpersonal character; the partners are mostly unaware of the latter. During the story the woman and the man address each other as equals. Some names given to the man are personal like 'beloved', 'friend' and 'brother'; others are more archetypal, like 'King' and 'Salomon'. The names given to the woman on the personal level are: 'friend' and 'beloved', and on a more archetypal level, 'bride', 'dove', 'sister', 'Shulamite' ('the peaceful', according to the Hebrew word *shalom* for peace; also the root of the word 'Salomon' is *shalom*; Shulamite in Greek is Salome). The fact that there are personal and transpersonal names means that the relationship is at the same time personal and transpersonal (archetypal, symbolic). This holds true for every deep man–woman relationship: it is on a human and at the same time on a Godly level. The sacred union between God and the Shekinah in the Kabbala corresponds to the union of the opposites as described by Jung (1957).

Figure 17.1 explains what is meant.

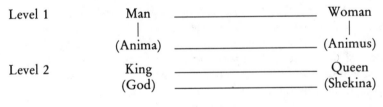

Level 1	Man ———————— Woman
	| |
	(Anima) ———————— (Animus)
Level 2	King ———————— Queen
	(God) ———————— (Shekina)

Figure 17.1

Level 1 corresponds to the conscious relationship between the partners and the mutual projection of the contrasexual part, anima and animus. In level 2, the partners are seen and experienced unconsciously as archetypal images, like king and queen, and may express this verbally, and non-verbally by caressing, stroking, kissing. When the partners are in level 2, the relationship becomes transpersonal and symbolical. Non-verbal expressions carry consciousness more deeply into the archetypal realm. In the moment of climax, king and queen, meaning God and Shekina, copulate; the respective 'egos' are, so to speak, non-existent, 'dead', for a moment, thus giving spiritual meaning to the sexual act. The man–woman relationship *is* then the relationship of God and the Shekina. Cohabitation of man and woman *is* cohabitation of God and the Shekina. The sexual act *is* the creation of the world, a continuing process of creation. It can give an experience of the transpersonal reality of the soul or the repeated realization of the transcendent roots of the human being. The union with the animus or anima, of the soul with the Self, can be experienced in a (sexual) dream. In the climax, ego consciousness is suspended for a moment; it is, so to speak, dissolved into the unconscious and will evolve again after the climax. In this moment the all-powerful aspect of God, the divine, the unconscious, the archetype, is *experienced*.

Jung has extensively dealt with the symbolism of the union of masculine and feminine archetypes in his book *Mysterium Coniunctionis* (1957). From a psychological point of view the union of the archetypal images, of male and female, is a symbol of the Self. The two are paradoxically one! This is the paradox of the Self, which can also be expressed by the following opposites: King and Queen, Adam and Eve, Heaven and Earth, Sun and Moon, Brother and Sister. In the union of man and woman the Self can be experienced in its wholeness, containing the opposites. The union of opposites expresses symbolically on an *inner* level the relationship of the ego to the inner countersexual part, to animus or anima in their numinous, transcendental meaning, which is a mystical experience of the archetype of the Self. Jung (1954: para. 218) comments: 'Mystics are people who have a particularly vivid experience of the processes of the collective unconscious. Mystical experience is experience of archetypes.' Von Franz (1990:198) has formulated this as follows (my translation):

> In the creations of the unconscious ... it is a matter of a 'unio mystica' with the Self, which is experienced as a union of the cosmic opposites .... One finds the experience hinted at ... in the words of the Song of Songs. It is an experience which frees the human being into cosmic expanse .... Only a few human beings today experience this level of individuation.

The result of the union can be a feeling of oneness, of peace with oneself.

As pointed out above, Chagall (Chagall and Mayer 1990) expresses in his paintings in general and on the Song of Songs especially the correspondence between the upper and lower world.

The union of God and the Shekina also brings forth the birth of the Godly child. Von Franz (1978:132) writes (my translation): 'If man does not grasp the eternal which dwells in love ... then the "Godly child" of the transcendent pair cannot be born, the child which is the symbol of achieved individuation.' One could add that every child born is a Godly child, the numinous result of love and sex of man and woman!

The analytical psychologist Edinger (1986) divides the story into a sequence of ten pictures 'for the purpose of exposition', as follows:

1. The Shulamite, burned black by the sun, labors in her brothers' vineyards and yearns for the Bridegroom. (1:1–2:7)
2. The Bridegroom comes to the Shulamite like the coming of spring. (2:8–17)

3. The lonely Shulamite rises from her bed and searches the street for her Beloved. (3:1–3)

4. The Shulamite finds the Bridegroom. He comes like a royal procession of King Solomon. (3:4–11)

5. The Bride and Bridegroom meet in the garden. The Bridegroom praises the Bride but is wounded by her. (4:1–5:1)

6. The Bridegroom knocks at the Shulamite's door but she is slow in answering and he is gone. (5:2–5:6)

7. The Shulamite again goes in search of the lost Bridegroom. (5:6)

8. The watchmen beat the Shulamite and steal her cloak. (5:7)

9. Bride and Bridegroom find each other and unite in the garden of pomegranates. (6:1–8:3)

10. The united lovers are sealed to each other in eternal love. (8:5–7)

He says that the Song of Songs is a *coniunctio* poem, a love drama expressing the union of opposites. His commentary is a classical Jungian interpretation. He sees the climax of the Song in the consummation of the *coniunctio* with the union of bride and bridegroom (7: 11–13). The protagonists of *his* interpretation are Salomon and the Shulamite, which is not clearly stated in the text, as mentioned above and below, but is taken for granted by many commentators as the Song of Songs opens with the words: 'The song of songs, which is Solomon's'. Edinger (1986:144) further comments:

The coniunctio is consummated with the union of Bride and Bridegroom symbolizing all pairs of opposites. Now is established the eternal alliance between Yahweh and Israel, the millenial marriage between Christ and his Church, or, according to the Kabbalah, the sacred union between 'the Holy one, blessed be He and His Shekinah'.

DISCUSSION OF SOME PASSAGES

The power of the archetype of love is hinted at in 2:5, which reads: 'I am faint with love.' The Hebrew original speaks of love-sickness, which is a stronger expression than 'faint with love'. Love-sickness expresses a state of mind in which one suffers because one has fallen in love and wants to be united with the loved one; one cannot tolerate the separation from the partner. One is, so to speak, the victim of the archetype and has lost the power of the ego. Psychologically it can also be explained as a possession by the countersexual archetype. Yet, behind this possession lies the striving for unity, the conscious or unconscious need to overcome the split of feminine and masculine in order to unite with the Self. The mystical experience of the oneness of existence is sought for.

Verses 3:1–5 (and also 5:2–7) are looked upon as a dream, because 3:1 says: 'By night on my bed I sought him', and 5:2: 'I sleep but my heart waketh.' From a psychological point of view one could say that an unconscious content breaks into consciousness, be it in a dream or in fantasy or imagination. Bride and bridegroom find each other and unite in the garden of pomegranates (7:11–13). The marriage is consummated (see Edinger 1986). Scholem (1946:152) mentions that in the Book Bahir the palm tree, a masculine symbol, stands opposite the Ethrog, but also opposite the bride of the Song of Songs. The *coniunctio*-symbolism is obvious.

In 7:6 we read: 'The King is held captive in the tresses thereof' (of the woman, the anima, the queen, the Shulamite), which is a metaphor for the psychological state of the lack of freedom of the ego. The archetype of love represented by the union of animus and anima has tremendous energy and can obsess the ego (as in the case of Samson and Delila). If this possession becomes an addiction, we speak of Don Juanism and nymphomania.

The possession by love expresses itself also in suffering. Goethe (1795–6) said: 'only the one who knows yearning understands my suffering' ('Nur wer die Sehnsucht kennt, weiss was ich leide'). This is only *one* example of the literature regarding love and suffering. Goethe extended the poem in June 1785 to a *Lied*, which was set to music by Beethoven (1810), Schubert (1827) and Schumann (1849).

One yearns and is longing for the partner with whom one cannot be together for some reason. Yearning can also be understood as a longing for union, whereby animus and anima are projected. Union, to become one, is from a psychological point of view a yearning of the ego for the Self.

The feeling of having fallen in love is described in 4:9:

> Thou hast ravished my heart, my sister, my bride;
> Thou hast ravished my heart with one of thine eyes,
> With one bead of thy necklace.

The beloved woman is called sister and bride, which alludes to the motive of incest (brother–sister), psychologically to a union with the anima or animus, the contrasexual part within. The symbolic understanding of incest in the individuation process is described by Jung (1957, passim), but it basically has a deep significance as a mystery. Also in the Kabbala, an incest-dream points to the process of individuation: sleeping with the mother, for example, is a very good sign, as it points to the union with the divine mother.

In 4:12 it says:

A garden shut up is my sister, a spring shut up, a fountain sealed.

This is clearly an allusion to the fact that the 'sister' is still a virgin, not ready yet for consummation of the marriage. Sister (and bride) are the anima.

Only in 7:1 is the friend, sister, bride called by the name of Shulamite. Her description in this chapter is especially poetic and rich. The comparison with nature alludes to the earthly, symbolic, archetypal aspect of the Shulamite.

266

The power of the archetype of love is also expressed in 8:6:

> For love is strong as death,
> Jealousy is cruel as the grave;
> The flashes thereof are flashes of fire,
> A very flame of the Lord.

By comparing love and death this verse expresses a psychological truth: when one is caught by the archetypal energy of love, of the God of love, there is a potency at work which one cannot escape, like death. One is overpowered by the archetype. It is a defeat of the ego. Love is connected with the negative emotion of jealousy and is cruel 'as the grave'. The Hebrew text speaks of the underworld (not the grave), thus emphasizing that man can be delivered to the forces of the underworld, of the unconscious. There is the 'flame of the Lord', the devouring power of the archetype of the Self.

The woman of the Song of Songs is called by the name of Shulamite only twice, in 7:1. The man of the Song of Songs is named Solomon three times, in 1:1, 8:11 and 8:12. But, as the first chapter starts with 'The Song of Songs, which is Solomon's', the whole poem is often looked upon as an interaction between Solomon and Shulamite. Incidentally, this seems to me artificial, because it tries to bring order to the story similar to the two rabbis' attempts to structure the text (see above). Verse 1:5 says: 'I am black, but comely.' This expresses an opposition: the woman is black, dark in appearance, which is an allusion to the shadow, yet inside she is comely, fair, white. From the point of view of the man, she represents the dark anima, yet in her soul, in her other side, she is comely. Does this mean that through the relation to his dark anima he may discover her fair side? There is a connection between Shulamite and the Queen of Sheba. They are different images of the archetype of the feminine. Shulamite herself is not always black; this is only one of her personalities. Like Kali she represents different types of female energies. Shulamite in the Song of Songs represents a part of the Queen of Sheba in a certain phase: she is black in a fallen state after the expulsion from paradise and then becomes Malkat Sheva. Hence it is mentioned that she is darkened. She is exiled, i.e. disconnected from the masculine. And thus the Song goes back and forth, between union and separation.

CONCLUSION

According to the Kabbala the erotic relationship between man and woman corresponds to the union of God and the Shekinah, the Holy Union, *Sivug ha'kadosh (hieros gamos)*. Thus, the sexual union between husband and wife gets a spiritual, transcendental significance and meaning. When husband and wife unite in this world, God and the Shekina unite in the other world. The two become one: Man–God unites with his inner Woman–Goddess, and the Woman–Goddess unites with her inner Man–God. Thus the sexual act can be looked upon as a symbol, but it is basically the *experience* of the oneness of man–woman, and animus–anima, of God and the Shekinah. It recreates wholeness after the split of the original man (Adam Kadmon, original man, Hermaphrodite) into two: man and woman. According to one story of the creation of man (Genesis 1:27) 'And God created man in His own image, in the image of God He created him; male and female created he them', man and woman are directly created by God. The Midrash, also quoted by Rashi, expands on this and explains that man as first created consisted of two halves, male and female, which were afterwards separated. Psychologically speaking, the hermaphrodite is a symbol of wholeness. By the separation man and woman are only parts of a whole, which explains the attraction between man and woman. From a mythological point of view the original oneness is symbolized by the motive of the World Parents (Neumann (1954:18)), who 'are the perfection from whence everything springs; the eternal being that begets, conceives, and brings itself to birth, that kills and revivifies. Their unity is a state of existence transcendent and divine, independent of the opposites – the inchoate "En-Soph" of the cabala, which means "unending plentitude" and "nothingness."' The *experience* of the mystical union in the here and now is the paradox of the two, man and woman, conscious and unconscious, which are one in the Self, and this cannot really be expressed in words. Understood this way the Holy Union is an experience of the oneness of existence of the individual, the collective, the world and the cosmos.

Von Franz (1957:71–2) discusses the Song of Songs, with regard to the alchemical tractate of 'Aurora Consurgens', which St Thomas Aquinas quoted in a state of ecstasis while on his deathbed. She calls it 'the most beautiful portrayal of the Hieros Gamos in our western tradition'. She continues that 'the alchemists regarded this text as a portrayal of the completion of their opus, it is at any rate the portrayal of the accomplished individuation, a final becoming one of the psychic opposites, a freeing of all egocentricity and an ecstatic going into a state of Godly wholeness'. Von Franz further relates, in her 'Aurora Consurgens' (1957: para. 614) that in the Kabbala death is described as the experience of a mystical wedding and quotes from Mueller (1932:390) that the disciples of Rabbi Schim'on bar Jochai heard at his funeral a voice which said: 'Come and assemble for the wedding of Rabbi Schim'on: May peace come and may they rest on their encampments.' Awareness, all over the world, of the deeper meaning of love and sexuality, namely its relationship to cosmic consciousness, could potentially become a unifying factor of mankind.

To sum up, the Song of Songs is a beautiful love poem which circumambulates the mystery of love. The interpretation on the archetypal level (Jungian depth psychology) and/or on the mystical level of the Kabbala comes nearest to a true understanding of the irrational experience of love.

REFERENCES

Brod, Max (n.d.) Foreword to the libretto of *Song of Songs – Oratorio for Soloists, Mixed Choir and Orchestra*, by Marc Lavry, based on the Song of Songs, Israel Music Institute (IMI), Tel-Aviv. See also Brod, Max: *Heidentum, Christentum, Judentum*, vol. 2, part 8, Munich: Kurt Wolff, 1922.

Carlebach, Joseph (n.d.) *Das Hohelied, uebertragen und gedeutet*, Frankfurt am Main, Hermon Verlag [printed *c.* 1925 and based on lectures held between 1923 and 1924; Carlebach, Chief Rabbi of Hamburg and Altona, was killed by the Nazis in Riga in 1942].

Chagall, Marc and Mayer, Klaus (1990) *Wie schön ist deine Liebe*, Würzburg: Echter.

Cohen, A. (ed.) (1946) *The Five Megilloth, The Song of Songs*, Hindhead, Surrey: The Soncino Press.

Edinger, Edward F. (1986) *The Bible and the Psyche*, Toronto: Inner City Books.

Falk, Marcia (1977) *The Song of Songs, Love Poems from the Bible*, translated from the original Hebrew, New York and London: Harcourt Brace Jovanovich.

Franz, M. -L. von (1957) 'Aurora Consurgens', in C. G. Jung's *Mysterium Coniunctionis*, part 3, Zurich and Stuttgart: Rascher.

—— (1978) *Spiegelungen der Seele*, Stuttgart and Berlin: Kreuz Verlag.

—— (1984) *Traum und Tod*, Munich: Koesel-Verlag.

—— (1990) *Psychotherapie*, Einsiedeln: Daimon.

Goethe, Joh. Wolfgang von (1795–6) *Wilhelm Meister's Lehrjahre*, book 4, ch. 11.

—— (1819) *Noten und Abhandlungen zum Divan*.

Idel, Moshe (1988) *The Mystical Experience in Abraham Abulafia*, New York: State University of New York Press.

Jung, C. G. (1954) The Tavistock Lectures, On the Theory and Practice of Analytical Psychology, The Symbolic Life, CW 18.

—— (1957) *Mysterium Coniunctionis*, CW 14.

Mueller, E. (ed.) (1932) *Der Sohar*, Vienna.

Neumann, Erich (1954) *The Origins and History of Consciousness*, New York: Pantheon Books.

Pool, David de Sola (1945) 'The Song of Songs which is Solomon's', *The Menorah Journal* 33(1) (Spring).

Scholem, Gershom (1946) *Major Trends in Jewish Mysticism*, New York: Schocken Books.

—— (1962) *Ursprung und Anfänge der Kabbalah*, Berlin: Walter de Gruyter.

Turner, Bruno (1986) Foreword to EMI compact disc.

When not mentioned otherwise in the text, all places referring to the Kabbala are from notes taken during private lessons with my teacher Joel Baks.

INDEX